Making Waves

Grassroots Feminism
in Duluth and Superior

Elizabeth Ann Bartlett

MINNESOTA
HISTORICAL
SOCIETY PRESS

Page 30: "Beaver Island Jubilee/For the Birds/Replenish," by Claudia Schmidt, used with permission.

Page 109: Power and Control Wheel, Domestic Abuse Intervention Program (DAIP), www.theduluthmodel.org, used with permission.

Page 253: "Heroes," music and lyrics, Ann Reed, Turtlecub Productions, Inc., © 1992. FFI: www.annreed.com. Used by limited permission.

www.mnhspress.org

The Minnesota Historical Society Press is a member of the Association of American University Presses.

Manufactured in the United States of America

10 9 8 7 6 5 4 3 2 1

♾ The paper used in this publication meets the minimum requirements of the American National Standard for Information Sciences—Permanence for Printed Library Materials, ANSI Z39.48–1984.

International Standard Book Number

ISBN: 978-1-68134-011-1 (paper)
ISBN: 978-1-68134-012-8 (e-book)

Library of Congress Cataloging-in-Publication Data available upon request.

This and other Minnesota Historical Society Press books are available from popular e-book vendors.

The publication of this book was supported, in part, by gifts from

Pamela Mittlefehldt
Joan C. Mork
Tineke Ritmeester

and

In honor of Mary Martin, a Minnesota feminist—from
Mary Graff, Sandy Christian, Nancy Tubesing, and Gloria Singer

and

In honor of all the women who made these organizations
and this book possible—Elizabeth Ann Bartlett

*To all those who have given their lives and their love
to the creation and sustenance of feminist
organizations and community in the Twin Ports
and to making the world a better place.*

Contents

Preface

I moved to Duluth in 1980, while I was still a graduate student at the University of Minnesota Twin Cities working on my dissertation on nineteenth-century feminism. During my first week here, I attended a Women's Coordinating Committee Brown Bag at the University of Minnesota Duluth (UMD). There I met and was immediately welcomed into a group of women who were creating a women's studies program. One connection led to another, and I was soon embraced by other feminists in the community, with whom I began working on a variety of political and legal projects and facilitating consciousness-raising groups. After interviewing coast-to-coast for teaching positions a year later, I chose to stay in Duluth, because the feminist community was unlike anything I experienced or witnessed elsewhere. Those early days of feminist organizing and friendship in Duluth were exhilarating, energizing, and inspiring. For me, this is still a community without equal, and I am both humbled and honored to share its story.

This book has been a collaborative venture, from its initial conception with my dear friend Susana, to the Women's Studies departmental collaboration in framing the project, to all the individuals who gave of their resources and time to be interviewed, and so many others in the community who gave me helpful suggestions, connections, and continuing enthusiasm. Even coming up with the book's title was a collective effort. After posting a request for title ideas on the UMD Women's Studies Alumni Facebook page, I received many wonderful suggestions, all of which had one thing in common: all agreed that the title should somehow reference Lake Superior. The resulting title, *Making Waves* (a variation on Helen Velishek's suggestion), carries the triple-entendre of significant impacts, the waves of feminism, and Lake Superior, which inspires these acts and restores the wave makers. From start to finish, this has been a project by and for the community.

Listening to the stories has been a rare privilege. I am honored by the trust and openness with which people shared their stories. The entire process has been the source of wonderful camaraderie in sharing memories of those early days, even if we were just meeting for the first time, or in our shared passion for feminism. I wish I had been able to include all the many stories and organizational histories in their full detail in this book. Though not included in this volume, they are available electronically at Archives and Special Collections, the Kathryn A. Martin Library, University of Minnesota Duluth (http://www.d.umn.edu/lib/), along with the original interviews and transcripts.

I have so many people to thank for their help and support in the creation of this book. Thanks first of all to Beth Olson, who planned the conference where the idea for the book came into being. This book would not have happened without my friends and colleagues in the Women's Studies program at UMD—from the Women's Coordinating Committee who originally invited me to join them in creating a women's studies program to all my students who have taught me so much over the years and whose insights influenced the writing of this book. I am especially grateful to those who first collaborated in conceiving of this project: Susana Pelayo Woodward, who was with me when we first together decided to create this book; Tineke Ritmeester, Njoki Kamau, Cindy Christian, and Joan Varney, who collaborated in the initial design of the study and the interview questions; Susana, Tineke, and Joan for conducting interviews; and Susana and Tineke for continuing to talk through issues and providing feedback about the book.

Thank you to the University of Minnesota Duluth for funding several small research grants that enabled us to hire research assistants and for my sabbatical leave, which provided the time and support to complete the project. My thanks as well go to research assistants Jen Chamberlain and Cheré Bergeron for their early transcriptions of interviews and Em Westerlund for culling archives and conducting interviews.

Many thanks to Pat Maus and Mags David with the Archives and Special Collections at the Kathryn A. Martin Library at UMD, who graciously and enthusiastically assisted me with archival material and have arranged for storage of and access to the interviews, transcriptions, and smaller histories that were part of the original manuscript, and to UMD librarian Jodi Carlson Grebinoski, who helped me in locating resources. I am also so grateful to the many organizations and individuals who took it upon themselves to collect and store herstory documents and records and generously shared them with me: American Indian Community

Housing Organization (AICHO), Aurora, the Northcountry Women's Coffeehouse, Program to Aid Victims of Sexual Assault (PAVSA), Safe Haven Shelter and Resource Center, Joyce Benson, Jean DeRider, Sadie Green, Kathy Heltzer, Stephanie Hemphill, Mary Ann LucasHoux, Caroline Pelzel, Sharon Torrison, and Tina Welsh.

Thank you to Pam McClanahan at the Minnesota Historical Society Press, who supported this endeavor with great enthusiasm. Many thanks as well to Tineke Ritmeester, Joan Mork, Pamela Mittlefehldt, Gloria Singer, Nancy Tubesing, Sandy Christian, and Mary Graff for their generous support of this project and the press. I am most grateful to Josh Leventhal, my editor at the Minnesota Historical Society Press, who believed in this project from the outset and advocated for it. With his careful and thoughtful editing, patient listening, and thoughtful responses to my questions and concerns, he shepherded this project into the book that it is with grace and care. Thanks as well to freelance editor Mary Russell and to Shannon Pennefeather at MNHS Press, who painstakingly went over manuscript details.

Many others helped with the editing. Rosemary Rocco, Tina Welsh, and Coral McDonnell were particularly thorough and helpful in commenting on and providing corrections and additional material on drafts of the chapters on PAVSA, the Women's Health Center, the Building for Women, and the Domestic Abuse Intervention Programs (DAIP). Many others responded quickly and graciously to my many queries about historical details. I am very grateful as well to Dianna Hunter for acting as a reader and giving thoughtful feedback on several draft chapters.

I give my deepest heartfelt gratitude to Pamela Mittlefehldt, who has been my main reader, friend, and very much a co-collaborator on this book. She read multiple drafts with great care, always providing thoughtful comments that have helped to make this a better book. Through countless e-mails and conversations, she read, listened, and talked through concerns, dilemmas, frustrations, and possibilities with me. She has been my main supporter and cheerleader for the book and has kept me going throughout.

Other friends have provided invaluable support. Kris Simonson has been so much a part of writing this book, literally walking with me through my dilemmas, delights, and questions, listening to each week's progress, acting as my sounding board, and being my good friend. My dear friend and advocate Mary Martin was such a supporter of this project and of me in my life. She was an important part of the feminist community, and I wish she had lived long enough to see this book completed.

Joan Mork has believed in this book and listened to and supported me throughout this project, offering helpful suggestions and consistently lifting me up. Mary Tennis and Jody Anderson, my musical partners first as a trio, and then with Barb Hanka as Wild by Nature, have contributed to and supported this book from the outset. They have been the mainstays of my friendships and connections with the feminist community through the Northcountry Women's Coffeehouse. Many of the people I interviewed for this book I met first through the Coffeehouse, and I can't imagine what my life would have been without my deep connection with this community.

My family has offered continual support and encouragement. My nephew, John, who was finishing his PhD dissertation as I was finishing this book, was my main commiserator. We paced each other with updates on our progress, celebrated each completed chapter, talked through ethical dilemmas and transcription trials, and shared mutual understandings of the nature of the process (as well as the importance of Twizzlers in facilitating that process) that could only be grown from a lifetime of deep connection and shared humor. My sister, Jeannie, has been my main cheerleader all my life and has always believed in everything I have done 1,000 percent. She listened and enthusiastically supported me throughout the process of writing this book, celebrating every triumph, large and small.

My son, Paul, who was in high school when this project began, is now grown, and is the finest example of a feminist man I know. He continually inspires me with his insight, his wisdom, and the way he lives his life, and I am grateful for his enduring love. My husband, David, who with good humor put up with my being, in his words, "the statue on the couch" during the writing process, has been a consistent source of good cheer, comfort, and love. And throughout I have had the constant companionship of my dog, Charlie, who sat beside me every moment, lending quiet support, and who, whenever he heard the sound of the laptop shutting down, would get up excitedly to take me out for a much-needed walk.

Finally, I am deeply indebted to all those who generously and graciously gave their time to this book, and to this community, and without whom this book would not have been possible. They are its inspiration. I am moved by their courageous and ceaseless dedication to making the lives of women in this community and the world better. We are all better for their efforts. For their wisdom, insights, memories, stories, passion, laughter, and generosity, I am forever grateful.

A Note on Methodology

The bulk of the research for this book was based on semi-structured, open-ended interviews with people who are or were working in or associated with the organizations. In addition to a snowball approach, I also took steps to include voices of those whose names came up often or that others in the organization identified as being central to the organization, and to include a diverse range of voices across class, race, age, and eras of the organizations. Because the interviewing process for this book has spanned almost ten years, some of the people initially interviewed were re-interviewed later. I also corresponded via e-mail with many subjects to clarify details.

Additional material came from letters, newsletters, flyers, memos, and old news items faithfully collected over the years by some of the organizations as well as by individuals who took it upon themselves to organize and store documents in their homes. Additional information was gathered from newspaper accounts.

All of those interviewed were sent chapter drafts, so they had a chance to correct, delete, or provide additional information.

Limitations and Subjectivity of the Interviews

Though many people were involved in designing the study, only five of us conducted interviews. In most cases, those of us conducting the interviews had some previous acquaintance or association with those we interviewed, either personally or professionally.

The sampling of interviews is not all-inclusive by any means. Many of the people we had hoped to interview had long ago left the area, and we were unable to locate them. Some declined interviews. Others had died before we had the opportunity to gather their stories. Undoubtedly, key people have been missed, and I apologize to those who were inadvertently left out or otherwise did not have the opportunity to have their voices included.

Nearly every organization had some periods of time that few remember and for which no good records or contact persons were available. The interviews often required that people recall events that took place twenty, sometimes thirty or more, years ago. Individuals often had difficulty remembering specifics. On occasion, people's memories of events, dates, and names conflicted with one another's, and I have tried to reconcile these as best I could. I have also supplemented personal accounts with archival data, newsletters, and newspaper accounts.

The initial study was limited to eighteen organizations. As the study took shape, persons associated with several smaller related organizations were also interviewed. While all of them inform the book, in narrowing its focus, several of these histories were shortened or left out altogether, though they are all available electronically at Archives and Special Collections, the Kathryn A. Martin Library, University of Minnesota Duluth (http://www.d.umn.edu/lib/). The study does not encompass all the grassroots organizations in the Twin Ports over the past forty years. Undoubtedly we have missed some.

Voice

It is a widely accepted practice in feminist interview methodology to let those interviewed speak for themselves, as much as possible. As I began putting the manuscript together, some of the chapters relied almost entirely on direct quotes from interviewees to tell the stories of the organizations. As I began a winnowing process, I provided more of my own summary of events and occasional analyses and interpretations.

A Word about Names

The typical practice in scholarly writing is to refer to people by their last names. The tendency to refer to men by their last names and women by their first names has been criticized as minimizing the status of women by being too familiar. After much reflection, I chose to refer to the individuals in this volume primarily by their first names. I came to the conclusion that referring to individuals by last names inappropriately reinscribes patriliny. Women renaming themselves has a long tradition in feminism—from Sojourner Truth to Starhawk to bell hooks. Similarly, many of the women in this volume have taken on names of their own choosing. So rather than refer to the women by their father's or their husband's names, I chose to refer to them by the name they call themselves, and asked each to tell me their preferred name. These are also the names by which they know one another, and it is such knowledge, friendship, and partnership that allowed these organizations to flourish.

After having made this decision about names, I was gratified to discover this letter from Elizabeth Cady Stanton to a friend in 1847:

> You differed from me on the ground that custom had established the rule that a woman must take the whole of her husband's name. . . . But you are mistaken in this. It is the custom now, since women have commenced forming themselves into independent societies, to use names of the feminine gender. . . . You will find no Miss and Mrs., and no Joseph, or Ichabod, but Elizabeth and Rebecca. . . . I have serious objections to being called Henry. There is a great deal in a name. . . . The custom of calling women Mrs. John and Mrs. Tom . . . is founded on the principle that white men are lords of all. I cannot acknowledge this principle as just; therefore, I cannot bear the name of another.[1]

A Note on Authorship

This book began as a joint endeavor, first with Susana Pelayo Woodward and myself, and then with all the other members of the Women's Studies Department at UMD. Initially, each of us agreed to interview and write chapters on two to four of the organizations. Ultimately I was the one to write the book, but I still regard this as a joint venture. All the initial decisions that gave the book its character and shape were made collectively, and Susana, Tineke Ritmeester, and I continued to have conversations about the shape and content of the book. I also regard all those interviewed to be coauthors. Without their stories and comments, this book would not be possible. Ultimately, I have been the one to weave together the stories into each of the individual histories and into the collective history of grassroots feminism in the Twin Ports. Any errors are mine.

Making Waves

Introduction

We need to know the history of our sisters—both for inspiration and for accumulating a full arsenal of ideas—and adopt what translates into the present.

GLORIA STEINEM

On October 25, 2002, hundreds of feminists gathered at the University of Wisconsin–Superior for "Making Women's History Now: The State of Feminism in the Twin Ports," a conference that brought together feminists from a variety of organizations and across generations to talk together about the pressing issues facing the feminist community. In her keynote address that morning, longtime activist Tina Welsh, director of the Women's Health Center, chronicled the early days of feminist organizing in Duluth, from the development of the first rape crisis center to the trials of establishing and sustaining an abortion clinic. In her afternoon keynote, Ellen Pence, well known for her work in the battered women's movement, regaled the crowd with her humorous rendition of the early efforts of the battered women's movement in Duluth to work with the criminal justice system to set up a coordinated community response to domestic violence. As Ellen began to tell her story, my friend and colleague Susana Pelayo Woodward and I, moved by the power, poignancy, and significance of these stories, turned to each other and said, "We need to write these down!" The seeds of this project were sown.[1]

A few minutes later the joviality turned to stunned horror as Ellen's talk was interrupted with the news that the plane carrying Senator Paul Wellstone and Sheila Wellstone, their daughter, and three staffers had crashed. There were no survivors. Paul and Sheila Wellstone had actively worked to end violence against women, and were personal friends of many in attendance. The conference ended quickly and quietly. This tragic event is what most remember from that day, and it was not until a few years later that Susana and I picked up the idea of writing the histories of these grassroots feminist organizations. The conference had reminded us of what we had always known—that the programs and policies developed by feminist organizations in the Twin Ports of Duluth, Minnesota, and Superior, Wisconsin, had been groundbreaking. Many pioneering organizations began here, including one of the earliest rape crisis programs and one of the first battered women's shelters in the country. The Domestic Abuse Intervention Project, home of the Duluth Model, is known worldwide for its innovative approaches to domestic abuse, including the first mandatory arrest law in the country. Mending the Sacred Hoop was the first domestic assault Training and Technical Assistance provider for tribal nations across the United States. The Women's Health Center has been a national leader in ensuring reproductive rights, and the Building for Women in which it is housed is one of only three in the United States. The American Indian Community Housing Organization developed the first urban shelter for Native women. Women in Construction was the first on-the-job training program for women in the trades. And these are only a few of the innovative and influential feminist organizations that developed in the northland. We knew that the abundance and significance of the organizations clustered here were noteworthy and deserving of recognition.

The conference had also reminded us of the passion, vitality, tenacity, and resilience of the feminist activists and organizers, and the friendships, camaraderie, and love that gave birth to and sustained the organizations. For those who were here when it all began, it was a time like no other, filled with vision and possibility. The stories inspired us, and we knew we did not want them to be lost or forgotten. We wanted to gather and record them both for ourselves and for future generations of feminist activists. Over a hundred interviews and more than a decade later, the book begun from a seed planted on that fateful October day has come to fruition.

The purposes in writing this book are three. First and foremost is to record the stories of the grassroots feminist organizations of the Twin Ports so that the vision, courage, efforts, and resilience of the women (and a few men) who grew and nourished these organizations will be known and remembered. As feminist historian Stephanie Gilmore has said, "When activists' papers are not archived, oral histories are not recorded, and assumptions about our shared and different pasts as feminists (and paths to feminism) prevail, students, scholars, and activists of the current and next generations are left to assume that feminism simply happened and operates around us." The second is to inform future generations of feminist activists, and to pass along the lessons and the wisdom of those who have gone before. The final purpose is to analyze those factors that contributed to the confluence of so many groundbreaking, visionary, and influential feminist organizations in the Twin Ports.[2]

At the outset, Susana and I invited the other members of the Women's Studies Department at the University of Minnesota Duluth (UMD) to join us in this project. Cindy Christian, Njoki Kamau, Tineke Ritmeester, Joan Varney, Susana, and I together developed the parameters of the study, as well as the questions that formed the basic framework of our interviews. We decided to limit our investigation to long-lasting grassroots feminist organizations. By "long-lasting" we mean those that endured for at least a decade; most have survived more than twenty-five years, some more than forty. We defined "grassroots" as those organizations that grew from the ground up through the efforts of local individuals, as opposed to regional or national organizations that established branches in Duluth.

Feminist is more complicated to define. Feminism has so many different forms that it is difficult to arrive at an all-encompassing definition. The best may be bell hooks's simple statement that feminism is the movement to end sexist oppression. We initially decided to include those organizations that self-identify as feminist. However, while most of the organizations and individuals we studied refer to themselves as feminist, not all of them do. Ultimately, we expanded our concept to include organizations whose mission and work in the world is primarily to empower women and girls.

The Twin Ports has been home to dozens of feminist organizations, ranging from local branches of established national organizations to local political, artistic, service, educational, and business endeavors. We sorted through them to determine which organizations met our study's parameters. The most obvious were those involved in work to end violence against women. This included the Program to Aid Victims of Sexual Assault (PAVSA) and organizations that worked in the field of domestic violence—Safe Haven Shelter and Resource Center, the Domestic Abuse Intervention Programs (DAIP), Mending the Sacred Hoop, Praxis International, Women's Transitional Housing, American Indian Community Housing Organization (AICHO), Women in Construction, and the

Center Against Sexual and Domestic Abuse (CASDA). Another obvious organization to include was the Women's Health Center, which provides reproductive health care and abortion services for women, as well as the Building for Women, where it and other organizations are housed. Other organizations clearly within the parameters of our study were the North-country Women's Coffeehouse and Aurora: A Northland Lesbian Center, which provided resources and support for lesbian women. While these organizations are at the center of this study, we recognize the importance of many feminist groups and enterprises that contributed to the flourishing feminist community in Duluth. Some of these stories are recounted briefly as well.

Second Wave Feminism: National and Regional Perspectives

The rise of feminist organizations in the Twin Ports did not occur in a vacuum. The tidal wave of Second Wave feminism, to use historian Sara Evans's metaphor, had been sweeping inward from the coasts since the 1960s. Many studies have been done of the history of Second Wave feminism in the United States, both as a national movement and in its particular manifestations in cities across the country. According to most narratives of the national movement, Second Wave feminism in the United States grew from two cohorts: an older branch of mostly professional women who had met in government-based commissions on women, and a younger branch of students and activists who had come of age politically in the civil rights movement and the New Left. The first cohort arose from state commissions on women established by President John F. Kennedy in 1961. Following a meeting with Eleanor Roosevelt where she expressed her concerns about the status of women in the United States, President Kennedy created the Presidential Commission on the Status of Women, which Eleanor Roosevelt chaired, to advise him on women's issues. At that time he also established fifty state commissions on women to investigate the status of women in each state. As women in these commissions met, they not only gathered data on women in their states, they also shared stories of their own lives. In so doing they discovered rampant and ubiquitous sex discrimination.[3]

From these commissions would grow such organizations as the National Organization for Women (NOW), the National Women's Political Caucus (NWPC), and the Women's Equity Action League (WEAL). Their main strategy for change was political, and in what Sara Evans has characterized as "the golden years" they rode the wave of legislative reform—the Equal Pay Act (1963), Title VII of the Civil Rights Act (1964), and the passage in Congress of the Equal Rights Amendment (1972, and still unratified). The year 1960 also brought FDA approval of the birth control pill, and the 1965 Supreme Court decision in *Griswold v. Connecticut* affirmed married women's rights to use birth control. These factors led to an increasing number of women joining the workforce. In addition, more women were winning elective office.[4]

The second cohort arose a few years later as young activist women involved in the civil rights and student movements found themselves discriminated against and dismissed by the men in those movements. As they met and shared stories of their lives in what came to be known as consciousness-raising (CR) sessions, they uncovered shared histories of sexual assault, unintended pregnancies and illegal abortions, abuse, and love for women. From these conversations grew such groups as New York Radical Women, Chicago's West Side Group, D.C. Women's Liberation Movement (out of which came the lesbian collective the Furies), and Boston's Bread and Roses. The organizing slogan "the personal is political" was used to indicate the recognition that so-called "personal" problems ranging from body image to domestic abuse in fact had to do with power relationships, and thus required political solutions rather than therapy. This characterized the central issues of this cohort. They were more likely to use tactics such as direct-action campaigns and mass demonstrations than to work with policy makers. While the older cohort sought an appropriate case to challenge illegal abortion in the courts, activists in the younger cohort marched in the streets to legalize abortion. When the National Organization for Women called the Second Congress to Unite Women in 1970, radical lesbians from the younger cohort, wearing T-shirts emblazoned with "Lavender Menace," disrupted the proceedings to challenge homophobia within the older cohort. One of their more famous actions was the 1968 protest of the Miss America Pageant, during which "objects of female torture," such as bras, girdles, and hair and eyelash curlers, were tossed into a "feminist trash can," and a live sheep was crowned.[5]

Spurred by consciousness-raising groups and two critical books, Susan Brownmiller's *Against Our Will* and Susan Griffin's *Rape: The Power of Consciousness*, this cohort reconceptualized rape as a crime of dominance enacted by men to control women, and formed a movement to resist violence against women. They redefined sexual assault and wife battering as crimes. They held Take Back the Night marches, educated police departments, worked to change state rules of evidence, developed national networks engaged in anti-rape advocacy, and opened battered women's shelters across the country. The first shelter, Women's Advocates, opened in St. Paul in 1971. Radical feminists established a plethora of organizations and services—from rape crisis hotlines to pregnancy and abortion counseling. The movements on the coasts spawned similar movements regionally and locally, with local branches of NOW and NWPC springing up alongside women's centers, women's bookstores, women's studies programs, women's health collectives, and rape crisis programs in cities and towns across the nation.[6]

However, by the 1970s, the national movement was plagued with schisms between and within the cohorts. Growing dissension arose from lesbians and women of color who felt excluded and dismissed by the movement. Many women of color separated from a movement defined by white women's issues to form their own organizations. Radical women of color, including Audre Lorde, Barbara Smith, Cherríe Moraga, Gloria Anzaldúa, and bell hooks, among many others, would become some of the most important voices of Second Wave feminism.

At the same time an alternative feminist culture of women-identified art, music, poetry, spirituality, literature, and film was blossoming. It drew much of its energy from the new visibility of lesbian feminism in living collectives, cultural events, coffeehouses, and businesses. As feminist historian Estelle Freedman has argued, "Lesbians created within North American and European women's movements a positive, even celebratory, alternative space in which they met, organized, and explored sexual desires. Their separate culture nourished not only lesbians but any woman who felt comforted by women-only spaces." Myra Ferree and Beth Hess point out that lesbians created places "to live out some of their hopes for a woman-centered, woman-friendly environment."[7]

This time saw the advent of music festivals, which historian Sara Evans sees as the most important venues for cultural feminism. The first national music festival was held in Champaign-Urbana, Illinois, in 1974, and the Michigan Womyn's Music Festival, which became the largest and most well known, began in 1976. Many smaller yearly festivals and a multitude of local events were held, including feminist concerts, writers' workshops, and conferences. With the rise of feminist presses and bookstores, a plethora of local and national newsletters and other publications appeared, and feminist speakers hit the lecture circuit.

A backlash hit the feminist movement in the 1980s as the antifeminist Reagan administration dismantled the state women's commissions and defunded programs like the Comprehensive Employment and Training

Act (CETA) and the Law Enforcement Assistance Administration (LEAA) that had funded many of the feminist service organizations. In response to growing governmental and media attacks, the fractured feminist movement consolidated. Distinctions between radicals and liberals became blurred. With feminism itself under attack, differences became secondary. Radicals increasingly engaged in the legislative and policy work more typical of liberals, and became more institutionalized as social service providers. Liberal organizations addressed previously taboo issues like lesbianism and adopted some aspects of the radical groups' collective structure. The hostile national political climate encouraged cooperation among feminists and the development of coalitions on the state level.[8]

Nevertheless, the period beginning in about 1980 saw the demise of many autonomous local women's organizations; those that survived were more likely to be service providers with bureaucratic structures and allied with the state. On the other hand, feminism grew more visible and acceptable, in some ways, in the 1980s. National organizations were well known and secure; feminist perspectives on sexual assault, sexual harassment, and domestic violence were becoming increasingly accepted by mainstream society; and local organizations that survived were receiving foundation and government funding.[9]

In the 1990s the rising tide of what Rebecca Walker christened Third Wave feminism disrupted the focus on women-centered culture and bonding. In reaction against identity politics, it raised questions about racial and sexual boundaries and unsettled notions of a unique women-centered experience. The emergence of genderqueer and more fluid notions of sexual identity pushed to the periphery the lesbian-centric focus that had characterized the movement in the 1980s. Gender became a more central organizing concept than sex. Women's studies programs increasingly became gender studies, organizations targeting violence against women increasingly became gender inclusive, and lesbian and women-only spaces disappeared. Though women's studies programs—now increasingly known as gender studies—introduced a new generation to feminist organizations where older generations of activists could show them the ropes, increasing dissension between the generations left both feeling more disconnected than connected. A new generation of young activists regards their movement as everywhere and nowhere, focused not so much in organizations as on the Internet, in social media, and in pop-up actions.[10]

The nationally based narratives tell only one part of the story of Second Wave feminism in the United States. This study joins a growing body of work focused on local grassroots feminist movements and organizations in large and midsized cities across the nation. These studies provide a corrective to the nationally focused narratives that draw sweeping conclusions primarily from feminist organizing in large cities on the East and West coasts. Seeking to "end bi-coastal arrogance," they tend to be studies of feminist movements and organizations in the interior of the country. Many scholars agree that the nationally based narratives fail to capture the nuances and particularities of how the movement was enacted in a variety of locales, which often tell quite a different story. As Stephanie Gilmore has noted, studies of local movements both uncover their distinctive qualities and give space for the voices of ordinary activists to be heard. These scholars argue that feminism became the largest social movement of the twentieth century thanks to the diverse ways it manifested across the country. These studies provide a fuller and more accurate account of the feminist movement in the United States.[11]

Many scholars who study local grassroots feminist movements emphasize the importance of geographical context and stress the effect place has on the character of those movements. As feminist geographer Anne Enke says, "feminist activism took shape around particularities of local geographies." Invoking Adrienne Rich's concept of a "politics of location," Gilmore reminds us that attention to place deepens our understanding of the politics of feminist organizing, allowing us to see "in what ways and around what issues feminists were able to create and sustain women's movement and feminist activisms."[12]

Until now, virtually all of the published studies on the women's movement have focused on feminist organizing that took place in cities that were among the sixty largest in the nation, most within heavily urbanized regions. This is the first study of feminist organizing centering around two small cities located at a remove from other metropolitan regions, on the edge of the northern coast and wilderness. I argue that the cities' size and location contributed to the unique character of the feminist movement here.

As Ferree and Martin note, the character, constraints, and opportunities of grassroots feminism are deeply affected by not only the place, but also the time in which they develop. Similarly, I argue that in the Twin Ports, committed moral feminists came on the scene at the perfect time, as two distinct waves of Second Wave feminism crashed in at once. The organization-building and consolidating phase of the feminist movement in the 1980s, along with the rise of lesbian and women-identified culture, hit the Twin Ports at the same time as the energy, enthusiasm, and excitement of the initial years of 1960s Second Wave feminism. The big small-town character of the Twin Ports, combined with the particulars of its culture, politics, and geographical location, created just the right conditions to harness the energy of those two waves into what would become one of the more influential and innovative centers of feminist movement in the state, nation, and world.[13]

Overview of the Book

In the first chapter, I address how and why the Twin Ports came to be the home of such a prolific and pioneering feminist movement. The second chapter provides a brief overview of the history of feminist organizing in the Twin Ports from the 1970s to the present. The bulk of the book is devoted to individual histories of each of the organizations, arranged in the chronological order of their origins. Chapter 13, "Lessons Learned," gathers together the wisdom gained by those involved in feminist organizing, while the concluding chapter includes a discussion of common themes that emerged in the course of this study and final reflections on the successes, the difficulties, and the future of feminist organizations.

The organizations chronicled here began with women sharing their truths and the stories of their lives with each other. It is fitting that this volume also arose from their sharing of their stories, and became a collection of the reflections and insights they so openly and eagerly shared. This book is their story. Like all stories, it has its characters, plot twists, struggles, sweetness, tragedies, and triumphs. Mostly it is a love story, a story of a love that gives birth to passionate and compassionate action for justice, a love that leads individuals to dedicate their lives to making the lives of others better, a love for the work and for each other that in the best and worst of times sustains the struggle. May it be an inspiration to those who follow.

{ 1 }

There Is Something Special in Duluth

There is something special in Duluth. Some of it is about a big
small town. Some of it is about all the hematite in that rock.
That lake. There is something about the women . . . women,
individually stepping out, stepping up to make it happen.

ROSEMARY ROCCO

In the late 1970s and early 1980s, Duluth/Superior was teeming with
feminist activism. Women were talking—in support groups,
consciousness-raising groups, meeting rooms, living rooms, kitchens, coffeehouses, and in the woods. They were reading—*Ms., off our
backs, Dream of Common Language, Sister Outsider, This Bridge Called
My Back*. They were listening to women's music—Chris Williamson,
Holly Near, Alix Dobkin, Meg Christian. They were visioning, planning,
organizing, marching, lobbying, and creating change. Local grassroots
feminist organizations were springing up everywhere.

At first glance, it might seem that the story of feminist organizations
in the Twin Ports is no different from that of dozens of similar organizations that were created throughout the nation during the Second Wave
of feminism. Feminist organizations in the Twin Ports followed many of
the same patterns of development as similar organizations around the
country. As elsewhere, they began with women talking with each other,
sharing their stories and their truths, discovering common issues and
struggles, and acting to address needs and transform society. Most began
as relatively structureless, consensus-based, and mission-driven collectives with a commitment to equal pay, equal voice, and rotating positions,
and suffered similar frustrations with seemingly endless discussions to
resolve organizational minutiae. Like many other feminist organizations,
an initial period of euphoria, energy, and growth was followed by the

difficulties that came with expansion and reliance on foundations and government agencies for funding. Abandoning collectives, most developed bureaucratic structures and moved away from their radical roots and into the mainstream. In addition, feminist organizations in Duluth, like their counterparts across the nation, grappled with issues of race and class. Most were established and initially staffed by white women with structures, policies, practices, and programming that were framed from white perspectives. These often failed to meet the needs or incorporate the perspectives of the women they served, many of whom were women of color and poor women. Nor could women of color relate as well to or feel as understood by white staff as they might with women from a similar background. Bringing more racial and class diversity to the membership and staff of the organizations was only a first step toward addressing these disparities, and issues of race and class continue to be part of ongoing conversations as organizations seek to incorporate perspectives and values of working-class women and women of color.[1]

However, feminist organizations in the Twin Ports did not experience the same schisms, fragmentation, and isolation that led to the demise of so many feminist endeavors nationally. Unlike many feminist enterprises that burst onto the national scene in the 1960s and '70s and then fizzled after a few years, most of the feminist organizations in Duluth lasted decades; most are still thriving thirty to forty years later. Moreover, many of these organizations have been national leaders, forging policies and initiatives that have served as models and inspiration far beyond the Twin Ports. Activists and organizers agree: "Duluth is one of those communities [that] . . . allows people to take an idea and run with it." "Duluth is a community without par." "Duluth's a creative and inspiring place." As Ellen Pence said, "If you want to make something happen, if you live in Duluth, that's where it can happen."[2]

Why Duluth? How did such a fruitful, robust, and influential feminist community come to flourish here? The confluence of the right people and the right time and place created the conditions to foster the innovative, influential, and enduring feminist community that calls the Twin Ports home. The timing was such that the institution-building era of the feminist movement hit the northland at the same time as the enthusiasm and excitement of the initial years of Second Wave feminism and the vitality of women-centered culture. Their coincidence created a tsunami of sorts that brought together the knowledge and resources needed to create feminist organizations with the energy, culture, and community to sustain them. Factors of place—size and location, as well as the physical, political, and cultural environments—made the Twin Ports ripe for the building and sustenance of grassroots feminist organizations. The women-honoring culture of the Anishinaabe along with a progressive political tradition of community organizing provided the context, and the big small-town atmosphere fostered cross-pollination, collabora-tion, and genuine community and feminist friendship. The awe-inspiring lake and surrounding wilderness of the area replenished and sustained.

Something about the Women

The smart, savvy, committed women who established the array of grass-roots feminist organizations in the Twin Ports were well known for their unusually strong spirit and persistence. "There is something about the women," said Rosie Rocco, a founder of Program to Aid Victims of Sex-ual Assault (PAVSA). That something is a fire, a passion, a collaborative spirit, commitment, clarity, and tenacity. The phrase "They don't give up" has often been used to characterize the women of this community. As Winona LaDuke said at an organizing meeting in Duluth in 2015, "We're northerners. We're plucky." *Plucky*—meaning brave, courageous, bold, daring, fearless, intrepid, spirited, dauntless, audacious, determined, mettlesome—describes the feminists in the Twin Ports to a T.[3]

Feminist historian Alice Rossi's description of First Wave nineteenth-century feminists as "small-town morally committed crusaders" is just as apropos for feminist organizers in Duluth: impelled to "give a 'call,' hold meetings, draw up resolutions, form local societies to implement the resolutions, and organize the network of local societies. . . . [They] developed their ideas in social interaction and delivered them in lec-tures, convention speeches, and legislative committee hearings." The many powerful feminist movers and shakers who were located in Duluth/Superior formed organizations, drew up resolutions, and spoke before legislators, city councilors, and local, state, and national agencies.[4]

These spirited, powerful women happened to find each other at just the right moment in time. Many dynamic duos and trios of these women came together in the initial creation of the organizations. Feminist or-ganizations in the Twin Ports had their share of dynamic familial con-nections as well. Sisters, mothers and daughters, spouses and partners had interweaving memberships in many of the organizations. The strong connections helped to establish a firm foundation on which these orga-nizations and the movement as a whole could thrive.

The reputation of the women caught the attention of and attracted

other feminist women to the Twin Ports. As Inez Wildwood, an early
director of PAVSA, said, "What drew me to Northern Minnesota was
the incredible strength and vision of women at a time when [that] did not
exist anywhere." Feminist organizing here was made possible through
the dedicated work not just of a few, but of hundreds. As Rosie Rocco
noted, "There were women who moved in many, many places—a lot of
women behind the scenes." "There's many heroes in this city of women,"
echoed Tina Welsh, "who are unsung heroes, who have done a great
deal." Committed individuals and joiners who answered a call, invited
others, inspired and supported each other—the spirit of the women here
was as magnetic as the hematite in the rock.

The Right Time

The timing was right. By the early 1970s, the national Second Wave
feminist movement was fracturing and losing momentum. Divided
along ideological lines from the beginning, the movement was prone to
schism. Divided along lines of ideology, race, class, and sexual orientation, it was slowly falling apart. Feminist organizations in the Twin Cities
suffered similar factionalism. The solidarity that had characterized the
early years was shattered as lesbians, women of color, and working-class
women confronted those organizations on their lack of inclusivity. While
funding challenges and inability to keep up with their own growth contributed to the demise of several feminist organizations in the Twin Cities, internal dissension was a key factor in "one group after another . . .
closing its doors in the late 1980s."[5]

The fact that Duluth was about ten years behind the times worked to
the advantage of the feminist movement there. Many of the schisms that
had plagued the national movement in the 1960s and 1970s had already
been fought out, worked through, or abandoned by the time the movement reached its heyday in the Twin Ports. The reformer–radical divide
did not define the feminist political culture in the Twin Ports. Feminists in local branches of established women's organizations such as the
YWCA and AAUW and the reformist nationally based National Organization for Women (NOW) worked alongside and often were the organizers of the rape crisis organization, women's health center, and battered
women's shelter. At the same time that they ran consciousness-raising
groups and formed organizations based on the radical perspective that
the personal is political, they engaged in mainstream political efforts,

working with state legislators and county and city officials to create policy reforms.[6]

Similarly, the gay–straight split was not a factor in the local feminist political culture. Feminist organization scholar Nancy Whittier contends that by the 1980s, the gay–straight split that had plagued the national feminist movement in the 1960s and 1970s was no longer an issue, and lesbians became "more indispensable than ever to the women's movement. . . . [Furthermore,] lesbian feminist communities construct and support a feminist collective identity that is not limited to those communities or to lesbians, but is important to the survival of the women's movement as a whole." This certainly was the case in Duluth, where far from being marginalized, lesbians were at the forefront of establishing many of the feminist organizations in Duluth.[7]

The growing lesbian feminist movement contributed significantly to the growth and sustenance of feminist organizations in Duluth. The movement there, especially in its origins, was defined by a women-centered perspective that largely can be attributed to lesbian feminism. Feminist scholar Janice Raymond defined this perspective as "equality of women with our Selves . . . being equal to those women who have been for women, those who have lived for women's freedom and those who have died for it; those who have fought for women and survived by women's strength; those who have loved women and who have realized that without the consciousness and conviction that women are primary in each other's lives, nothing else is in perspective." Independently, Native women's organizations also were reclaiming their women-honoring heritage.[8]

Feminist projects in Duluth placed women's experiences and interests at the center of theory and practice and grounded political action in addressing concrete needs discovered through listening to women. Their actions both in service of women and in seeking institutional change in the society at large were premised on honoring and valuing women and women's experience. They acted out of a context of feminist community and a concept of feminist solidarity that sought the collective empowerment of women and societal transformation rather than individual status and inclusion within the patriarchal status quo. The organizations have been strongest when they have been able to maintain their women-centered mission; when this foundation has been eclipsed by internal or external forces, the result has often been disorganization, dysfunction, and, in some cases, demise.

Another serendipitous effect of the timing of the rise of the feminist movement in the Twin Ports was the confluence of the institution-building phase of the women's movement with the rise of women's culture and lesbian feminism. As the one built, the other nourished and sustained.

Robin Morgan described the national women's culture and spirituality movement as "lifeblood for our survival." Nancy Whittier has made the important point that feminist cultural events were "not just apolitical entertainment" but rather were "an expression of feminist collective identity that rejuvenates committed feminists, recruits new women, and contributes to social change in the wider world by challenging hegemonic definitions of women." They were an integral part of what sustained the movement nationally as well as locally. The feminist art, music, and literary culture that has been a vital element of feminism in the Twin Ports has long served as a main point of connection for many individuals and has helped to nourish and sustain feminist community building and organizing in the area.[9]

The Right Place

Factors of place—the size of the Twin Ports, as well as its cultural, political, and physical geography—all contributed to the flourishing, creativity, and resilience of feminist organizations in the Twin Ports. The size of the community has been a key factor in creating the conditions for the cross-pollination of ideas that made feminist organizations there unusually innovative. The city is large enough to garner a variety of resources of people, knowledge, expertise, connections, and finances and small enough that people can readily connect with one another, whether at the grocery store or at rallies. As Nancy Gruver, the founder of *New Moon Magazine for Girls*, has pointed out, because Duluth/Superior is a relatively small metro area, it is easier to meet and develop friendships with people unlike oneself than in larger metro areas where most people tend to stay within their own communities. The nature of Duluth is such that it cultivates the personal associations and cross-pollination that create fertile collaborations.[10]

Significantly, the size of the community also protected feminist organizations from the isolation that led to the demise of organizations elsewhere, such as the Twin Cities, where Judy Remington found that "the groups' isolation from each other—their inability to share knowledge and strategies and to break out of a situation in which they were competing for the few funding dollars available for women's organizations and issues" exacerbated the difficulties and challenges they were facing.

She found that Twin Cities' organizations did not communicate well with one another and over time became more private, tending to keep their problems to themselves in order to preserve their public image. Sue Miller of Chrysalis noted the tendency "to be off in your own little world instead of aligning and at least talking to other organizations that might be going through the same stuff." With increased isolation, organizations lost opportunities for fresh perspectives and support. Ellen O'Neil of the Minnesota Women's Fund cited the "absence of community that these organizations can call on for help or ideas." Judith Ezekiel found that a similar lack of connection characterized the feminist movement in Dayton, Ohio, in the late 1970s.[11]

Such was not the case in the Twin Ports. The women involved in feminist organizing in the Twin Ports were likely to be active in many organizations on multiple fronts, and in a town of this size, the multiple and overlapping memberships of those involved in the Duluth/Superior movement served to weave a web of connections that enabled ideas and efforts to spread easily and strengthen the whole. Many moved from organization to organization; many who were employed by one organization sat on the boards or volunteered for others. Overlapping memberships in local branches of national women's organizations provided vital connections. Some worked together on political organizing and supporting feminist candidates for office.

The growth and flourishing of the feminist community there was also nourished by its cross-fertilization with other progressive and reform movements—peace, the environment, racial and economic justice, Native sovereignty, and others. In particular, as was true of the feminist movement nationally, many feminists in the Twin Ports area had connections to the peace movement and to the feminist peace movement in particular. Whether standing in silent vigil, marching in peaceful protest, or organizing more formal reform efforts, many in feminist organizations have joined their efforts with women's peace organizations such as Women's International League for Peace and Freedom, Grandmothers for Peace, Women in Black, or Women Against Military Madness. Others were part of international peacemaking initiatives, such as Duluth's sister cities programs, which seek to foster peace by creating bonds and relationships between people in communities around the world.[12]

The alliance between activists and academics in the Twin Ports is particularly noteworthy. Elsewhere, academics, who often were involved in early feminist organizing efforts, eventually retreated to their ivory towers. However, the separation of academics and activists chronicled by Sara Evans did not happen here. From developing the Northcountry Women's Center together to the present day, academics and activists have worked side by side in the Twin Ports. When the Women's Studies program began at UMD in 1981, it brought to campus new feminist scholars and students eager to learn, and they became involved in newly formed feminist organizations. Faculty spoke at the Northcountry Women's Coffeehouse and students were part of creating a women's radio show on the public radio station housed on the UMD campus. Faculty formed close ties with the community. Former Women's Studies director Susan Coultrap-McQuin said of her colleague Tineke Ritmeester, "she connected with the community in new ways. . . . She was the one who said we should be having some community people on our board. . . . She got to know the community people." Feminist activists have expressed their appreciation to Women's Studies and the Women's Resource and Action Center (WRAC) at UMD for being the "feminist link" to the community by providing programming where they could connect with feminist scholars and each other, revitalize and restore, and remind themselves of why they are doing the work. Faculty and staff have been integral members of organizations as participants, board members, collaborators, friends, and allies while community members have been involved in campus programs and curricula. The UMD Women's Resource and Action Center partners with many community organizations.[13]

The student connection has been especially important for the vitality of feminist organizations in the Twin Ports. Nancy Whittier has argued that feminist organizations will not survive without incorporating younger generations of feminist activists. The Women's Studies program and Women's Resource and Action Center at UMD, along with similar programs at other universities in the area, have nurtured generation after generation of younger activists who have revitalized and replenished the organizations as volunteers, interns, and employees. Students regularly volunteer and serve as interns in community organizations, and many go on to work for them, infusing the organizations with feminist scholarship. "The work we do is so much connected with the work that is happening in the community," said faculty member Njoki Kamau. "The fact that most of our students also flow over to work in the feminist organizations downtown shows the connection. . . . You could say we have been the theorists and women downtown do the actual practice. There's a direct connection."[14]

The relatively small size of the city also contributed to organizations being in fairly close physical proximity to one another, which in turn fostered collaboration among not only individuals but also organizations. Most of the feminist organizations are located within a few blocks of each other, easing collaboration as well as conversation. Certain locations in town have acted as hubs and gathering places; the Damiano Center, which is a center of activity for folks working on housing and poverty issues and which houses the soup kitchen and clothing exchange program, the Duluth Community Health Center, the Building for Women, and the building that was home first to the YWCA and then Gimaajii, have all at various times housed a variety of grassroots feminist organizations, often simultaneously. Many feminist events—from Take Back the Night rallies to International Women's Day celebrations—have been held in the Y's Trepanier Hall, and as part of Gimaajii it continues to be a gathering place for community forums and events. The Northcountry Women's Center, the Northcountry Women's Coffeehouse, the lesbian cooperative Chester Creek House, and gatherings at Gimaajii have all served to connect feminists in the Twin Ports.

More importantly, the collaborative work and the gathering places fostered the feminist community and friendships that have been so vital to the strength of Twin Ports grassroots feminist organizations. As organizer Judith Niemi said of the Northcountry Women's Center, "One of the impacts [of the center] was all of the people who got to know each other that way, the friendships and various relationships that came about that wouldn't have if you didn't have a place where they all showed up together at the same time." Many said the Northcountry Women's Coffeehouse and the lesbian center Aurora were places where they made some of the most important friendships of their lives. And as longtime resident Linda Estel said of Chester Creek House, one of the main things it offered to the community was "just a place for people to hang"—a place where women could connect, form and sustain relationships, celebrate, relax, relate, question, vision, and create.

The friendship of women, the love of women for one another, was one of the most important elements of vitality of the feminist movement nationwide. As Winifred Wandersee notes, the internal dissension within the women's movement is "just part of the story." The common thread missing from the record is "an overriding sense of love—a burst of energy related to a sense of loving one another." In Linda Gordon's words, the women's movement brought female friendship "into a position of honor." A female ethic of care promoted the primacy of women's relationships with one another. This was often something new for women, and was a large part of what motivated and energized the movement.

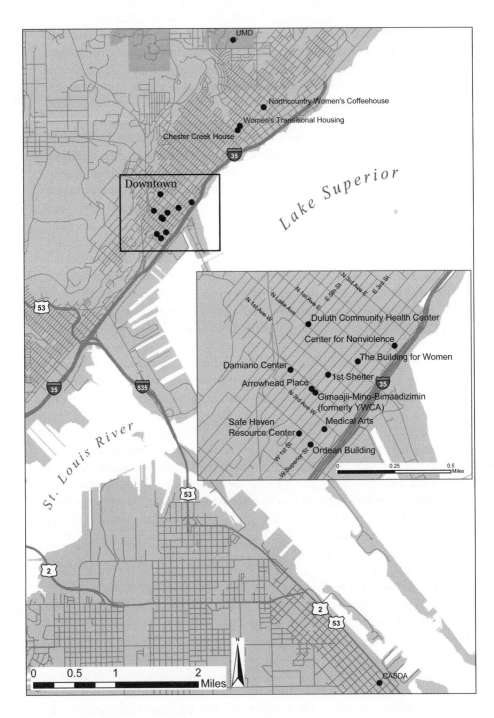

Locations of feminist organizations in the Twin Ports

Historian Ruth Rosen points to the euphoria of simply being listened to and accepted, and knowing that others shared similar stories. It created a deep sense of belonging and community. As scholar Verta Taylor states, women in feminist organizations were motivated by the "joy of participation, love and friendship of other women, and pride in having maintained their feminist convictions in the face of stunning opposition."[15]

The downside was that if relationships turned bad, the resulting pain and hostility was equally intense. Sometimes deep and irreconcilable woundings led to dysfunction or the demise of organizations, with women mirroring the oppression they had experienced and turning it toward other women. Feminist activist and scholar Jo Freeman warned against friendship as the basis of feminist organization, arguing that such a basis carries the potential of negative consequences, among these being organizations becoming closed to new members because of the time required to develop the same level of trust and the maintenance of relationships and solidarity becoming more important than action.[16]

While feminist organizations in the Twin Ports occasionally suffered such negative consequences of feminist friendship, for the most part bonds of friendship contributed to the depth and durability of the organizations. Feminist scholar Janice Raymond has argued that feminist ventures failed when there was nothing to hold them together beyond a community of resistance. Without what she termed "gyn/affection," feminist politics and political struggles remain superficial and more easily short-circuited. She argued that female friendship, on the other hand, gives depth to a political vision of feminism and is a profoundly political act. "The best feminist politics proceeds from a shared friendship. . . . Politics and friendship are restored to deeper meaning when they are brought together . . . where political activity proceeds from a shared affection, vision, and spirit, and when friendship has a more expansive political effect." Such friendship infuses the feminist community with the energy of affection and imbues sisterhood with spirit.[17]

Other elements of place, in particular the indigenous and political culture, also contributed to the nature and thriving of grassroots feminist organizations in the Twin Ports. The influence of the Anishinaabe was fundamental to the women-centered approach that sustained feminist organizing efforts in the northland. Just as the equality and respect accorded to the indigenous women of the Haudenosaunee nation inspired the first wave of feminism in upstate New York in the nineteenth century, the deep roots of women-honoring culture of the Anishinaabe are at work in the culture that supports feminist organizing in this area.

With colonization, Native women lost nearly all the freedoms, respect, and equality they once knew. Native women now experience higher rates of sexual assault and domestic violence than any other ethnic or racial group. Their spiritual traditions, language, and voice have been stripped away through forced assimilation efforts. Much of the land and water from which they drew their physical and spiritual nourishment has been mined, polluted, paved over, and desecrated in the name of "development." So the work of Native women and Native women's organizations in Duluth has been that of reclaiming what they have lost. As the mission statement of Mending the Sacred Hoop states, their aim is to *restore* the "safety, sovereignty, and sacredness of Native women," as well as their traditional leadership roles. Celebrating and teaching others about the sacredness of women is central to their daily lives and to their work.[18]

Valuing the sacredness of women has been an important piece of the feminist work in the Twin Ports community. I have heard it in the voices of the women in the Women's Action Group—"We were believed, we had value, we had wisdom"; in the lyrics of the women's music at the Coffeehouse and on Wise Women Radio; in women's studies classes where young women have found their voices and their truths honored and respected. It is repeated by the members of these organizations who have spoken of the importance of being guided by the voices and wisdom of the women they serve. This respect for women has been critical to defining the feminist movement in the region. It underlies what Victoria Ybanez has called "creating sister space"—the idea that when a woman is in crisis, the appropriate response is to create a space for her and treat her as a sister.[19]

This is not to say that the Twin Ports' feminist organizations have escaped their share of power struggles and undermining, but the predominant message at the core of the work and to which the organizations return when they have strayed from it is the importance of empowering and respecting women. It is a message that was inspired and continues to be renewed by Anishinaabe ikwe (women). A poster for Mending the Sacred Hoop pictures three women dancing, "celebrating the sacredness of women." It is integral to their work and to their lives. When it is integral to society and the sacred hoop is mended, then the goal of all of these organizations will have been realized.[20]

Another key element in the growth of feminist organizations here is the political culture in the Twin Ports and in Minnesota at large. As historian Rhoda Gilman has written about the political climate in Minnesota, "most would agree that it has been a seedbed for cultural and political movements that have changed the country." Without that climate, much of the successful work of the feminist organizations that developed in Duluth would probably not have been possible. Kelly Burger of the Superior-based Center Against Sexual and Domestic Abuse (CASDA) noted that when they began they simply could not do many of the things that organizers in Duluth could because they did not have the state legislation in Wisconsin to support it.[21]

The Minnesota political climate enabled activists to convince legislators to enact such legislation as the Displaced Homemaker Act, the Domestic Violence Act, sexual assault legislation establishing degrees of sexual assault, and Safe Harbor legislation for minors who have been victims of sex trafficking. A strong feminist movement in the Twin Cities, including pioneering work in sexual assault and domestic violence services, provided inspiration, models, resources, and support for feminist organizations in the Twin Ports. "There's a pretty big pipeline between Duluth and the Twin Cities in terms of resource gathering and outreach," noted Nancy Tubesing. PAVSA, the Women's Coalition, AICHO, the Women's Health Clinic, Women's Transitional Housing, and the Building for Women all had strong partnerships with organizations in the Twin Cities. Most continue to be part of state and regional coalitions.

Progressive political movements in the Twin Ports come from a strong political tradition of community organizing and collective action. The Finnish socialists who settled in Duluth and Superior at the turn of the twentieth century were one of the main influences contributing to this rich heritage. They were the backbone of socialist political organizing and a strong labor movement, as well as community building and cooperative activity ranging from consumer cooperatives to Finn halls where the community came together for dances, concerts, plays, lectures, and social gatherings. The plethora of Finnish socialist newspapers published in Duluth and Superior and the Finnish Work People's College in Smithville (now a part of Duluth), where curriculum was geared to training socialist and trade union activists, were major influences. This all contributed to an understanding of collective action that is alive and well today. Women were an integral part of the movement and engaged in every aspect from labor organizing to writing for the Finnish newspapers.[22]

Having already gained suffrage and greater recognition and rights in their native Finland, Finnish immigrant women formed a strong feminist movement both among the Finnish socialists and in connection with the national suffrage movement. Not only did the Finnish feminist movement create a heritage of strong, independent, and assertive women, it established a tradition of women working collectively to address issues. As historian Hilja Karvonen noted, "they had learned that a group could exert more energy and have more power than could the individual alone." As Finnish historian Marianne Wargelin Brown stated, "Finnish American feminist activity rarely operates on an individual basis; individual women quickly become groups of women who organize a female support network to solve problems at hand." These elements of this cultural and political legacy are apparent in the ways women came together in the grassroots feminist organizing efforts in Duluth and Superior decades later.[23]

The School of Social Development at the University of Minnesota Duluth, with its mission to train future community organizers, also helped foster the culture of community organizing in the area and prepared the way for the feminist organizations that followed. Many of its faculty and graduates were part of the early formation and ongoing growth of those organizations and did much to address the needs of women, those living in poverty, and the homeless population.

Finally, the distinctive culture of feminist consciousness raising in the Twin Ports played a significant role in the success of feminist organizations there in transforming the culture of the entire community. According to Alice Echols, by the 1970s, the feminist politicos of Second Wave feminism were concerned that consciousness raising was taking the place of action. In analyzing factors that led to the erosion of Second Wave feminism, Sara Evans has also argued that the political nature of consciousness-raising groups changed as they took an inward turn and migrated from political action to therapy. Rather than the informal, spontaneous consciousness-raising groups that arose around the country in the 1960s and '70s, the critical consciousness groups that were developed in different forms in Duluth—through the local NOW branch and the curricula of the Domestic Abuse Intervention Project (DAIP), as well as by feminist therapists—were deliberately structured to be educative and politicizing with a goal toward moving participants to action. Groups that helped develop DAIP's *In Our Best Interest* curriculum for critical consciousness (see Chapter 5: Domestic Abuse Intervention Project), and the groups that followed that used that curriculum, were a unique and fundamental piece of raising the feminist awareness of women in the Twin Ports. That curriculum has since come to be used around the world. All the groups were crucial not only in creating community, but also in creating political change.[24]

Another key piece in the distinctive character of consciousness raising in the Twin Ports came from a community of feminist therapists who took on an educative role in the community, training not only feminist organizers but also local law enforcement, social service workers, and health care professionals in feminist organizational principles. Many of the therapists specialized in organizational and group dynamics, and several organizations brought them in to help work through issues. Others modeled the practices and techniques the therapists used in groups organizers attended. The result was the creation of a culture that supported positive, collaborative, egalitarian relationships. "We trained a lot of women in how to have their own voice . . . and to have egalitarian [relationships]," said Nancy Tubesing, one of the therapists. They also worked with the medical community, police, educators, and clergy, both on organizational dynamics and on issues of sexual and domestic abuse.

Duluth being Duluth, the effect they had was exponential. "Think about the number of people in the community who've been touched by our thinking," said Mary Graff. "That's probably an underestimated thing in any community, but *in a community this size, you can change the culture.* You can support what is happening out there by training the next generation, or training the current generation of institutions so they're receptive to the ideas" [emphasis mine]. These feminist therapists did change the culture, and played a critical role in creating an environment that was open and receptive to feminist ideas and egalitarian organizational practices.

They also helped to sustain the organizations by providing support and guidance for people in the trenches. "I was a beneath-the-scenes cheerleader, encourager, supporter, tender of the people who were at the forefront . . . encouraging their gifts, shoring them up, teaching them," said Nancy. In addition to helping the women in the fledgling grassroots organizations work through organizational issues, they also helped them cope with the stresses of working with victims of sexual assault, domestic abuse, and entrenched male systems. The willingness of women in these organizations to find and seek support and healing was crucial to their ability to persevere.

The therapists modeled support in their own practices. Five of them had formed a work support group that many in the feminist community emulated. "We were a living model of feminism—living consciousness and awareness, supporting one another," said Sandy Christian. Nancy also thought they played an important role in modeling the fact that "people who are at the forefront need to gather together and give each other support." Accordingly, women working in the feminist organizations took the time to be that type of support to each other.

The vitality of the feminist movement in the Twin Ports has been sustained in part by the geographical location of the Twin Ports on Lake Superior and the edge of the wilderness. Surrounded by forests, rivers, and the lake, and within a hundred miles of the Boundary Waters Canoe Area Wilderness (BWCAW), the place facilitated friendships through women camping, hiking, canoeing, and being in the wilderness together. Spending time in the wilderness together not only led women to develop independence and inner strength, but also was a way that women connected and bonded as friends.[25]

In the early 1970s, a group of about fourteen women who had been part of forming the Northcountry Women's Center, Judith Niemi and Rosie Rocco among them, saw an ad in the *Duluth Herald* (now the *Duluth News Tribune*) for an island for rent in the north woods. "We chipped in fifty bucks a piece and had ourselves an island retreat. . . . It became an organizing place in itself," said Judith. "The Island" carried a certain mystique in the feminist community here, and was known as a place where some of the strongest and most radical feminist women in the community would gather, organize, relax, and renew—and still is.

While many women organized their own feminist camping and canoeing trips, others went on trips organized by Woodswomen or Wilderness Ways. Phyllis Cook, who owned Wilderness Ways, had for a time worked for PAVSA and been on the board of the Women's Coalition, and often did trips for "pure fun" with several women who had been colleagues and friends in those organizations in Duluth. "It was great bonding," remembered Phyllis. Undoubtedly many of the bonds that made this area such a special place for the growth of feminist organizations happened on those trips into the woods.

Those trips also provided a place to renew from the difficulties of the work, a practice essential to the sustenance of the organizations and the people in them. Sheryl Boman remembered that every year after the Take Back the Night march, a group of them would go into the Boundary Waters with Phyllis. Occasional breaks from the daily grind just to have fun together, especially in the restorative waters and wilderness of northern Minnesota, helped to nurture relationships, which so many have found to be an essential component of the success of their organizations.

But one does not need to take trips into the wilderness to experience the inexplicable energy that pervades this place. "That rock. That lake." The power of the ancient rocks and the vast, brilliant sea to inspire and empower is undeniable. The experience of awe, so much a part of daily life here, "leads people to cooperate, share resources, sacrifice for others, all of which are requirements for our collective life," and leads to a greater persistence in the creation of paradigm-shifting change. No doubt that spirit is at work in this place. The physical beauty and the energy in the natural environment that surrounds the Twin Ports—the majestic Lake Superior, the ancient volcanic bedrock, the pine and birch forests, the many rivers and tumbling waterfalls that course through the city, the deep blue of the sky mirrored in the lake, the northern lights—all inspire and renew. So many people have mentioned the incredible endurance of the women in these towns. I sincerely believe one of the main reasons for this is the capacity of the natural environment to replenish us. I am continually in awe of the power of natural beauty to cleanse me of cynicism, despair, and weariness, to compel me to look upon the world afresh.[26]

It also inspires. It seems next to impossible not to do extraordinary things here. As Nancy Gruver noted, this place provides a kind of "time space and mind space" that allows for creativity. "For people who have an inner creative drive, Duluth is an amazing place. People find each other because of that and are drawn by something." Perhaps it is, as Rosie said, "all the magnetite in the rock."

Many of us were drawn here by the power of the lake. For the Anishinaabe it is Gichigami, home of the Gichi Manidoo, the great spirit. Anyone who has watched the sunrise or the moonrise or the northern lights dance over this great body of water, or its waves crashing over rocks, or has been bathed in the serenity of its stillness or dived into its crystalline waters knows its capacity to calm, to strengthen, and to heal. To quote Winona LaDuke, "It is the most magical place on earth."[27]

Joan Chittister has said that "we do feminism because we cannot morally do otherwise." That kind of moral imperative lives in the very fiber of those hundreds of individuals in this place who have so dedicated their lives to the work of creating a more egalitarian, just, and peaceful world, a world in which women's voices, wisdom, bodies, and spirits are valued and respected. Every day they engage in the energizing and often exhausting work of fighting for recognition and voice, repairing and restoring what has been broken, and enacting a different vision—and at the end of the day, they go to the lake.[28]

%% %% %%

We go on, canoe under hot sun, the upturned paddle guides
    liquid to our dry mouths, water within us, water surrounds us,
    a great mystery, our becoming dry at all.
Replenish, all must be replenished, the water within and without,
    all that fills us, all that surrounds.
The great whistling pines, the tenacious beaver, the ancient loon,
    the rush of the young eagle's wings as it dips low over our
    canoe . . . the heron's wing and the hope in our souls.
We go on, our paddles dance with the lake water to the music in
    our throats.
We will go dry again, perhaps leap into the water, a small and
    symbolic celebration of a great and endless task which,
    gracefully undertaken, might allow us all to go on, and on, and
    on.

–Claudia Schmidt, "Replenish"

{ 2 }

A Brief History of Feminist
Organizing in the Twin Ports

The Second Wave feminist movement had grown out of and alongside political and social justice movements of the 1960s and 1970s—the civil rights movement, the student movement, the environmental movement, the farm laborers' movement, and the movement against the war the United States was waging in Vietnam. The same was true of the feminist movement in Duluth and Superior. "It can't be understood except by thinking of what it was like in the '70s and the ferment," said early feminist activist Judith Niemi. "It was the Vietnam protest, civil rights, boycotting grapes, the founding of HMOs, trying to get Women's Studies going at UMD, environmental things, and food. It's not separable from all of that. . . . In the '70s, you just had an idea and did it. . . . People were passionate about change."[1]

At the center of many of these activities locally was Chester Creek House, originally formed as a social justice–oriented intentional community in 1970. Household members were involved in antiwar activities and draft resistance. They operated a buying club out of the basement that was the beginning of the Whole Foods Co-op. Many were involved in the establishment of the Duluth Community Health Center, locally known as the Free Clinic, that among other things provided pregnancy testing and counseling, and after *Roe v. Wade*, abortion counseling.

Faculty and students from the School of Social Development (SSD) at the University of Minnesota Duluth (UMD) also infused the community with progressive activism and organizing. The school, which operated throughout most of the 1970s and until 1982, drew dynamic and innovative faculty who came with a vision, a philosophy, and a curriculum for a systems and social development approach to social change. They were, in the words of former SSD faculty member Judy Dwyer, "intellectual radicals" who trained students to advocate for people by enabling them to articulate and achieve those things that would be helpful to them in attaining a better life. Faculty and graduates of SSD, many of whom stayed in the area, became actively involved in forming and building social change organizations throughout the larger community. "It's that Alinsky organizing where you start with small issues in people's self-interest, vacant lots, that sort of thing, and when you see progress there you can move on to bigger things. So we worked on a lot of little issues here in Duluth," remembered Angie Miller, an SSD graduate.[2]

SSD's faculty and graduates helped to develop programs within the Duluth Community Action Program (CAP)—including West End Community Action, the Senior Coalition, Broad-based Organizing for a Newer Duluth (BOND), and the CAP Weatherization Program—as well as social service programs at the Fond du Lac Reservation. They also created the Loaves and Fishes Catholic Worker Community in Duluth and Citizens Organized Acting Together (COACT)—a direct-action, citizen-based organization that empowers individuals to take action in their own lives on social justice issues.[3]

Feminist Organizing: The Early Years, 1970–1980

The feminist movement in Duluth arose in the midst of this climate of activism and community organizing. While the women's liberation movement had been sweeping the nation since the mid-1960s, Duluth's earliest efforts in feminist organizing began in the early 1970s. One of the first of these efforts occurred when a group of UMD faculty, including Judith Niemi, Susan Johnson, and Caryl Bentley, along with student Rosemary Frye and other women from the community—Barb Neubert, Nancy Massey, Rosemary Rocco, and others—decided to form a joint campus/community women's center called the Northcountry Women's Center. At first operating out of a small office in the YWCA, it was as much a clandestine lesbian center as a women's center. They held support groups for lesbians, had a small lending library, and also worked with the city's Human Rights Commission to include sexual orientation in a Human Rights ordinance (though it would be many more years before this would pass). They held a women's conference and organized a workshop for local therapists on how to give better service to their lesbian and gay clients.[4]

Around the same time another group of women, among them Barb Neubert, Diane Skomars, and Sharon Torrison, were beginning to meet in what was essentially a consciousness-raising group. They talked about the new women's liberation movement and the issues in their lives, and read everything they could get their hands on, from Simone de Beauvoir's *The Second Sex* to every issue of the new monthly magazine *Ms.* Calling themselves Women's Liberation of Duluth, they went into the community to speak with church groups, community organizations, and college classes about the issues of women's liberation. They even taught classes in karate and self-defense.

In November 1972, Women's Liberation of Duluth, along with representatives from several long-established women's organizations in Duluth—the American Association of University Women (AAUW), the Junior League, the League of Women Voters (LWV), the AFDC (Aid for Families with Dependent Children) League—organized a major event for the budding feminist community. According to organizer Claudia Daly, the Woman to Woman Conference, held at Pilgrim Church, was "for and about women" and addressed itself "not to the particular interests of any group or organization, but rather to all women as individuals, women whose common bond is that they are women." Workshops included such topics as "Sexuality, Health Rights, and Contraception," "Women as Single Heads of Households," and, exclusively for black women, "Soul Talk."[5]

In 1973, Randi Goldstone from the Neighborhood Improvement Center, a rape crisis shelter in the Twin Cities, held a workshop in Duluth for the Duluth and Superior Police Departments and others who might be interested in the shelter's work. At that workshop were some of the women from the Northcountry Women's Center, including Rosemary Rocco and Nancy Massey, and others from the local Planned Parenthood, including Tina Welsh. That workshop and the meeting of these individuals were pivotal in galvanizing much of the feminist organizing in Duluth. The conversations begun there would lead to the creation of a rape crisis program. (See Chapter 3: Program for Aid to Victims of Sexual Assault.)

The Northcountry Women's Center, now known as the Women's Growth Center, had by then moved to an office in Old Main on the former UMD campus. In addition to serving as a resource and outreach center, the Women's Growth Center housed the first rape crisis line for the group that would become the Program to Aid Victims of Sexual Assault. Many of the women involved in the center were beginning to teach courses at UMD that would be considered "women's studies" courses. Among these were a course taught by Judith Niemi, Contemporary Literature by Women, and another called Women and Madness, where students read books that were hot on feminists' lists at the time—Phyllis

Chesler's *Women and Madness*, Sylvia Plath's *The Bell Jar*, and Charlotte Perkins Gilman's *The Yellow Wallpaper*. Caryl Bentley taught a course on women through the Sociology Department, and at the urging of undergrads in the Psychology Department, grad student Sharon Torrison taught the first women's studies course in the regular curriculum, Psy 3221: Changing Roles of Women.

Recognizing that several courses relating to women's studies were being offered across different departments, a few of the faculty decided to approach the Interdisciplinary Studies Committee at UMD to have their courses designated formally as Women's Studies courses. "But even the Interdisciplinary Studies committee argued about this," remembered Judith. "They weren't sure it was a good idea to have a Women's Studies concentration." Ultimately they did agree to have some sort of designation, but as Judith noted, "it was fascinating how even your allies were very reluctant to do that." From these courses, UMD student Joyce Benson constructed the first Women's Studies major through the Interdisciplinary Studies major and became the first Women's Studies graduate at UMD.

In 1974, UMD provost Ray Darland called together a Special Committee on Women's Studies, later called the Women's Studies Task Force, to investigate the need for a Women's Studies program and a campus women's center. The committee for many years simply investigated, though in 1976, a "Wo/men's Resource Center," which primarily provided books and pamphlets on "changing sex roles and alternative lifestyles," opened in the UMD library. According to the newspaper account, "the odd spelling of Wo/men is intentional to let persons of both sexes know they are welcome."[6]

Also in 1976, a local branch of the National Organization for Women (NOW) was created in Duluth. Joyce Benson had attended a meeting of NOW in Chicago, and returned excited to form a chapter in Duluth. All she needed was to find ten interested people, which she did fairly quickly, and from there "it just took off." Established mainstream national organizations—such as the AAUW, the Junior League, the YWCA, and the League of Women Voters—had existed in Duluth since the late 1800s and early 1900s, but this was the first local branch of a specifically feminist national organization. The local chapter had an initial membership of about fifty people. "Women were just beginning to have a voice during those years," said Joyce. "They needed an organization that would represent women and NOW did that." The group studied NOW cofounder Betty Friedan's *The Feminine Mystique* and other feminist works, and began tackling issues of workplace discrimination and reproductive rights. "That was the beginning of so many changes that occurred over the years," Joyce reflected. Superior, Wisconsin, soon followed suit when Jan Conley began a local branch of NOW there.[7]

Feminist activism in Duluth also grew spontaneously from the Community Action Program (CAP) when it began a weatherization project for low-income households in Duluth. The intent of the program was to break the cycle of poverty, but an unintended result was that it became an organization that empowered women. The CAP board supported hiring women for construction jobs and hired Susan Askelin, one of the founders of the construction cooperative Builders and Laborers, to head the weatherization program. Susan, who had been instrumental in hiring and promoting women in the trades, hired many women laborers for the weatherization program. Run as much as possible as a collective within the constraints of being a city project with unionized workers, it provided one of the first models of a women-run organization in Duluth. They employed circular rather than hierarchical decision-making methods, utilizing empathetic practices. Program participant Shary Zoff described their process: "You put on the cloak of what the other person was talking about, and you advocated for that. Then you put yourself in a position, 'What would it take for me to agree with what they're saying?'"[8]

The program also provided highly visible examples of women in nontraditional jobs. "Women on the street, in the neighborhood, working in homes and doing carpentry . . . you just didn't see that. It made a tremendous impact in the community," said another participant, Shirley Duke. Kelly Ravenfeather, who also worked with CAP, recalled, "I loved it when little girls would be on the sidewalk and they would look up and go, 'It's a girl.' We would look down and smile and say, 'Yep, and you can do this, too.'" Working in nontraditional jobs that challenged them physically, mentally, and emotionally, and required them to problem solve, they developed an inner confidence and a Rosie Riveter-esque "We Can Do It!" attitude that inspired countless other women in the community.[9]

"There was so much support there to be able to succeed," said program participant Mary Tennis. Connie Gunderson said she felt "embraced by women who gave me a chance." They learned to appreciate other women and came to recognize themselves in the experiences of other women. "I felt like I'd met kindred souls," said Linda Ward. "It felt like coming home. Finally people like me—women like me." The kind of support and solidarity of women for women fostered in the weatherization program would come to characterize the nature of feminist organization building in the Twin Ports. Confidence in the strength and capacity of women, the valuing of women and of working with women, and of equality in relationship were all principles the women in the program lived out and passed on to the community. These principles were extended either by their direct involvement in feminist organizations or indirectly through the model and inspiration they provided. Many of the women continued these efforts in their later work as healers, farmers, gardeners, social activists, and educators.

Another organization that broke from traditional stereotypes of women's roles was Woodswomen. Founded by Judith Niemi, Elizabeth Barnard, Shirley Hayer, and Trudy Fulton in 1977, Woodswomen was a women's outdoor adventure company that organized trips for women, at first primarily canoe trips into the Boundary Waters Canoe Area. Judith never set out to create feminist trips; she just wanted to do trips in ways that were the most fun. She wasn't about teaching survival skills, and she was not in the business of teaching women self-esteem. Her only agenda was that "women should be free and happy." But that kind of freedom and happiness gave women perspective on how life could be, as well as how capable they could be. "It's a confidence-building thing for women who are doing it," she noted. She witnessed how, without expectations of who they were supposed to be, even the most conventional of women became freer on her trips.

For a while Woodswomen worked with women's groups to teach leadership skills. In the wilderness, women learned their own capacities, strengths, and realities. "It was my job to see that any mistakes were within the realm of safety, but women did not want to be taken care of," stated Judith. "They did not want too much running by rules. They could figure it out." Carolyn Shrewsbury, director of Women's Studies at Mankato State University, once told Judith, "What we do in Women's Studies is the theory and you're the practice." "It was a way to create society the way we wanted society to be," reflected Judith. "[The fact] that women were doing this mattered to other women who weren't part of it. . . . It caught people's imagination."

A few years later, Phyllis Cook also developed a business taking women on outdoor trips, Wilderness Ways. She took women, primarily from this area, on backpacking trips, canoe trips, and a winter dogsledding and skiing trip. "My purpose in taking women into the wilderness," she said, "was [for them to learn] that 'I can do this and I don't need a man.'" All-women trips into the wilderness continue to be an important part of the women's culture in the area.

By the mid-1970s, a group of feminist therapists had brought a new model of therapy to the region that had a significant impact in the community. Maggy (Peg) Anderson, Sandy Christian, Mary Graff, Mary Martin, Rosemary Rocco, Gloria Singer, and Nancy Tubesing, among others, formed support groups, ran training sessions and workshops, and otherwise nourished the budding feminist community and did much to shape and support feminist organizing in the Twin Ports. One of the truly radical and radicalizing aspects of their work was a new model of therapy they brought into the community. "It was a change in the whole therapeutic understanding of what people needed to do and what their issues were," said Nancy Tubesing. Unlike "that patriarchal model of psychoanalytically-based therapy of us as experts with someone who was 'less than,'" feminist therapy was based on a model of a "shared and egalitarian relationship where relationship and respect were emphasized." Their therapeutic process was one of "listening to women's stories and paying attention to what came up," said Gloria Singer. This new model opened the door for people to turn to therapists to help sort out the issues of their lives. For women, many of these issues centered around relationships, as well as dealing with traumas of sexual assault, incest, and domestic abuse.[10]

When feminist therapists at the Human Development Center began holding support groups for women, these conversations quickly made evident that many women suffered from physical and emotional abuse in their homes and that there was a dire and urgent need for some kind of shelter where battered women could go to be safe. Three women who had met in these support groups—Shirley Oberg, Jean DeRider, and Pat Hoover—decided to do something about it. With the help of many others, by 1978 they had formed the Women's Coalition for Battered Women (later the Safe Haven Shelter), and opened the doors to the first domestic violence shelter in Duluth. (See Chapter 4: The Women's Coalition for Battered Women/Safe Haven Shelter.)

Because of her work with the Women's Coalition, Shirley Oberg was appointed to a statewide advisory task force on domestic violence shelters. The task force was run by the Minnesota Department of Corrections, which administered funding for domestic violence shelters in Minnesota. On the task force, Shirley met Ellen Pence, who was the director at that time. The two of them began talking and visioning about more effective ways to address domestic violence, and by 1980, Ellen had moved to Duluth, where she and Shirley, in conjunction with the Women's Coalition, began using new state legislation to try an experiment with mandatory arrest in cases of domestic assault, known as the Domestic Abuse Intervention Project (DAIP). Together they would go on, through a process later known as the Duluth Model, to create training programs for the criminal justice system, a program for men who batter, and groups for battered women that provided education for critical consciousness. (See Chapter 5: Domestic Abuse Intervention Project.)

The Heyday of Feminist Organizing: 1980–1990

By the early 1980s, many other grassroots feminist organizations were springing up in the Twin Ports. In addition to PAVSA, the Women's Coalition for Battered Women, and the DAIP, other direct service organizations for women began, including a displaced homemaker's program and the Women's Health Center, and professional and political organizations were established. Chester Creek House, the social justice housing cooperative, became a lesbian collective, and faculty and staff at UMD finally established a Women's Studies program. In addition, the women's arts and culture scene was burgeoning. Along with the founding of the Northcountry Women's Coffeehouse, the early eighties saw the rise of women's bookstores, a women's radio show, and a women's music production company.

The Duluth and Superior chapters of NOW were involved in several local and national projects. Their main focus was passage of the Equal Rights Amendment (ERA). In 1979, the Duluth chapter of NOW "had this big rally and parade down Superior Street, with big banners with 'Pass the ERA,'" remembered local NOW president Joyce Benson. About a hundred marchers joined together in support of the ERA, to a mixed reaction of "support and stares." While some onlookers gave them the thumbs-up sign, others decried the ERA as contributing to "the breakdown of the family unit." In the spring of 1980, about thirty members of the Duluth and Superior chapters of NOW traveled together by bus to Chicago to join the roughly 200,000 who had gathered there from across the country to march and rally in support of the ERA. They marched to Grant Park, where they listened to speeches by among others Betty Friedan, Bella Abzug, Jesse Jackson, and Gloria Steinem. "It was quite a trip," remembered Joyce. "It was rewarding. Everybody thinks of that trip fondly." The Superior chapter of NOW had several issue-oriented task forces. Among these was a Violence Against Women task force that held discussions on the need for a domestic violence shelter in Superior and organized one of the first Take Back the Night marches in the Twin Ports area. In 1980, the Duluth chapter adopted the national organization's project of forming consciousness-raising groups, with well-developed process guidelines and discussion topics, and trained facilitators to lead them. "People could open up and talk about things. It was good for women to have a forum for letting loose and sharing some of their experiences with others," said Joyce. The sessions were designed to empower women to create change, and each session ended with strategizing for action.[11]

In that same year, Joyce began looking into developing a displaced homemakers' program in Duluth. Displaced homemaker legislation—to fund programs to support and serve women who had been homemakers all their lives but suddenly found themselves without income or means to support themselves due to separation, divorce, disability, or death of a spouse—had recently been enacted on both the state and federal levels. The state of Minnesota was funding sites throughout the state, but did not yet have one in Duluth. So, for her senior project for her Interdisciplinary Studies/Women's Studies major at UMD, Joyce decided to develop a displaced homemaker program in Duluth. She formed a task force with other interested individuals, including women from the Women's Coalition and the YWCA, to develop a program. They had models of other programs around the state, but wanted theirs to be better. They worked on every detail. Tina Welsh, the YWCA board chair at the time, remembered, "Joyce Benson and I, along with others, sat with [state senator] Sam Solon working on legislation that would enable displaced homemakers to get revenue from state taxes on marriage licenses."[12]

Run first out of the basement of the YWCA, Project SOAR (Service, Opportunity, Action, Responsibility) provided training, education, and supportive services for women entering the workforce for the first time. Pat Gosz, who had been interning with the Women's Coalition as part of her work toward her degree from the School of Social Development and was part of the SOAR task force, was hired to direct the program. Pat hired staff and developed a curriculum for the program and also did outreach to the community to find referrals for women to be in the program and to educate the community about it. The program worked with women to access the tools they needed to find employment. The overall goal of the curriculum was to develop increased self-esteem and self-confidence, and to enable the women to recognize how the skills they had acquired as homemakers translated into employment skills. They offered ten-week training sessions, with about fifteen to twenty participants in each.

They began with sixty-one participants and the program grew from there. Fairly soon Project SOAR incorporated into its own organization and moved across the street into a suite of offices in the Arrowhead Building. While displaced homemaker programs throughout the state were highly successful, with more than 80 percent of program participants being placed in employment or education and training, the program in Duluth had an even higher success rate, with nearly all of the women finding employment, even during difficult economic times. Pat, who stayed on as the director for the first five years, remembered Project SOAR as being "well supported [by] a lot of caring people who sincerely cared about getting the project going and helping the women who were struggling. . . . It was good morale, good team spirit, we had a good board." They also had good working relations with the county job training program. "It was a good experience," said Pat, "[with] a positive, committed group of women."[13]

Another unaddressed need for women in the northland was for accessible abortion services. Abortion services had been available at St. Luke's Hospital in Duluth for a few years immediately following *Roe v. Wade* (1973), but increasing controversy over abortion rights had left the area without an abortion provider for several years. Women from the area seeking abortions had to travel one hundred fifty miles to the Twin Cities. With a desire to make women's health services more accessible, abortion rights pioneer Dr. Jane Hodgson, who had established the Midwest Health Center for Women in the Twin Cities, hired Tina Welsh to direct a clinic in Duluth, and together they cofounded the Women's Health Center. The center provided, and continues to provide, abortion services as well as family planning, contraceptive, testing for STDs, and other services for women throughout northeast Minnesota, Wisconsin, and the Upper Peninsula of Michigan. (See Chapter 6: Women's Health Center and the Building for Women.)

A variety of grassroots women's professional networking and political groups also sprang up in the area at this time, among them the New Women's Network and the Greater Minnesota Women's Alliance. The New Women's Network was a loose affiliation of several hundred women that had been formed to provide information about job openings, careers, and resources as women joined the professional workforce in large numbers in the 1970s. Begun in 1978 from a conversation among six women seeking to promote careers for women in education, with the support of secretary of state Joan Growe it grew to include women in a variety of careers. Meant to be an alternative to "the old boys' network," the monthly meetings offered information on job openings and qualifi-cations, but also acted as a support network. As Mary Ann Lucas, one of the founding members, said, "We are often dealing with exchanges of how to handle things (faced by women in jobs and at home)—what to do and the best method." Carol Tierney, another member, said, "Women need this outlet for information, conversation, and support." The net-work was fairly short-lived but fulfilled an important role at the time.[14]

The Greater Minnesota Women's Alliance (GMWA), a bipartisan group of women dedicated to promoting a feminist political agenda, sprang up for a few years beginning in 1981. It began when a busload of women went to the state capitol to lobby on women's issues, which meant "anything that affects women and that's more than 50 percent of the population." They had not made appointments, and when they went around to legislators' offices, some legislators were willing to meet with them, others were not. "Someone was told, 'Why aren't you all home with your families? Why are you coming down here and bother-ing us?' . . . They were surprised to see all these women come to talk to them. . . . Some of them were impressed. . . . No other group had done this. . . . We made a real impact," remembered Joyce Benson, one of the organizers. Their debriefing session on the bus on the way home revealed that while some had had good experiences, others left furious. Some of the legislators' intransigence and complete unwillingness to listen was eye-opening. However, most of the women felt empowered, aware of how much more informed and knowledgeable all of them were on the issues than were the legislators. Taking women to spend a day lobbying at the state capitol continued for several years.[15]

The first trip to the legislature convinced them of the need to continue their efforts, so several of them met and agreed to form the Greater Min-nesota Women's Alliance. Their big kick-off event was held October 4, 1981, with Gloria Steinem as the keynote speaker. There they held work-shops to train women for precinct caucuses and to network. "We were issue-oriented. We did not have regular meetings, but when something came up that we should work on, we would get together," remembered Joyce. Getting more people in office who were sympathetic to feminist issues became their main focus. The group identified individuals they thought would be good. "We would interview the women we wanted to support to see if they had the same values, and if they did then we would work for them," remembered Tina Welsh. They encouraged them to run for office and supported their candidacies. Their first effort was to fill an opening for St. Louis county commissioner. Looking to their membership, they decided Marilyn Krueger would be a good candidate, and they worked to have her elected. She served on the county commission for many years. Soon after, they decided they needed to get a supportive woman on the city council. They hoped Gail Huntley would run. "She was interested," said Joyce, "but she said her children were too young. She was not in a position to do it, but she said, 'I'll offer my husband. I think he would be good at it.'" Tom Huntley successfully ran for city council and later ran for the state legislature and served as the representative for District 7A in Duluth from 1992 to 2015.[16]

In addition to supporting candidates for office, GMWA organized hundreds of women and men to turn out in support of women's issues at local political party caucuses. GMWA worked closely with other women's organizations in the area that consistently turned to them for help and lobbied for their needs. GMWA lasted about five years and dissolved as people became more involved with other organizations in the community.[17]

Feminist peace and nonviolence organizations, a significant part of the feminist political presence in the Twin Ports, also formed in the early 1980s. Recognizing the connections between militarism and violence against women, members of these organizations were often the same as those involved in movements to end sexual and domestic assault. Jan Conley, who had spearheaded Superior NOW's investigation of the need for a domestic violence shelter in the early 1980s, founded the Superior chapter of Twin Cities–based Women Against Military Madness. Among their many endeavors, WAMM held the first war toys picket in the Twin Ports to emphasize the importance of children learning that violence is not an acceptable approach to conflict resolution. Many of those who marched together in Take Back the Night marches could also be found marching together in antinuclear marches sponsored by Duluth-based Women Speak for a Sane World. Jan Provost, inspired by her sister, Barbara Wiedner, who founded the international antinuclear organization Grandmothers for Peace in an effort to preserve a future for all children and grandchildren, established a chapter in Superior. In the Twin Ports, the Grandmothers have marched and held vigils in support of peace and nonviolence, actively engaged in efforts to promote anti–domestic violence legislation in Wisconsin, and annually donate toys from their holiday peaceful toy drive to local domestic violence shelters.

When the women's and lesbian cultural movement blossomed nationally in the 1970s and 1980s, it did so locally as well. The most significant component of this in Duluth was the opening of the Northcountry Women's Coffeehouse in 1981. Hosting educational and entertainment programming twice a month in its first few years, the Coffeehouse was the center of women's culture in Duluth. Providing a venue for local women musicians, artists, and speakers, it brought women's music and culture to the Twin Ports. More than this, it was the central gathering place where feminists met, shared information, made connections, and renewed their spirits. (See Chapter 7: Northcountry Women's Coffeehouse.)

In the same year that the Coffeehouse opened, a women's radio program, Wise Women Radio, began on the public radio station on the UMD campus. In the fall of 1980, during a pledge drive marathon for WDTH (now KUMD) radio, Cathe Hice-Hall ran a long segment of women's music that had such a positive response that she suggested it be a regular ongoing program. The following February, Jean Johnson (now Stephanie Hemphill), the Outreach Coordinator for WDTH, organized a meeting "to explore the possibilities" for women's programming on WDTH that would combine music with public affairs material. She suggested Brenda Dziuk (now Latourelle), then a student at UMD, become one of the main volunteer coordinators and be responsible for organizing more volunteer involvement in running the program. Brenda remembered Jean asking if she would be interested in putting together a weekly women's music program: "I remember thinking, 'Wow, how cool is that!' At that time, women's music was pretty new, and you never heard any of it on any of the mainstream airwaves. . . . It was so exciting to think we could get some of this music out on the airwaves."[18]

They met several times, set a tentative schedule of topics including sexual assault, alternative lifestyles (which was code for lesbian issues), "the new abortion center in Duluth," and more. They decided to name the project Wise Women Radio, with Kay Gardner's "Wise Woman" as the theme song. Wise Women Radio ran its first broadcast on May 10, 1981. Brenda remembered: "KUMD was so supportive. . . . They spent hours with us, teaching us how to use the equipment. We did it, just like we did everything else in those days, by the seat of our pants."[19]

Their purpose was "to promote awareness of women's music, issues, culture, and history," and Katrina (Deconcini) Tobey, one of the volunteers and a regular listener, remembered how important the show was in connecting and inspiring women in those early days of feminism in the community. "All these isolated, in a sense, women listening to the radio and listening to women's music. . . . It was unifying."

The featured artists spanned generations and genres, from early recordings of Edith Piaf and Bessie Smith to the latest generation of women's music, such as Chris Williamson and Margie Adam; from the folk music of Buffy St. Marie and Joan Baez to the gospel and blues of Odetta and Bernice Reagon, to international artists and the popular artists of the day. The public affairs topics covered a wide spectrum of interests and concerns.[20]

By 1982 WWR had a dozen regular volunteer announcers. During those first years they held an annual arts fair benefit to promote the radio program, but also to showcase women artists in the community. The benefit featured local women's visual arts, poetry and literature, dance and theater, and live music. WWR also sponsored two major concerts in 1982. Looking back on the early days of Wise Women Radio, Stephanie Hemphill reflected, "It was a popular program, evidenced by success in the pledge drives." And while levels of volunteerism fluctuated, at the beginning "there was a golden age—we shared what you could call synergy and shared a vision." In 1984 some women approached KUMD to add a lesbian-specific show. The regular Tuesday evening program, *Ruby Red Slippers*, aired for a few years. KUMD also had a regular program on GLBT issues called *This Way Out*. That same year, Wise Women Radio decided to focus on music programming, which is "easier and quicker and more fun for a lot of people to do a music show than to do a public affairs interview," said Stephanie. The radio show, now called the *Women's Music Show*, has continued every Sunday afternoon to this day.[21]

WWR did not sponsor any more concerts, but others, primarily Artemis Productions and later the Northcountry Women's Coffeehouse, picked up that task. Artemis Productions was formed to bring nationally known lesbian performers to the Twin Ports. Four women—Rosemary Frye, Shirley Lundquist, Donna Haggert, and Linda Estel—began the music production company by each putting in $100. "The community rallied behind us," remembered Linda. "Community members would do the ushering, they'd do the sound, they'd take tickets, sell tickets. . . . We had a lot of good concerts; lots of fun times."[22]

Their first concert was Alix Dobkin, who was "the most radical person we ever brought. . . . She was pretty separationist at the time. She did not want men in the technical side of the concert—no men allowed," said Linda. Other performers included Teresa Trull and Barbara Higby, Marvea, Sue Fink, Kay Gardner, Jenny Clemmons, and Heather Bishop. "People would come because it was an Artemis concert. There wasn't a place to get women's music of that caliber unless you got to Michigan or the Cities. It was very well received," remembered Linda.[23]

Artemis fell apart, for personal reasons, about two years later, but during those few years it created events that brought together hundreds of local women in ways that galvanized and energized the feminist community. Several years later, the Northern Lights Womyn's Music Festival similarly invigorated the community as it brought local and regional women musicians to the area for a two-day celebration for several years.

To support the growing feminist culture in Duluth in the early 1980s, a few women decided to open a feminist bookstore. Named simply A Woman's Bookstore, the store was run as a collective in a small storefront on First Avenue West. They carried a small selection of feminist books and magazines, as well as children's books. When that store slowly fizzled out in the mid-1980s, Jan Conley and Cheryl Wiltrout opened another, Journeys Bookstore, with a focus on New Age, ecology, and affirmative children's books. After a short time, Linda Beatty (now Darcy Seezaday), who had been the volunteer coordinator, took on the business and made books, literature, magazines, music, and other media available to the feminist and the LGBT communities at a time when these were not otherwise accessible. She worked with a representative from Lady Slipper (a women's music supplier) and was one of the few, if not the only, places in town that carried women's music. Journeys was more than a bookstore. Darcy wanted it to be a community resource, and held several special events there, especially during Pride. She was an affirming presence for a mostly closeted LGBT community. She said that it was with some regret that the business closed, "but when I think of those moments that I provided a place where people could be affirmed no matter who they were—makes me cry sometimes."

One of the most significant events for the lesbian and feminist communities in the early 1980s was the establishment of Chester Creek House as a lesbian collective. At the end of the 1970s, Beverly Berntson, one of the members of the original Chester Creek community, began talking about her desire for Chester Creek to become a lesbian community, and by 1981, when the last man from the original community had left, Chester Creek officially became a lesbian housing cooperative. Linda Estel, one of the first women to join the cooperative, recalled, "I moved into Chester Creek House because it was a community and because it was lesbian. We felt very strongly that there needed to be a lesbian space available that was just lesbian space—space for women to be without men and space for lesbians to be without heterosexuals regardless of their gender." Some lived there for many years; others were transient. In the early years, many of the women who lived at Chester Creek House were students. In later years, long-term residents tended to be older and more established, though the house always had a mix of generations.

The house also served as temporary housing for women in transition, for women needing short-term housing, such as visiting scholars, or for women in dire straits. "We were an emergency house," said Linda. "We had women come who were getting out of abusive relationships or women who just needed a place to live for a while. We often had temporary residents who didn't plan on staying there, but were going to be there for a period of time."

In the communal living environment at Chester Creek, residents convened regularly for house meetings, and group meals were encouraged. They shared expenses and chores, as well as a "political ideology that was distinctly anti-establishment and anti-war, and strongly women-identified," said longtime resident Tineke Ritmeester. Over the years, residents of Chester Creek House have played important roles in many of the grassroots feminist organizations in the Twin Ports. It was an important center for lesbian and feminist community building and community activities for many years.[24]

The biggest event at Chester Creek House was the annual winter solstice gathering. More than a hundred women and a few children would gather to celebrate the solstice and honor its traditions, which included sharing the solstice legend, lighting thirteen candles to represent the thirteen lunar months, and a ritual jumping over the fire to leave behind the ills of the past year and leap with hopes for the year to come. Lutheran church potlucks had nothing on the solstice potluck at Chester Creek, with tables upon tables of everyone's best—from the classic Minnesota hot dishes to smoked fish and vegetarian dishes, soups, salads of every imaginable sort, and desserts beyond compare. Tables were set up all around the house for conversation; friendships were renewed and begun. Community happened there.

Meanwhile, on campus during the late 1970s and early 1980s, more and more Women's Studies classes were being taught and efforts were underway to develop a minor. After five years, the original task force formed by the provost in 1974 was doing nothing more than studying the issue. It took the infusion of new energy to make Women's Studies at UMD a reality. A core group of new energized and dedicated feminist faculty members and staff broke off from the Women's Studies Task Force and formed the Women's Coordinating Committee. Bilin Tsai in Chemistry and Mary Zimmerman in the Medical School did the bulk of the research to support the proposal for a Women's Studies minor and move it forward, but they had significant support from campus minister Margaret Morris, Marge Grevatt in the School of Social Development, myself, and dozens of other UMD faculty and staff. In the fall of 1980 the proposal for a Women's Studies minor, with a program to be housed in the College of Letters and Sciences, was approved. In the fall of 1981, Susan Coultrap-McQuin came on board as the first director of the Women's Studies program.

The program quickly grew, and by 1986 had become a department with a major. At that time they also received funding to hire their first full-time faculty member, and Tineke Ritmeester joined the department in 1987. The Institute for Women's Studies began that same year. The institute included the Women's Studies Department, the Center for Research, the Women's Drop-In Center, and the Office of the Sexual Harassment Educator and Advocate. By March of 1988, the plan for the women's center had finally borne fruit, and officially opened as the Women's Resource and Action Center. All of these created vital resources and connections for feminist activists and organizers in the community, a collaboration that continues into the present day. Similar programs began at the College of St. Scholastica, University of Wisconsin–Superior, and Lake Superior College in the late 1990s and early 2000s.[25]

As needs arose that existing feminist organizations could not fill, another wave of service-oriented organization building began in the late 1980s. Recognizing that women who had experienced domestic abuse often would return to their abusers simply because they had no alternative, a number of women in the community came together to create Women's Transitional Housing in 1988. Women's Trans gave women experiencing domestic violence a longer-term solution to homelessness, as well as supportive programming to enable them to become self-sufficient. Many years later, when women in the program were having difficulty finding jobs that paid a living wage, Michelle LeBeau, one of the founders of Women's Trans, formed Women in Construction to provide training for them and others to get jobs in the trades where they could earn decent wages. (See Chapter 9: Women's Transitional Housing and Women in Construction.)

Also in 1988, women in Superior formed the Center Against Sexual and Domestic Abuse (CASDA) from two other organizations in order better to consolidate their efforts to fight violence against women. (See Chapter 8: Center Against Sexual and Domestic Abuse.) Lesbians whose need for a more public and political presence was not addressed by the Coffeehouse formed Aurora: A Northland Lesbian Center. Aurora provided a gathering space, resource center, support groups, and programming for lesbians and education and outreach on lesbian issues for the wider community. (See Chapter 11: Aurora: A Northland Lesbian Center.)

1990–2000: Continued Creation and Growth of Feminist Organizations

Organizations continued to be formed throughout the 1990s. In the late 1980s and early 1990s, a group of Native women and men, in collaboration with Ellen Pence of DAIP, had been meeting to discuss how best to assist Native women experiencing domestic abuse whose needs were not being met by domestic violence organizations in the community. This led to the creation of Mending the Sacred Hoop (MSH) in 1991. After the passage of the Violence Against Women Act in 1994, Mending the Sacred Hoop would become the first training and technical assistance provider on domestic abuse issues throughout Indian country. (See Chapter 10: Mending the Sacred Hoop.)

While MSH provided advocacy for Native women experiencing domestic abuse, Native women with immediate needs for safety and shelter still needed a Native-specific alternative to the shelters in Duluth and Superior. Three Native women—Victoria Ybanez, Toni Sheehy, and Mary Ann Walt—organized efforts to establish a Native-specific shelter and transitional housing in Duluth. In 1994, they launched the American Indian Community Housing Organization (AICHO) to address this gap. (See Chapter 12: American Indian Community Housing Organization.)

After leaving DAIP to pursue her PhD, Ellen Pence began Praxis International as an offshoot of DAIP. The focus of Praxis was conducting institutional Safety and Accountability Audits, a method of analysis Ellen had created in order better to assess how things like racism or sexism or safety or lack of safety are built into institutional practices. (See Chapter 5: Domestic Abuse Intervention Project and Praxis International.)

Finally, Men as Peacemakers, which has partnered with many of the feminist organizations in Duluth, though the organization itself is not a women's nor a specifically feminist organization, began in response to a series of thirteen domestic murders that occurred from mid-1992 to mid-1993. St. Louis County created the Violence Prevention Initiative, modeled on a similar program in Ramsey County. The main purpose of the initiative was to reach out to the community and involve people in violence prevention activities. However, when mostly women and very few men volunteered, Frank Jewell, the violence prevention coordinator, worked with Vicki Gowler, editor of the *Duluth News Tribune*, to involve more men. "It was seen as a women's issue and not something men should be concerned about," said Frank, "but nobody was asking [men] either." Following a retreat on the issue with men who were leaders in the community, Men as Peacemakers was formed. Its main purpose was to get men involved in the prevention of violence. The group worked closely with schools, state corrections, and the police department. The name, Men as Peacemakers, was a statement of their vision. Despite initial skepticism about Men as Peacemakers, feminist organizations now actively partner with them, participating in restorative justice circles in cases of intimate partner violence, and Men as Peacemakers has become an important ally in the work of feminist organizations in the community.[26]

On the cultural front, At Sara's Table, a feminist bookstore and soup and sandwich shop, opened in 1991. Co-owner Barb Neubert, who had been part of Women's Liberation of Duluth and the Northcountry Women's Center twenty years earlier, said of the bookstore, "I did not want a lesbian bookstore. I intended it to be a woman's bookstore owned by a lesbian, but immediately the rumors had us labeled as a lesbian bookstore. We were accepted by out-of-town tourists and college and university employees, but Duluthians were more apt to peek in and some of their comments, as they looked through the door, led me to believe they just wanted to see what a lesbian looked like." After a few years, the bookstore/coffee shop, now owned by Barb and Carla Blumberg, moved for a short time to a spot just over the Aerial Lift Bridge on Park Point. In 2001 they moved to their current location on East Eighth Street. Though it no longer operates as a bookstore, stacks of feminist and other books still line the "library" of the thriving restaurant featuring locally grown organic food. It is a favorite gathering spot of local feminists and other progressives in town.[27]

Another feminist cultural enterprise galvanized young feminist girls in the area. A variety of factors coalesced to give Nancy Gruver the idea of starting *New Moon Magazine for Girls* in 1992, not the least of which was raising twin eleven-year-old daughters. Concerned about girls traversing the transition time from girlhood to womanhood, she found a resource in Carol Gilligan and Lyn Mikel Brown's study of adolescent girls' psychological development, *Meeting at the Crossroads*. "One of the key points was that there was an alternative for women to become allies of girls who are in that transitional time of life, rather than fulfilling the culturally approved role of teaching girls to accommodate themselves to the patriarchal culture as they were getting older. It was a radical idea that women would change the relationship we had with girls." She began by exploring the idea of beginning some kind of mentorship program with girls through the YWCA, where she sat on the board, but one day had the idea of starting a magazine for girls, by girls: "a *Ms.* for girls." For her this meant "bringing girls' voices into the world and being presented in a way that created respect for what the girls knew, what the girls were saying, what the girls needed."[28]

Gruver, with her daughters, put together a board of twenty-five girls, ranging in age from eight to fourteen, to make decisions about everything for the magazine, including the size, the content, and the name. Though rejecting Nancy's initial idea of "Artemis," the girls liked the idea of the moon associated with the goddess Artemis, and they settled on "New Moon" as the name for the magazine. By the time they printed the first issue they had five hundred paid subscriptions, without a bit of advertising. The first issue received positive and helpful responses from Gloria Steinem, Nikki Giovanni, Toni Morrison, Louise Erdrich, and others. They got the attention of *Ms.* magazine by flooding their office with letters, and *Ms.* "did a lovely review." Linda Ellerbee ran a story about *New Moon* on the children's news show *Nick News*. By the end of 1993, they had 5,000 subscribers, built by word of mouth and public media.

The magazine has been publishing six issues a year ever since, covering topics of interest to the girls on the editorial board who now come from all over the world and hold editorial board meetings online. Every day they hear from readers and their parents about the need for this media alternative.

Nancy said her work was inspired by the feminist community in Duluth and how "they kept going." *New Moon*, in turn, inspired the feminist community of Duluth, which shared enthusiasm for the magazine and the way it involved girls at a young age in creating positive messages and broadening their interests and awareness beyond the typical tween magazines. It inspired a youthful energy in the feminist movement in the Twin Ports. Undoubtedly many women who read *New Moon* when they were growing up now work in the local grassroots feminist organizations. It was an important part of the cultural scene that fed and inspired the ongoing work of feminist organizations in the Twin Ports.

Feminist writers were always an important part of creating the women's cultural movement in the Twin Ports. They got a boost in the summer of 1993 when Joan Drury, owner of Spinsters Ink, one of the oldest lesbian publishing houses in the country, established Norcroft: A Writing Retreat for Women, in Lutsen, Minnesota. Norcroft drew even more feminist creative energy to the area, nurturing more than six hundred women writers over its ten-plus-year existence. A few years later, Joan moved Spinsters Ink to Duluth, making Duluth a center for lesbian and feminist authors.[29]

In the years from 1992 to 1994, the feminist community came together to support the Women's Health Center, which, due to constant harassment and picketing, was facing its third eviction. Individual feminists and feminist organizations collaborated to create the Building for Women in 1993 that would provide a safe and secure home not only for the Women's Health Center, but for PAVSA, the YWCA, the League of Women Voters, the Coffeehouse, Aurora, and more. It was a major milestone in this community and stands as a proud landmark in this community of women. (See Chapter 6: Women's Health Center and the Building for Women.)

2000s and Beyond

The 2000s saw the creation of some organizations and the demise of others. The Northland Birth Collective, begun by Jana Studelska in 2002 and modeled on and in association with the Minnesota Birth Collective in the Twin Cities, provided information and resources for women and families about birthing options, midwifery, and doula support. The Birth Collective held monthly Parent Topic Nights, which covered such issues as postpartum care, getting to know your newborn, and birth hormones. Among its most notable achievements was its successful effort to secure permission for doulas to attend hospital births. With the help of Susan Lane, a Twin Cities–based doula and activist, the Collective pushed for a change in legislation, and Minnesota became the first state in the nation to include a statement specific to birthing women that allowed them to have a companion of their choice with them throughout labor and delivery. During its ten-year existence, the collective helped to create a community of doulas in the area, and effected a significant change in the care available during childbirth. Since its end in 2013, other groups, such as Women Circling Women, have arisen to meet some of the needs. Women's Transitional Housing and Women in Construction suffered from economic problems and ceased operation in 2010. Due to the successes of the LGBTQ movement in gaining rights, visibility, and respect for LGBTQ people, the Northcountry Women's Coffeehouse and Aurora—which had been formed to provide resources for lesbians who were for the most part closeted in the 1980s—died natural deaths in 2009 and 2012, respectively. However, the rest of the major organizations studied in this volume have continued to grow and adapt to changing needs, and create innovative programming and policies to this day.[30]

Grassroots feminist organizations continue to spring up with new endeavors. The North Central Windows Program, begun by Susan Meyers and Jennifer Salo in 2010, partners with CASDA, Safe Haven Shelter, UMD's Women's Resource and Action Center, and others to provide art enrichment programming for survivors of sexual and domestic abuse. The Native Sisters Society grew from the work of Mending the Sacred Hoop and AICHO and works to raise awareness about and to bring an end to trafficking of Native women. Hildegard House, a Catholic Worker house of hospitality specifically for women who have been sexually exploited through trafficking, opened in 2014. The idea for the house grew out of conversations Michele Naar-Obed had with PAVSA, the Native Sisters Society, the Benedictine Sisters of St. Scholastica, and Anishinaabe ODay—a grassroots organization that helps the Native community of Duluth with a variety of issues. Nine women came together to create Hildegard House, and in their first year they had a consistently full house. Grassroots feminist organizations will continue to sprout wherever there is an injustice to be confronted or a need to be addressed. Feminism in Duluth and Superior is alive and well.[31]

{ 3 }

Program for Aid to Victims
of Sexual Assault

I n the early 1970s women in the Twin Ports, in small, often spontaneous conversations among friends and associates, began the simple
yet revolutionary act of sharing the truths of their lives. "Women of
all ages, younger and older, were getting together and talking . . . about
how enraged they were about rape, domestic abuse, and they were really
fired up. . . . We were up for anything," recalled Nancy Massey, one of
the pioneers of the movement in Duluth to end violence against women.
Those early conversations marked the beginning of the organization that
for forty years has supported victims of sexual assault and worked to
eliminate sexual violence through education and activism: the Program
to Aid Victims of Sexual Assault, or PAVSA.[1]

Origin Story

In 1973, Randi Goldstone from the Neighborhood Improvement Center
in Minneapolis, the first rape crisis center in Minnesota, came north to do
a workshop for the Duluth and Superior Police Departments. In addition
to Mary Potter from the Superior Police Department and Jan Laine and
Donnetta Wickstrom from the Duluth Police Department, among the key
players who came together at this workshop were Nancy Massey, Susan
Gillespie, Arlene Bjorkman, and Nancy Biehl. Also in attendance were
Rosemary (Rosie) Rocco and others from the Northcountry Women's
Center, and Tina Welsh and others from Planned Parenthood. It was the
beginning of a beautiful feminist friendship and partnership. "Rosemary
Rocco and I were soulmates from the very beginning," said Tina. "She has
a very good sense of humor. She liked my anger, to put it very bluntly."[2]

"Every woman in that room had been affected by sexual violence in
one way or another," said Candice Harshner, PAVSA's executive director

since 2000. "Whether it was a friend, themselves, a family member—everyone had been touched by it, and they realized that this is something that we need to stop." The coming together of those women at that particular workshop was the catalyst for putting thoughts into action. The initial relationships, alliances, and ideas that led to PAVSA were forged there. "For us, that workshop was like, 'Wow, this is a huge problem. Somebody should do something about this!'" Rosie remembered. "Being presented with the scope of the problem was what pushed us to action."[3]

Following the workshop, Tina, Rosie, and Nancy traveled to the Twin Cities to be trained at the Neighborhood Improvement Center as crisis-line advocates. "A few of us got training for eight hours," recalled Rosie, with a laugh. (Today the training is forty hours.) From that initial training, they established the original crisis line through the Northcountry Women's Center, which operated out of Old Main on the former University of Minnesota Duluth campus. For many months before PAVSA even began, the three of them and many other volunteers staffed the crisis line. Volunteers took first names and phone numbers from callers, and Nancy, Tina, or Rosie would follow up, often going to the hospital to be with the victims.[4]

In 1974, when the federal government made grant money available to establish rape crisis centers through the Law Enforcement Assistance Administration (LEAA), the original core group of women held a community meeting at the Duluth YWCA to discuss establishing a rape crisis center for northeastern Minnesota. They applied for the LEAA grant but were turned down on the grounds that there were too few rapes in the region to warrant funding. In the previous year, only thirty-five rapes had been reported in all of St. Louis County. "What we learned out of that," said Rosie, "was our first issue was the level of reporting."[5]

The women worked with Peggy Spector, director of Victim Services in the Minnesota Department of Corrections, along with the assistant director, initially Eileen Keller and later Sharon Sayles Belton. The women from Victim Services advised them that the reporting system was not friendly to victims, so numbers were artificially low, and suggested that they could get a more accurate accounting by talking with clergy, counselors, therapists, and other professionals. During the next year, 1975, they connected with members of the broader mental health system in the county, as well as with some faith communities and friends in law enforcement, to get a clearer sense of the scope of the problem in St. Louis County. They also kept records of their crisis-line calls to document the prevalence of sexual assault in the county.

By 1976, Tina, Rosie, and Nancy had gathered enough information to show a sufficient number of sexual assaults in St. Louis County to get funding from LEAA. LEAA required that the funds be handled through a governmental unit, so initially they operated through the county attorney's office as an advisory board called the St. Louis County Aid to Victims of Sexual Assault Program. Susan Gillespie became the first program director. Though she was officially an employee of the county attorney's office, the advisory board set her agenda. The original group from Duluth was joined by people from northern St. Louis County, including Sue Neuttila from St. Louis County social services and Debbie Knoke from the Hibbing police department.

Early Years: 1976–1985

In the beginning, PAVSA's focus was advocacy and education for the right of victims to be treated respectfully by police, the courts, and medical personnel. "There literally were hundreds of people who we had to have on board at various points, not only to get money, but also to change people's perceptions," said Rosie. Susan Gillespie remembered "racing all over St. Louis County, Carlton County, Cook County" talking to law enforcement and health administrators and doing community education in the colleges and high schools. "Law enforcement trainings were the most challenging because of some of the attitudes and stereotypes," recalled Susan. Tina put it more bluntly: "We ran into total indifference, outright hostility. The police department, judges, and doctors in the ER had no training in compassion or understanding."[6]

It took PAVSA eleven months even to get a case brought forward within the justice system—though admittedly this was some progress, because in the past it would not have been charged at all—"and that's when we were under the County Attorney's office!" Tina noted. Rosemary remembered that during the trial, which was the only rape case prosecuted that year, the defense attorney was particularly hostile. "Imagine the scene: He's sitting at the defense table, and he sets a Coke bottle spinning. The victim is on the stand. He takes a pencil and he is trying to jab it into the neck of the spinning bottle. While he's doing that, he says to her, 'You mean to tell me that a woman can't run faster with her skirts up than a man with his pants down?' And the County Attorney did not object." The defendant was found not guilty.[7]

One of the most disturbing things for Tina was the lack of support from other women. "I can remember the first time we had an all-female jury and they came back with a 'not guilty' [verdict]. That shook me to the very foundation of my being. I just could not believe that they didn't find this man guilty." Rosemary also had been certain they were going to get a conviction. When they didn't, she looked for a reason, and came to believe that the women on the jury had to make the victim the Other, somehow different than themselves, in order to keep their own vulnerability to rape out of their consciousness.

Despite these setbacks, PAVSA did find tremendous support. They connected with feminists in community organizations and with the consciousness-raising groups that were emerging in Duluth. "In the beginning, there weren't feminist organizations; there were feminists within organizations, and there were feminists who met as a group," said Rosie. "Because of Duluth being Duluth, you knew who those people were." They had connections with women's groups like Business and Professional Women, the Junior League, and the League of Women Voters, as well as women at the University of Minnesota Duluth (UMD). Those associations helped PAVSA get invitations to speak around town and spread the word. They were also helpful in fundraising. Those allies, Rosie noted, "came together and worked together and made things happen."[8]

Hundreds of people volunteered as advocates, many of whom went on to become community leaders in business, counseling, and education. The volunteer advocates ran the crisis phone line through St. Louis County's Information and Referral service, which in turn would route the calls to the advocates' home phones. The volunteers printed up red cards with "Rape Crisis Line" and the phone number to call and put them in bars and other places around town where women in need might pick them up. Rosie remembered, "We were overwhelmed with calls."

Tina and Rosemary realized fairly early on that services and education, while worthy in and of themselves, would not be sufficient to bring about the kind of change necessary. "Most of us were civic-minded," said Tina. "We were politically active. . . . What became clear very quickly was we needed to organize politically or we weren't going to move ahead." PAVSA worked with the League of Women Voters to educate the community on issues of sexual assault, to help get out the vote, and to find like-minded people to support their efforts. They also supported the efforts of colleagues working on sexual assault issues at the state legislature. "People who were down at the Capitol would call us up and say, 'We need x number of calls to this person and this person and this person [state legislators] by tomorrow,'" Tina recalled. PAVSA had developed a phone tree, so they always got the calls they needed and more—"a hundred, a hundred and fifty calls"—in less than twenty-four hours.

In 1975, PAVSA had worked with Peggy Spector to develop sweeping and revolutionary legislation that changed state statutory law on sexual assault. Formerly in Minnesota, all sexual assaults had been lumped into one category. The new legislation divided the crime of sexual assault into four degrees. Having different degrees made it easier for courts to determine the extent of the crime and appropriate sentencing. The laws defining sexual assault were also changed so that the victim no longer had to show signs of struggle and resistance to prove non-consent, and some of the first rape shield laws ensured that a victim's past sexual history was no longer admissible in court. Minnesota has been a leader in progressive sexual assault legislation, and PAVSA has been a key player in making that happen. Over the next several years, PAVSA continued to work to develop and refine sexual assault legislation.[9]

In 1978, PAVSA officially incorporated as the Program to Aid Victims of Sexual Assault (PAVSA), a 501(c)(3) nonprofit organization. At this time, Susan Gillespie left as director, and PAVSA was led by two co-directors, with Tina Welsh responsible for programs in Duluth and southern St. Louis County, and Peggy Metzger responsible for the Iron Range and northern St. Louis County, with an office in Virginia, Minnesota. The organization's eighteen-member board comprised nine women from the Iron Range and nine women from Duluth. With the shift to nonprofit status, PAVSA was no longer supported by LEAA grant money, and the ongoing search for funding began. Tina went to the St. Louis County Board for funding and told them, "If you give us just five cents for each woman who's your sister, your mother, your wife—we'd have money to do this." They got their funding, but in retrospect, Tina said, "Five cents per woman—that's kind of degrading when we think about it."

In 1980 PAVSA hired Inez Wagner (now Wildwood) to be its first executive director. PAVSA had been closed for several months due to a lack of funding when she first came on board, so her first order of business was hiring staff, sorting out the finances, and getting the program up and running again. She was impressed that, "even though the office was closed, many of those women volunteered their time to continue to take calls and . . . to go support women going for exams for rape and finding resources."

The previous year, PAVSA had moved out of the county attorney's office and into its own offices in a house on Lake Avenue and Fifth Street. The Community Health Center (commonly known as the Free Clinic), of which Nancy Massey was the director, was located on the first floor, and PAVSA moved onto the second floor. As Phyllis Cook, PAVSA's program director at that time, remembered, "Inez Wagner was in the front bedroom. . . . I was in the living room." The Domestic Abuse Intervention Project (DAIP) moved in shortly thereafter. (See Chapter 5: Domestic Abuse Intervention Project.) "They needed space," recalled Inez, "so Nancy kicked us out of the kitchen."

PAVSA's new location facilitated relationships and collaborations with other organizations. "I remember working closely at times with the clinic, helping women get appointments," said Phyllis. "Nancy Massey was on the board for PAVSA." Inez, Nancy, and Ellen Pence of DAIP did a lot of collaborating. Cathy Tickle Curley, from the Women's Coalition, also would show up from time to time to join the conversations. (See Chapter 4: The Women's Coalition for Battered Women.)

Inez remembered that the shared space also created some tensions: "As they [DAIP] started services with men who battered and we had women who were victims coming up our stairs . . . it caused some stressful moments and lots of fiddling around, figuring out how to do things in order to have shared space." The incest survivor groups would meet off-site, at the Human Development Center, to avoid any possibility of contact between victims and perpetrators.

PAVSA continued to rely heavily on volunteer advocates and held nine-hour training sessions two to three times a year. "It was a huge part of our structure," said Phyllis, who was in charge of the training. "We had a lot of advocates from the college [UMD]. . . . It was a vital time."

Within a year of Inez coming on as executive director, PAVSA reopened the office in Virginia, which served all of northern St. Louis County. PAVSA also received grants to provide services to Lake, Carlton, and Itasca Counties, as well as a bit of Aitkin, making it the largest victim-advocacy service provider in the state. PAVSA then connected with the Cook County Collective, an all-volunteer organization providing services to victims of sexual assault. "We had a huge geography for volunteers [to cover], so we focused right away on building the volunteer network," Inez remembered.[10]

The organization was focused on building advocacy and training medical personnel, law enforcement, and social service professionals. Phyllis could hardly believe some of the comments police officers made during the training, though some, like Donetta Wickstrom, were "won-

derful." A couple of men in St. Louis County social services also challenged them in ways that impeded the progress of the program. "I think
it might have been [a difference in] style," said Phyllis, because "we were a
woman-run organization." When Inez first came on board, PAVSA relied
on two women in the police department who, in her words, "were very
good about referring women. . . . The nurses in the emergency rooms,
and a few social workers, were very good."

Inez also spent a lot of time on the UMD campus "working to get a
discussion going about violence on campus and [developing] services—
everything from escorts to training with the campus police." However,
she largely relied on what she called the "underground network of
women" to spread the word about what PAVSA was doing and why. "My
passion was to get the message out to all women and to professionals."

PAVSA had support from two young attorneys in the county attorney's office, Mark Rubin and John DeSanto. "Mark helped us, as part of
our advocacy training, by getting us into the courtroom and having attorneys and judges come in and talk to advocates about how that process
works," remembered Inez. "Our advocates really understood the legal
process. We did the same in turn. I went down many times and spoke
at the state judicial conference with others about it. All the new county
attorneys came through our place and attended the advocacy trainings
because of those partnerships."

PAVSA's extensive outreach and programming required monetary
support, and in 1981 it held its first annual art auction, featuring a dinner
and a silent auction of works donated by local artists. "It was a crazy idea
concocted by Nancy Massey, Sue Mowbray, and Patricia Pearson, who
were all on the board," Inez recalled. About a hundred people came to the
auction, which was held at the Chinese Lantern restaurant. The auction
raised between $1,500 and $2,000, which at that time seemed like a lot of
money. "By the time I left PAVSA, we were well in the high double dig-
its," said Inez. "[The auction] was a great contributor to our budget every
year." The auction continues to be one of PAVSA's biggest fundraisers.

Together with the Women's Coalition and others, PAVSA cospon-
sored Take Back the Night marches first in 1981 and again in 1982, with
more than 2,000 people participating in the 1982 march. "It was successful beyond our wildest hopes," said Inez. "That, combined with training
we were doing with the County Attorney, and the police, and the sheriff's
department, and raising the level of understanding of professionals, is
what allowed the program to move into being a routine part of the response [to sexual assaults]." This included the police notifying PAVSA

about reported assaults, and emergency rooms calling for an advocate before an exam happened. "Minnesota was in the forefront of creating good collaborations with the police and the medical [community]," said Kim Storm, PAVSA's program director from 1984 to 1988. PAVSA also partnered with the Human Development Center, Range Mental Health, and independent therapists in Itasca County to start incest and rape survivor groups throughout the area.[11]

Once it had developed a strong advocacy and response network within the medical, social service, and criminal justice systems, PAVSA began work on a child sexual abuse prevention program for the schools. The pilot project was so well received that PAVSA obtained funding to hire two educators to continue to take this specialized curriculum into the schools. The curriculum, called *Good Touch Bad Touch* and originally developed by Illusion Theater in Minneapolis, was designed for elementary children to learn about their rights to their bodies. Once PAVSA had established that program in most of the schools in the region, it brought in *No Easy Answers,* a program for middle school and high school students, also built on an Illusion Theater curriculum that, in Inez's words, had "more candid age-appropriate discussions about touch and sex—no easy answers."[12]

In 1983, PAVSA became the first sexual assault program in the country to produce public service announcements (PSAs) that dealt with issues of sexual harassment, sexual assault, and child sexual abuse. The PSAs were broadcast on television and radio throughout the region. A series of vignettes featured local law enforcement agents, judges, advocates, and others encouraging women and children to report incidents of assault or abuse and make the system work for them. "We did that to stir up controversy and conversation, and we got a lot of it," Inez remembered. People wrote letters to the editor of the *Duluth News-Tribune & Herald* (now the *Duluth News Tribune*) in protest. Even a regular columnist for the paper wrote about "these uppity women and all of their issues," remembered Inez. Inez stressed that the whole point of the PSAs was "to go public and not be an underground support network." PAVSA ended up selling their PSAs to other advocacy programs around the country. Soon after, PAVSA partnered with women at the Fond du Lac Reservation to produce an educational video for Native American communities on childhood sexual abuse and incest called *The Bridge* (1986). It was the first film of its kind in the country.

PAVSA also worked on public policy issues at the state and national levels. "I was fortunate to be part of the group that wrote the sexual exploitation by professionals laws," said Inez. PAVSA was also part of organizing the National Coalition Against Sexual Assault, or NCASA, and helped bring its second national gathering, keynoted by Gloria Steinem, to Minneapolis. This gave PAVSA more support and visibility on the state level.[13]

As PAVSA continued to grow and expand, tensions emerged between board members from the northern and southern areas of the county, partially stemming from a feeling that more resources were being directed to the southern office. Finally, in 1984, the board made the decision to divide PAVSA into two independent programs. Because of the sheer geographical size of St. Louis County, creating separate organizations for the northern and southern regions helped to make the program more manageable. The division allowed each organization to develop more community-oriented programs that better served local needs and interests, which also made it easier to raise money from within the community. It was a difficult time for director Inez Wagner, who was caught in the middle:

> I laughed about and still laugh with some of the people who were on the board at the time, about being the child of the divorce, because it was a very stressful, unpleasant experience for me reporting to a board of directors that was trying to sort all this out. . . . We needed to have the base that we had and the strength in numbers that we got by being one [organization], but it did need to be individual communities providing these services and getting more support from their communities than they could from a centralized base.

It didn't make economic sense to have a separate office for Carlton County, so PAVSA continued to serve Carlton County as well as Duluth, with separate volunteers for each community. PAVSA also worked with women in Superior, Wisconsin, who were forming a program there: the Center Against Sexual and Domestic Abuse (CASDA). (See Chapter 8: Center Against Sexual and Domestic Abuse.)

1986–2000

In 1986, PAVSA moved its offices into the Ordean Building in downtown Duluth, a move that made sense both for PAVSA and for the Free Clinic, which needed more space. Soon after, Inez Wagner left to take another position in St. Paul. Susan Askelin, who had been the chair of PAVSA's board, became executive director, a position she held until 1991. PAVSA's focus during that time was maintaining services and educating the community. It also once again partnered with a range of local groups in sponsoring a Take Back the Night march and rally in 1990.[14]

Rosemary Rocco came on as PAVSA's executive director in 1991 and remained until 1996. Rosie worked on building up some aspects of PAVSA that had begun to decline. Enthusiasm for volunteering had waned, so PAVSA strategized ways to increase the number of volunteer advocates. Also at that time, Rosie noted, "it was clear that victim-blaming was still running around and that we needed to focus there," and PAVSA put more efforts into community education. In the early 1990s, the national movement was deeply divided over whether the focus of sexual assault programs should be on prevention or advocacy, and MNCASA (Minnesota Coalition Against Sexual Assault) put pressure on PAVSA to pursue prevention efforts more actively. Generally, PAVSA has regarded the services versus prevention issue as a "false argument," because, according to Rosie, "it was dichotomous, and of course, it [the program] needed to be all of it." It was and continues to be a balancing act.

Rosemary Rocco is nothing if not a mover and a shaker, and under her leadership, PAVSA took some courageous and controversial stances. It led a face-off, first with Victim Services in the State Department of Corrections, and then with the state legislature, over monetary support for sexual assault advocacy programs. The Department of Corrections had begun making unusual requests for personal information about victims as a condition of funding, far beyond the required level of reporting. Rosie said the DOC's reviews were simply a way of "looking for what we were doing wrong as a 'gotcha,' rather than working with programs to develop and evolve." Bringing together several programs across the state, PAVSA led the movement to call out Victim Services on this. Ultimately several employees were removed and new procedures put in place. "We needed that statewide strength," said Rosie. "We certainly needed more evenhandedness in the people who were dispensing the money, or we were going to be so at each other's throats that it would undermine programs across the state. Programs that were struggling needed help, not punishment."

Rosemary recalls the battle with the state legislature with humor, but also as a "not-so-nice thing." PAVSA had gone to the legislature seeking $150,000 in additional state funds that would enable it to access federal funds to set up data systems. The legislature turned down PAVSA's request, then immediately afterward appropriated $160,000 for a lunch for sportswriters who were coming to the Twin Cities for the NCAA men's basketball Final Four. Rosie was absolutely furious. She waited outside the senate chambers for Senator Sam Solon, who when he came out patted her on the shoulder, saying, "I know you're mad, Rosie, but calm down. It's a hard year." Standing by the railing in the capitol rotunda, Rosie shouted her frustrations at Senator Solon, and her words echoed throughout the building. "I turned on my heel and walked away. He shouted after me. Two days later we had our money."

Another focal point of PAVSA's work during the early 1990s was defending the rights of Indian women and men. "We had to stand up for the rights of Indian men, too," said Rosemary, "even if they were perpetrators [of sexual assault]. The reality was that if an Indian was charged, he was going to get convicted. Not only were they going to get convicted, but their sentences were going to be incredibly harsher. It put a huge barrier for Indian women to report, especially on incest." As part of the effort to support the Native community, PAVSA turned over the royalties from *The Bridge* video project, which at the time were about $10,000 a year, to the women from the Fond du Lac Reservation. That move was not without controversy in the organization at a time when money was tight, but as Rosie said, it was "one of the best things PAVSA ever did. . . . It was the right thing to do."

Due to constant harassment from anti-abortion protesters, the Women's Health Center (WHC) was facing eviction for a third time, and its only hope of finding a home for the clinic was to buy its own building. (See Chapter 6: Women's Health Center and the Building for Women.) In 1992, PAVSA, along with the YWCA, made the bold and courageous choice to partner with the WHC in building and then sharing space in the Building for Women. Not only did this involve financial risk and hardship, but because the WHC performed abortions, sharing space with the center meant literally putting the lives of PAVSA staff and clients on the line. The Building for Women was made possible through the collaboration and support of dozens of feminists and feminist organizations, but only PAVSA and the YWCA were willing to be partners in the building. In addition to helping in the fundraising campaign, PAVSA moved its offices into the Building for Women in 1994, where it remains to the present day. "They came together to create space that was primarily for the Women's Health Center, but was a testament to their support for women's rights in general," said Candy Harshner. She continued: "I have profound respect for Rosemary Rocco saying, 'We believe in women's rights enough that we will suffer the consequences.'.... It shows you that unity that women can have and the belief that women get to make their own decisions, whether it's about abortion and reproductive health, or about whether or not to report a sexual assault, or whether to go on with their education."

Rosie said the building stood as a model for action and PAVSA's commitment to supporting the right of every woman to make her own decisions about her body, which, she asserted, is "a fundamental right" and at the heart of PAVSA's work. Rosie wanted to ensure that women truly have "the power and the right to say no."

Because of its location in the Building for Women and its partnership with the Women's Health Center, PAVSA became a target of opposition, and although this has diminished over time, being headquartered there continues to bring challenges. "I know that we lose clients at times," said Candy. Some people who seek PAVSA's services do not want to come to the building or may be traumatized by the protesters who regularly picket there. The advocates try to prepare the women and will escort them into the building. Advocates also offer to meet women at alternative locations off-site. Candy recalled a woman who had come to see her who had been told not to go to PAVSA because of its association with the WHC. "She'd been told that anybody who works here can't be a good person because we work in the building." Undaunted, PAVSA values and continues to stand by its association with and support of the Building for Women.

Rosemary Rocco left PAVSA in 1996. Tammy Feige, who had worked at PAVSA for several years as the advocacy coordinator, succeeded Rosie as executive director. In that position, Tammy "played a critical role in solidifying PAVSA financially," recalled Candy Harshner, who was then the educator at PAVSA. "She did all she could to improve our fiscal and business practices and got the management side of things up to date." During those years, PAVSA received grants from large foundations, as well as ongoing commitments from local funders, particularly the Ordean Foundation and the United Way. Tammy stepped down in 2000, and Candy became the new executive director.

2000–2015

The new century would bring many changes to PAVSA. New programs were launched, such as the Sexual Assault Nurse Examiner (SANE) initiative and the Sexual Assault Multidisciplinary Action Response Team (SMART), and the organization became more focused on bringing racial and gender inclusivity to its mission and staffing. It has at the same time remained committed to providing the best possible services and to the empowerment of those who come to them for services. During her time as executive director, Candy Harshner has seen PAVSA evolve in many ways. It has grown exponentially in size and visibility, as well as in the services it offers. "It's not always been a well-known organization," Candy admitted. "People found out about it when they needed it." From a staff of three, they have grown to fourteen, and they still could use more staff. "I need a grant writer—put that in there," said Candy, smiling. Candy elaborated on how PAVSA's focus has changed over the years:

> In the very beginning with the rape crisis centers, everybody called us. We were the initial line of services and sometimes the only line of services. Women have a lot more options now. They may call us to come to the emergency room with them, but they may hook up with a therapist on their own, or someone in their family, or a student support group. . . . They have better resources. But we still have an awful lot of people in our community who don't have those resources. We've become much more of an advocacy organization for people who don't have multiple resources, for women living in poverty, women who are homeless, women who have severe and chronic mental health issues, chemical dependency issues. . . . They not only get services, they get the best services.

PAVSA has evolved by being on the cutting edge in the sexual assault field. "When adult survivors of child sexual abuse started to be identified in the '80s and the '90s, PAVSA was right there doing that work," said Candy. "When we first started looking at prevention of child sexual abuse, working with children in the schools, PAVSA was right there. [They have been] willing to grow and educate themselves and change and try to meet the needs of the community and meet the needs of victims—and those needs have evolved."

As PAVSA was growing, the staff members met to discuss how they wanted to improve services to best meet victims' needs. They asked themselves, "If we could have a perfect world, what would we want?" They arrived at three areas that needed improvement: the medical response, the counseling response, and the legal response. They addressed each in turn. "One of the things that we were experiencing at the time was bad medical exams," said Candy. "Women going into the hospital, girls going into the hospital, and doctors telling them, 'Do you know that you're ruining someone's life?'; or accusing them of lying; or not being offered emergency contraception." The advocates had to spend so much time reminding doctors and nurses what to do that they were not able to be there fully for the victim. "It wasn't that physicians didn't care," she continued. "They didn't do enough [sexual assault exams] to feel competent, and when they felt incompetent, they took it out on the victims." This happened often enough that PAVSA saw the need for a medical response specific to sexual assault. That's where the SANE (Sexual Assault Nurse Examiner) program came about.[15]

PAVSA, in collaboration with St. Luke's Hospital and St. Mary's Medical Center and law enforcement and social service agencies, developed the SANE program to provide specially trained nurse examiners to respond to the emergency room when a victim of sexual assault is admitted. In addition to training in advocacy and addressing the emotional and physical needs of the victim, SANE nurses are trained in the proper collection of evidence, so that "nothing gets lost," said Candy. Cizzarie Schomberg, one of the SANE nurses, said, "It's the most patient-centered nursing you can give. We are there only for that one patient. For the time that they are there, we get to attend totally to them. . . . To know that you're delivering quality care to that person and helping to start the healing process is really empowering, really rewarding." Sarah Fries, the first SANE program coordinator, said, "By providing this best-practice model of care to victims of sexual assault, SANE nurses are not only insuring a standardized means for collection of evidence that will ultimately increase the likelihood for prosecuting perpetrators, they are also providing a victim-centered service that focuses on the needs and wants of the victim first and foremost." PAVSA also collaborates with CASDA in Superior, so that victims who go to CASDA also have access to SANE nurse examiners. The SANE program in Duluth is unique, compared to others in the nation, in that it is run through PAVSA, whereas other such programs typically are run through hospitals. Though hospitals give financial support, PAVSA employs and trains the nurses.[16]

PAVSA has been more successful in recent years in getting cases to trial, and the testimony of the SANE nurses has been critical to that. Another development, in 2008, was PAVSA's work with the Duluth Police Department and the St. Louis County Attorney's Office to develop an anonymous reporting option, which allows victims of sexual assault to file a report, have evidence collected and stored, and receive a SANE exam without having their name attached to the report. Duluth was the first community in the nation to develop such an option, and in 2009, the organization End Violence Against Women International, a national training agency on sexual violence, recruited PAVSA to educate other communities across the country on anonymous reporting. By 2010, seven jurisdictions in Minnesota and Wisconsin had adopted anonymous reporting, now considered a national best practice.[17]

To address the counseling response issue, PAVSA hired a staff therapist to be available to victims. Before this, too many of the women using PAVSA's services were unable to receive outside therapy because their insurance was inadequate, or they couldn't get an appointment for many weeks. "With this kind of crisis," remarked Candy, "if people need to get in, they need to get in, otherwise you miss the window when they're willing to go in." PAVSA now offers professional therapy free of charge. "We felt very strongly that victims of crime shouldn't have to pay to heal from that crime," Candy added. PAVSA also ensures that victims are seen by the therapist within a week of coming to them. Finally, to address the legal response issue, PAVSA hired a legal advocate who helps victims negotiate the criminal justice system. The advocate also works with police and attorneys to examine and create policies and protocols to make sure they are victim-centered.

With the continuing expansion and broadening of its programs, PAVSA provides a holistic approach, offering a wide range of services for victims and their families, from the crisis line and hospital visits to providing SANE nurses, working with law enforcement, and providing therapists and legal services. It also runs a variety of support groups, including therapy groups run by the staff counselor and support groups held throughout the community at locations including Life House, a resource center and street outreach program for homeless youth, and the Arrowhead Juvenile Center.

PAVSA continues to focus on education and building awareness of the societal issues surrounding sexual assault. Social change is an important piece of the mission, because "we want this crime to end," said Candy. "We want this organization to not be needed. We say we want to work ourselves out of a job, but we do, because it needs to change. It hasn't changed enough in the time we've existed." As part of this effort, after a gap of more than a decade, PAVSA reinstated the Take Back the Night march in 2001, on the initiative of advocate Beth Olson. This annual multi-organization collaboration continues to the present day.[18]

In 2002, in collaboration with law enforcement and the Duluth public schools, PAVSA led an initiative to create an improved protocol for the resolution of sexual assault and sexual harassment complaints in the schools. The protocol provides step-by-step procedures to follow when complaints are filed against either school employees or other students. According to Deb Anderson, formerly the Duluth school district's violence and harassment prevention specialist, the protocol was the first of its kind in the nation to be employed in public schools.[19]

PAVSA has also maintained a long association with the Women's Resource and Action Center (WRAC) at UMD. WRAC interns are all trained PAVSA advocates, and they provide on-campus sexual assault advocacy for students. "It's just a great relationship," said Candy. One consequence of this alliance has been changing attitudes and greater responsiveness toward sexual assault on campus. "I see the student contact staff being more sensitive and accessible to the needs. I see college administrators paying attention," said Candy. Emphasizing the importance of college administrators acknowledging the problem of campus sexual assaults, she said, "We know that college girls are being sexually assaulted. It's a given. To give parents and students a false sense of security makes no sense whatsoever." She believed it was better to be upfront and state publicly how the campus is addressing the problem, as well as ensuring that any student who is sexually assaulted "get[s] the very best of services and care."

While the expansion in PAVSA's ability to provide a range of services has been an undeniably good thing, it has brought greater funding pressure. "Funding is always a struggle, no matter how big or small you are," said Candy. "It's been one of our biggest challenges." Like most nonprofits, PAVSA has relied primarily on grants for funding. Federal grant money has made it possible to develop longer-term projects, and both large and smaller local foundations have been supportive of PAVSA's work. The main issue, one echoed by every organization, is that support from granting agencies and foundations is "project-driven." Candy emphasized that the message the organization tries to send to funders is, "help us *continue* projects. Don't always ask for something new and exciting, because the continuation of projects that you start is so important."

PAVSA's biggest hurdle, both in raising funds and raising awareness in the community, has been the issue of sexual assault itself. "Our biggest issue is our issue," said Candy. "It has 'sex' in the title, which right there shuts people down." PAVSA worked for a short time with a professional development officer, who after several months came back and said, "I don't know how to help you. . . . It's an unattractive issue. People don't want to talk about it."

PAVSA does not ask the women who have come to it for services to raise money or talk at fundraisers to solicit financial support for the programs. "Sometimes we discourage them when they've said they want to talk at fundraisers, because it's traumatizing," said Candy. Nor does PAVSA use victims' stories to promote the organization. Candy said that every time she talks to a reporter about sex trafficking, they ask, "Do you have a victim we could talk to?" Her response is always, "No, because that's a horribly personal thing in their life and I don't want you to retraumatize them by asking intrusive questions."

While Candy gave kudos to community entities such as the county prosecutor, law enforcement, and UMD for acknowledging that sexual assault is a community issue and supporting the organization that helps its victims, she felt individuals were more reluctant to confront such a difficult issue. A general avoidance of talking about the issue as well as the pervasive attitude that "it's never going to happen to me" inhibits broader societal change. Candy pointed out the lack of progress within society: "We haven't changed the statistics. Just as many women are being sexually assaulted now as they were in 1975, if not more. They're getting help faster, and maybe they're reporting to people who are more sensitive, but we haven't changed as a society. . . . It's insidious in our culture. It's challenging to do away with."

In 2001, PAVSA began working with a multidisciplinary team approach called SMART: Sexual Assault Multidisciplinary Action Response Team. SMART involves professionals from all the systems in the community that PAVSA works with, including law enforcement, hospitals, the county prosecutor's office, and other advocacy groups and victim service agencies. SMART is one of eight such programs in the state set up through the Sexual Violence Justice Institute of the Minnesota Coalition Against Sexual Assault (MNCASA). The model works on a cyclical basis. It begins with surveys that are used to discover what victims experience in the community and to identify what the biggest needs are for the victims. From there they do a community needs assessment, and then work with the various systems and agencies to enact policies and protocols to address the needs. They repeat all the steps every seven years and evaluate the effectiveness of the policies and protocols. As of 2015, PAVSA has been through the cycle twice. The victims' surveys in 2008 showed the experiences to be very different from those in 2001. Candy noted that the SMART surveys have identified critical changes and gaps in the system: "In 2001 we talked about SANE; in 2007–2008, we recognized the need for Native women to be getting better services. . . . The team serves to set that course, determines where we grow and how we develop programs."[20]

The recognition that Native women need better services grew from an initiative of Mending the Sacred Hoop (MSH), a training and technical assistance provider for Native tribes based in Duluth. (See Chapter 10: Mending the Sacred Hoop.) In 2006, MSH initiated an audit of cases of sexual assault of Native women. The audit team did extensive interviewing of women who reported assaults, as well as people in the reporting agencies, and reviewed the records of both PAVSA and the Duluth Police Department. "We had lots of interviews," said Candy. "They looked at our paperwork. They looked at everything we did." The team also looked at how Native women who reported were treated by law enforcement. "It was atrocious," said Candy. "They weren't believed. They were accused of prostituting themselves. They were accused of lying . . . of being drunk. They didn't receive services, and hardly any of them reported." None of the cases found in police reports went forward in the criminal justice system. As a result of the audit, the police department radically changed its practices. "They took some risks during this study. They opened themselves up to some examination. . . . It was a courageous thing to do." The audit team recommended that PAVSA have Native staff and do more to ensure culturally sensitive practices. As a result, PAVSA hired its first advocate who was Native American, Paula Morton. "That one thing made a huge difference," said Candy. "When . . . a Native woman walks in, she breathes a sigh of relief because there's someone there who looks like her."[21]

The audit as well as the work of Kelly Kurst, PAVSA's outreach coordinator, revealed the issue of trafficking of Native women in Duluth. Recognizing that the port city had become a major hub for trafficking in Minnesota, PAVSA collaborated with Dabinoo'Igan (a shelter for Native women) and the American Indian Community Housing Organization (AICHO) to develop the Duluth Trafficking Task Force to examine trafficking, primarily of Native women and girls, in the area. (See Chapter 12: American Indian Community Housing Organization.) The task force brought together service providers, systems personnel, advocates and community organizers, elders, civic leaders, and others to hear from focus groups, identify service gaps, and develop protocols and curricula.

In 2010, PAVSA hired a human rights advocate with a specialization in sex trafficking, Shunu Shrestha, to head the task force.

One of the goals of the task force was "to redefine prostitution as sexual violence against women." The task force has played an important role at both the state and local levels to change laws, policies and practices, and ultimately attitudes. Minnesota as a state has one of the highest rates of sex trafficking in the nation. An estimated 8,000 to 12,000 women and children are sold for sex in the state annually. While Minnesota had fairly progressive and forward-thinking laws that correlated trafficking and prostitution, it did not take into account some specific vulnerabilities of the minor population, especially of homeless youth who often are running away from abusive situations but are then forced to use sex as a tool for survival. "Gender plays a huge role as well," said Shunu. "Transgender folks, primarily girls and women, [are at risk]." Because the sex trafficking law did not take these factors into consideration, the burden of proof still remained on the victim, even if they were minors, to show that somebody else was pimping them out.[22]

Many state and local agencies, including PAVSA, came together to draft new legislation that takes these factors into consideration and addresses the sexual exploitation of vulnerable youth. The Family Partnership and the Advocates for Human Rights, both based in the Twin Cities, played pivotal roles in drafting the law and bringing it to the legislature. With a variety of local agencies regarding this as integral to their work, Shunu saw the initiative as a collaborative accomplishment "in true Duluthian style." The legislation, called Safe Harbor, passed in 2011 and went into full effect in August of 2014. It excludes sexually exploited minors—youth who are exchanging sex for food, drugs, and shelter for survival—from the legal definition of "delinquent child" so that they will not be charged with a crime. The legislature also appropriated funds to provide services and advocates for sexually exploited youth.[23]

St. Louis County was one of only four counties in Minnesota that put Safe Harbor practices into effect before they were mandated by the Safe Harbor Law. In a joint statement at a press conference in May 2011, county attorney Mark Rubin and Duluth mayor Don Ness, chief of police Gordon Ramsay, and sheriff Ross Littman said, "Our practice, even without legislative mandates, has been to look for protection instead of juvenile delinquency charges." Shunu called it "a huge development. We fought to make Safe Harbor happen."[24]

The Minnesota Department of Public Safety's 2013 report *No Wrong*

Door offered a model of the services sexually exploited youth would need, including regional "navigators" to provide needs assessment and referrals to services. PAVSA houses the regional navigator for a seven-county region in central and northeast Minnesota. Together with Life House and Safe Haven Shelter, they provide shelter and services for trafficked youth in Duluth. PAVSA runs a program called My Life My Choice to intervene with youth before they are exposed to sexual exploitation. Developed by the Justice Resource Institute in Boston, this ten-week prevention program for at-risk youth educates them about what trafficking is, as well as about things like developing self-esteem. They have about a 20 percent success rate. "Even if we get two people out of ten, it's still a success," said Shunu.[25]

Because of the Safe Harbor legislation and the accompanying funding, PAVSA has added staff for its trafficking program—the regional navigator and two part-time counselors—to help youth navigate the complex systems and to provide a 24-7 crisis response. PAVSA also played a large part in putting together a men's group focused on combating sex trafficking in Duluth, called MAST, Men Against Sex Trafficking, which is now formally a program at Men as Peacemakers.[26]

The Native women's sexual assault audit also alerted PAVSA to issues of inclusivity within the organization. For many years, PAVSA had been run and staffed primarily by white women and was known in the community, according to Shunu, as a "white agency." This "whiteness" manifested itself in different ways. "It [could] mean you impose your mainstream approach to things on your clients and your staff, or it could physically mean that you're a lot of white people at the agency," continued Shunu. She commented that lack of diversity among the staff has been one of PAVSA's biggest barriers in attracting women of color to use its services, whereas, she said, "If I see somebody like me, then I'm more comfortable." In 2015, about half the staff were people of color—"a big accomplishment for a small nonprofit in Duluth," noted Shunu—and the positive impact can be seen in the fact that more people of color are coming to PAVSA to seek services and support.

PAVSA also found that its focus on gender-based violence, and even feminism, were barriers for people in communities of color and the transgender community. Some perceive "feminism" as a white women's movement that does not take the values of communities of color into consideration, or does not take into consideration men and boys who also are victimized. The term "gender-based violence" is perceived by many in the trans community as not being inclusive of them. According to Shunu, even though most of the people that PAVSA serves are women and girls, the organization has reframed its mission to be "inclusive of men . . . women . . . folks in trans communities . . . [and of any] sexual orientation, whether they define themselves as lesbian, gay, bisexual, intersexed people, or people defined in certain cultures as having multiple spirits."

Through all the ways that PAVSA has grown and evolved, one key value that has endured is that of empowerment, "that women are their own best decision makers," as Candy put it. "As soon as that person has contacted us, we want them to start healing. Empowerment is a big piece of that." One of PAVSA's strategies of empowerment is to let the clients make their own decisions about what steps they want to take, while at the same time offering guidance when asked and supporting them in the decisions they make, even if it's not the choice the advocate would make. "Our role is to inform, educate, give resources and options and choices," said Candy. "They need us to be there to be empathetic, offer them options, and support them in the options that they choose. . . . That's core to our work." Another element of PAVSA's work that has remained unchanged is the strong reliance on volunteer advocates. PAVSA trains about thirty-five volunteers annually, ranging from college age to people in their sixties, and over its history PAVSA has had more than 1,300 volunteer advocates. Advocates donate more than 13,000 hours every year. The volunteer advocacy program is what enables the organization to provide services twenty-four hours a day. The volunteers answer calls around the clock and are available to meet victims' needs whenever they arise. "I always go to the volunteer training on the first night," said Candy. "I tell them that we now have this very well-developed program, but if everything fell apart, the thing that would be left is our volunteers."

Volunteer advocate Meredith Fifield said, "I love being able to work with the people one-on-one by being able to help them through a difficult time or trying to make a visit to the hospital less traumatic." Another volunteer, Melissa Perpich, said, "I love working with survivors, offering support and validating their concerns. The survivors I speak with make me a stronger woman. They are taking the power back by speaking out on their injustices and getting help."[27]

Overall, an enduring value and practice of PAVSA is that "we've always wanted to serve people and serve people well," said Candy. "It's an organization that's always been very involved in knowing what victims need and having the most up-to-date techniques and most up-to-date standards . . . [and then] giving people what they need—well-informed staff members and people who care deeply."

Conclusion

Begun with a handful of dedicated individuals who wanted to do something about sexual violence against women, PAVSA has grown from a crisis line and a few volunteers to an agency that assists eight hundred to a thousand individuals each year and has brought about significant change in local, state, and national policies regarding sexual assault. It has had an impact on thousands of women and men "whose lives were made perhaps just a bit easier because PAVSA was there after they were victimized." "People often say to us, 'that's got to be such a hard job.' It's not a hard job. It's an amazing job. I feel lucky every single day," said Candy. "People share their lives with us in such a unique way. They feel we're safe for them in such a vulnerable time in their lives. That's an honor. That's a privilege. . . . I love what I do." Others who work for PAVSA echo those sentiments. "My workmates are incredible [people] because they've chosen to do this," said Candy "The people who choose to work in this field, on whatever level, have a passion for justice."[28]

PAVSA has worked with women who have suffered terrible abuse and violence. Rosemary Rocco reflected that while she felt sorrow for the parts of the victims "that have been killed off, probably forever," she is continually "in wonderment at the incredible bravery and resilience of women." When Rosie received an award from President Bill Clinton in 1994, in recognition of her work in the sexual assault field, she told him that while receiving the award was a "wonderful thrill," she could "only imagine what it would be like for victims of violence to receive awards for their bravery and courage in speaking out, because . . . ultimately it was victims speaking out—women subjected to ridicule and shaming and ostracizing in their families—that allowed me to do that work."

PAVSA's larger purpose has been to bring about a shift in cultural attitudes. Rosie has come to recognize that the culture and attitudes that foster sexual violence and the underlying gender oppression are deeply embedded in generation after generation, and that the road to full equality will be a long one. "A large amount of sexual violence on the continuum rises out of our psychosexual socialization—the [expectation that] 'boys will boys,' and 'girls are to remain virgins, but boys are to sow their wild oats,'" she said. Like so many who began this work with the idealistic belief that simply by raising awareness they could change the world, Rosie, too, thought, "surely, if we just made people aware, we could change things around in three to five years." The greater lesson is that such deep cultural change takes much longer. "Pretty quickly I understood it was going to be a lifelong commitment," she said.

Nevertheless, she has witnessed change. Statements by politicians and public figures about sexual assault that may have been acceptable in the past are no longer heard. For Rosie, it is important to recognize the "distance that we've come . . . and understand what we were up against, and that it took many people to move those barriers aside. . . . I do believe we're in a time of a quantum shift in terms of understanding."

Looking to the future, Candy hoped PAVSA's legacy would be "that somewhere along the line, this organization worked with enough people and worked effectively enough in the community to change some of the values in our community and eradicated sexual assault here." As is true of the women they have served, the story of PAVSA as an organization has been its resilience and perseverance. "We once called ourselves 'the little agency that could,'" said Candy. "That was when we had four people and we were steamin' ahead. We wouldn't give up. We don't give up, and the reason we don't give up is because of the women we work with. . . . They don't give up." With such determination, perhaps they will indeed, some day in the future, achieve their dream.

{ 4 }

The Women's Coalition for Battered Women/Safe Haven Shelter and Resource Center

Before the 1960s, domestic abuse was rarely talked about publicly, and certainly not as a problem that needed to be addressed by society at large. Indeed, at one time the use of physical force on a wife was legally prescribed under laws of coverture, and considered normal. Though it had been an issue for feminist activists for well over a hundred years, spousal abuse was generally considered by society to be, for the most part, a private issue, a "domestic dispute." Then women began talking with each other, and the personal became political. So it was in Duluth in 1976 when a few women in a support group began talking about their experiences of physical and emotional abuse, and the seeds of what is now Safe Haven Shelter were sown.

With its philosophy of "helping women help themselves; empowering them to make their own decisions and to take control of their lives," Safe Haven Shelter and Resource Center, originally the Women's Coalition for Battered Women, has provided a safe place, support, and assistance for women in abusive relationships and their children to heal and begin to transform their lives.[1]

Origin Story

In 1976, Shirley Oberg, Jean DeRider, and Pat Hoover met in a support group run by Maggy Anderson, a feminist therapist, at the Human Development Center. "It was in the support group that the consciousness raised. There were many stories about women who had been battered," said Shirley. Jean agreed: "We were getting to know each other, supporting each other. It was like a consciousness-raising group, too."

In January 1977, the three of them attended a speak-out and workshop on domestic violence in Duluth that several area women had organized in honor of their friend Mary Chagnon, a woman known to be in an abusive relationship who had disappeared under suspicious circumstances a few years earlier. Among the speakers was Monica Erler from Women's Advocates in St. Paul, the first battered women's shelter in the nation. Battered women, including Shirley, spoke as well. The city and county attorneys talked about how women typically would drop charges, and representatives from St. Louis County social services revealed that their response to calls from battered women was to put them up for twenty-four hours in the Lincoln Hotel, which by 1975 had deteriorated from its original 1920s grandeur and had become a haven for recovering alcoholics. In essence, no effective services for battered women existed in Duluth.[2]

The workshop "was the spark that lit the flame," said Shirley. She and Jean and Pat were inspired then and there to establish a shelter in Duluth. They formed a task force that included Paul Gustav from Victim's Witness, Brian Brown from the city attorney's office, Cindy Clauson with Family Services, Claire Dettmers, Kathie Moore, and others, that first met in March 1977. The group decided that the first step was to establish a hotline. "The various task force members got enough money together to get us a red phone—of course it had to be red—so we had a phone and a hotline number," remembered Jean. They took turns answering the hotline, which was housed in a small office space in the YWCA, and at night the phone calls were forwarded to their homes.[3]

When the task force held an open meeting at the YWCA to raise interest and gather input into developing a shelter and resources for battered women, Michelle LeBeau, who had recently moved to Duluth after leaving an abusive relationship, attended the meeting thinking it was a support group. As it became clear that it was not, she started to leave. "I was heading out the door, when this woman came running over," Michelle recalled with tears in her eyes. "She said, 'Come on in! My name's Shirley Oberg. I'm glad you're here.'" Michelle recalled that, by the time she left, Shirley had signed her up to be on the hotline.

Her turn to answer calls was the very next night, and she received a call from a woman who needed to leave her home "right then and there." Because they didn't have a shelter yet, Michelle invited her to her home, where the woman and her two children stayed for three days. Michelle recalled, "I just did with her what my sister did with me. I sat up and talked to her, listened. We cried together."

Michelle asked her friend Cathy Tickle (Curley) to join the group of women interested in forming a shelter. Years later, Cathy explained that she had recently witnessed one of her friends in an abusive situation. "It was serendipitous when Michelle asked me if I would like to be involved, because I didn't feel like I helped that friend of mine very much." Cathy would be with the shelter for the rest of her life.

"This was truly a grassroots movement," Shirley recalled. "The women who were involved were all working class, students and waitresses. . . . We didn't have resources. I don't think there was a degree among us at the time. There were several on AFDC. . . . We had the dream of a shelter . . . so that women had a safe place to stay."[4]

Many people from the community provided resources. Rosemary Rocco, who helped found the Program to Aid Victims of Sexual Assault (PAVSA) a few years earlier, recalled, "the Women's Coalition was emerging, and we worked directly with them." Her partner, Maggy Anderson, who had led the galvanizing support group, also helped the group get off the ground. "They let us carry the ball," said Jean. "It wasn't like they did it for us." Claire Dettmers helped get a small grant to pay Shirley and Jean. The county attorney gave them models to follow to fill out the forms they needed to become a 501(c)(3) nonprofit, and in June 1977, the group officially incorporated as the Northeastern Minnesota Coalition for Battered Women, later to become the Women's Coalition.

The Coalition began holding support groups for battered women and made an arrangement with the YWCA to use some of its single room occupancy housing, if available, for women and children in need, and the women from the Coalition occasionally opened their own homes as well. In September they began formal volunteer training sessions. Through it all, they boosted each other up. "We told each other endlessly we could do this," said Shirley.[5]

Serendipitously, that same year the Minnesota legislature allocated $500,000 to the Department of Corrections to start model programs for battered women. The Duluth women applied for and received a $50,000 grant. "We paid ourselves four dollars an hour," said Shirley. The United Way provided paper, postage, and printing and helped them make their first brochure, and after the first year became a regular contributor.

After three months, the Coalition moved the drop-in and outreach center into the basement of the Free Clinic, with an office consisting of an old typewriter and the hotline. The organization received referrals from the police and hospitals, and women called the hotline directly. Jean recalled that they would give the women information and support "and help them through whatever process they were going through."

It wasn't long before they realized that taking women into their homes or putting them up at the Y were not adequate solutions. They would need an actual shelter. They sought advice from shelters in the Twin Cities, including the Harriet Tubman shelter and Women's Advocates, which provided training. The Housing and Redevelopment Authority (HRA) gave them free rent in a three-bedroom duplex on Second Street and Second Avenue East (currently the Churches United in Ministry, or CHUM, homeless shelter). People donated furniture and household items.

On March 1, 1978, the Women's Coalition opened the doors to the first battered women's shelter in Duluth, and only the third such shelter in the nation. "The newspaper said we're in the vanguard of the country," said Shirley. The women took turns staying at the shelter. "I did the very first overnight," Cathy recalled. "One woman called and came in. We stayed up all night, ate popcorn, and talked. We had someone every night since then." That first year the Coalition provided shelter to two hundred fifty women and children. "We were flying by the seat of our pants," said Jean. They would help the women who came in whatever way they could. "Shirley had a hard time not giving away half of her stuff," said Jean.

The original shelter was always crowded, and the rent-free arrangement with HRA was temporary, so the Coalition began looking for a permanent location. Fortuitously, in August 1978 a woman who had been battered and was divorcing her husband needed to sell her house, so she asked the Coalition if they wanted it. They did, and were able to purchase the home with a no-interest loan from the Ordean Foundation. The house needed a lot of renovation before the Coalition could use it as a shelter, and the staff and others from the community did much of the work themselves. In February 1979 twenty women and children moved into the new shelter. Shirley recalled, "We had no running water, the kitchen wasn't done, plaster was hanging from the ceilings," but they were glad to be there, and the shelter filled up quickly. In addition to providing shelter, the group provided advocacy and ran support groups for women at the shelter and in the community. Two women showed up at the first meeting, and the groups grew from there. The Coalition encouraged women to come back to the support group even after they had left the shelter because ongoing support was so important.

Early Years: The Collective

As the Women's Coalition became more established, figuring out how to operate became a daunting task. "We did not have one bureaucratic bone in our collective bodies," said Shirley, laughing. They decided that operating as a collective would suit their energies well. "It was such a 'woman' thing. We're more cooperative than competitive." They also were impressed with the collective model of Women's Advocates in the Twin Cities and wanted to replicate that. Believing Duluth to be too conservative to back a shelter run as a collective, however, the board at first imposed a two-director model. But when the women who ran the shelter insisted on functioning as a collective, the board gave in, and the group officially established itself as a collective. "Our idea of the collective was that we're all equal value, whether someone did administrative work or worked with the kids," said Jean DeRider. "We're all necessary." The staff rotated jobs, took turns doing overnights at the shelter, and received the same pay.[6]

Cathy recalled that one reason they chose to become a collective was "to model for the women in the shelter that we could work together collectively and make decisions together. It didn't have to be hierarchical and it could work." Trish O'Keefe, who joined the collective some years later, said the women wanted to "model equality in relationships, so that one person because of their gender or their title didn't get to tell you what to do."

They made decisions by consensus and would talk through everything for hours. "We tried to give everybody a voice. . . . It took a long time to hear everybody and work it through," remembered Jean. Even the smallest thing had to be agreed upon by all. The example everyone recalled—now with humor, though at the time it was frustrating—was whether to serve wheat or white bread. "We heard it all the way out, and of course we came up with, 'We'll buy both!'" said Jean. Trish acknowledged that "there were times it was very frustrating and slow . . . but I think the decisions that we finally came to were good because they had the input of a lot of voices. People would be behind them."

Michelle recalled "a lot of crazy meetings and arguments." Sheryl Boman, who joined the collective shortly after it began, remembered her first staff meeting well: "People were arguing and crying, and I'm wondering what did I get into? Then there would be a support group [of the staff] after the staff meeting." Jean reflected, "It's going to be rocky at times. There's going to be disagreements. When you're doing work that is passionate to you, it's hard not to react passionately about things that are going on in the organization, too." Cathy felt good about the mutual commitment to dealing with conflicts as they arose. "We continuously made pledges that we were going to keep working through our conflicts."

As part of that pledge, they sometimes brought in feminist therapists to help them work through their struggles. That helped them survive as a collective for two decades.

At its outset, the Women's Coalition had two major purposes, according to Jean: "We wanted to offer women who were in abusive relationships shelter and support. We also wanted to change the response the system had toward women who were abused." But as Cathy Curley said in her remembrance of the first twenty-five years of the shelter, "The larger vision was clear: We would end violence against women."[7]

The Coalition addressed its first goal through its shelter program, but it also provided support for hundreds more women who called the hotline, working with them to develop safety plans or finding other ways to help them. "Many of our own had been abused, so the stories were clear to us," said Jean. "The idea was to help them in some way." They helped women obtain resources to enable them to leave, connecting them with Legal Aid for divorce and custody issues, or to the displaced homemakers program if they needed help getting education or finding employment. They even had people who would help women move. "Once they're out [of the abusive relationship], they're pretty much on their own," said Jean. "If they can make a couple more connections in the community, it really helps them."

The Coalition made up the program as it went along, developing programs and adding services based on the needs of the women who came to the shelter. "We didn't have a clue what we were doing," said Michelle. "We had to base it on our own experience and what felt right, and what women told us they needed." She continued: "We had the best interests of the women and children at heart. That shaped everything that we did. The goal was to let the women know there were alternatives and give them a sense of hope." As Shirley explained it, "the women were informing the next step that we would take."

Women needed supportive services for their children. Michelle recalled that, in the era before shelters were regulated by the state, members of the collective would sometimes take kids home with them on the weekends, "to give their moms a break. . . . It was fun—just being able to have that experience of watching kids play where they're not afraid and they're around grown-ups who are being happy—taking them out of that trauma for a while." Eventually the Coalition developed a children's advocacy program and hired an advocate specifically to work with the children to help them deal with the trauma they had experienced and set them up with schools and other community resources.

The Coalition's mission, however, "wasn't only about helping women create change in their own lives," said Michelle. "It was also about creating change in how the community saw and understood [the issue of domestic violence]." To that end, the Coalition took a two-pronged approach, focusing on education and public policy. Members of the Coalition did outreach, speaking at churches, community groups, and schools and universities. "We were always out there educating people, doing radio spots and newspaper articles," said Michelle. They also provided education and training for the Duluth Police Department, which was far from supportive at first. "It was a hostile climate," said Cathy. She recounted a story of their first training with the police that has since become legendary: "This one officer stopped me while I was speaking and said, 'Are you going to tell me that your husband never slaps you around?'" Cathy thought he was joking, but he wasn't, and when she responded, "no," the officer said, "Well he's a damn fool." Cathy added that, a little while later, the same officer shouted out, "You women with your alligator mouths and your hummingbird brains." "That was the climate for us in that arena," said Cathy.

They experienced similar attitudes with every agency with which they worked. Cathy remembered that when they made a presentation to the United Way, hoping to receive funds, she felt like "there were potential batterers on those panels, just by the questions that they would ask. They were hostile questions." Sheryl remembered people coming back from the trainings saying, "We need combat pay to do this."

By 1979 shelters were being established all over the state, and members of the Coalition provided training and support for developing programs elsewhere in the region, including Range Women's Advocates in Virginia and Carlton County Advocates.

The second prong of the Coalition's efforts to effect change in systems and attitudes was through public policy. As Shirley put it, "Women didn't have to make coffee anymore. They had to make policy." Locally, they worked with the police and a variety of social service agencies to create victim-friendly policies. As members of the Minnesota Coalition for Battered Women, they worked on developing legislation to address the needs of battered women and to support battered women's programs and domestic assault advocacy. During 1978 and 1979 the state coalition saw two major breakthroughs. First, 1978 was an election year, and women from the state coalition attended both major parties' candidate rallies and continually asked the candidates, "What are you doing for battered women?" This effort worked to convince Al Quie, the ultimate winner of the election, that "this was *the* issue," and he made funding for shelters part of his agenda as governor. Second, in 1979, the state coalition helped to move two critical pieces of legislation into law: the Domestic Abuse Act, which contained a provision regarding orders for protection (OFP), and the Probable Cause Arrest Law. These two laws profoundly changed the work of the shelter.[8]

Shirley remembered that they lobbied for the Domestic Abuse Act as an "anti-divorce bill." They told legislators, "Women don't want to have to divorce their husbands, but they cannot stay because of the violence, but if they [the legislators] passed the civil order for protection, a woman could go to court and get a civil order for protection and that way save the marriage." Before OFPs, a woman's only option to escape abuse was to leave. With the advent of OFPs, women and their children were able to stay in their own homes, with some assurance of protection, and the batterer had to leave. Shirley called it "quite a piece of legislation." Trish O'Keefe said, "It was a total shift in beliefs about who gets to do what. It meant that so many more women could stay in their homes, versus hauling all their kids and all their stuff someplace else and uprooting everybody." Now able to make that choice, many women preferred to stay in their own homes, and soon fewer women needed to come to the shelter, but the Coalition needed to dedicate several staff members to writing orders for protection. Eventually, legal advocates were added to the staff to address this need.[9]

However, "orders for protection weren't a panacea," said Jean. Their effectiveness depended on the respondent. "Some [respondents] had no regard for authority. Others maybe had a job on the line or wanted to be more discreet," said Jean. Nor did police respond consistently to OFPs. If the respondent wasn't there when the police came, no charges were filed. "It wasn't a cure-all, but it did empower women," said Jean.

The second major legislative provision, the Probable Cause Arrest Law, brought profound changes to the shelter and to the approach to domestic abuse in Duluth. At the time, Shirley sat on a task force with Ellen Pence, who headed the Department of Corrections, and when the law passed, Shirley and Ellen partnered up for a project they called the Domestic Abuse Intervention Project (DAIP). It was an experiment designed to observe the differences in outcomes for victims of domestic violence when the partner was arrested versus not being arrested. The shelter in Duluth was a good fit for the experiment, and the program was of benefit to the shelter, which regarded it as a way to take the onus off of women to press criminal charges. Shirley recalled, "Our role would be to follow up on arrests, be the access point for women walking, jumping, or being pushed into the criminal justice system, and last, and most importantly, to educate every woman we came into contact with as to the political reality of violence against women—where it came from, what was the purpose, and what she can do about it."[10]

Ellen and Shirley began the experimental program with the Duluth Police Department in 1980. Half the police officers were told to make arrests on domestic violence calls and half were not. The Women's Coalition sent follow-up advocates and tracked the arrests. After the police picked up a batterer, they called the Coalition, which then sent an on-call volunteer advocate—alone and often in the middle of the night—to follow up and check on the victim at her home. These were not always the safest situations. Advocates were warned not to go in the house if something didn't feel right, and they were told not to go on calls at locations above the Cozy Bar or in the Seaway Hotel at night. Remembering her days as a volunteer on-call advocate, Tina Olson said, "I could tell you stories for hours about being dispatched to a house in Central Hillside in the dark and being chased by dogs, or sitting with a woman in a hospital for four or five hours in emergency—a Native woman who didn't have any insurance, so they made her wait forever . . . this was an elder—and finally having to get up and say, 'Can somebody see this woman, please!'" The day after an arrest, the Coalition would receive the police report and pass along information from the on-call advocates to the court and attorneys. "We saw that as an opportunity for teaching," Jean recalled. "They [the judges and lawyers] didn't understand women's fear, or how isolated they get, or how they can easily be influenced."

The Coalition followed up on every call, whether or not an arrest had been made. The advocates visited the women in their homes and, if necessary, took them to the hospital and continued to visit them there. Setting procedures that are now standard, the on-call advocates kept records of their interviews and conversations with the women, which they used to help the cases through the criminal justice system. "I was able to say [in court], 'This time she had a mark on her face and three years ago he broke her jaw,'" said Jean. They took photos of victims' injuries, which along with the written records allowed them to see patterns and to document histories of abuse. The advocates supported women through the criminal justice system. "The court system is very intimidating for people," said Sheryl. "Having that support system for women was crucial." They also helped police understand why a woman might strike out herself, or strike back—that she was scared or defending herself.

As a result of the study, the city of Duluth adopted a mandatory arrest policy, the first city in the nation to do so. This also shaped the nature of the Coalition's work. Since the organization was now dealing with the criminal justice system on a regular basis, it established on-call advocacy, criminal advocacy, and legal advocacy programs.

The downside of the mandatory arrest policy was that, as more women fought back, more women were arrested, with negative consequences. "You get arrested, you're not going to call the police anymore, because they might arrest you again. So, that gave [the abuser] more power over her," said Cathy. Women were being arrested even when they were clearly striking out in self-defense. Sheryl said, "I'll never forget one woman who was arrested because she bit his tongue. We said, 'Did anybody stop to think of why his tongue was down her throat?' . . . He was on top of her and was trying to rape her, and she bit his tongue. She was arrested and he wasn't." They had to train officers to look at the whole picture. Years later, the mandatory arrest law was amended with "predominant aggressor" legislation. Under that policy, police responding to domestic assault calls are charged with screening for self-defense and predominant aggressor injuries, with the purpose of arresting only the predominant aggressor.[11]

The other facet of the collaboration between the Coalition and DAIP was running women's education and consciousness-raising groups, both at the shelter and throughout the Duluth community, to educate women about the political realities of violence against women. Among other things, conversations with these groups led to the development of DAIP's Power and Control Wheel. (See Chapter 5: Domestic Abuse Intervention Project and Praxis International.) One of the Coalition's most significant contributions to the Power and Control Wheel was its discovery of the role that sexual violence plays in maintaining power and control. After going through several orders for protection, Jean had noticed that in many cases, sexual assault, either of women or children, accompanied the domestic abuse. When she and others researched the link between sexual abuse and other forms of physical battering, they found that sexual violence had a significant role in upwards of 80 percent of battering situations. After the Coalition presented its findings to DAIP, DAIP included sexual violence in its representation of the violence holding the wheel together.

Growth and Changing Needs: 1980–2000

In the beginning of the collective, everyone did a little bit of everything. The Coalition even did its bookkeeping by committee. Cathy recalled,

"We were keeping our notes and our receipts in a shoebox." The Department of Corrections said that was not adequate, and the organization would need to improve its financial record keeping. Anne Marshall, Ellen Pence's mother, trained Cathy how to do the books. This was just the beginning of increased specialization of roles for the staff. In addition to women's advocates and the children's advocate, the Women's Coalition now had legal and trial advocates as well as an education coordinator. When it became clear that all the staff members couldn't do overnights and continue to function, they stopped rotating tasks. As a result, the advocates' jobs became specialized, and, explained Cathy, "the daytime advocates learned a lot about the [community and legal] resources because they worked on that during the day, and the night advocates spent a lot of one-on-one time with the women because they had the time to do that. It just evolved that way."

In about 1980, the Coalition received a Community Development Block Grant to add on to the shelter. As more women were being served at the shelter, the Coalition hired more staff, and the job specialization increased further. "We had grown so large that we now had two tiers," said Cathy. "We had a collective, and we had non-collective staff, because we a) couldn't make decisions with as many people as we had—it was too cumbersome—and b) we didn't have funding for us all to get the same wages."

Though they were part-time, the so-called casual staff worked regularly. Some women in the collective felt they should be considered regular staff, and receive better salaries and benefits, but in order to implement that they would need to reapply for their jobs. The casual staff responded by forming a union, "which is unusual for any shelter," noted Jean, who believed the union was a good thing. Cathy, on the other hand, felt that the union was "a big blow for all of us who had been in the collective, definitely not a part of our model in our head about how this was going." While the formation of the union created some internal hostilities at first, it did force the collective to establish clearer policies, many of which previously had been murky or were constantly changing.

Additional challenges arose over time, with both the staff and the residents. One of the main ones was with regard to race. Michelle recalled that the Minnesota Coalition for Battered Women began talking with them about racism and the importance of having women of color in leadership roles. At its inception, the collective was all white, but many of those who came to the shelter were women and children of color, and the staff needed to better reflect the people they served. The Coalition became more deliberate in hiring people of color. "We ended up with a fairly diverse staff," said Jean, "but that doesn't mean the problems went away."

To paraphrase Peggy McIntosh, an underlying issue was that it doesn't work to just add staff of color and stir. Because the perspectives of women of color were not accounted for in the original formation of the Coalition, the very nature of the organization reflected that homogenous point of view. As Sheryl Boman, a white staff person, put it: "The organization was framed and built from a white cultural perspective. As women of color came into the organization, that didn't necessarily change." Even when women of color's voices were included, "their voices and their experience didn't drive the decisions that were made or the policies that were put in place," Sheryl continued. "We were asking women of color to do their job from a white cultural framework, even when working with their own communities, and that didn't make sense to them." She gave the example of the shelter's policy that a staff person could not have a personal relationship with someone who had utilized their services for six months after they left the shelter. That practice did not fit with the ways people from communities of color related with one another. "A lot of the African American women who were coming to our shelter were coming from other areas," said Sheryl (increasingly, women were coming from the Twin Cities metro area and Chicago), "so they didn't know anybody from their own community, except for the African American women who were working at the shelter. We set up this framework where they couldn't have a relationship and support this woman as a friend when she left the shelter. That caused a lot more isolation for women of color who had come into our community."[12]

Tina Olson, a Native woman who volunteered at the shelter for ten years, witnessed Native women being treated differently than white women at the shelter. They were held to rules more strictly, and were more likely to be told to leave if they broke them. She also saw Native women being talked about in a "gossipy" way by staff. She understood that advocates needed to pass along pertinent information to other advocates, but, as she explained, "when you tell other advocates about someone's personal journey, you're breaking her confidentiality. You're not treating her with integrity. I saw that happen a lot with Native women. There was judgment. . . . It would fall just short of racism, because racism is too strong a word. Individually they weren't racist. Their intent wasn't to put women down or to create a judgment, but in their behavior and approach they did."

The difficulties extended to staff of color as well. Sheryl noted that just as men had the "good old boys club," the early collective of white women had formed close bonds and had in a way developed their own "good old feminists club." She felt that the women of color coming onto the staff were never fully extended that same level of trust. "It seemed that women of color's work performance was looked at more critically, that their voices were not heard to the same degree as white staff."

Tina perceived a strong sense of entitlement and white privilege among the white staff at the shelter. On various occasions she felt that her values and beliefs, while not criticized, were not accepted by white staff. "I felt like they were trying to teach me to be like them. I didn't want to be like them," said Tina. She witnessed a similar attitude in how the white staff approached the ways Native women raised their children. Differences also arose over parental discipline of the children. Sheryl observed that "white women would have issues with how African American women would speak about spanking their children." (The shelter prohibited spanking, so this was more about verbal threats.) On the other hand, "Native women would parent nonverbally, and when the other women wouldn't hear them saying anything, they would get upset because they didn't think they were dealing with issues." Trish agreed that the shelter "struggled a lot with racism and parenting." The shelter had a no-hitting policy, but mothers coming to the shelter often had different beliefs about how best to discipline their children. As the shelter grappled with how to deal with that, the women of color on the staff explained that women of color had to discipline their children in a way that would ensure the children understood clearly what they can and can't do, because they are much more susceptible to police response than white children are. The staff ended up bending on the no-hitting policy because, as Trish said, "Women are going to raise their children the way they decide to. They have the right to do that." However, the staff continued to raise the idea that hitting may not be the best way to respond to behavior issues, and provided alternatives. It was a learning process. Sheryl said, "I give credit to women of color in that organization that continually tried to work with white women to help them understand their reality. It was through them and their being willing to share that that helped me."[13]

Lesbian battering raised a new set of challenges for the Coalition, such as determining which of the partners to take into the shelter. "We always just believe women," said Trish. When a woman would call for their services, the shelter agreed to take her in and didn't question her about whether she was truly being battered. But in the case of lesbian couples, when both women claimed they were being battered and that the other partner was the batterer, the staff wasn't sure how to handle the situation at first. "Finally, we came to the conclusion that we would take the first one who called, and if the other one called and needed shelter, we would find her a shelter somewhere else," said Cathy. "If it became obvious that we were housing the wrong one, then we would ask that person to leave. It does become obvious pretty quickly who's the batterer and who isn't." If the partner who was the batterer contacted them, they advised her to contact DAIP, which held support groups both for batterers and their partners.

Some in the community criticized the Coalition for its policies regarding lesbian battering, but they also garnered support. In January 1990, members of Aurora: A Northland Lesbian Center extended a formal letter of support to the Coalition: "The lesbians of the Aurora Task Force recognize and appreciate the energy and sincere effort that the Coalition has contributed to this difficult and complex issue. We applaud the fact that you are one of the few organizations in Duluth that is actively confronting homophobia and lesbian battering." A few months later, the Coalition began running support groups specifically for victims/survivors of violence in lesbian relationships.[14]

Increasingly, shelter staff also had to deal with women coming to the shelter with serious chemical dependency issues. In order to better address those needs, the Coalition collaborated with Liberalis, a women's chemical dependency agency based in Carlton County. While the shelter educated Liberalis about the specific needs of women who were abused, Liberalis worked with the Coalition to develop better policies for dealing with residents with chemical dependency issues. Liberalis helped the Coalition realize that they needed to take more seriously the issue of women being intoxicated or high. "We were reluctant to send [the women] to detox, yet we should've been doing that," said Jean. "We didn't know what kind of history they had. If they blacked out, it could be life-threatening for them. It was extremely important for us to follow through on that." With a grant from the Department of Corrections, the shelter hired a half-time staff person to work with abused women who also had drug or alcohol issues.

Over the years, the Coalition had to come up with solutions, resources, and policies to deal with a variety of situations. They sometimes had to deal with women who wanted to have contact with their abuser. "We were worried when current residents would see their abuser and have their abuser drop them off at the shelter. It compromised our safety and revealed our location to him," said Trish. Increasingly the staff had to deal with women with mental illness. They also began to see more women who had been trafficked into prostitution. One year they had a number of women who had been victims of satanic cults. Each of the changing populations came with its own unique set of considerations and needs, and the staff and board often had to work through disagreements about how best to address those issues. "Rules were always a big fight," Michelle remembered, "because you either had people that wanted to try to regulate everything women and kids did, or you had people who [thought], this is their home, we need to respect them as adults and just provide food and shelter and services."

Despite the challenges, working with the women who came to the shelter was the most rewarding part of the work for staff and volunteers. Trish felt honored to have women share with her such intimate stories and details about their lives. Battering had been a secret and private issue for so long, she said, and "women knew this was a place where they could talk about it without being judged or blamed. . . . I didn't know the intimacies of this, the level of violence, and . . . the incredibly cruel and horrible things that women were going through. That was a real eye-opener for me."

The Coalition also continued its efforts to effect legislative changes and influence public policy. It took busloads of women who had been battered to the state capitol in St. Paul to meet with legislators in their offices. Eventually they set up listening sessions where the legislators came to them and the women told their stories. The Coalition's work contributed to improvements to the Domestic Abuse Act, orders for protection, and child custody laws, and to the passage of the Indian Family Preservation Act and several appropriation bills to help fund shelters.

The Coalition also continued its partnership with DAIP, but over time, tensions arose between the organizations. As DAIP's prominence grew, the shelter began to feel like the "poor cousin." Trish, who had worked with both DAIP and the shelter, remarked, "the work at the shelter was unrecognized, poorly paid. The work of the DAIP was innovative, creative, and got national attention. People [at DAIP] got to go to conferences and have their own hotel room, and when we went to a conference we would share a bed with each other because we were so broke. There was always a bit of this tension between the shelter and the DAIP."

Women in the Coalition also came to feel as though people from DAIP sometimes acted as the "shelter police." Occasionally the Coalition and DAIP worked with the same woman, and if the woman wasn't happy about something at the shelter, DAIP would call the shelter on policies

or behaviors they perceived as not being in line with feminist principles. Trish felt that DAIP didn't have to deal with "the realities of living
situations. They could be these purists theoretically, but when you have
people in that kind of living situation, it doesn't always work that way."
She recalled an example of helping some women pack up their things
and taking them to the bus station, only to realize later that they had
stolen items from the shelter. When they created a policy dictating that
certain items needed to be locked up, some people at DAIP thought
that was "oppressive and wrong." Trish said, "We were faced with dealing
with the reality of needing to provide food and clothing and basic living
essentials. . . . Advocates often felt like they just did all the dirty work."[15]

Competition for funding also put the two organizations at odds.
"Shelters were so vulnerable. Everybody was always focusing on . . . what
we did and didn't do right; how we could do this better. There was not a
lot of funding, so for another organization to come and start competing
for that funding and for that attention . . . was difficult for me," Michelle
admitted. While members of the Coalition valued their involvement with
DAIP, and many had friends at or even worked for DAIP, the relationship
was made difficult by these divisions, and after years of collaboration, the
organizations for the most part went their separate ways.

A highlight for many in the Coalition came in 1998, when six women
from Duluth's sister city, Petrozavodsk, Russia, came to Duluth and four
women from Duluth—Mary Ness, Cathy Curley, and Trish O'Keefe from
the Coalition and Vicki Ybanez from AICHO—traveled to Petrozavodsk
to share ideas about domestic violence. They differed over philosophies
and approaches to domestic violence. "Most people in Russia believed
battering was because of psychological problems, alcoholism, and lack
of financial resources," Cathy explained. "We believe it has to do with
sexism, power, and control." The women in Petrozavodsk were working
to open a shelter there, where the resources for battered women were
minimal. Only two other shelters existed in all of Russia at that time. "It
felt like they were where we were twenty years earlier," Trish recalled.[16]

Trish recounted a meeting with a police chief there that was reminis-
cent of Cathy Curley's encounters with Duluth police officers two decades before. When the police chief said, "We have a saying in Russia: 'If
he doesn't beat her it means he doesn't love her,'" everybody in the room
laughed, except the Duluth women. Instead, they pulled out a poster,
developed by the Minnesota Coalition for Battered Women, that showed
a picture of a woman's neck and shoulders covered with stab wounds.
The poster said, "My boyfriend says he loves me. This isn't love." Trish

recalled this as "a very awkward moment," but that it was safer for the women from Duluth than the local women to push those points, "and maybe some of it would sink in."

For Cathy, the highlight of the trip was meeting with women in rural villages. "They were welcoming, loving, and seemed hungry to talk to us about domestic violence and battering. There were disagreements, tears, energy, hope, and motivation to work towards some relief. There were also personal stories about their mothers and grandmothers, what they have endured, and continue to endure."[17]

1998: A New Shelter

By the mid-1990s, the Coalition had outgrown the house that served as the shelter, and the organization decided it needed its own building to accommodate the expanding demands of the shelter. The Coalition began the multiyear project of finding a location, raising funds, and managing the construction for a new shelter. It took two to three years to raise the $1.6 million budget and another eight months to build the building. Trish, who was in charge of writing the grant and managing the construction, said that building such a large facility changed the nature of the shelter and the shelter program considerably. For the safety of the residents, the shelter had operated in an unknown location for many years, but the new building made this impossible. "We couldn't build a building like that and not have people know what it was," said Trish. Being in a known location required increased security. A few years earlier, a woman had been abducted from a different shelter and raped at gunpoint, and the Department of Corrections mandated that all shelters install elaborate security systems, which was expensive. The Women's Coalition, however, took the more public profile of the shelter as an opportunity to change its image, from one of being hidden and isolated to being a community matter that should be openly acknowledged. "That was a big shift and people took it on," said Trish.

In addition to security concerns, neighborhood relations became a major issue with the more public location. The shelter faced opposition from its new neighbors, who were concerned about how the shelter would affect the neighborhood. "They were not happy at all," said Trish. One objection was that the shelter was to be built on green space, which the neighborhood residents wanted kept open. As summarized in the *Duluth News-Tribune*, "Residents near the proposed shelter . . . wish the Women's Coalition would find another place to build. It's not a 'not in my backyard' kind of thing, they insist. They just want to keep the land open as a place for their children to play."[18]

Residents were also concerned that the shelter would bring crime into the neighborhood. Though crime had never been an issue for the shelter, many neighbors feared it nonetheless. One resident who operated a daycare expressed concern that the shelter would "attract crime," and she claimed that parents had told her they would send their children elsewhere if the shelter was built. Another resident made an offer to buy the property and turn it into a park; others tried to find alternative locations for the shelter.[19]

Opponents of the shelter's construction sent dozens of letters to city hall and took their concerns to the city council. Nevertheless, the city council ultimately granted the Coalition the zoning variance necessary to build the shelter. After moving in, the Coalition continued to work toward improving neighborhood relations. It responded to neighbors' concerns about traffic and lighting by putting a stop sign in the parking lot and dimming the lights. "We're doing our best to be a good neighbor," said Cathy.

The new shelter opened in 1998. Its capacity was triple that of the previous shelter, with space for thirty-nine occupants, and it had a large industrial kitchen, common living and dining spaces, offices, and meeting rooms. Built to be a housing facility rather than a home, the new shelter has a more institutional feel than the former shelter. According to Trish, the previous shelter had been "much homier and cozier" and was more conducive to fostering relationships among the residents, since women and families often shared rooms and typically spent more time in the common areas. With more bedrooms in the new shelter, people have a greater tendency to stay in their own spaces. Trish commented that "there's always trade-offs," and while the larger facility "changed a lot of the feeling" of the shelter, it enabled them to meet the needs of a far greater number of women.

2001–2015: The End of the Collective and the Beginning of Safe Haven Shelter

In its first twenty years, the Women's Coalition had grown from a small collective with a $50,000 budget to a large operation with an annual budget of more than $1.2 million. The new shelter required more staff, and by 2001, the staff had become so large and specialized that the collective model became problematic. "The ideal group for a collective is seven," said Jean. "Once you get up to thirteen, you get more divided." She thought the organization had not understood how to adapt the collective model as its numbers expanded and had no model of a successful collective to look to for guidance. Others thought the structure was working fine and wanted it to stay intact. However, following a personnel crisis, the board concluded that the current model was no longer working, and ended the collective structure. With the exception of Cathy Curley, all the members of the collective left the Coalition. They did so for a variety of reasons, some due to the change in structure. Susan Utech was hired to serve as executive director, and because the organization was no longer a coalition, the name was changed to Safe Haven Shelter for Battered Women.[20]

Simply meeting the needs of the women they served took the bulk of Safe Haven's resources and attention, but the organization did take on several new initiatives. In 2002, the shelter participated in another international exchange, this time with women from the Coalition on Violence Against Women in Nairobi, Kenya. At that time, there was only one domestic violence shelter in all of Kenya. Four activists from Kenya came to Duluth to train with Safe Haven and DAIP and four women from Duluth traveled to Kenya to exchange information and ideas.[21]

A major initiative was developing a resource center modeled after family justice centers. In the mid-2000s, the Bush administration made large grants available to support the development of family justice centers. The concept was to provide a "one-stop shop" for victims of domestic violence, where, as Cathy described, "the services and the people come to the woman, rather than her having to find all the services and get child care, and transportation, and wait a month to talk to somebody." Police, attorneys, therapists, and others would provide services at the center.

Safe Haven compiled a team to put together the grant proposal. Such a program was already in existence in San Diego, and Cathy went there to learn about it. A Safe Haven employee who had worked at the San Diego Family Justice Center also contributed her practical knowledge to the proposal. In the end, Safe Haven did not receive the grant, but by that time the organization was fully committed to the project and decided to go ahead with it. It would, however, need to find other sources of funding.

A building on First Street across from the county courthouse became available. The location was ideal. Safe Haven held fundraising events and received major grants from the Bush and Bremer Foundations. It also received a $100,000 donation from the building's owner. An anonymous donation of $240,000, made through the Ordean Foundation, made the dream of the Family Justice Center a reality. "I don't think we could have raised the money in the time period without that gift," Susan Utech said.

The center had its share of controversy, primarily over which agencies should be included. Keeping in mind the wisdom she had gained in San Diego—that conflict was a given and that what mattered was staying focused on the dream—Cathy remained undaunted. In 2008, the Family Justice Center opened its doors with a community-wide reception and celebration. It is a beautiful space, with meeting rooms, private consultation space, offices for staff and partners, two kitchens, a shower, a lounge with computers for client use, childcare facilities, and even a hair salon. Here women work with Safe Haven legal advocates, police, and attorneys on OFPs, filing charges, and divorce and custody issues. They can also meet with advocates from PAVSA and professional therapists. A representative from DAIP comes to the center to talk with the men. Childcare is also provided. Agencies located in house include the Duluth Police Department, Arrowhead Regional Corrections (Probation), Legal Aid, and the county and city attorney's office. When the Resource Center first opened, police chief Gordon Ramsay said that the establishment of the center kept Duluth a leader in the work against domestic violence and violence against women.[22]

As its first director, Cathy wanted to infuse the center with the original vision of the collective. "I'm wanting it to have a collective flavor . . . where everybody's voice is heard and considered," she said as it was opening. For many in the community, the Resource Center stands as a legacy to Cathy, who gave her heart and soul to its creation but died just two years after its opening.

The Safe Haven Resource Center continues to work to enact its vision "to provide a safe location where all the needs of victims are met, children are protected, violence stops, families heal and thrive, economic justice increases, hope is realized, batterers are held accountable, and all professionals work together." The center has broadened its offerings beyond the original vision. In addition to assisting with legal matters, the Resource Center is home to four weekly support groups. "We have an empowerment group that does a lot of work with education, getting people their GEDs, but also helping them apply to colleges, helping them get scholarships," said Susan. Safe Haven also offers a self-sufficiency program, which helps women to become independent through securing employment and new housing and furthering their education.[23]

Since the opening of the Resource Center, the majority of the work of Safe Haven has occurred through the center, which serves more than 1,300 people each year, averaging 258 victim visits per month. About two-thirds of the visits are victims walking in looking for help or accessing the Resource Center's other services without an appointment. A dream for the center is to provide mental health services and counseling. The women who come to the center are dealing with emotional trauma, and as violence becomes more severe, issues of physical disability compound the emotional issues.[24]

Safe Haven's shelter provides temporary housing to about six hundred women and children annually, with an average stay of about twenty-two days. However, some women and families stay up to six months, largely because they have nowhere else to go, especially since the demise of Women's Transitional Housing. (See Chapter 9: Women's Transitional Housing Coalition.) Thanks to a provision in the funding for the new shelter, Safe Haven is able to house a certain portion of the women longer than what is considered transitional.

Safe Haven values its volunteers. In 2015, 181 volunteers performed over 6,000 hours of service for the organization. Volunteers serve in a variety of capacities, from on-call advocates who contact and visit with victims in their homes or at the hospital after a domestic violence arrest, to food servers, tutors for adults and children after school and during Empowerment Group, and childcare workers. Professionals also volunteer their time, offering such services as spiritual direction, massage, and art therapy.[25]

The enduring philosophy of Safe Haven is reflected in the five core values they hammered out by consensus in 2013–14: safety, equality, teamwork, empowerment, and compassion. Though the organization has been pressured by funders to become gender neutral, it intends to keep women the focus. "You can't let that erode," said Susan. "It's important to have those feminist ideals. The feminine is a part of the equation. . . . The people who started this had deep feminist principles. To honor that is a big enough job for us."[26]

Conclusion

A few years before her death, Cathy Curley reflected on her thirty years with the shelter:

That this first group of women who had no clue about how to start a nonprofit, or experience doing grant writing, or how to work together as a team, came together and made this happen [is an achievement]. That thirty years later we have a shelter that has room for thirty-nine women and children, and we'll be opening this new Justice Center, and hoping to serve 2,000 to 2,500 women, just based on some women meeting together in some women's living rooms with a dream, is a huge achievement to me, a testimony to what we can do if we put our minds to it.

Since its origins, the Women's Coalition/Safe Haven Shelter has provided shelter, safety, and support for thousands of women and children affected by domestic violence. "We've saved hundreds of lives," said Cathy. "That's an achievement that is beyond measure."

"Safe Haven began with a vision of changing the world," reflected Cathy, "of bringing about a cultural shift to a society where men would treat women with dignity and respect and shelters would be a thing of the past." And though violence against women has not decreased, the attitudes and society's response toward it have changed in significant ways. As Cathy noted, "When we first started out, there wasn't much awareness about domestic violence. . . . It was still pretty much in the closet and [there was] a lot of shame attached to it," but today, societal awareness is much greater. Rather than being ignored or even condoned, domestic violence is a crime. The community of Duluth embraces and celebrates its role as a world leader in fostering a community response that is supportive of women dealing with domestic violence. "When you're doing this day to day, it feels like there's still so much to change," said Trish. "But people's attitudes have changed a lot. The relationships with people that we work with in the courts, the police, and social services have changed." The fact that domestic abuse is no longer a private and silenced issue but rather one that the society as a whole is addressing openly is a huge achievement for which Safe Haven and others in the battered women's movement around the country are in large measure responsible.[27]

The shelter's work was life-changing for countless women and families who have benefited from its services, and for all those involved. "They gave me a great opportunity," said Tina. Jean agreed: "The amount of insight and things that you learn is incredible." "Working at the shelter . . . helped me to value the experience of women working together—understanding the value and support of women, and what they can accomplish," said Sheryl. "The friendships I made back then are still strong today," said Trish.

To conclude with the thoughts of Cathy Curley: "I will always be proud and grateful to be a part of the grassroots group of women that started that shelter. Miracles really do happen there. Women finding the courage to come or call in the first place—lives are saved. Many women find their way to healing and independence against great odds."[28]

{ 5 }

Domestic Abuse Intervention Project and Praxis International

T he Domestic Abuse Intervention Project (DAIP) was the first community-based project to coordinate the interventions of key agencies in the criminal justice system in cases of domestic abuse and is best known through "the Duluth Model," the Power and Control Wheel, and the mandatory arrest policy. The community-response model that DAIP created, generally referred to as the Duluth Model, calls on agencies that are part of an integrated response to develop policies and protocols that emphasize victim safety, are accountable for that safety, provide a supportive community for battered women, and offer rehabilitation and education services for batterers. The Duluth Model has been adopted and adapted around the country and the world. By centering its work in the voices and lived experiences of women, DAIP has changed communities' responses to violence against women and has helped to create a shift to a more victim-centered approach to addressing the problem of domestic violence.[1]

Origin Story

The Domestic Abuse Intervention Project began with women who had experienced verbal and physical abuse talking about "the problems they had with the police . . . problems they had with clergy . . . about how the institutions in the community kept them in these [abusive] relationships." They were talking in the battered women's shelter and in the many groups run by the Women's Coalition for Battered Women. "The idea for the Domestic Abuse Intervention Project came out of the women's groups," said cofounder Shirley Oberg.[2]

Shelter activists around the country had also been exploring how to provide legal, civil, and social remedies to intervene in domestic violence.

In Minnesota, they had developed civil and criminal legislation to provide greater safety as well as legal recourse for women living in violent relationships. Through more than twenty bills passed in the Minnesota state legislature, activists helped to create a "dual-track" system: a civil track to meet the needs of women living in abusive situations (shelters, child support, orders for protection); and a criminal track, which activists regarded as necessary "to make the use of violence in the home as [criminally] sanctioned as its use in the public sphere."[3]

A pivotal piece of this legislation, probable cause arrest, became the centerpiece of the Domestic Abuse Intervention Project. The law allowed police officers to make a warrantless arrest if they had probable cause to believe a crime had been committed, and activists believed that it might be applied effectively in domestic violence cases. Shelter activists wanted to find a community where they could put this to the test and coordinate the intervening agencies to implement the new legislation in such cases. Shirley Oberg and Ellen Pence, who had met through their work on the Minnesota Department of Corrections' advisory task force on battered women's shelters, agreed that Duluth would make for a great test site, given its size, the nature of the community, and the receptivity of the Women's Coalition's shelter. "I don't think the DAIP could have been started under the auspices of any other shelter at that time," said Shirley. In her opinion, it was "the only program in the state fertile and open enough" for the project. After Shirley and others from the Women's Coalition convinced shelter activists from the state coalition to attempt this in Duluth, she and Ellen partnered to start the DAIP. "The partnership between Ellen and myself was a praxis where we put the theory and the practice together," Shirley recalled.[4]

Shirley and Ellen wrote a grant to fund a six-month trial and approached the Duluth police chief about doing an experiment in which half the officers answering domestic abuse calls would make an arrest if they had probable cause to believe an assault had occurred, and the other half would respond as they normally would. It became clear that left to their own discretion, most of the officers would not make an arrest.[5]

The Women's Coalition was a key partner in the experiment. "The DAIP was organized as an ally of the shelter," wrote Ellen. The shelter would follow up on arrests, be the access point for women coming into the criminal justice system, and educate women about the political reality of violence against women. The focus of the project was always "what to do for *women* to keep *women* safe."[6]

Creating the Duluth Model

The DAIP began in 1980 in a kitchen above the Free Clinic at Lake Avenue and Fifth Street. Shirley and Ellen asked Coral McDonnell, who had been volunteering at the shelter, to join them as administrative coordinator. "I did various activities: administration, on-call advocacy, women's groups," Coral recalled. Months later they hired Dale Brown to follow up with men who were arrested and to facilitate a men's group. With just enough space for a typewriter, file cabinets, copier, and an extra desk, DAIP worked out of the kitchen for a year and then moved into larger rooms in the basement of the Free Clinic. A year later they moved to the Damiano Center, where they also had room to hold meetings.

DAIP began as a hierarchy, with Ellen as director, and Shirley and Coral working under her. There was also a board of directors. However, Ellen recalled, once they recognized that "the source of all of the violence against women was the hierarchal relationships," they began asking themselves, "Why are we one?" Within a year or two, they transformed into a collective model. "Everyone had an equal vote on any policy issue, and we tried to make all of our decisions together," she explained. They eschewed consensus decision-making in favor of majority rule, except in cases of major policy decisions, which required a two-thirds vote. Once DAIP became a collective, all salaries were equalized.

Shirley used the metaphor of the "spinning plates" act on the *Ed Sullivan Show* to describe the work of DAIP at that time. "All these plates twirling on all of these poles—that was the Domestic Abuse Intervention Project." "It was fun. It was exciting. It was filled with possibilities. We could do this," she said. DAIP had three spheres spinning simultaneously, each with its own stack of plates and each responsive to the other. One was working with agencies in the criminal justice system to develop a coordinated response and policies and procedures that would be responsive to the needs of battered women. The second was working with batterers who had been arrested. The third and core piece was listening to the voices of women. As stated in the values supporting the mission statement: "We listen to battered women: Our work involves active engagement with women who have experienced violence so that our efforts are guided by their realities and concerns." The shelter and DAIP collaborated in running women's groups. The wisdom gained from listening to women provided the substance of the policies, programs, and curricula that became the core of DAIP's work.[7]

DAIP's efforts to establish a coordinated response to domestic abuse were intended to "link all the intervening agencies in a community to a common philosophical approach." This involved shifting the onus of holding offenders accountable from the victim to the community and changing understandings of domestic violence to include power and control as causal factors. DAIP also sought to "introduce ways for the different agencies to cooperate and so improve the community's ability to hold offenders accountable for their violence" with the guiding goal being the safety of women.[8]

The first step was to organize with the police. The story of that first meeting is recounted often by those in Duluth's domestic violence movement. In her version of the story, Ellen recalled that the training officer introduced them as "the girls from the shelter," and it went downhill from there. The room erupted with laughter when one of the officers made the infamous remark that women were hit because "they let their alligator mouths outrun their hummingbird brains," and then again when another officer said, "You know, there is something about a battered woman that just makes you want to hit her." Stunned, the advocates and the women from the shelter asked for a break. One of the women asked, "Why do they hate us so much?" No one could answer, and they left.[9]

Shirley and Ellen came to recognize that the resistance they encountered was due in part to a conceptual distinction those in the criminal justice system were making between harm against the public, whom it was their duty to protect, and harm against women in their homes, which they regarded as a private matter. Ellen was struck by the chief jailer saying, "That law regarding *threat to the public* means the public. . . . It means that . . . if you would let some guy out he might just randomly shoot people or be a general threat to 'Joe Blow citizen.' It's not about his wife!" They met similar resistance from officers who said that if they arrested the batterer, his partner would just bail him out. Prosecutors complained that battered women often chose not to testify. With crowded court dockets, judges often dismissed domestic assault cases. Ellen said, "It became our task to build an assumption into the daily work routines of every practitioner that touched these cases that 'Sallie Blow wife' was, in fact, a citizen, and that while protecting her safety might be difficult because of her relationship with her assailant, it should not be impossible."[10]

To accomplish this, Ellen, Shirley, and Coral immersed themselves in the details of the criminal justice process—the 911 dispatcher, the police, the jail, the courts, and probation. They observed, took notes, went on ride-alongs with police, went to trials and hearings, and read every policy. They took note of hundreds of institutional steps used to process a case. Every step of the way, they would check in with battered women. They organized a group of formerly battered women to meet monthly to discuss every proposal, and they either reworked or threw out proposals based on the women's input. "We talked to hundreds of women about their experiences and analyzed each institutional action from the woman's standpoint, with her safety in mind," Ellen noted. Analysis and proposals in hand, they talked with police, judges, probation officers, and others about how best to work with them in facilitating these processes. Jean DeRider of the Women's Coalition recalled, "They worked with nearly a dozen different agencies, and eventually found at least one person in each who would work with them as an ally." As they worked with the various systems, they found multiple ways to enhance women's safety. Ellen later wrote, "We proposed changes at every stage of a case's journey through the system. We proposed new legislation, new notions of practitioners' job duties, new department policies, new interagency protocols, and new administrative forms."[11]

Within two years, they had developed a comprehensive policy on domestic abuse responses for all the intervening agencies, and as each agency came on board, the "Duluth Model" emerged. The intervention model came to be known formally as the Coordinated Community Response (CCR). Among the outcomes were a 911 system that gave priority status to domestic violence calls, a mandatory arrest law in Duluth, an agreement to hold offenders in jail until a court hearing the next workday, aggressive prosecution, and presentence investigations on all domestic cases. By 1986, domestic homicide and assault rates in Duluth had dropped dramatically.[12]

Programs and Curricula

While the needs and safety of women were the core of DAIP's work, another key piece of its philosophy was providing effective communication, response, and education to men who battered. Early on, DAIP started the Jail Visit Program, through which a community volunteer would visit a man the morning after his domestic assault arrest to talk about the consequences of his use of violence, what might happen next, and the services available to him. A group of women in the community compiled a list of about a dozen men whom they believed could serve as jail-visit volunteers, and nearly all the men agreed. Among them were Brooks Anderson, who later joined the DAIP board, and Michael Paymar, who later became an integral part of DAIP as a men's group facilitator, the men's program coordinator, coauthor of the men's education curriculum, and a national trainer. DAIP was one of the few feminist organizations to recruit men early on. Coral recalled that bringing men into the organization was difficult for her at first, but over time she came to see its necessity: "Men needed to take responsibility for men's violence." They were clear that men had to take leadership from women, and she felt fortunate to find men willing to do so. Nevertheless, the male/female dynamic has not always been an easy one and remains complex.[13]

Advocating for mandatory arrest for batterers did not mean that DAIP regarded locking up batterers as the solution to domestic violence. They were cognizant of the misogyny of the prison system. Ellen wrote, "If a man does not enter prison feeling hostile to women, he will almost surely leave that way." Jail time would not create the conditions for men to reflect on why they use violence against the women in their lives, nor give them tools to stop, so DAIP sought a different approach. They worked with local mental health counselors—such as Norm Herron and Chris Ketelsen of Family Services, Shirley Levine and Dick Stepp of the Human Development Center, and counselors from Lutheran Social Services and the Vet Center—to provide groups for men who were ordered into the program by the court. In 1982, DAIP began running follow-up groups for men who had completed their required time at the counseling agencies. Bob Brenning, John McBride, and several other men from the community facilitated these groups, which focused primarily on anger management, based in part on a Batterer's Anonymous model. After two years, DAIP decided that having only men facilitate the men's groups was collusive, and that women should co-facilitate. Since then, male/female teams co-facilitate all DAIP men's groups. Carol Thompson, who has co-facilitated men's groups since the beginning, shared that a highlight was witnessing the men begin to think differently about themselves, their partners, and their actions.[14]

As partners in the mandatory arrest experiment, the Women's Coalition also provided advocates to follow up with domestic violence victims after their partners were arrested, and they invited the victims to biweekly women's group meetings. Run as consciousness-raising groups, the early groups for women at the shelter were political and empowering, but gradually they took a more therapeutic approach. Not satisfied with this, DAIP began experimenting with a consciousness-raising educational approach based on the feminist premise of each woman sharing her truth. Later DAIP incorporated the work of Brazilian educator Paulo

Freire to create a model for a curriculum based on problem-posing, and by 1985 it had fully adopted Freirean methods. A significant element of both feminist and Freirean pedagogy was the fundamental belief that, as Shirley expressed it, "teaching and learning were the same deed." She explained that, as a facilitator, "I had to go in knowing that everyone in there would have a piece of the truth. The purpose was to build to a higher truth of how we would be with each other." The process was based around posing problems and dialoguing about the truths that emerged. "There's quite a difference between a women's support group . . . and an education group," said Jill Abernathy, who had been in one of the groups and later went to work for DAIP. "An education group changes the way you see yourself and move and act in the world." DAIP ran groups for women at the shelter, for women whose partners had been arrested, and for Native women, as well as educational groups at community centers throughout the city. DAIP provided transportation and childcare to facilitate attendance.[15]

A key component of DAIP's women's curriculum called for each group to take some action in response to their newly raised awareness. In 1984, one of the women's groups decided to focus its action against the Neon Parrot restaurant. On the restaurant's menu was an item called "battered mushrooms," the description of which read, "We got the recipe from a social worker at the shelter for battered mushrooms." Not surprisingly, battered women and their allies found this offensive. They wrote a letter to the restaurant management, with no results other than an apology from the company that had designed the menu. They next decided to picket the restaurant publicly and called on women from the Coalition and the DAIP to join them. The battered mushrooms were eventually withdrawn from the menu, and a year later, the restaurant closed.[16]

From that action grew the Women's Action Group (WAG), with Shirley Oberg as facilitator. Though run through DAIP, WAG incorporated as a separate organization, Silkwings Incorporated. The group met weekly at a house kitty-corner to the Damiano Center. Marvella Davis, one of the members, recalled how she would walk there with her baby in an old baby buggy, or Shirley would pick them up. "Our kids were always with us." Another member, Babette Sandman, said, "I don't think we ever missed a time because that group became so important to us. We were waking up." What kept the women coming back was a feeling of being valued, and a love and sisterhood among women. "We were believed," said Babette. "We were valued. We had wisdom. We had a piece of the truth. We were carrying around a gem. It felt like a jewel inside of us that we didn't even know we had. People were interested in us. We had sisters." After experiencing years of abuse and battering, Babette continued, "I didn't even know I was a human being, I was so dehumanized by the time I crawled into the Women's Action Group." The group brought her back to life. All the women in the group credited Shirley with facilitating their ability to see that they were, as Babette said, "people of wisdom. . . . It was a gentle, loving education that valued our entirety as human beings, which made us feel fully human again." Having grown up with cultural messages that taught them to distrust and regard other women as "the competition," the women were amazed by the acceptance they experienced from women in the group. "The beautiful thing back then is we were actually sisters," said Babette. "It was not just words."[17]

A skilled facilitator, Shirley could draw out each woman. "She'd be on edge listening and wanting to hear," said Marvella. "If you said [something], she was so excited to hear from you and would write it down." "That was the first moment that I felt valued," remembered Babette, "so I always write down what people say." Both Marvella and Babette credited Shirley for teaching them to trust their guts and to ask questions. "She embraced women, and every woman thought she was her best friend," Lee Hemming said of Shirley.

As the members of the group became more aware of the political nature of the issues and struggles of their daily personal lives, and how the system suppressed their power as women, they became more politically involved. They began by speaking at local high schools and colleges. Babette remembered Shirley encouraging them, "Get out there and tell your story. . . . Other people will learn from you." Soon they were telling their stories to state legislators in St. Paul and were amazed by the reception at the capitol. "We were treated like queens," said Babette. "We were valued for our knowledge of what it's like to be in poverty and on AFDC and be threatened by welfare reform." They also worked with local police on fostering awareness of the realities of being a battered woman and in developing policies that were victim-centered rather than victim-blaming. They spoke at conferences and battered women's shelters regionally and nationally. They performed skits about their lives as battered women and afterward would dialogue with audience members about what they had learned. Babette said, "It was a great way to communicate with other women who had been battered, or to women who themselves hadn't been battered but could get a sense of the feelings of women who had been." By example, they showed women how to be supportive of one another. Lee remembered that when they visited battered women's shelters, the women would be "bowled over" by how loving the women in WAG were with one another.[18]

One of the social change conferences they attended featured Paulo Freire himself. He had heard about how DAIP, and WAG in particular, was using his methods, and he came to Duluth to teach and learn from the group. Freire's visit was a highlight for many involved with DAIP, though the women in WAG were at first put off by his academic language. Marvella recalled, "I got in an argument with him about his language. Why do we need to learn the elite language? Why can't he learn my language?" He responded, "Do you want to beat them at their game? . . . Then you need to learn their language." Laughing about it now, she said, "It took me a while to get there, but I finally understood what *The Pedagogy of the Oppressed* [the title of his book] meant."[19]

The role of the church in perpetuating domestic violence came up often in WAG's group discussions and in the work at the shelter. Babette recalled, "We were constantly hearing how the clergy were sending people back into their relationships using Biblical phrases and shaming." So the group engaged local clergy to discuss domestic violence. They believed their efforts were ultimately successful because they stopped hearing of clergy sending women back into abusive relationships.

Following their protest of the Neon Parrot, WAG engaged in several other direct actions and protests. They put information "help" cards in bars around town—cards with an insert saying, "Being beaten? Call . . ." They wanted a card small enough that women could hide it from the men—"something simple that women could stick in their pockets," said Marvella—but still have it for their safety if and when they needed it.

Lee recalled that they did a lot of protests. "We would do marches up and down Lake Superior. . . . We did one with pots and pans because that was an old tradition." At the state capitol, they set up mock graveyards and hung T-shirts with the names of women who had died due to domestic violence that year. When a Native woman was being held in the county jail for killing her husband, WAG held a silent vigil outside the jail. Her husband had attacked her in the kitchen and she had grabbed a kitchen knife to defend herself and ended up killing him, and WAG wanted to bring attention to the fact that she was a battered woman. Jill remembered that at the vigil a woman handed her a sign to carry. "I turned it around to look at it, and it read, [*choking up*] 'This could happen to me.' I was blown away realizing it could've happened to me."

Shirley Oberg's departure from DAIP in the late 1980s left a huge hole in the Women's Action Group. Lee took on the role of coordinator for a

while, though she admitted that after Shirley left, "it was never the same."
"There was no leader like Shirley Oberg," said her sister, Jill, admiringly.
While some of the women went on to own a farm together, WAG itself
faded away. In those few years of its existence, it changed the lives of all
the women involved. "I don't think I'd be the woman I am today without the Women's Action Group," said Marvella. Babette echoed, "I don't
know where I'd be without it. . . . The Women's Action Group was one of
our mothers." "It was good for our soul," added Marvella. "We were opening. Our butterflies were growing"; to which Babette responded, "It was
our wings, our silkwings." Said Coral, "The Women's Action Group was
the highlight for all of us." Ellen called it "the best work I ever did." "I
learned to love women," said Shirley. "To love our weeping, gnashing,
wailing. . . . It was extraordinary."

DAIP also wanted to create groups for men like those they had for
women, based in a dialogical educational approach to raise awareness in
men of how the culture creates the conditions for men's violence against
women. In creating the men's curriculum in 1984, as in everything it did
in those early years, DAIP turned to women. Ellen recounted: "We went
to the women's groups and said, 'If we can get these guys for eight or
ten . . . weeks . . . what do you want us to teach them?' Out of that came
the Power and Control Wheel." Shirley pointed to the Power and Control
Wheel as a key example of DAIP's model of praxis: using women's voices
to create the theory. In all, more than two hundred formerly battered
women contributed to developing the Power and Control Wheel.[20]

At the time, DAIP had been teaching Lenore Walker's cycle of violence theory, but one woman's remark led them to shift that paradigm.
"If you live with a batterer," she said, "it [violence] is not cyclical. It isn't
something that comes and goes. . . . Even when he's being nice to you,
it's a part of the violence. If he's raping you and telling you, 'You're no
good and you're ugly,' and then three days later he's telling you, 'You're
beautiful and I need you and I want you,' it's all part of the same thing."
She enabled them to see that violence and abuse are part of "a constant
relationship with him, one in which he is trying to mess with your mind,
your heart, your feelings, or your thoughts." The new paradigm inter-
preted battering as a set of behaviors that continually contributes to the
batterer having the power and control in the relationship.[21]

In the discussions with the women's groups, the DAIP facilitators explored the question of what tactics batterers used, and they discovered
common tactics, like batterers not letting women see their friends and

calling them names. They grouped these into categories such as "isolation" and "emotional abuse." They came up with more than twenty recurring tactics and behaviors that batterers implemented, in a context of violence, to maintain power and control. "If every woman in the room had a story that fit this thing, then we knew it was a core tactic." As they refined the results, the facilitators focused on eight core tactics and presented them as a wheel, with a ring of violence on the outside that held them all together. They added "sexual violence" to the outer ring after women at the shelter presented their research on the strong correlation of sexual abuse and battering.[22]

As they presented the Power and Control Wheel around the community, the women from DAIP realized they had to address the defensive response they frequently got from men. While giving presentations to high schools, Jill found that young men believed they were supposed to do these things because "that's what a man is." When discussing with colleagues how young men lacked better models for how to be a man, she remembered Coral saying, "We have to have an equality wheel." Similarly, in co-facilitating the batterer's groups, Carol Thompson found that when presented with the Power and Control Wheel, men would get so defensive it inhibited their ability to learn. She and her co-facilitator, Bob Brenning, also were concerned about the suppressed anger that some of the women at DAIP carried toward the men, and they told their co-workers, "If you don't care about the men, don't love them at some level, you shouldn't be doing the work. It works against you." Carol remembered a particularly tense meeting at McCabe Renewal Center where Bob, John McBride, Michael Paymar, and Ellen battled over this point. Eventually Michael and Ellen were convinced that they needed to create a new model, and together they created the Equality Wheel, designing its components to correspond with those of the Power and Control Wheel. To this they later added the Equality Log to deepen their conversations.

According to the values supporting DAIP's mission, "An educational process of dialogue and critical thinking is key to our efforts to assist women in understanding and confronting the violence directed against them, and to our efforts to challenge and support men who commit to ending battering." To achieve this, DAIP developed curricula with a goal of raising awareness. The women's curriculum was designed for women's liberation, in the deepest sense of that term, as opposed to the trivialized phrase it has become today.[23]

The women's curriculum, *In Our Best Interest*, argues that the process of education requires that theory continually be informed by reality. In keeping with that, all the curricula and teaching tools created by DAIP were informed by the real-life experiences of women in the groups. "DAIP always acted like they cannot write a manual without us," said Babette. They ran all the material by the women for input on what did or didn't work and what changes they would make. Incorporating the Power and Control Wheel as a centerpiece of the curriculum reflected DAIP's commitment to the women who helped shape it.[24]

By the mid-1980s, DAIP knew that "something was amiss" with the anger-management focus they had been using in the men's groups. Their work with women's groups deepened their understanding of how battering is culturally constructed, thus helping them to recognize that in order to effect change, they needed to address the deeper cause of men's violence: the long history of a patriarchal belief system shared around the world. The basic underpinning of the Duluth curriculum was that "if he doesn't change his attitudes, he's going to continue to batter her." Hence a more appropriate approach would be cognitive, raising critical awareness to help men understand the basis of their beliefs and the intentionality of their actions.[25]

To get men to think critically about their behaviors, Ellen and Michael designed a curriculum that would engage men in dialogue. It was based on a belief that if you ask sincere questions of men in the group, with genuine curiosity about why they think the way they do, then that process of dialogue has the capacity to change beliefs. They sought to challenge the men to stop using the behaviors on the Power and Control Wheel and shift to a radically different belief system about themselves as men, and to teach them the skills they needed to change their behaviors. The Native men's group used a different, culturally appropriate power and control wheel, which recognized their battering as an outcome of colonization that had supplanted the indigenous belief of men and women living in balance. Years later, Barbara and Ty Schroyer, in conjunction with DAIP, developed a curriculum specifically for Christian men who batter, based on conversations with focus groups of women who had been battered by Christian men.[26]

From a Project to Multiple Programs: MPDI

Over time, individuals who had developed or worked at DAIP went on to establish other related programs in the community, including the Duluth Family Visitation Center (1987), the National Training Project (1989), Mending the Sacred Hoop (1991), and the Battered Women's Justice Project (1993). Minnesota Program Development, Inc. (MPDI), the official name of the nonprofit that was DAIP, was the umbrella organization that housed these various programs.

The National Training Project grew out of DAIP's increasing focus on training. As it became better known in the community, DAIP began doing more and more training locally in schools and civic organizations, and as the work gained the attention of those working on domestic violence elsewhere in the country, DAIP started training nationwide. "Because we were the first city in the country to get a mandatory arrest policy, to get prosecutors to consistently prosecute wife beaters, to get

the courts to sentence them with something other than marriage counseling or a fine . . . Duluth became quite well known," said Ellen. "People
from all over came to Duluth to get trained and we were going all over
the country training people."

The Family Visitation Center was begun in order to address the needs
of women in the shelter who had children. Conversations with women in
the shelters revealed how central their children were to their responses
to situations of domestic abuse. "Half were leaving for the kids; half were
staying for the kids," said Cathy Curley. Separation did not end the violence, conflict, or uncertainty in the lives of the children. In fact, children
seemed to be drawn in even more as custody and visitation were negotiated. Police records and women's testimony underscored that abusive
partners often used visitation as "an opportunity to harass or physically
assault their estranged partners." "Women would talk about [how] they
were under threat when the men would pick up the child, or when they
would pick up the children," said Shirley. "We started the Visitation Center because this is what women needed."[27]

The Visitation Center opened in the YWCA building in 1987 as a
place where parents could exchange children without having to interact directly with each other, and as a space in which fathers could have
supervised visitation with their children. The center provided a solution
for men who were frustrated about lack of access to their children and
allowed the men to interact with their children in positive ways. In addition, the center staff were indirectly involved in custody decisions and
provided advocacy for a just and child-centered community response to
custody and visitation issues.[28]

Mending the Sacred Hoop was formed in the late 1980s in response
to Native activists in Wisconsin and Minnesota who worked with
DAIP to develop a project specifically for Native women who were battered. Originally begun to provide advocacy for Native women, Mending
the Sacred Hoop expanded its work considerably after the passage of the
Violence Against Women Act, when the organization became the first
Training and Technical Assistance (TA) provider on domestic abuse to
tribes across the country. (See Chapter 10: Mending the Sacred Hoop.)

In 1993, domestic violence activists around the state used DAIP as
a home base to create the Battered Women's Justice Project, a national
library and resource center on criminal justice reform. The project provides training, technical assistance, and other resources related to civil
court proceedings and the criminal justice system, as well as information
on orders for protection, custody, divorce, post-separation violence, and
other matters.

With growth came other changes. Like many other organizations, DAIP increasingly lost its grassroots focus and became more hierarchical and institutionalized. Operating as a collective became more difficult. "It worked well as a collective for a long time," said Ellen, "but as it got big, it got awkward to do." Coral agreed: "It got to be quite cumbersome . . . to communicate as much as you needed to to make good decisions." Slowly the organization grew more hierarchical. "We started to have these differences," said Ellen, "like [between] people who were in the collective and who weren't." People hired for short-term projects were not invited to join the collective. For a while DAIP operated with a team management system, in which each program had a team coordinator who represented it in management meetings. Eventually, wage and salary differences between team leaders and staff grew larger, as did the sense of hierarchy. "We still had this idea that some work was more valuable than others," Ellen lamented.

The changes brought gains and losses. Coral thought their improved advocacy came at the cost of the "grassroots spirit." Increased specialization prohibited the staff from picking up and following through on things that weren't part of their responsibilities, even if they saw a need. Increasing demands made finding time to talk together as a staff more difficult. Many from the original collective felt the loss of camaraderie and collective spirit. Increasing professionalization formalized advocates' relationships with the women with whom they worked. Jill said that the early days at DAIP "was like getting together with your women's groups. . . . Ellen was the number one sociable person you have ever met. . . . She'd train all day and be up all night with everybody socializing." The need to set clear professional boundaries changed that atmosphere.

The climate at DAIP had begun to change when Shirley left in the late 1980s. The Women's Action Group and other women's groups in the community disbanded shortly after. Ellen Pence left a few years later to pursue further education, though she remained involved with DAIP.

Praxis International

While pursuing her PhD at the University of Toronto, Ellen, in her words, "came under the spell" of Dorothy Smith, a sociologist who originated a form of sociology called "institutional ethnography." In her years at DAIP, Ellen had found that there was quite often a "gap between the reality of women's lives and what they need, and what human services do for women." She said, "You have to recognize that if you're going down to the police department or the courthouse . . . [with] the same problems, woman after woman, there is something wrong there." Smith's work gave Ellen a way of analyzing that gap—what produces it and why institutions so consistently fail women. "It affirmed, in many ways, the things that we were doing at DAIP, but it also gave me a way of looking at institutional change a bit deeper than I had been."

In research for her dissertation, Ellen created a concept, adapted from Smith's work, of an "institutional audit" to assess how things like racism or sexism, or safety or lack of safety, are built into institutional practices. She used this to develop a method of analyzing how institutions process cases in ways that do or do not centralize safety for battered women. She called it the Safety and Accountability Audit. It examines whether battered women are being protected in a particular system. Ellen explained, "You watch the processing of the case from the moment it comes in until it's all done. Every single interchange between the institution and the woman you're asking the question, 'Is safety built into this process? How is it and how isn't it?'" The audit has four components: reading case files; reading all the documents in the system (rules and regulations, administrative forms); interviewing people involved in the cases; and observing practitioners doing their work. The process reveals how safety is compromised when it is not structured into the system and points to things that need to be changed.[29]

Ellen had been envisioning an organization that would use the Safety and Accountability Audit to analyze how institutional practices contribute to the safety of battered women, or lack thereof, and where and how systems could change. She had put the phrase "Praxis Lives" on her computer screensaver so it would be the first thing she saw when she started working. "It only lived in my imagination at the time," she said. People would ask her what it was, and she would respond, "That's an organization I'm going to start one of these days."[30]

The actual work of Praxis began in 1996 when Ellen returned to DAIP after completing her PhD. The U.S. Coast Guard requested that she do an analysis of its handling of domestic assault cases. Using $40,000 from the Coast Guard, she got a small board together and incorporated Praxis. When she called the state to incorporate, they told her there were already two organizations in Minnesota with that name and suggested she add another word. Thus the organization became Praxis International.

Ellen had intended for Praxis to be something she did on her own, a sideline to the work she was doing at DAIP, but circumstances surrounding a project DAIP had with the Marine Corps changed that. The Marine Corps had contracted with DAIP to set up an intervention program for spouse abuse cases at eighteen of their bases. In the fourth year of the five-year contract, the Marine Corps rescinded the contract, and the group of experts that Ellen had brought together to work on the project were suddenly out of a job. Fortunately, the timing coincided with the federal Office of Violence Against Women (OVW) announcing a large grant program for organizations to provide training and technical assistance for a new initiative in rural domestic violence programs. Ellen saw this as a good potential transition period for her team. It also meant that anyone who was getting grants from OVW for the first time would be trained by Praxis. With that grant, they went from a one-person operation to an $800,000 program overnight.

Ellen hired seven women, mostly from DAIP—Janice Wick, Shelly Stoffel, Amanda McCormick, Casey McGee, Maren Hansen (now Woods), Julie Tilley, and Ellen's mother, Anne Marshall—to begin Praxis International in October 1998, with herself as executive director. According to Janice, Ellen was clear that the organization was not going to have the same structure as DAIP, "that it was a hierarchy and not going to be run as a collective."

In addition to the OVW rural technical assistance project, Praxis continued to do Safety and Accountability Audits. "That's her [Ellen's] passion," Janice remarked. In doing the audits, Praxis continued the DAIP practice of developing theory and practices based on listening to the experiences of women. "We say you can't start the process without talking with women to hear about their experiences," said Maren. "It's at the front, the middle, and the end." The lived experiences of women with the intervening agencies frame the investigation. When Praxis auditors read case files, forms, and documents and observe procedures, they take what they know of women's actual experiences and analyze how this is represented. "As auditors, as activists, and people who are working in the battered women's movement, we bring that knowledge with us all the time," said Maren. The rules, regulations, and administrative guides and checklists affect what police officers and others in the system see or don't see, so it is important to develop these from the standpoint of battered women.

One of the first audits was with the St. Louis County Sheriff's department in Duluth. It has been referenced thousands of times since. When traveling to other places and reading sheriffs' policies, more often than not, Ellen found they were "word for word what we made up in that little room in the St. Louis Sheriff's department." It has become a national model for law enforcement policies on domestic assault.

Two years after starting Praxis, Ellen retired from MPDI and DAIP. Wanting to separate herself, she moved the Praxis office and the now twelve-member staff to a house she had bought on the shore of Lake Superior just north of Duluth. "It was a dog and human office," remembered Maren. "Trish O'Keefe had her dog [Maggie], Casey McGee had her dog, Emma, I had Gracie, and Anne was upstairs with her two dogs. We'd take breaks and go swimming; we'd run our dogs up and down Scenic Drive." Although they felt isolated from the larger feminist community, being set apart helped them to develop a strong sense of community amongst themselves. They cooked meals together and discussed feminist issues over lunch. "It felt radical," said Maren. "It was literally women around a kitchen table trying to figure out how to end violence against women across the nation." They had their feminist community on the shore for about five years, until Praxis moved back to the Damiano Center in Duluth.

A few years later, Praxis received another grant to oversee OVW's Safe Haven Supervised Visitation program (not to be confused with Safe Haven shelter in Duluth), through which Praxis has "completely influenced the way visitation centers work." They built into the practices of visitation centers a method of analyzing a center's impact on the lives of battered women and their children.[31]

This expansion necessitated a second office in St. Paul. As more of the staff moved to the Twin Cities, Praxis shifted its base to the Wellstone Center, a hub of progressive activist organizations, while only three staff members remained in Duluth. Because Paul Wellstone had been one of the main authors of the Violence Against Women Act (VAWA), and he and his wife, Sheila, played central roles in the domestic violence movement nationally, it has been particularly meaningful to the Praxis staff to be working in a building that is a living memorial to them and their work.

Praxis has gone on to develop other influential programs, among these the Blueprint for Safety—"the Duluth Model on steroids," as Ellen called it—for the St. Paul police department, and the Advocacy Learning Center, an eighteen-month experiential course that works with advocates to develop their knowledge about what makes for good advocacy, while also providing opportunities for them to practice advocacy skills.

From MPDI to Domestic Abuse Intervention Programs

When Ellen had been on leave from DAIP, her mother, Anne Marshall, began working at the organization. For many years, Anne had been working with women who had been arrested for using violence in domestic assault situations, and she saw a need for a program and curriculum for this group of mostly battered women. Anne spoke of "how devastating being arrested is for a woman who is the victim of ongoing abuse. The woman usually was treated like a batterer and brought to court in an orange jumpsuit and shackles." Even though the women had struck back in self-defense, they also often felt ashamed that they had "stooped to using violence—just like their batterer." Assistant city attorney Mary Asmus had seen women plead guilty without seeking a lawyer's advice because they wanted to get the case over with. She said the women didn't always realize the long-term consequences, for example that having a criminal record would hurt their job prospects if they wanted to work in health care or childcare. Jill Abernathy said she had seen women plead guilty thinking they could then get back to their kids. Instead, they ended up in jail. Once arrested, the women were at even greater risk of harm. "He [the abuser] would have more control over her than ever," said Jill, "because she'd be on probation."[32]

In 1998 Anne and Mary together created a deferral program called Crossroads, for which a woman is eligible on her first arrest for domestic violence or if she's been convicted on a misdemeanor assault. The women in Crossroads are court-ordered to attend nonviolence classes. Drawing from the experiences of women who used illegal violence, Anne and others at DAIP developed the classes, which Anne co-facilitated with Yvette Farrow, an advocate at the Women's Coalition. "Mainly what we try to do is get them to think about what will happen [to them and their children] if they use violence," said Anne. Jill was particularly impressed by the effectiveness of their training for probation officers: "All of my women in this group [Crossroads] have probation officers that are like advocates for them. That's phenomenal."[33]

By 1998, MPDI had grown to more than twenty staff members. Needing a larger space, MPDI bought and renovated a building on Superior Street in downtown Duluth. Said administrative coordinator Denise Lisdahl: "This will allow us to have adequate office space, adequate space to do our classes and trainings, and allow all of our programs to be in one central location." They named the building the Center for Nonviolence.[34]

Like all groundbreaking work, the policies and programs developed by DAIP have not been without criticism, and as its reputation has grown, the organization has had to spend considerable energy and resources responding to its critics. The mandatory arrest policy generated controversy within the feminist community, as many argued that it took discretion and choice away from women and worked against rebuilding relationships that women might desire. It has also been criticized because it made women of color even more reluctant to call the police in domestic assault cases, due to a general distrust of law enforcement. Likewise, immigrant women may be reluctant to call police out of fear of deportation. DAIP's focus on men, but not women, who batter has spurred debates on women's use of violence and what constitutes battering.[35]

In addition to these external stresses on the organization, tensions emerged from internal changes as well. Ellen's departure from the organization left a large hole. As MPDI struggled to find a workable management model, it decided to become more of a traditional hierarchy and hired its first executive director, Linda Riddle, who came to MPDI in January 2007 and served in that capacity until 2013. "Having an executive director was a big change for the organization, welcomed by some and resisted by others," said Linda. Linda and the staff worked to develop strategies and methods to build communication and positive work relationships, and to examine their internal values surrounding nonviolence and how better to put these into practice.[36]

The board charged Linda with making DAIP as well known in Duluth as it was in other parts of the country and the world, and to make it more integral in the Duluth community. To this end, in 2007 the organization changed its name from Minnesota Program Development, Inc., to Domestic Abuse Intervention Programs. It also undertook a marketing campaign featuring a new logo and the tagline, "Home of the Duluth Model: Social Change to End Violence Against Women." Linda brought new people from the community onto the board and sought to create a more diverse board.[37]

DAIP worked to expand the coordinated community response beyond the criminal justice system to other experts in the community in order to share information and build alliances. DAIP worked with Safe Haven, PAVSA, AICHO, and others on a project to develop better responses and services for women with disabilities who are victims of domestic and sexual assault, and collaborated with PAVSA, Safe Haven, the Duluth Police Department, and others in an in-depth study of system responses to domestic assaults when the victim is sexually assaulted by her abusive partner.[38]

Because the Blueprint for Safety developed by Praxis International with the St. Paul police department in 2007 extended the work of the Duluth Model, in 2011 Duluth was chosen as one of three sites in the nation for an OVW demonstration project initiative on the Blueprint. As

Bea Hanson, principal deputy director of OVW, said, "The whole idea for the Blueprint . . . was built on the work that happened in and emanated from Duluth," making Duluth a fitting choice. According to assistant city attorney Mary Asmus, the Blueprint would help them identify the most serious cases of abuse more quickly. Linda saw the Blueprint for Safety as "the perfect tie-in for making the organization well known in the community and building relationships in the community." It was fully adopted by the city of Duluth and St. Louis County in January 2015.[39]

DAIP's National Training Project put energy into revising the men's curriculum to make it more in line with the practices DAIP had developed at the classroom level and that hadn't yet been written down. DAIP also brought changes to the Family Visitation Center. The center had been serving families who had not experienced domestic violence in addition to those who had, and the staff was severely overextended. Coming from the standpoint that neutrality is dangerous for victims, DAIP refocused the Visitation Center on families impacted by domestic violence. The center also took on more work relating to custody issues. It created the Transitions program, in which "fathers had to do some work, show some change, before they could have offsite visits." In addition, conversations with focus groups of formerly battered women who were struggling with visitation and custody disputes led the Visitation Center staff to develop policies and procedures for responding to men's post-separation violence, as well as a "post-separation power and control wheel." In conjunction with the National Training Project, they also developed a set of educational resources on men's post-separation violence and its effects.[40]

DAIP continues to have an impact around the world. In 2014, the Domestic Abuse Intervention Project was awarded the Future Policy Award for Ending Violence Against Women and Girls by the United Nations' World Future Council. The award, which recognizes policies rather than people, was given to the DAIP in recognition of the model it has created for implementation of intimate partner violence legislation and the coordinated community response.

Michael Paymar sees prevention as the "next frontier" of DAIP's work. "Our culture creates men who batter, rape, buy women for sex. We need to change the culture in which we live," he said in a 2014 webinar training. In that regard, it is significant to note that one of the main lessons Ellen had learned in doing the work was that, in order to change not only individuals but an entire culture that enables domestic abuse, multiple and more far-reaching approaches are needed. Reflecting on her life's work, she said: "If I'd known this was going to be a thirty-year project, I would have done things that take longer to do. I put all my eggs in the criminal justice system basket and that was a huge mistake. . . . The criminal justice system is a reactive institution that responds to something that is already well entrenched. . . . Many institutions allow this violence to go unchecked and create the conditions for it. I wish I had understood the longevity of the struggle. I would have taken different approaches."[41]

In the late 2000s, Ellen was diagnosed with breast cancer. Despite her declining health, she continued working practically up until her death in 2012. Ellen was charismatic, dynamic, and a large presence in the organization and the world. She had been the visionary and driving force of Praxis and for many years of DAIP, for which she remained a board member after she stopped working there. Her death came as a great blow to everyone associated with both organizations and to the organizations themselves. They have each experienced and struggled with that loss in their own ways as they work to redefine themselves.

Conclusion

Begun as an experiment by three people with a good idea in a kitchen above the Free Clinic, the Domestic Abuse Intervention Project evolved into an internationally recognized organization that established policies, practices, and curricula that have changed the shape of domestic violence work in the state, the nation, and the world. The model has been adopted in seventeen countries and countless cities in the United States. Its pioneering combination of feminist and Freirean methodologies to create an education for critical consciousness has the potential to foster deep cultural change and paradigm shift, as does the continual grounding of its work in the lived experiences of women. The multitude of curricula—from the groundbreaking *In Our Best Interest* to the newly revised *Creating a Process of Change for Men Who Batter*—have been used by thousands of people across the globe. DAIP was revolutionary in its work with men, "helping them figure out how they can change, helping them see from the inside, the value of it for them, and not writing them off," said Laura Wedge of the National Training Project. The iconic Power and Control Wheel has been translated into twenty-two languages and adapted for thirty-three different cultural contexts. In a tribute to Ellen Pence, friend and colleague Shamita Dasgupta wrote: "Advocates use the wheel to encapsulate a battered woman's narration; experts use it to testify in court; specialists write reports based on the wheel; and even battered women, from whom it originally surfaced, use it to organize their experiences when retelling their stories to others. . . . It has permeated our popular culture, a verification of deep penetration in society. I am often delighted to detect it in the décor of a movie scene."[42]

The Safety and Accountability Audit extended the early work of DAIP and has been implemented across the country. It has changed the way domestic violence work is being done. "That whole notion of auditing has replaced the idea of people coming together around a task force for domestic violence," said Ellen. "Now people are saying, 'Let's come together and analyze what's wrong.'" While giving credit to the work of others upon which the work of DAIP is built, Ellen said that DAIP's contribution has been "to demonstrate how to organize in ways that build women's safety with daily work practices of legal and mental health agencies and to show that agencies can work cooperatively with community-based advocacy groups."[43]

Reflecting on the overall work of Praxis and DAIP, she concluded: "We've had a big impact on the field of domestic violence. We've kept a lot of notions that feminists wanted to put into this field in the beginning alive, made it credible, made it mainstream." They have changed the concept of domestic assault from a norm to a crime. "In every community across the country, domestic violence is known as a crime, whereas before it was [considered] a fight in a home that wasn't any big deal," said Jill. Dramatic changes have taken place over the last thirty-plus years in increasing knowledge about domestic violence and providing more services and better training for people in the criminal justice system. As Michael Paymar put it, "We have made significant progress and domestic violence has declined."[44]

Shortly before her death, Ellen shared these reflections on the significance of the Domestic Abuse Intervention Project: "In the end the DAIP's greatest contribution was its demonstration of how a local advocacy group could reshape institutional responses to male violence. . . . It insisted on a system that intervened beyond the incident and understood the whole context of violence, and it showed a way for activists and allies in the system to work together. We made gender visible in a justice system that purported to be blind to all of the privileges it routinely maintained."[45]

{ 6 }

Women's Health Center and the Building for Women

efore the 1973 *Roe v. Wade* Supreme Court decision legalizing abortion, thousands of women in the United States died each year from self-induced or back-alley abortions. At great personal risk, activists, physicians, and clergy across the country joined together to form underground networks to help give women access to safe, though still illegal, abortion. In Duluth, activists and clergy also set up an underground. In relays, they drove women to points where someone else would pick them up and drive them to South Dakota, where Dr. Charles Munson performed abortions, or to the Minneapolis airport to fly to Sweden or Mexico for abortions.[1]

Since *Roe*, physicians and other health care providers and activists who seek to provide women with safe, legal abortion still do so at great personal risk. In the face of these risks, the Women's Health Center has been providing reproductive health care for women in Minnesota, Wisconsin, and northern Michigan for over thirty years.

Origin Story

In 1972, a small group of community activists established a free clinic, the Duluth Community Health Center, in the basement of Sacred Heart Church in Duluth's Central Hillside district. Soon after, the center relocated to a former grocery store on Lake Avenue and Fifth Street. The Free Clinic, as it was known, served many needs, providing health care for people who otherwise couldn't afford it. In a time before over-the-counter pregnancy tests, it was also a place women could go for confidential pregnancy testing, as well as sexually transmitted disease (STD) screening. Following *Roe v. Wade*, volunteers did abortion counseling and referral. "I had no official training or medical training," recalled Joyce

Benson, one of the volunteers, "but I worked with the women that came in. It was a very heart-wrenching, rewarding job."

In 1973, hospitals in seventeen counties in Minnesota provided abortions. In Duluth, only Dr. Bill Lundberg and his wife, Dr. Kay Lundberg, who was the anesthesiologist, were performing abortion procedures at St. Luke's Hospital. The procedure required general anesthesia and a hospital stay and was very expensive. When Dr. Lundberg's wife died in a tragic accident, it was difficult for him to find another anesthesiologist willing to do this work, and the availability of abortions in Duluth became even more scarce. Most people from the Duluth area in need of abortions had to travel to the Twin Cities, one hundred fifty miles away.[2]

With increasing pressure from anti-abortion forces, the number of hospitals in Minnesota providing abortions dwindled rapidly, and by 1979, 98 percent of all abortions in the state were performed in Hennepin and Ramsey Counties, but less than half of the abortions performed there were for residents of those two counties. Well over half of the women seeking abortions in St. Louis County were unable to get one. The unmet need in the surrounding rural areas was even higher, ranging upwards of 80 to 90 percent in Aitkin, Cass, Itasca, Cook, Koochiching, and Lake Counties.[3]

In 1980, Dr. Jane Hodgson, a pioneer in reproductive health care and administrator of the Midwest Health Center for Women in the Twin Cities, began looking into opening an abortion clinic in Duluth. "She was tired of seeing women thumb a ride down to the Cities for an abortion," Tina Welsh remarked. The center approached various people in Duluth about opening a clinic there, and offered the position of director to Joyce Benson. She recalled, "It was an agonizing decision." Weighing this exciting possibility against the significant challenge and very real dangers of starting up a clinic, Joyce decided against it. She did, however, help the center find "the right person for the job": Tina Welsh. Tina, who was then with Planned Parenthood, had worked with Joyce in the abortion underground prior to *Roe v. Wade*. She also had to wrestle with the decision of whether to accept the challenging position at the new clinic. "After serious thought and talking to my kids," Tina recalled, "I decided that I would go for it." It was not a decision to be made lightly, as the unfolding events would make clear. Tina began her work as director of the Women's Health Center (WHC) in 1980.[4]

In 1981, with a three-year $98,000 grant from the McKnight Foundation and a matching grant from the Midwest Health Center for Women, the Women's Health Center in Duluth incorporated as a 501(c)

(3) nonprofit with a mission "to provide medically safe, legal, and afford-able reproductive health care in a professional setting." The center had from January to March to get set up. In that short time, WHC needed to find a place to house the clinic, purchase the equipment, and hire nurses, counselors, and a receptionist. Tina called everyone she knew who had worked at Planned Parenthood and the Free Clinic. "A lot of women here had experience in pregnancy counseling and referring women," she said, "but nobody had ever been an abortion counselor before, or 'patient edu-cator' as we call them now." They were able to find offices for the clinic in the Medical Arts Building, and the staff went to Minneapolis for training at the Midwest Health Center for Women. They had quite the rude awak-ening when they returned.

While the staff was in the Cities, anti-choice people had gotten wind of the plan to open an abortion clinic, and by the time staff returned to Duluth, the opposition was quite organized. "They had about 5,000 sig-natures on a petition that they didn't want us in the Medical Arts Build-ing," said Tina. "They didn't want us in Duluth." However, the clinic had strong support from the Alworths, who owned the building, as well as from several doctors who had practices there, and the clinic opened as scheduled on March 30, 1981.

Ever since *Roe*, abortion providers have been under attack from abor-tion opponents. Due to concerns about harassment from protesters, the clinic staff had arranged for escorts to drive women to the clinic. "We had sent patients to the YWCA, and we had escorts pick up the women at the YWCA and drive down to the Medical Arts Building and bring them in through the garage," Tina recalled. As it happened, the day the clinic opened was the same day President Ronald Reagan was shot, so with all attention on that, the clinic went through its first day without incident.

The understanding with funders was that the clinic needed to prove itself in three years. It did not take long. Despite the fact that the only ad-vertising the clinic had done was to send letters to physicians and other clinics to make them aware of its services, the clinic was very busy and within six months had demonstrated a clear need for abortion services in the region. The original needs assessment had not taken into account northern Wisconsin or Michigan's Upper Peninsula; the closest clinics for women living there were in either Madison or Detroit. Nor had they considered that women from Canada might come to Duluth for an abor-tion. On the other hand, given the large service area covering northern Minnesota, northern Wisconsin, and the UP, the clinic became a target of the anti-choice movement. It also fell victim to a concerted nation-wide campaign against clinics in small cities like Toledo, Ohio; Fargo, North Dakota; and Appleton, Wisconsin. "One of the tactics of people who wanted to restrict choice was limiting access," commented Karen Diver. As a result, the clinic was subjected to regular harassment from the time it opened.[5]

Protest, Harassment, Threats

Tina looks back on the first few relatively peaceful years in the Medical Arts Building as "pure bliss." But in the years that followed, the clinic and its staff "came under siege." Tina detailed the harassment in testimony in a suit against the protesters:

> Shifts of individuals took turns blocking the entrance and harassing people at the street level and on the sixth floor, where WHC was housed. They would stand or kneel with their rosaries and grab a hold of individuals trying to gain access to the clinic. They would attempt to block people getting off the elevator. On one occasion a protester entered the clinic and began tearing posters off the wall. When confronted by a clinic employee he turned and threw her across the waiting room. The landlord had to solder our mail slot as protesters would reach between the legs of an off-duty police officer and shout "please don't kill your babies" through the open slot. . . . Patients utilizing services of other medical facilities were stopped and asked to boycott the providers in the building because they were sharing space with "baby killers."

Tina recalled how the protesters "would follow people all the way up to the sixth floor and outside of the clinic doors, and they'd pray and tell women they were having a sin. Patients and their support people often arrive[d] at WHC upset, terrified and angry."[6]

The clinic also had its allies, sometimes unexpected ones. "One day the clinic door opened up and two of the biggest men I've ever seen walked in," remembered Tina. They had been walking by the building and were angered by seeing the picketers. Being gay truck drivers, they were sensitive to others being bullied and offered to be escorts. Garrett and Bob escorted patients and Tina for a long time.

The local Catholic diocese began organizing protests against the clinic. They put out flyers saying, "Do you realize that half of the people who go into the Women's Health Center don't come out alive?" and "Do you realize that they're murdering babies?" Tina remembered the Catholic church putting out bulletins that said "We want the arrow of truth to pierce Tina Welsh's heart." Tina did admire Father James Crossman's persistence: "He never missed a week. He was there for twenty-nine years. He was getting very physically handicapped, but he'd still be there and he'd still pray."

The protests and threats intensified as the WHC became a target of the national movement Operation Rescue. The movement had a strong following in Duluth that they were able to mobilize against the clinic. "They had wooden crosses that must have been ten feet high," Tina recalled. "They would take the cross to make sure that the shadow of the cross would fall over you and they would pray for you. They would surround me walking to my car." Among the big-name anti-abortion protesters Operation Rescue sent to Duluth was Joe Scheidler. A large man, he barged into the clinic demanding that they hand over patient and staff files. Tina remembered clinic staff standing spread-eagled in all the doorways to stop the protesters from entering.[7]

As was the case throughout the country, threats against physicians made it especially difficult to find doctors willing to perform abortions at WHC. No doctors in Duluth would do it. "They were frightened. They didn't want to get involved," said Tina. While some local physicians admitted to being opposed to doing abortions even though they were pro-choice, others said they were intimidated by the opponents. Tina said she would have to fly physicians in. Others would drive from the Twin Cities. "We had some very loyal physicians," she continued. One was harassed so badly that escorts would meet her outside the city to drive her in. Similarly, after picketers surrounded the plane of one of the physicians, the clinic arranged to have people at the airport to meet the plane. Some physicians were harassed in their hometowns. "One of my physicians from a small town was totally surrounded. His wife couldn't get out of the house for four or five days." The clinic nearly turned away a physician who called saying that she wanted to learn how to do abortions, fearing that she was a plant, but ended up training her. She's now the medical director of numerous clinics throughout Minnesota. Compounding the problem, St. Mary's Medical Center, the largest health care provider in Duluth, wouldn't give privileges to any WHC doctors, making it difficult for the clinic in case of a medical emergency.[8]

The harassment and threats of violence toward Tina were especially vicious. She received many threatening letters, and protesters threatened her at the clinic. Tina recollected two large men shaking their fists in her face, saying, "When you are dead and the maggots crawl in and out of your eyes, then you will know the wrath of God." Out of fear that protesters would use her license plate number to find her home, the clinic provided her with a leased car. Nevertheless, the protesters "were at my house all the time," said Tina. They made her life miserable. They made scenes in drugstores and grocery stores, telling people she was selling shampoo with placenta in it, and using their carts to block her in. "It didn't make any difference what the profession was, when it came to abortion, all of their ethics could be put on the shelf," she said. "I would get calls to say if I believe in murdering children, that maybe my children wouldn't come home from school." Anti-abortion activists made threatening phone calls to her children, saying things like, "If your mother likes to kill babies, maybe she wouldn't feel too bad if you got killed." Tina eventually filed a restraining order for her home. "Usually all you do is go down and sign a few papers. Mine went all the way to district court because they [the opposition] felt the more expense I would have to incur, the more likely I was to drop it." She later said, "I still had a lot of support from the community. My name was the only name that was out front, and we were very careful to try to protect the rest of the staff."[9]

One day, someone else parked in Tina's spot at the clinic, and shortly after he drove away, the wheels came off his vehicle as he drove over the High Bridge, a two-mile span across St. Louis Bay between Duluth and Superior. "That's when the FBI got involved," said Tina. "They had taken the lugs off of the wheels. They were pretty serious about getting rid of me."

As the harassment grew increasingly vicious and violent, WHC trained two hundred volunteers to help maintain safety. "We had to have spotters making sure that they [the protesters] didn't follow our clients." Once the staff came to work to find that protesters had emptied the holding tanks from their RVs into the building. "The smell was so bad," Tina recalled. "They wanted the stench of death throughout the whole building. It was a mess."[10]

After five years of constant harassment and picketing, the landlords at the Medical Arts Building refused to renew the clinic's lease. Supporters financed a move to the Arrowhead Place building, but there the picketing only intensified. WHC filed a trespassing case against the picketers, which took eighteen months to go to trial, in part because no local judge was willing to hear the case. WHC won the case, but protesters were only fined $100 per count. The protests didn't stop, and they scared away other potential leaseholders in the building. The county decided against housing the Women, Infants, and Children (WIC) program in Arrowhead Place because WHC was there. County commissioner Bill Kron said, "Some of those people who use the WIC program are against abortion and will be less willing to use the service if it's housed in the same building." Crimes against the property continued, including bomb threats, spray paint, and bear scent, which spreads an obnoxious smell. The Arrowhead Place building was the first in the nation to be hit by a butyric acid attack, an anti-choice tactic designed to disrupt clinic operation that later became widespread throughout the country.[11]

WHC had received bomb threats since it opened, and as more and more clinics around the country were being bombed, the threats seemed more real. Between 1977 and 2011, at least 41 bombings, 175 arsons, 100 attempted bombings and arsons, and 656 bomb threats were directed at abortion providers nationwide. The owner of Arrowhead Place also was subjected to harassment, including picketing and bomb threats at work and at home. After five years, in 1992, the Women's Health Center was evicted from Arrowhead Place. "Once again we were homeless," said Tina.[12]

The Building for Women

Realizing that leasing clinic space was no longer an option, the WHC board of directors decided they needed to own their own building, but knew they could not afford to do it on their own. They called a meeting of all the allied women's organizations they could think of. Twenty-three organizations and three community members attended that first meeting. Tina told the attendees that "we'd given the old college try and the only thing we knew is that we would have to buy a building and that we could not do that alone." Rosemary Rocco, the director of PAVSA at the time, had been talking for years about women buying a building, and she encouraged them all to support the project. The WHC board and staff agreed and began the monumental task of purchasing a building for women.[13]

The group met several times throughout the summer, discussing the mission, purpose, possible tenants, fundraising, and implications of having an abortion clinic in the building. "It was very stressful for Tina, who was trying to work with other organizations but also had to deal with the eviction deadlines," remembered Rosie. Tina also sought advice from Heidi Timm-Bijou, a member of the WHC's advisory council who worked for the city, and from Peg LaBore of Family Tree Clinic and Ann Ricketts of the Face to Face Clinic in the Twin Cities, which had built their own buildings. They advised Tina to put in what money she could and that other organizations needed to do the same, and suggested she work with developer Susan Sands.

A dedicated group of five women—Marge Whitney, Phil France, Ruth Frederick, Mary Ellen Owens, and Hommey Kantor—to whom Tina referred as "the blue bloods of Duluth," could leverage significant sources of money. The five met with Tina and Rosie weekly to strategize fundraising for the building and to provide not only financial but moral support. Tina also once again met with the organizations to ask for financial commitments. Only PAVSA and the YWCA were willing to make that commitment. "Rosie was in with both feet," said Tina. A building for women had long been Rosie's dream, but she was also acting in solidarity with Tina and the other women involved with the clinic. Years later, she still teared up remembering the threats they had withstood: "What those women endured . . . to serve this community, to take care of women I referred to their clinic. How dare I have stood apart from them all that time? And how dare the community stand apart?" She could do so no longer.[14]

Concerned with protecting their endowment, the YWCA board agreed to become a limited partner in the Building, but nevertheless played a large role in its development. Karen Diver, executive director of the YWCA, commented, "The YWCA nationally was a pro-choice organization. The YWCA has always been progressive on tough social issues like racism and diversity, so the Y Board signed on." She felt that, as the oldest women's organization in Duluth, the YWCA brought "stature, longevity, and stability" to the project. In addition, Karen said that being part of the Building for Women "fired up some passion that was sorely lacking—that there is a real purpose in the YWCA's advocacy, that we were willing to take strong stands that were controversial and that our support of women and girls was more important than approval."[15]

Tina, Rosie, and Karen were quite a force. They had been crossing paths for years as workers, volunteers, and advocates for women and children, and "Now that they had decided to come together in one spot, however besieged, nothing was going to stop them." They were joined by the five women Tina had first called upon, the "blue bloods." Together they became the "fundraising committee," which met weekly for the next five years.[16]

The committee conducted a needs assessment and developed the mission statement: "The Building for Women will provide a welcoming atmosphere, a safe and accessible place in which organizations and individuals serving primarily women can grow and thrive." The vision was a multipurpose facility, with offices for nonprofits, incubator spaces for start-up organizations, and rental space for small community groups, in addition to larger office suites for the YWCA and PAVSA and clinic space for the WHC. They would need to raise nearly $2 million, with the bulk going to acquiring the property ($330,000) and renovations ($1,072,000).[17]

Raising the funds was no small task, made possible only by the women's perseverance, the generosity of donors large and small, and being in the right place at the right time and knowing the right people. Lee Roper connected Tina and Rosie with Joan Drury, who committed $400,000 at eight percent interest, with only Tina's and Rosie's houses for collateral. "What impressed me most was their chutzpah," Joan said of Tina and Rosie. "That they believed so strongly in their vision and in their ability to make it happen that they would come to a total stranger and ask for a ridiculous amount of money as if it were a perfectly normal, ordinary request."[18]

Tina recalled, "Rosie and I were just dancing out of there," but Susan Sands reminded them they still had to find the money to pay Joan back. Many people helped—Dale Lewis, a banker at Park State Bank, Ruth and Harold Frederick, and Jan Davis, "who stood up at the first fundraiser waving her check for $2,000, challenging the rest in the room to open their wallets and 'give until it feels good.'" A chance encounter garnered the support of Mort Phillips, whom Rosie described as "a staunch supporter" who contributed both financially and with regular moral support. They received anonymous gifts of $25,000 to $50,000. "In those first weeks of fundraising, it seemed we were going to steam along, raise the money and keep construction on schedule," said Rosie. "Of course we would soon learn that all was not going to go quite so smoothly."[19]

Construction began at a time when violent attacks on abortion clinics were increasing nationally, with incidents occurring almost weekly. "Then the unthinkable happened," said Tina. "One of our colleagues got murdered. It was a chilling effect throughout the whole country." Dr. David Gunn, whom Tina characterized as a gentle family man, was murdered by an anti-abortion protester in Pensacola, Florida, in 1993. Tina went to Florida to attend the funeral, and when she walked into the hotel, she saw Paul Hill, "the best-known anti-abortionist intimidator," Tina explained. "He believed that it was justified to kill . . . anyone who worked with abortion." When she saw him, Tina kept going and walked right back outside; she didn't return until her colleagues arrived. For their protection, their entire floor at the hotel was blocked off and filled with security guards. Tina recalled that in the middle of the night, the security personnel had alerted all those attending the funeral that a truck with bombs had been found and that protesters were planning to blow up the clinic where Dr. Gunn had worked. The next morning the women walked through a police gauntlet to get to the bus to the funeral, with police officers three to six deep surrounding the bus. At the funeral, police snipers were all over the buildings on the lookout for potentially violent anti-abortion activists. "They believed they were going to kill all of the abortion providers that were there." Tina reflected, "That's the first time I realized that they absolutely did not have a bottom line. They truly believed that murdering any abortion provider would be forgiven by their God and that they had every right to do it."[20]

The situation became increasingly dire back at the clinic. The Feminist Majority Foundation and the Department of Justice both sent security consultants to work with WHC on insuring safety for the clinic and its staff, especially since one of the doctors was on the national hit list. Tina and the physicians had to wear bulletproof vests. Rosie recalled a security consultant telling her, "Your license plate has been blocked. You need to change your home phone number. You need to vary your route from home. And you really should consider wearing a bulletproof vest." Rosie was baffled that she needed the same level of security as Tina, but he told her, "I understand you are a key spokesman. I understand that you are one of the key fundraisers. They will shoot you." In retrospect, she reflected, "That's the moment I realized . . . how extreme it was."

Though the women had secured enough funding to begin construction, they needed considerably more money to complete it, and the new security measures required another $50,000. Grant proposals to major foundations—Bush, McKnight, Kellogg, Phillips, and Kresge—totaling $1 million were pending when everything fell apart. They had been going about their fundraising quietly, and "a little bit underground," said Karen, because if word got out before they had secured the grants, they might lose them due to pressure from anti-abortion forces. The local Catholic hospital, St. Mary's, had a far reach in the community, and the small pro-life movement in the area could also impede their efforts, so WHC held small invitation-only fundraisers in people's homes. When someone invited Janice Pilon—wife of Dan Pilon, the president of the local Catholic college, St. Scholastica, and sister of Roger Schwietz, the bishop of the Duluth Catholic diocese—their quiet efforts suddenly became quite public.

Bishop Schwietz "denounced them from [the] pulpit." The diocese distributed flyers to parishioners; ran ads in the newspaper listing names, addresses, and phone numbers of those working on the building; and contacted foundations, city offices, the general contractor, electricians, plumbers, and labor unions on a daily basis, all as part of a campaign to bring work on the project to a halt. It had been difficult enough to find an architect, contractors, and others willing to work on the building, and the threats only made it harder. "The Catholic diocese told Dan Holmes [the contractor] that they would never work with him in a Catholic facility again, period," said Tina. Both Rosie and Tina credited architect Noel Knutson for going above and beyond, making weekly, sometimes daily trips to city building inspectors as opponents were filing concerns about code violations, or complaining about construction blocking First Street, or anything else they thought would shut down construction. "Noel kept documenting that we were doing everything first rate and in full compliance with all codes," said Rosie. Protesters carrying signs with pictures of aborted fetuses and chanting "Stop abortion!" and "Future death camp!" showed up at the construction site. When protesters began entering the site, salaried and volunteer security guards were brought on-site around the clock. Some of the contractors wanted to wear WHC T-shirts in counter-protest. "All these guys would come to work with Women's Health Center T-shirts on, just to walk by them, because they got tired of being harassed," said Tina.[21]

Janice Pilon took her story to the *Duluth News-Tribune.* In a letter to the editor entitled "All Should Know Abortion Clinic Had Role in Building for Women," she recounted that when she attended an informational fundraiser for the Building for Women, seeking help in garnering support, "we were advised to do this quietly because grant requests pending with several foundations imply that there is broad community support for this effort." She urged readers to let the boards of the YWCA, PAVSA, and the United Way know of their objections to the building where abortions would be performed.[22]

Protesters showed up outside the YWCA. Because hundreds of children came to the Y daily, Karen asked the person in charge of the protest to carry signs with words only, not pictures of aborted fetuses, which disturbed the children. "The response I got was, 'Better to sacrifice one to save millions,'" she recalled. "I remember being so incredibly angry that there was no care for the life that they wanted to preserve." She continued: "The kids we served . . . were 98 percent low income, 50 percent kids of color, well over 50 percent from single-parent homes. These are exactly the sort of kids that need a stable afterschool environment, academic enrichment, positive adult role models, a nutritious snack, advocacy. It seemed so incredibly counter-intuitive to me that you would take it away from children who are at risk, that are actually born—that you would take it out on them because of your dogma. But they did."

The United Way was inundated with phone calls from donors objecting to its financial support of PAVSA's *Good Touch Bad Touch* program and the YWCA's after-school program. JoAnne Axtell, president of the United Way board, said, "They don't see our policy as being neutral anymore," even though the board included people on both sides of the abortion issue.[23]

Bishop Schwietz resigned from the United Way board in protest. He stated publicly, "I encourage all people who believe in the sacredness of life to write or call the board members of PAVSA and the YWCA to express their outrage. PAVSA and the YWCA have been willing accomplices with the Women's Health Center in attempting to create a respectable front for the perpetuation of abortion." The bishop's resignation set off a maelstrom in the community and the press for months. Letters to the editor appeared in the paper almost daily. A letter signed by a dozen Twin Ports ministers who supported the Building said: "We would like the community . . . to know that religious leaders are willing to speak out on the side of women who need all of the services that will be offered in the women's building, be it protection from abuse, education, reproductive health care, resource development, or an abortion." The WHC received private letters and donations from people objecting to the bishop's decision. One couple wrote: "We are a Catholic couple who believe in a woman's right to choose. We are disturbed at the recent controversy with the Duluth Bishop and the United Way, and we want to show our support for your organization with this donation." Rosie said they received "scores of small donations over the first weeks of the controversy, many with notes that expressed shock at how over the top they saw the opposition behaving." Allan Apter donated $1,000 in honor of the bishop's resignation. When the United Way instituted a donor-choice plan so donors could designate where their contributions should go, Bishop Schwietz restored his support.[24]

Due to pressure from the diocese and protesters, the Knight Foundation rejected the women's grant proposal, and grants requiring "community support," while not being denied, were stalled. (All the other foundations eventually funded the project, though some not until months or even years later.) Nevertheless, the women needed to pay the contractors and laborers. If they could not come up with $275,000 by the end of January, construction would stop.

Harold and Ruth Frederick and Allen Apter came up with the idea of selling "grant anticipation notes," to be paid back with interest when the women received their grants. Joan Drury, Park State Bank (what is now Wells Fargo Bank), and the Feminist Majority Foundation were among the first to buy these. All in all, they obtained $400,000 through grant anticipation notes, and the Fredericks offered to secure them. Tina was overwhelmed by the support. Others, like Betty Ramsland and Tiss Underdahl, well known in the community for their work with charitable and civic causes, also solicited support for the Building.

Construction continued, and the women did some of the work themselves. Lindy Askelin, the building manager during the first year of construction, was a carpenter and a willing teacher, as was Sue Lawson, who took over when Lindy had to quit for health reasons. "Both Lindy and Sue made it possible for all of us who would live in the building to 'build' some small aspect of our future offices and meeting spaces. They were 'can-do' women who made us all feel we 'can do,' too," remembered Rosie. With everyone's help, the top floor that was to house the clinic was ready by the end of December 1993.

In anticipation of protesters who were geared up to block the move, police closed the streets at about two o'clock in the morning. At 3:00 AM on that forty-below morning, nurses came with a U-Haul, and dozens of people—doctors and lawyers, teenagers to octogenarians—showed up to help. The clinic was completely moved in long before the picketers arrived at 7:00 AM.

Shortly after the clinic reopened, the clergy who had written in support of the Building placed a congratulatory ad in the *News-Tribune*: "The reality of the Building for Women is the result of a generation of dreams and hard work by many people in the community. It ensures a literal stake in the future and a foundation for real justice. We encourage all people who support the exciting possibilities in this endeavor to show their support in generous and tangible ways, through presence, prayer, and donations to the respective organizations." Three days later, a letter to the editor signed by ninety-four male clergy and deacons encouraged the community to be "pro-woman" and "join them in working to close the doors of the health center." That spring, several ads from "concerned individuals and organizations" appeared weekly, including one from Feminists for Life of Minnesota that featured a photo of an infant with the heading, "Why isn't she essential to feminism?" The ads ceased when the state attorney general's office found the supporting organization, Life Ad, to be in violation of the law for soliciting funds without registering with the state.[25]

Partner organizations continued to be targeted. "It took a great deal of courage for those boards to vote to go with us for the simple reason they did have threats of losing their funding," said Tina. In February 1994, Sister Kathleen Hofer, director of St. Mary's, withdrew the hospital's sponsorship of the YWCA Mother's Day walk/run for breast cancer research. "The day that Karen lost her funding from the hospital she called the newspaper," Tina recalled. "It was on the front page the next day." Organizations and private individuals rushed in to fill the funding gap. "Within three hours Karen had more money than the hospital had ever given them."[26]

Partners faced greater threats than the loss of funding, however, and from individuals and organizations far beyond Duluth. In her role as WHC director, Tina had dealt with personal threats to her home, life, and safety for years. Marge Whitney recalled, "the first time I hugged Tina and she had on a flak jacket, I burst into tears. . . . Why should she have to live this way?" Karen also "worried about all those women. . . . I saw Tina Welsh wearing a bullet-proof vest, being taught to check her car for bombs with a little mirror on the end of a stick." Now Rosie and Karen faced similar threats.[27]

Karen recalled, "We got hate mail at the Y. They would call and say nasty things on the phone." St. Mary Star of the Sea church printed the women's home phone numbers in its bulletin. Karen remembered coming home from work one day and her eleven-year-old daughter asking her, "What have you got yourself into now, Mother?!" Someone had called looking for Karen, and when her daughter asked to take a message, the caller said, "Do you know your mother's helping them kill babies?"

"I truly did not have a full depth of understanding of what we were signing onto," said Rosie. "The forces arrayed against that clinic were vicious, underhanded, and absolutely single-minded." For Rosie, the attacks by the diocese felt personal. A Catholic and a graduate of St. Scholastica, Rosie knew many of the priests and nuns who came to the construction site each month to pray. "None ever harassed me," she said, "but invitations to dinner with friends at the Priory disappeared. I had several conversations with one of the priests at the diocese about the level of threat that their actions were raising among fringe groups and more than a couple unbalanced individuals. He simply kept to the line, 'It was the price we had to pay.' . . . It felt like a personal abandonment as well as a public attack."

The intensity of the campaign waged by the diocese was unlike anything any of them had ever experienced. "I was used to a lot of hostility," said Tina, "but the level of anger directed at us in such a righteous way was . . . frightening." "Anybody who was involved in it, whether it was the small donor who could only afford five dollars or the women who didn't have money and gave time . . . was an advocate," said Karen. "It was a courageous thing because of the level of vitriol." Years later, Bishop Schwietz expressed regret, saying that were he to do it again, he would stress the dignity of every person, "whether the person is an abortion provider, a woman who has had an abortion, or a member of the pro-life movement," and he would make sure his stands were not taken as encouraging violence of any kind, including violent words.[28]

The women continued their fundraising undaunted. They found support from donors outside Duluth, including former governor Elmer Andersen. Gloria Steinem spoke on their behalf at a Twin Cities fundraiser: "The Building for Women is . . . the only one outside a major metropolitan area. They are also the only facility to house a clinic that provides abortion services. We believe that this project is a national model for securing reproductive rights." At a luncheon for Dr. Jane Hodgson at the Women's Club in Minneapolis, Jane said: "You always ask me what you could do for me. . . . I want your money. I want the building in Duluth. I want the Women's Health Center to be secure."[29]

Altogether, they managed to raise $3.5 million for the Building for Women. Throughout, they had the ongoing support of their sister organization, the Building for Women in St. Paul, and many individuals like Cathy Curley, who volunteered to do the bookkeeping. "We had some of the most hard-working, creative women in Duluth working on this issue," said Tina. Rosie noted, "There were so many who did little and big things that all added to the success of the Building for Women." Mostly they were buoyed by the support and dedication of the group of five women who "met every single week for five years."[30]

By January 15, 1994, the Women's Health Center was fully operational, and a dedication ceremony was held in October. The *Minnesota Women's Press* honored Tina, Rosemary, and Karen among the 1994 Newsmakers, saying: "The Building for Women surely is a miracle, having been built on lots of prayers and very little money. It provides more than a safe place for reproductive rights; it also provides peace of mind for a group of advocates who simply wanted to give women in need a place to go." In addition to the WHC, PAVSA, and the YWCA, the building has been home to the Northcountry Women's Coffeehouse, Aurora: A Northland Lesbian Center, the League of Women Voters, and others. Karen drives by the

Building every now and then, causing her to reflect, "I'm still just as proud of it now as I was then. . . . The stability is incredibly important."[31]

The Building secured its place in history as the third women's building in the country. Eleanor Smeal of the Feminist Majority Foundation sang its praises: "Duluth's Building for Women is an inspirational model, because it rallied the whole community to take responsibility." "It wasn't just about putting up a building," Karen reflected. "It was about creating that level of community support and participation, whether it is with your physical body, your willingness to get trained, your cash, and asking people to say, if you believe that this is something that's a woman's right, now is the time to step up."[32]

Not only was the Building created *by* the community, it was created *for* the community. "The name was chosen consciously as a play on words denoting both a physical building and a verb indicating the building of something, in this case, community. . . . It was always seen as a vehicle with which to cement community relations between all women in this region, but particularly between women's organizations that are run by women to serve women's needs, expanding women's choices and opportunities." "This community made sure, and a group of women made sure that this was going to happen," said Tina. The Building stands as a legacy to the courage, dedication, and solidarity of the community of women and men who, against all odds, persisted in their vision, and of those in the community who supported them.[33]

In the years that followed, violence against clinics continued. Close to home, a Planned Parenthood clinic in Brainerd, Minnesota, was destroyed by firebombs in 1994. Eight years later, after it had been rebuilt, somebody fired five bullets at the clinic. Three weeks after that, a clinic in Grand Rapids, Minnesota, was struck by seven bullets. In succeeding years, abortion opponents across the United States murdered three doctors, one escort, a security guard, and two clinic receptionists. In May 2009, Dr. George Tiller, a longtime friend of Tina's, was murdered while attending church. About that time, Tina wrote: "We were naïve to think that the opposition would not mobilize in the political arena and we could not comprehend that after finally gaining a freedom, the right to choice, we could lose it. We never imagined the extent of the violence. We never truly believed that we would be the victims of harassment, stalking, fire, bombing, or murder. Who would have thought that our doctors would be wearing bullet proof vests, carrying cellular phones for safety, cameras and tape recorders to document the harassment, traveling and checking into hotels using assumed names."[34]

The dedication of the clinic staff was phenomenal. "During all this time, I never had a staff quit," said Tina. "I never had a physician that left. I have been very fortunate through all these years that I worked with some of the most courageous and dedicated women and men."

After President Bill Clinton assumed office in 1993, new laws were enacted to protect clinics and patients from harassment. The Freedom of Access to Clinic Entrances Act (FACE) was passed in 1994, establishing federal civil and criminal penalties for anyone who uses force or threat of force to injure, intimidate, or interfere with access to reproductive health services. In Minnesota, a state statute protecting access to medical facilities providing abortion was enacted in 1993. The Minnesota attorney general's office and the City of Duluth Police Department were also supportive. Protests have lessened in their virulence since the Building for Women opened, but picketing outside continues. Protesters have a regular presence on days the clinic provides abortions.[35]

In 2012, the Women's Care Center opened kitty-corner to the WHC. According to its director, Angie Wambach, the aim of the Women's Care Center—which offers pregnancy testing, counseling, and services for new parents and women facing unplanned pregnancies—was to help young mothers make the best decisions for themselves, not to change anyone's mind. However, a fundraising letter referenced helping "abortion-minded" women keep their babies. According to the National Abortion Rights Action League (NARAL), placing anti-abortion clinics next to or near abortion clinics has become a new tactic of anti-abortion organizers. Current WHC director Laurie Casey said, "When clinics have similar names, there are problems. . . . Crisis pregnancy centers like to be near abortion clinics and try to confuse women. They try to get them to come to their place by mistake. Usually, they give inaccurate medical information and try to change a woman's mind." The Care Center director said the location was chosen because that's where the greatest need was. However, another pregnancy crisis center, offering similar services, is just three blocks away. Laurie feared that the Care Center's presence would only add to the harassment against the WHC.[36]

Since the Women's Care Center opened there has been no "outward" harassment of clinic clients on the street, but sometimes the harassment is more subtle. Sometimes WHC clients go to the Women's Care Center by mistake and are not told at first that they are at the wrong building. The women may divulge personal information to the Care Center staff before they realize they are in the wrong place, and sometimes the Care Center staff will contact them later.[37]

Political, Legal, and Financial Challenges

The Women's Health Center has been on the front lines of several legal and political battles, and a significant part of its work has been to maintain legal access to abortion in Minnesota. Ever since *Roe v. Wade*, abortion opponents have been trying to find ways to deny access to abortion through restrictive state laws. Though the Supreme Court has struck down many of these, four significant rulings opened the floodgates for such laws. In addition, several bills restricting access to abortion have been introduced into the Minnesota legislature, and some became law. In 1981, the state legislature passed a parental notification law requiring that before an abortion provider can perform an abortion on an unemancipated minor, both parents must be notified. As director of Midwest Health Center for Women and WHC, Dr. Jane Hodgson challenged the constitutionality of the law and sued the State of Minnesota, arguing that the parental notification law violated a woman's constitutional right to access abortion. In 1989, *Hodgson v. Minnesota* was heard by the U.S. Supreme Court, with WHC as lead plaintiff. Although the court upheld the constitutionality of the statute, it held that without the option of a judicial bypass, requiring parental notification would violate constitutionally guaranteed rights. The law was amended to include a judicial bypass in cases of sexual or physical abuse, or neglect, or if a court determines that the minor is mature and capable of giving informed consent. "We lost [the case]," said Tina, "but we got the court bypass."[38]

A few years later, the legislature passed a statute prohibiting the use of Medical Assistance funds for abortion. Once again, the WHC sued the State of Minnesota, and this time WHC won. The Minnesota Supreme Court ruled in 1995's *Jane Doe v. Gomez* that Medical Assistance statutes that permitted the use of public funds for childbirth-related services but withheld them for services related to therapeutic abortion violated a woman's right of privacy under the Minnesota Constitution.[39]

The Minnesota Woman's Right to Know Act, passed in 2003, requires physicians to inform women of the medical risks associated with the abortion procedure, including, "when medically accurate, the risks of infection, hemorrhage, breast cancer, danger to subsequent pregnancies, and infertility," as well as the medical risks associated with pregnancy and childbirth, and the probable gestational age of the fetus, at least twenty-four hours prior to an abortion. "That's another barrier just to have women jump through hoops," said Laurie.[40]

Opponents of abortion persist in their political efforts to restrict access to abortion, so WHC continues to spend resources on being a political watchdog for reproductive rights. It helps fund a NARAL staff person to lobby on abortion issues. WHC also belongs to the Reproductive Health Alliance (RHA), an association of family planning clinics throughout the state, whose paid lobbyist works on behalf of family planning issues, but not abortion issues. "We have found that some legislators are friendly towards family planning, but they don't have those same feelings for abortion," said Laurie. Legislation severely restricting access to abortion began sweeping the country in the 2010s, and Laurie has felt fortunate to have the support of the Minnesota legislature and the governor. She has, however, been disheartened by the political apathy of the clinic's clients. "They take this service for granted. They don't think it's ever going to go away." Those who grew up before *Roe* remember what it was like before access to safe and legal abortion, "but the younger generation doesn't remember. . . . That's what's hard to pass along," Laurie says. "People don't get out and vote, and they don't take an active [interest] in women's reproductive health in general."[41]

The cost of abortions also has always been a difficult issue. "Money is a real issue for some of these women," said Tina. "Some of our clients don't even have phones. Some of them don't have running water." In 2002, a group of women formed the HOTDISH (Hand Over the Decision It Should Be Hers) Militia, a local grassroots organization dedicated to ensuring reproductive justice for all. Over the years, it has held hot dish bake-offs to raise money to fund abortions for women who lack the resources to pay for them; in 2014 it received $5,000 in disbursements from the sale of the Midwest Health Center for Women.[42]

Every January, when protests increase around the anniversary of *Roe*, the WHC does a "sponsor-a-protester" fundraiser, in which donors pledge money for every protester in front of the clinic. The event was begun after Joan Drury, whose Spinsters Ink was located in the Building for Women, said she would pay $100 for every protester. The fundraiser is intended more to deter protesters than to raise money, but it has also served to bring funding to the clinic.

Legislative changes have increased access to abortion for women on Medical Assistance, which in Minnesota will pay for an abortion for health reasons—mental, emotional, or physical—so most of the women who come to the clinic are eligible. With the Affordable Care Act, more women qualify for Medical Assistance. Although this is a good thing for aiding women's access to abortion services, it has brought new financial strain to WHC, because the Minnesota Medical Assistance reimbursement rate is only half of the actual cost of the service. "We lose money on every procedure and this affects our cash flow," said Laurie. While funders are willing to pay for medical equipment, trainings, and public policy, few will fund abortion services, so the clinic relies on patients to finance abortion services. One of the biggest challenges is just keeping the doors open. "Each year it gets tougher to stay open," said Laurie, tearing up.[43]

Though WHC was solely an abortion clinic when it began, abortion services now comprise only a small part of the many medical and social services the WHC provides. "People still have a perception that we're just the abortion clinic," said Laurie. "They don't realize we do other things." The number of abortions performed at WHC has dropped drastically, from about 1,200 a year when they opened in 1981 to about 430 in 2014. "Hopefully it's because there are better methods of birth control," said Laurie. "Some of the barriers have been reduced for women accessing [contraception]. The Affordable Care Act has helped other women get birth control. . . . We also are getting better sex education in the schools. . . . All over the United States the abortion rates have dropped, which is a good thing."

The bulk of WHC's work is providing comprehensive services for women's reproductive health, as well as contraceptive and family planning services. WHC provides prescriptions for contraception and, thanks to a grant from the Healthier Minnesota Community Clinic Foundation, is able to provide IUDs at no cost. The clinic also provides free emergency contraception, screenings for breast and cervical cancer, and HIV testing, screening, and counseling. WHC offers a full-cycle health care program for women and girls, ranging from educational programs for preteens and their moms to estrogen replacement therapies and support groups for menopausal women.[44]

A Family Planning Grant from the State of Minnesota enabled WHC to extend its family planning services to five counties in northeastern Minnesota that otherwise would have been without those services. "Family planning services were . . . the most important services that we did," said Tina. "In small communities it was very difficult." According to Tina, the one pharmacist in Cook County refused to give birth control to women he thought were too young. Tina said it was "quite a coup" when WHC received unanimous support from the Koochiching County Board of Commissioners to open a family planning clinic there. They also opened a clinic in Carlton County, historically a difficult county in which to retain family planning services. With just a few administrators, two lab techs, two nurses, two doctors, and three patient educators, WHC provides family planning services to an area covering more than 10,000 square miles.

For a few years, WHC offered a successful program for young fathers, Boyz II Dads, later called Fathers and Children Together. It also works with the Lutheran Social Services Teen Clinic to provide pregnancy and STD testing as well as education, and it provides services to women at Safe Haven's Resource Center as needed. All these services together have enabled them to serve tens of thousands of women over the years.

Conclusion

One of the first clinics in Minnesota to provide abortion services, the Women's Health Center has protected the rights, health, and well-being of thousands of women. Its staff has provided training in medical abortion, assured access to contraceptive and family planning services throughout the region, and been at the forefront of reproductive justice battles in the courts. "The Women's Health Center has many things to be proud of," said Tina. "We have been leaders." And despite repeated threats to their lives and safety, attacks on their persons and their profession, persistent pro-tests and harassment of themselves and the women they serve, the center and its staff have endured. Laurie praised the staff's dedication. "Most of them are part-time, so they could do something else, make more money," she said, "but they believe in what they do. They're very kind and compas-sionate to the patients. . . . The clients that we see . . . are very appreciative that we're here. We know that we make an impact."

The WHC is one of only about a dozen independent nonprofit clinics remaining in the country. Every two or three years, another one closes. Laurie regards their staying open in such a hostile environment, and with little support from the local medical community, to be the clinic's greatest achievement. Tina believes that the reason the Women's Health Center has endured is "the community felt it was important that we were here. They have absolutely stood behind us." The Women's Health Center stands as a legacy of that commitment. It is a testament to the courage of those who, at great personal risk, have dedicated their lives to ensuring access to a woman's legal right to abortion and to safeguarding women's health, well-being, and lives.

{ 7 }

Northcountry Women's Coffeehouse

The 1970s and '80s were a very different time from today for lesbians living in Duluth. As was the case nearly everywhere in the country, lesbians were for the most part closeted and found it difficult to meet and socialize together publicly. "There was a small pocket of folks that knew each other and made community for one another," recalled Kathy Heltzer, "but . . . it was very difficult to find other gay and lesbian people."[1]

For over twenty-five years, the Northcountry Women's Coffeehouse made it easier for people to find each other. One of the main purposes of the Coffeehouse, as stated in its mission, was to "provide a meeting place for women." The initial vision was to offer a safe place where women, primarily lesbians, could meet, listen to music by women, and exchange ideas. Once a month, the Coffeehouse created a space that brought women together, built lesbian and feminist community, and sustained them for the journey.

Origin Story

In the 1970s, bars were one of the few places lesbians went to socialize, hear music, and dance, but the bar scene wasn't very conducive to lesbians getting together. Longtime Coffeehouse member Shirley Duke said of that time, "There were no women's bars. In fact, there wasn't even a gay bar." She remembered when she and her friends got up to dance at a local bar, a woman told them women couldn't dance together. They danced anyway, but as Shirley said, "That was the best it got. You didn't have a place to go in those days."

It was a little better for women living in the country outside of Duluth who had formed a sort of community of their own. "We just identified each other," Linda Estel remarked. The "country women," as she called them, had been part of the back-to-the-land movement of the 1970s. "There were a bunch of us out here deciding we were going to live in the woods."

Mostly, lesbians got together privately. Jody Anderson remembered a "loose-knit group," which Shirley remembered being called "Superior Women," that got together for coffee or a hike, bike riding, picnics, and so on. One of the women in that group, Rosemary Frye, who had been a part of the Northcountry Women's Center at UMD, wanted the group to be more established and visible. Throughout the country in the mid-1970s, women-identified women were forming coffeehouses for the purpose of meeting, listening to music, dancing, and socializing. A Woman's Coffee House had opened in Minneapolis in 1975, and it drew women and lesbians from all over the Midwest, including Duluth, to its weekend events.[2]

Rosemary, eager to create a lesbian/women's coffeehouse in Duluth, called together a group of people she thought would be interested in the idea. A handful of women, including Rosemary, Joan Tousignant, Dorothy Rapple, Jody Anderson, and Fran Kaliher, attended the first organizing meeting in January 1981 at Rosemary's house. The group posted flyers saying: "An organizational meeting for the development of a Women's Coffeehouse will be held: Wed. Mar. 18th, 6:30, 1113 East Fourth Street. All interested ♀ are invited to attend." The group quickly grew. "That critical moment had come where people wanted a place to meet and gather," remembered Jody. Over the next few months, the group met often to work through philosophical and logistical issues.[3]

The philosophical issues focused around identity and inclusion: Was this to be a women-only space, or would men be welcome? Would all women be welcome, or only lesbians? Would the Coffeehouse have a feminist agenda, or would it welcome all political and ideological views? The biggest discussion was whether or not to allow men. "A number of women had been in abusive relationships," Jody explained, "and they were at the point where they couldn't be around men. . . . They needed a safe place. There was conflict from the get-go [between] people who hadn't experienced that and didn't want to be exclusive and people who had and needed it to be." Fran remembered, "We were into boundaries. We did at first try to say that there would be no men," but then they needed to decide at what age boys would be excluded. Jody remembered making those distinctions of who was "acceptable" and who was not "terrible." "They were big issues back then," Jody added. Ultimately, the group agreed that the Coffeehouse would not be advertised as open to men, but if men showed up they would be "tolerated." In any event, being a public place, legally they could not exclude men. They did decide that the dancing after Coffeehouse events would be women-only. As indicated by flyers for the first Coffeehouse event and by Coffeehouse spokeswoman Lana Gunsell, men would be "welcome" at the performances upstairs, but "the coffeehouse downstairs will remain 'strictly women's space.'"[4]

The Coffeehouse also drew a line at only women "running the show." The Coffeehouse arose in a time when nationally the women's music scene burst forth as an alternative to the male-controlled music industry that monopolized every aspect of the music scene—from performers to sound technicians to recording companies. Women began forming their own record companies, such as Olivia, Pleiades, and Redwood Records. They started holding women-only music festivals—the most famous being the Michigan Womyn's Music Festival, first held in 1976—as places where women could make and enjoy music without the dominating interference of men. For these same reasons, "it was very important for [the Coffeehouse] to be all women in terms of women performers, women sound technicians, women doing the lights, women doing the publicity, women doing the emceeing, women, of course, making the coffee," said Kathy Heltzer. The Coffeehouse said even men who accompanied women couldn't play at the Coffeehouse, primarily because "they could play anywhere." The bottom line was that the women of the Coffeehouse wanted to offer a venue for performers and for women to get together in a women-only space. Adding men into the mix would change the entire dynamic.[5]

Discussions of whether the Coffeehouse would be welcoming of all women or lesbians only revolved around issues of sexuality and homophobia. The Coffeehouse was established primarily by and for lesbian women. While the Coffeehouse sought "to facilitate a sense of lesbian identity and power," they also sought to foster acceptance of all types of sexualities, whether lesbian, straight, bi, or asexual. Struggling to find a name for the Coffeehouse brought the issue to the surface. "Some people wanted it to be 'lesbian,'" remembered Shirley, "but it was decided to call it 'women's' coffeehouse in order to be more inclusive of the whole women's community, especially to allow a safe place for people who were questioning their sexual orientation but weren't ready to publicly declare it." Linda Estel added, "a lot of straight women come when they're straight and then it turns out they're actually bi. Then it turns out that they're not wanting to behave as a bi anymore; they'd rather behave as a lesbian. We wouldn't want to stop that from happening."[6]

Deeper considerations factored into the decision to name the Coffeehouse "women's" rather than "lesbian." According to Kathy, "women" was in fact "code for an organization that was in support of lesbians." "No matter what we called it, it was still what it was," agreed Linda. "It has always been a lesbian organization, but [has] never been identified as a lesbian organization." She felt that internal homophobia was at play in an "unwillingness to be comfortable . . . saying who we were," and that played out in "denial that it was a lesbian organization." Also, "we didn't want to exclude people by identifying it as lesbian because women who weren't lesbian wouldn't feel comfortable," she said. Others remembered the Coffeehouse as always intended for all women, recognizing that women "who weren't connected up to their community felt pretty isolated and not very empowered in this part of the world." As Dianna Hunter, who came later to the Coffeehouse, saw it, "the Coffeehouse was for women-identified women, whatever we saw ourselves as at that time, not just for lesbians, though it was predominantly lesbians who came and enjoyed the Coffeehouse."[7]

Whether the Coffeehouse intended to be feminist was debated then and now. Some thought that creating a feminist space had never been part of the Coffeehouse mission or programming. "It was lesbian and that was the point," said Linda. "Some of the women who were involved early on were feminist, but most that came probably weren't." Shirley saw it the other way around: "It happened to be that most of the feminists who got involved were lesbian, but not all of them." She argued that the Coffeehouse was part of a continuum of feminist thought and action. She pointed to lesbian separatism and said, "Without feminism, how would that have ever happened?" The flyer advertising the first membership meeting stated, "This is a feminist oriented Coffeehouse, [but] no specific political stance is held by collective members as a group." The Coffeehouse was feminist to the extent that it aimed "to support women's responsibility to each other" and "women's empowerment."[8]

However, its stated mission was also to provide a forum for discussion not only of feminist but also of "alternative" ideologies, which at that time was usually code for "lesbian." The feminist bent of the Coffeehouse was evident in early presentations on topics such as feminist therapy, feminist spirituality, lectures by feminist professors, as well as what was advertised as "the first feminist square dance." However, organizers who were trying to draw a larger audience seemed to back away from the term. As spokeswoman Lana Gunsell stated, "We want to stress that the place isn't specifically feminist based, or any other kind of base." In later years, as the Coffeehouse became geared more toward providing entertainment and less toward informational programming, it seemed to lose any specifically feminist focus.

Other issues were logistical and pragmatic. Finding a space for the Coffeehouse was difficult. Many places refused them. "Even though it was the top-secret underground lesbian organization, people figured out that that's what it was," said Kathy. The Unitarian church, on the other hand, was open to gays and lesbians, and welcomed the Coffeehouse being held in their building. Many lesbian/women's coffeehouses, including A Woman's Coffee House in the Twin Cities, ended up in churches because they were the only places that would take them. Opening their doors to diverse groups and women's coffeehouses was often a part of their social justice mission.[9]

Organizers decided to begin with two events a month, one educational and one entertainment, on first and third Friday evenings. Also, like many others, Duluth's coffeehouse would be alcohol-free. While not, as some thought, formed specifically for people in recovery, organizers were sensitive to the issue. "For many gay and lesbian people, bars were historically places that they would get together, and if somebody was struggling with an issue of addiction, that wasn't the best place for them to try to work on their recovery. . . . The Coffeehouse was offering an alternative to that." They provided refreshments, however, and coffee.[10]

Within a few months the Coffeehouse was ready to open. Women who had connections with the League of Women Voters and the YWCA used their mailing lists to send flyers announcing the opening to hundreds of women. On the first Friday in May 1981, the Coffeehouse opened its doors for the first time. Twin Cities–based singer-songwriter Ann Reed played a concert to a reportedly "standing-room only crowd."[11]

Early Years

In those early years, the Coffeehouse was the popular place to be. Events were held in the sanctuary, and afterward, as Kathy recalled, they went "down a very narrow, winding, completely non-handicapped-accessible stairway . . . into the basement, where there was a kitchen and a very small social hall," with space for dancing. The energy was "so high," recalled Fran. Jody agreed, "It was exciting. . . . The church was full because people really wanted to be there." The women were excited to be meeting new people and developing new connections, and they always provided a greeter to welcome new people. They felt they were a part of something important.

The Coffeehouse was run as an all-volunteer organization, and many people helped make it happen. A central committee—which initially included Rosemary Frye, Joan Tousignant, Dale L., Donna J., Linda Estel, and Fran Kaliher—made the major decisions about the running of the Coffeehouse. The Coffeehouse had committees for refreshments, arrangements, programs, publicity, fundraising, and nominations, with one or two people in charge of each. Jody and Fran provided refreshments for many years. Jody especially enjoyed being able to talk with people as they came in and making them feel welcome. For many years, Anne Tellett did the publicity, which was pretty low-tech—cut-and-paste stencils and taped-on photographs.

While the audience was experiencing the fun and excitement of those early years, those involved in running the Coffeehouse had their struggles. Making decisions using consensus was challenging. Linda reflected, "They just liked the sound of it. 'Let's do it by consensus' sounds so welcoming and warm and womanly, but we never knew what we were talking about." Meetings would often drag on late into the night, with attendees hashing out issues until everybody was in agreement. In retrospect, Fran thought consensus decision-making had been worthwhile, and Jody agreed, even though at the time, "you wish[ed] it could be the majority rules, because you just want[ed] to go home." "And go to bed," added Fran.

Early meetings were spent hammering out the process of registering as a 501(c)(3) nonprofit, without any prior knowledge of how to do this. Linda gave credit to Donna Jallonen (whom she called their "token straight woman") for the work she put into this. Sarah Phoenix, chair of the Community Development Coalition, held a training session on how to form a nonprofit. The lore is that they used the Articles of Incorporation of the Northcountry Women's Center as their template (and perhaps this is also the source of their name). Being a nonprofit required that the Coffeehouse have at least two officers. "Nobody wanted to be the person to put their name out there," recalled Deb Anderson, "but Rose Frye was the one who had, I don't know if it was the guts or the naiveté to be willing." At the time, a person could lose her job for being lesbian, and Rose was out to her boss and her job was secure. Despite its official status, the actual organization of the Coffeehouse was quite loose. No one had any desire to head the organization. They were simply a group of volunteers who managed among themselves to make the organization thrive.

The Coffeehouse provided a much-needed venue for local women musicians. Early performances included many "girls with guitars," such as Deb Anderson, Barb Hall, Kathy Heltzer, and Lynn Skelly. A favorite was Bloodroot with Mary Tennis, Jody Anderson, Rosie Rocco, and Kelly Ravenfeather. In those early years, performers played to packed houses of enthusiastic women, and new members were always joining. The organizers were concerned with making the Coffeehouse accessible to all, and so membership was $10 a year, with admission to events $2 for members and $3 for non-members. These were also suggested donations, so people who couldn't afford to pay could still attend. Women often traveled long distances to come to Coffeehouse events. Many came from the Iron Range, sixty miles to the north, where feminist activism was mushrooming with the creation of a battered women's shelter, Range Women's Advocates, and growing awareness of the struggles of women like Lois Jensen facing sexual harassment in the mining industry.[12]

Every other Friday the Coffeehouse held educational events. New feminist organizations were forming around Duluth, and the Coffeehouse served as a vital connecting point, informing people about issues and new organizations in the community. Rosie Rocco talked about the Program to Aid Victims of Sexual Assault (PAVSA). Others gave a presentation about the battered women's shelter. Donetta Wickstrom spoke about being a female police officer in a predominantly male police force. With such topics as the history of women's music, women and pornography, feminist therapy, Frida Kahlo, goddesses, and Woodswomen's Judith Niemi's Hudson Bay canoe adventure, the educational programs reflected the growing interest in women's history and culture. The Coffeehouse also showed films, such as *Amelia Earhart* and *Adam's Rib*.

The Coffeehouse nurtured local women's music and culture. Jody, who often performed at the Coffeehouse, said she had always thought about playing music, "but never thought that there would be a place to do that." Local favorites Kim Curtis-Monson, Karen Bauman, Barb and Sherry, Terrol and Jane, and Mary, Beth and Jody—later incarnated as Wild by Nature—performed regularly. The local women's cultural scene also included writers and poets—Sheila Packa, Ellie Schoenfeld, Greta Gaard, Dianna Hunter, Kate Basham, and Sadie Green, to name a few— as well as artists, such as Patricia Canelake and Linda Hallender. "That's what it was all about," noted Dianna, "giving an outlet for this community to be who we were and express ourselves." Jody said the Coffeehouse "provided a place for a budding musician or poet." Sara Thomsen and Rachel Kilgour, both now standard names in the local music scene and well known nationally, got their starts at the Coffeehouse. The Coffeehouse provided opportunities for many local musicians and other artists to perform, "even if you're not budding," joked Fran Kaliher.

Performers remembered Coffeehouse audiences as being the best—
enthusiastic, responsive, forgiving, and completely supportive. "No matter what you do, they're really happy," said Kathy. "I've heard [artists] that
perform in different spaces in Duluth or even around the country say
time and again how much they enjoy being there. You couldn't ask for a
better audience." Twin Cities–based storyteller Susan Delattre found this
to be typical of women's coffeehouses: "My experience in performing at
women's coffeehouses is that what you find is an incredibly supportive
audience. They're behind you 150 percent."[13]

The Coffeehouse played a significant role as a place of cultural connection, especially for those living isolated lives in the rural areas surrounding Duluth. Dianna Hunter, who was farming about forty miles
outside Duluth, appreciated that connection:

> It was an important political, social, and cultural link for me.
> I was starved . . . for those kinds of cultural, political, social
> links that you can only get by a gathering of a large number
> of people. . . . Little bits of acknowledgment of your cultural
> identity mattered at that time. The Coffeehouse was that kind
> of place, not just because of the lesbians, but because it had a
> feminist identity. . . . The dancing afterwards was important,
> too. You just couldn't get it anywhere else. . . . It was such a
> sweetness, the kind of connections that were forged there.

Before the Internet, e-mail, Facebook, and LinkedIn, the Coffeehouse
also served as the social medium for the local feminist community. "So
many of us so looked forward to those gatherings because you could connect with people. If you didn't know somebody's phone number or last
name, you could either find them at the Coffeehouse or you would find
somebody who knew them and could connect you," remembered Deb.
Before every Coffeehouse performance was a time for announcements
of "all the things that were going on in the community or even sometimes
places to rent or things for sale. . . . All sorts of needs got met thanks to
the announcements."[14]

However, the Coffeehouse functioned more effectively than social
media in connecting people because it was face-to-face. People met and
had genuine conversations, with all the nuances of tone and body language
that face-to-face conversation brings. They shared fun and food and laughter and tears, and developed real relationships. They organized and
strengthened each other in the political and social struggles they faced.

A particularly memorable example of this came during a time when the Duluth City Council was once again considering passage of a Human Rights ordinance, and many in the lesbian community were receiving death threats. Rosie Rocco got up and talked about this one night at the Coffeehouse and then began to sing Holly Near's "Singing for Our Lives." In a moment of solidarity, everyone started singing together. The power of music shared in that place and time to create political change was profound.

During the holiday season, the Coffeehouse held an annual talent show and, in later years, a potluck, at which many Coffeehouse favorites performed. Kathy Heltzer in her tux and red bow tie and cummerbund emceed with her inimitable humor and oft-requested rendition of "I Like It in Duluth." Between acts, women did mock public service announcements and commercials. Many fondly recalled the annual parody of the Popeil Pocket Fisherman commercials—"Popeil's Pocket Penis Pincher"—that always brought down the house with laughter. The holiday talent shows were everyone's favorite Coffeehouse event. "The talent shows were a scream," remembered Jody Anderson. Kathy called it "a time to see old friends." Caroline Pelzel concurred: "I loved the talent show . . . [and] enjoyed that part of what the Coffeehouse represents: women sharing their own talents with each other in whatever way, shape, or form." The Coffeehouse also held an anniversary celebration every year, on the first Friday in May. For many years, Ann Reed returned to celebrate the anniversary. Those celebrations were always special nights and drew large crowds of Coffeehouse supporters.[15]

After several fun and successful years, the excitement began to wane. Not enough people were coming and not enough were volunteering to sustain the Coffeehouse. For years, the same people had been doing most of the work. They began to tire of long meetings, and personality conflicts arose. Linda thought power struggles and "ego issues" were the cause of much of the conflict. "It's a common thing with feminist organizations to have power struggles," she said. "We're not all that good at using our power, at identifying it, and wisely using it." Some disagreed about the direction for the Coffeehouse. Whereas Linda wanted to bring in national names and have big concerts, others, she said, "seemed very satisfied that we get fifty people to come."

Though Jody remembered the meetings as "fun" and "pretty congenial," she also recalled that there were "personality conflicts" and one night in particular when there was "noticeable friction." Five years after the Coffeehouse began, the people who had been organizing it decided they couldn't do it anymore. "They called a big community meeting and said they were going to close the Coffeehouse," remembered Shirley Duke. "A few of us at that meeting said, 'No, we don't want to lose it. We'll take it over.'" A core group, including Shirley, Jody, Kayt Sunwood, Adrianna Soeters, and Bev Lorentzen, stepped forward. Shirley took on the programming and coordinated the productions. Kayt did publicity, Jody handled refreshments, and Bev served as treasurer. Jody credited Shirley with keeping the Coffeehouse going. "She just kept at it."

While recognizing that the Coffeehouse played an important role in offering local artists a venue, Shirley wanted the Coffeehouse to expand beyond the homegrown music scene. It was a time of a burgeoning women's culture, and Shirley wanted the Coffeehouse to give it maximum exposure. They showed films on Georgia O'Keefe, birthing alternatives, and feminist anime. They brought in women adventurers like Ann Bancroft, who led the first women's team to ski to the South Pole, and Ann Linnea, the first woman to kayak around Lake Superior. They expanded beyond the local music scene and regularly brought performers from "prestigious venues in the Twin Cities." Ann Reed, Ruth MacKenzie, the Wyrd Sisters, the Buffalo Gals, Zuni Mugozi, Deidre McCalla, and Ellis were just a few of the well-known performers hosted by the Coffeehouse. Concerned that most of the performers and speakers at the Coffeehouse were white, Shirley also brought in more culturally and racially diverse performers, as well as performers of different ages. "One of our presentations was this group of women in their seventies that did chorus girl dancing," she recalled. "That was a hoot! They were fabulous!" The Coffeehouse was also one of the first venues to offer interpretation for the hearing impaired.[16]

Eventually, the Coffeehouse picked up Linda Estel's vision of bringing nationally recognized performers to Duluth, and at least once a year they produced a major performance with a larger venue and audience. These included blues singer Heather Bishop, Casselberry-Dupree, June Millington, Sue Fink, Faith Nolan, and Teresa Trull, as well as big-name feminist comedians, such as Chris Cinque. It was a real treat for people involved with the Coffeehouse to interact with the performers. Others hosted the performers in their homes. Some became friends.

Turning Point: 1994 and Beyond

In 1994, the Building for Women opened in downtown Duluth. Built primarily to provide a permanent space for the Women's Health Center, the

Building was also home to other organizations that leased space. North-country Women's Coffeehouse was one of them. "We wanted to support the Building for Women and what it stood for and wanted to become one of the permanent tenants that could provide a little bit of income to that organization," recalled Kathy. She said changes at the Unitarian church also contributed to the decision to move. The church had put in new carpet, so people could no longer have coffee and refreshments upstairs, which "did cramp our style a little bit," she added. "We were a coffeehouse, and we wanted to have coffee."

The move was a major change for Coffeehouse audiences and per-formers. Even though the new place seated about the same number of people, it felt "smaller" and "limiting." Shirley said she second-guessed that decision several times. Politically, the move supported the Build-ing, "so from that perspective," she said, "it was a good decision. But on the other hand, the physical venue is not anywhere near as nice as the old Unitarian church. . . . It's so beautiful and the sound is so wonder-ful, whereas, at the Building for Women, you're in the basement. . . . It was a big change." The sanctuary of the church had the cozy feel of old dark wood and stained-glass windows, with a large elevated area for a stage and a rich-toned Baldwin grand piano. The new space in the Build-ing was stark by comparison and devoid of charm, as was the tinny-sounding spinet. Chairs needed to be set up and put away every time, requiring even more work on the part of volunteers. On the plus side, the kitchen was connected to the performance space and made for easier serving, and people were happy to be supporting the Building. In con-junction with the move, the Coffeehouse worked in cooperation with Aurora, a lesbian resource and support organization that was housed in the space next to the Coffeehouse and provided room for kids to play during performances.[17]

Leaving the church was a turning point. Audiences dwindled. De-creasing monetary resources and increasing costs were of growing con-cern. The Coffeehouse was losing money on every performance. The low admission price did not cover expenses, and the core committee had on-going discussions about raising it, which they eventually did. Funding relied primarily on Coffeehouse memberships and donations. "Had it not been for a generous donation the year before, we would not have been able to make our twenty-fifth year," said Caroline. The large mailing list was a major expense, and the question of whether to maintain it led to heated debates between those who found it impractical and those who saw advertising women's culture as part of their mission.

The dwindling audiences and declining interest in the Coffeehouse in general were of greatest concern. Dianna Hunter characterized it as "the 'taking it for granted' time of assuming it's always going to be a vibrant place and that it's there for you. We used to practically beg for people to help." Although the individuals changed over the years, generally only a handful of people kept the Coffeehouse going at any given time. Throughout the 1990s, Nettie Bothwell, Deb Anderson, and Trish O'Keefe set up, got the performers, and handled the sound system, Dianna Hunter designed and produced the flyers, and Sharon Schlarman took money at the door, set up contracts, made sure there were performers, and kept the Coffeehouse together.

By the 2000s, the Coffeehouse had become what Linda characterized as a "get-by" organization, doing the minimum needed to put on nine events a year. Lee Hemming, Paula Bergren, Lori Hutchins, Lorna Clark, and Caroline Pelzel kept the Coffeehouse going in the later years, but their dedicated efforts did not change the fact that fewer and fewer people were coming to the Coffeehouse. Those who did come were mostly the same people who had been coming for twenty years, and even many of the regulars rarely went anymore. The Coffeehouse was not attracting new audiences, and the audiences were aging. Younger people weren't as interested. "The frustration was that we didn't seem to mesh across the generations very well," said Dianna. The committee took initiatives to attract a younger crowd. They held a couple of inter-generational conversations to figure out how to bridge the generations. The conversations were followed on both occasions by a performance by Ellis (Delaney), who drew audiences from multiple age groups. Dianna recalled that "it was nice to hear voices of various generations." Through hosting these conversations, they discovered that the entire generation of "thirty-somethings" was missing. "They're all busy having babies," said Caroline, "and trying to keep their careers going." Though the Coffeehouse had toys and other things for kids in Aurora's office so moms could watch the performances while their kids played, the Coffeehouse did not provide daycare and had not even discussed it.

The Coffeehouse tried a variety of events and occasional changes in venue to raise interest. They brought Starhawk to the University of Wisconsin–Superior to speak in 2005 and moved the holiday potluck and talent show to a bigger and better space, but by its twenty-fifth year, Coffeehouse organizers were facing a major decision. Greater acceptance of the LGBTQ community in society at large and shifts in the feminist movement toward greater inclusivity had lessened the desire for lesbian separatism and the need for women-only spaces nationally and locally. "People don't want separateness [anymore]," reflected Deb. "They want integration." She noted that when it began, the Coffeehouse met a "fundamental need in women in the community to have a safe space to laugh and be who we were and love each other and share our lives and enjoyment of music," but the need for a separate safe space no longer existed. Lesbians now had many alternatives to the Coffeehouse. "Lesbians will go to any bar now," said Linda, "and there are lesbians performing in coffeehouses that are straight." Caroline commented that the local coffeehouse Amazing Grace "has a night that's open to a lot of queer kids who do their poetry and prose and perform. We have places in the community that bring in women performers, women lesbian performers, that are available to everyone in the community."

According to Caroline, the recurring questions for the Coffeehouse became, What is our function? Is the energy that we're putting into a women-only space still needed and wanted? How are we moving forward? Do we continue? Increasingly, it seemed the reasons the Coffeehouse originally came into being no longer existed, and some wondered if it was time to close the doors once and for all.

The Coffeehouse held a memorable twenty-fifth anniversary celebration at the original location in the Unitarian church in May 2006. Many of those who had performed over the years returned, the history was read, and hundreds of supporters filled the sanctuary. The evening ended with all the performers singing the Wailin' Jennys' "One Voice." "We made it through the twenty-fifth year," proclaimed Caroline triumphantly. "We got there, and we had one heck of a great performance." It was a particularly big deal, she added, because the women's coffeehouse in Chicago had its last performance in 2005, making the Northcountry Women's Coffeehouse the last women's coffeehouse remaining in the country. It continued a few more years, but in June 2009 the decision was made to close. They retained their nonprofit status, in case future generations wanted to reopen the Coffeehouse. The Coffeehouse would continue its annual holiday potluck and talent show, but the Coffeehouse ceased as a regular gathering place in 2009. That the Coffeehouse lasted as long as it did is truly inspiring. Only Chicago's Mountain Moving Coffeehouse for Womyn and Children, at thirty-one years (1974–2005), had a longer existence.[18]

On the first Friday of December 2014, the Northcountry Women's Coffeehouse came together once again for a holiday potluck and talent show. A few weeks before, Deb Anderson had said, "How many years of reinforcing friendships? Here we get to go this year to another holiday party under the guise of the Northcountry Women's Coffeehouse, and a lot of that energy will come back into whatever space we inhabit . . . and it will resonate again, and thirty years will evaporate, and we'll all be young again."

She was right. The years did indeed seem to melt away, and yet they also compounded in the deepening of those relationships in a way that happens over decades of shared memories, stories, and lives. All felt renewed by coming together. Some of the younger women expressed a wish that their generation had a similar way for them to continue to come together year after year, a place to develop those long-lived friendships. One, Rachel Kilgour, said that she was considering starting up something akin to the Coffeehouse. The Coffeehouse may yet find a new incarnation, inspired by the spirit of a new generation.

Conclusion

The Coffeehouse changed lives. For some it was the place where they were first able to come out to themselves and to others. For others it was a place to express their gifts and talents, even launch their careers. For others it was a place to develop lifelong friendships. Kathy Heltzer often wondered if she would have ever met the many friends she made through the Coffeehouse without it. "The Coffeehouse was such a catalyst for getting people together," she said.

The Coffeehouse played a key role in building and sustaining feminist community in Duluth. "The Coffeehouse provided such a wonderful focus for the women's community, the lesbian community," said Shirley. Fran expressed the sentiments of many: "It was the defining thing of the community at that time." It enabled people to meet, develop relationships, and enjoy each other outside their normal work lives. People networked informally there, shared news, strategized politically. As Deb Anderson said,

> It was another strong brick in a very well-orchestrated and
> built support system for women and families in this town
> that remains today. It's why things like the Duluth Model for
> domestic violence are out there, because there was a time
> when this incredible group of women with incredible energy
> for social change in this town looked at the role and the lot
> of women and said, 'Wait a minute,' and 'What can we do to

make this different?' . . . The Coffeehouse was a place those women came together to celebrate and to share and to have that lifeblood and have that support.

"Music was always a big piece of it," she continued. "So many of us found some sort of emotional strength or calming or energy in the music." Women's music inspired. To women who had grown up believing they were "the second sex," it offered the woman-affirming words of Alix Dobkin's "The Woman in Your Life" and Meg Christian's "Glad to Be a Woman." Chris Williamson's "Song of the Soul" had the power to lift spirits, and Margie Adam's "We Shall Go Forth" renewed solidarity and hope.

The Coffeehouse sustained people in those years of feminist formation in Duluth. In the exhausting days of the struggle to raise awareness and bring about actions and organizations to effect social change, it offered renewal and support. And it was fun. It provided the opportunity for humor and shared laughter that were such a necessary counterbalance to the serious issues of combating oppression and violence that filled our days. It offered a creative outlet for people to express their angst as well as their hopes and dreams, their love and longing—to express themselves in a world that did not always accept them. Once a month, on a Friday night, the friendships, connections, camaraderie, and music of the Coffeehouse brought inspiration and healing to war-weary souls and replenished spirits, enabling "us all to go on, and on, and on."[19]

{ 8 }

Center Against Sexual and
Domestic Abuse

"Why didn't she just leave?" "What was she doing out late at night by herself anyway?" These were the victim-blaming attitudes that early pioneers in the sexual assault and battered women's movements encountered when they first began to set up advocacy services and organizations. For more than twenty-five years, the Center Against Sexual and Domestic Abuse (CASDA) not only has provided victim advocacy, shelter, and programming, but has educated a community and changed perceptions in its ongoing work to end violence against women.

Origin Story

Begun in the office of the Human Resource Center (HRC) in Douglas County, Wisconsin, the organizations that formed CASDA grew from the vision of Rena Baumgardner, the director of HRC. In 1981, she formed the Human Resources Rape and Incest Victim Advocacy unit and hired Kim Storm and Katrina Tobey to be on-call advocates and co-coordinators. They provided and coordinated direct service advocacy, from crisis intervention to medical and legal advocacy and support services for victims of sexual assault, incest, and harassment. They carried beepers and responded to calls anywhere in the largely rural county. Calls came through the county office, but with no direct help line, the only way someone could activate advocacy services was to report the assault to the police or to the victim advocate in the district attorney's office. Even the hospital emergency room had to report to law enforcement. "That's a real problem under any circumstances," said Katrina, and it was complicated further by the fact that law enforcement lacked training in how to respond appropriately to victims of sexual assault. There-fore, one of the advocates' main tasks was to train law enforcement "that if someone did report, they got services right away, rather than trying to decide if services were needed." Kim and Katrina worked on developing relationships with physicians, the county attorney, and police, including Mary Potter and Herb Bergson in the Superior Police Department and Irene Greene, the first victim advocate in the county attorney's office. They also recruited, trained, and supervised individuals to be volunteer sexual assault advocates, and provided community education regarding sexual assault.[1]

After Katrina left HRC in 1983, Kim worked with Carol Stewart, who had been hired by HRC to be the domestic assault on-call advo-cate. Because Kim and Carol had a victim-centered, grassroots femi-nist approach to sexual assault and domestic violence advocacy, being housed in the mental health care program of HRC was not the best fit for them. Carol decided to break off from HRC, and she contacted a group of people to develop their own domestic violence advocacy program. Calling themselves the Coalition Against Domestic Violence (CADV), Carol, Fran Levings of the Superior branch of NOW, Bob Kinderman of Douglas County Human Services and the University of Wisconsin–Superior (UWS), Irene Greene, Sandy Fogo, and Jean Fisher formed a board and began developing the program. The Domestic Assault Task Force of Superior's NOW chapter—Fran, Jan Conley, Becky Kurtz, Mary Morgan, and Kathy Fogle—worked with CADV on raising public aware-ness of the need for a battered women's shelter in Superior.[2]

CADV was all-volunteer and operated without funds. A local land-lord donated a small office that housed the phone line. "All we had to pay for was the phone," remembered Bob, "and every board meeting, the board members would open up their wallets, look at the phone bill, and pay it." The volunteers offered consultation for people who called in as well as temporary shelter in "safe houses," which amounted to a room or a couch in houses all over town, mostly the homes of board members and friends. After about a year, using Concentrated Employment Program (CEP) funds, CADV was able to hire an office manager, who operated out of her home.

The group usually met and worked out of UWS's Women's Center, which Katrina had helped to start with Dr. Delores Harms a few years earlier. Brita Rekve, then a social work student at UWS, was interning for CADV on Bob Kinderman's recommendation. She recalled that the organization consisted mostly of a logo of a woman holding up the moon and "a cardboard box with some papers and a pager in it . . . and a collection of women who took turns dealing with the pager." Brita carried the pager and responded to calls for about six months. The experience lit a fire in her, and when she completed her internship, she stayed on as a volunteer.

The Human Resource Center continued to provide domestic assault advocacy, but the community was divided over having competing domestic assault programs. State representative Bob Jauch moderated a meeting between the two groups and invited the administrator of state funds for domestic violence programs in Wisconsin to work with them to come up with a solution. They decided that CADV would continue to operate autonomously, supported by state funds administered by the HRC, which also provided some general oversight. The HRC maintained its sexual assault program, now known as the Rape and Incest Victim Advocacy (RIVA) Program. Housed in Hawkes Hall, a dormitory at UWS, the program was run primarily by twenty-five volunteer advocates, with Kim Storm as the one full-time staff member. Kim recalled that she "maintained quite a distance" from HRC in order to have as much of a grassroots, victim-driven approach as possible within a social service bureaucracy. Because RIVA was housed separately, Kim was better able to stay close to those she served. She stayed on for a few more years, but eventually left to work for the Program to Aid Victims of Sexual Assault (PAVSA) in Duluth. Mimi Rappley was hired as the new sexual assault program coordinator.

Mimi at RIVA and Brita Rekve at CADV hit it off and began having conversations about bringing the two groups together. To do this, RIVA would need to split off from HRC. Bob Kinderman, who was then the director of HRC, recalled that, after discussions with the board, all agreed that it would be best for CADV and RIVA to work together, independently of HRC. Because domestic violence victims and sexual assault victims deal with similar issues and need similar services, the merger made sense. Brita remembered long discussions about what the organization would call itself, with the unspoken question of which was the greater priority—sexual assault or domestic violence—lingering in the air.

Reflecting on the highlights of those early years, Brita thought that their biggest success may have been "women learning how to work with each other and navigate through those choppy waters." Within that first year, the organization registered as a 501(c)(3) nonprofit and in February 1988, the Center Against Sexual and Domestic Abuse (CASDA) was launched.

Early Years

CASDA began with a staff of three: Brita Rekve, Jan Jenson, and Linda Kelly, who had been a volunteer advocate for RIVA. Grant funding required that they have a director, so Brita served in that position, but the three did their best to operate as a collective. The program operated as CADV had previously, with a few "safe houses" in the community, but eventually it had a suite of offices and shelter space in Hawkes Hall. After three years, CASDA brought on a fourth staff person, hiring Kelly Burger to provide case management and support services.

The early years were difficult for a number of reasons. For one, "we were up here on our own," said Brita. "We had no good example to draw from. We had these goddesses on a national level that we could aspire to, but there was nobody in our own backyard holding our hand saying, 'This is what you need to do.'" Unlike the organizations in Duluth, which had the models and support of organizations in the Twin Cities, Superior was a six-hour drive from Madison. Organizations in Duluth offered to help, but the state border was a tremendous obstacle. Brita recalled that the laws in Wisconsin regarding domestic abuse and sexual assault were "so far behind" those in Minnesota that when the Duluth organizations explained what they were doing, the women in Superior could only respond, "That won't work here." After Frank Boyle was elected to the state legislature, he worked with Brita to rectify this problem and helped craft mandatory arrest legislation in Wisconsin. Wisconsin Act 293, which among other things required arrest of perpetrators of domestic violence under certain circumstances, became effective in May 1990.

Another difficulty was lack of recognition and legitimacy in the community. CASDA struggled to be taken seriously. "The 'f' word [feminist] was a dirty word," said Brita. Linda Kelly remembered that domestic violence and sexual assault were things people didn't talk about, "so trying to educate folks and help them understand the importance of the service was huge." CASDA worked with law enforcement, the judicial system, and church and community groups and was often met with resistance and victim-blaming. Trainings with the Superior Police Department were difficult. With the exception of Mary Potter, who was very supportive of their efforts, the police officers stereotyped them as "women's libbers" who were trying to interfere in police matters. "They did not recognize what an ally we could be to them," said Kelly Burger. Advocates in Duluth had encountered the same attitudes a decade earlier, but by the late 1980s, "Duluth was eons ahead with regard to training law enforcement," said Brita. "We were just trying to get in the door."

As CASDA's efforts to educate the community gradually led to greater understanding of sexual assault and domestic violence, perceptions began to change, and advocates saw greater recognition of the need for their services and acceptance for the work they were doing. However, it would take them many years to be regarded as a reputable agency within the community. The highlight for Linda was the day the chief of police, the district attorney, the sheriff, and the head of the hospital waited for her to arrive before beginning a meeting because CASDA was an important part of the discussion. She reflected, "It was that day I went, 'We have arrived.'"

In the beginning, CASDA staff made decisions collectively, with everyone having input and an equal voice. The original staff was cross-trained and holistic in its ability to offer services. However, funders pressured CASDA to become more specialized and departmentalized in its work. Linda Kelly became the child abuse prevention coordinator in 1988. The high rates of abuse—verbal, physical, and sexual—that children were experiencing across all walks of life were just coming into the public eye, and CASDA's goal was to institute a community-wide child abuse prevention program. This eventually resulted in their use of the *Good Touch Bad Touch* program in the schools. School administrators were reluctant to allow CASDA to educate in the schools. The national *Good Touch Bad Touch* curriculum CASDA provided made parents, teachers, school counselors, and school administrators "very nervous [about] what we were going to be presenting to kids," remembered Kelly Burger. Linda also worked with local school districts and daycare centers to create awareness about child abuse, reporting requirements, services available in the area, and the need for prevention; to create partnerships with those agencies to provide training for teachers and staff to include child abuse prevention programming as part of their regular curriculum; and to develop a support and ongoing training network for staff that were providing this programming.[3]

Demands of funding agencies eventually forced CASDA to adopt a more hierarchical model, and Linda Kelly became the executive director in 1991. Securing funding, and the ways in which funding dictated programming, fostered other difficulties. "It felt like we were always scrambling to find money to support the program," remembered Linda. CASDA was able to pay only the bare minimum, which made it difficult to find and maintain staff. Time spent writing grants was time away from advocacy. The tendency of funders to link money to developing new programs around the latest hot topic, or what Kelly termed "the flavor of the year," also created instability and put CASDA in the position of spending time and energy creating new programs rather than maintaining existing ones.

In 1992, CASDA hired a staff attorney who provided legal representation for domestic violence issues, divorces, custody and child support, and child visitation disputes. The ability to obtain child support or income maintenance in the case of divorce helps women get back on their feet financially and enables them to move on with their lives. In 1993, CASDA added an outreach coordinator to extend services into neighboring Ashland, Bayfield, and Washburn Counties. The coordinator, who has a small office in Washburn, responds to crisis calls, offers peer one-on-one counseling, develops safety plans, helps women do the necessary paperwork to obtain restraining orders, and provides transportation to court or other victim-related services. She works with the attorney in the Superior office to provide legal advocacy and support to victims. "It's important to have the legal program extend their services in that capacity out there," said CASDA assistant director Erika Leif. "They're so rural. . . . There's not a lot of resources." The funding for the position only covers domestic violence services, but she provides referral services to victims of sexual assault.

The staff at CASDA saw a need for someone to work with the children who came to the shelter with their moms. "We were there to help the women navigate and map out their journey, figure out where to stay, and the kids were a very integral part of [that]." In 1996 they hired a children's program coordinator to provide basic support for child victims and witnesses of abuse and educate them on healthy communication skills, setting boundaries, and developing self-esteem.[4]

After several years, the staff running the shelter program had seen how difficult it was for women to figure out their lives in thirty days, which was the maximum shelter stay. While a small amount of transitional housing was available in the shelter, the staff recognized that women and families in transition have different needs. In 1997, CASDA began the process of raising funds and finding a location for a transitional housing program. With the help of a Community Development Block Grant and low-interest loan, as well as state grants, CASDA was able to purchase a fourplex on Ogden Avenue for about $95,000. Volunteers from local labor unions helped do repairs, paint, install new appliances, and lay carpet.

The new building, named Lightfoot House in honor of former director Linda Lightfoot Kelly, opened in June 1998. The program enabled

CASDA to provide safe and affordable housing, as well as advocacy, support groups, and classes in life and employment skills for women who had come out of battering relationships but were on a path toward self-sufficiency. It also freed up the shelter space that had been used for transitional housing, enabling CASDA to increase its emergency housing at the shelter to accommodate nine families. CASDA was able to provide transitional housing for about seven years until grant funding, easily available in the 1990s, abruptly disappeared. "One day you get the letter in the mail that they're not funding you anymore," said Kelly. "Yet you just bought a house, and you're working with four women that have their kids living there, and there's no money."[5]

1999: Crisis

In 1999, CASDA faced an internal calamity that had the potential to cause such a crisis of confidence in the organization as to lead to its internal collapse or to the demise of community support. During a routine audit, auditors found financial discrepancies that raised concerns of possible wrongdoing on the part of the executive director, Lynn Andrews. Previously a CASDA staff member, at this time Lynn had been serving as CASDA's executive director for two years. After the auditors reported this to the board president and vice president, Lynn confessed that she had not paid payroll taxes in six months. Late on a Friday, Lynn called together the staff and informed them that CASDA owed the IRS six months' worth of payroll taxes, that bills had not been paid, and that she needed to come up with more than $80,000 quickly. She planned to take a 50 percent pay cut and was looking at cutting the staff's health insurance. Several of the staff went back to Kelly's house afterward to process all this. "We were all devastated," recalled Kelly. "A lot of us are survivors, and all that victimization stuff started coming up." The staff gathered two days later and agreed they no longer felt comfortable working with Lynn. They wrote up a grievance and requested a meeting with board president Mike Simonson. They requested and he agreed that the executive director not be present at the emergency board meeting scheduled for the next day. Ten minutes before the meeting, Lynn submitted her resignation. The CASDA staff and board spent the next seven months trying to figure out what had been going on with the organization's finances. The board had not taken Lynn's keys prior to the emergency board meeting, and she had gone in and "shredded all the financials," destroying much of the evidence. What they were able to uncover was devastating. CASDA did not have enough money to meet payroll. Grant reports had not been submitted for six months. When they called the IRS, they discovered that CASDA owed a year and a half's worth of taxes, along with penalties and interest, totaling about $192,000. "The IRS came [to the board] and said, 'We can take your kids' college funds. We can take your houses, your cars,'" remembered Kelly.[6]

The first challenge for the organization was figuring out how to restore its financial footing. They had to go through all their bills and figure out what they needed to pay first. A financial consultant acted as negotiator with the IRS, which, given CASDA's situation and nonprofit status, was willing to work out a deal. They had to take out a second mortgage on the transitional housing units in order to pay the $40,000 the IRS had agreed would satisfy their obligations. From August 1999 through January 2000, several difficult meetings were held to map out a recovery plan to rebuild CASDA's financial health.[7]

The organization kept its situation quiet until it was prepared to navigate the next challenge: informing the community and dealing with the fallout. The only news that had been reported was that Lynn Andrews had left for "personal reasons," that Kelly Burger would serve as interim director, and that the organization would not hire a replacement director for a while in order to "save the program money." The CASDA board and staff decided to break the full story in January 2000. They first contacted Douglas County, the United Way, and the other grantors—who stood behind them—and then took it to the press. They presented the story in such a way as to acknowledge that though this was devastating, they had developed a concrete plan for recouping their losses and had put financial controls in place. The headline in the *Duluth News Tribune* was one of triumph: "CASDA Survives Financial Crisis." The newspaper account glossed over Lynn Andrews's role in the financial crisis and focused on CASDA's plan for recovery, which CASDA stated would be complete by the end of the year. CASDA was aided by Douglas County, which realized it paid CASDA only a fraction of what other counties were paying for similar services and decided to increase its payments to CASDA. CASDA also cut expenses by postponing the filling of two positions, restricting travel and other expenses, and vacating half of its office space in Hawkes Hall. The community responded generously. "Nobody turned on us," said Kelly. "In fact, we had people call and say 'We'll do a fundraiser.' They stood behind us. . . . They believed in us. They gave us a chance."[8]

Later in 2000, Kelly was hired as the next executive director, and one of her first tasks was to address the matter of the former director's accountability. "I believe in justice," she said. "This was truly victimization of an organization that provides services to victims. She needed to be held accountable." The investigators had discovered that Lynn Andrews had forged checks and embezzled funds, and had been doing so for the entire six years she was with CASDA. They could track $40,000, but the auditor estimated the actual amount was three to four times that; much could not be tracked because donations often came in the form of cash.

The staff expressed to the board their desire to hold Lynn Andrews accountable, and the board somewhat reluctantly brought the matter to the local district attorney, saying they wanted to press charges. Andrews was arrested in late November 2000 on charges of theft. According to the criminal complaint, "audits uncovered evidence of an ongoing pattern of theft by Andrews. It was discovered that Andrews had created a false set of books." The newspaper reported that she had embezzled more than $6,600 from CASDA by cutting herself extra payroll checks in 1998 and 1999, and by using CASDA funds to pay for her own washer and dryer. Because she was in a position of trust and power when the alleged theft occurred, she was facing a potential sentence of fifteen years in prison and a $10,000 fine. However, the district attorney wanted to go lightly on her. This concerned Kelly, who feared Lynn might go on to do similar harm to other nonprofits. Because CASDA received federal funding, it could ask the FBI to investigate, which Kelly convinced the board to do. By March, the local charges were dropped so that the FBI could pursue its investigation. The FBI found sufficient evidence for the U.S. Attorney's Office to charge Lynn Andrews with embezzlement in June 2001. She was facing up to ten years in federal prison. Andrews was found guilty and served six months in a women's federal prison in Illinois and paid a few thousand dollars restitution.[9]

The decision to press charges was not without repercussions in the small, close-knit community of Superior. "I remember us being in court," Kelly recalled, "and one of our past volunteer coordinators . . . walked up to me and said 'You're on a witch hunt. I will never forgive you for what you're doing to this poor woman. She's got kids. Our kids play baseball together.'" To which Kelly replied, "She did a number on us. . . . How do I run this organization and let this go?"

Those left in the wake poured the next nine months of their lives into rebuilding the organization. "It wasn't like you work eight to four and go home. It was ninety-hour weeks," Kelly recalled. She was willing to put so much of her time into saving CASDA because, as she said, "It saved my life many years ago walking in as a victim, and I believe in this organization."

The final challenge for CASDA staff was rebuilding their own sense of trust. They had trusted Andrews and felt deeply betrayed. It was especially disturbing that she perpetrated her crime in a field where the client population and many of the staff had been victims of trauma. Erika commented, "This individual . . . re-enacted all those dynamics on all of these people who were really trusting."

Rebirth and Growth

Not only did CASDA survive the financial crisis and public scandal, it thrived. The organization was rebuilt on integrity and regained the respect and trust of the community. It developed new programs and strengthened existing ones.

The attitudes of police and others in the community have evolved, largely due to CASDA's outreach, trainings, and community education. Kelly said that police have "started to recognize what an advocate truly is, what her role is, and how we could be an ally." CASDA has developed three law enforcement partnerships. Launched in about 2003 with the Superior Police Department and Douglas County Sheriff's Office, the Immediate Response Program was modeled after the program that PAVSA introduced in Duluth. Any time an officer responds to a domestic violence call and the alleged perpetrator is arrested, the officer in turn provides CASDA with the name and contact information of the victim. The advocates then immediately reach out to the victim to make her aware of their services. "Our Immediate Response Program with Douglas County law enforcement is a model," said outreach coordinator Kim Marble-Follis, who is developing a similar program in Bayfield County. "The response that CASDA has with law enforcement, the bond and the building of a working relationship, that's an achievement beyond belief."

CASDA also developed a program called DART (Domestic Abuse Reduction Team), in which an advocate and a law enforcement officer work together with the victims. A CASDA liaison in the police department reads all the domestic violence reports. Certain scenarios, like a weapon being used or if police have responded to a call at the same location more than three times, automatically trigger a DART response. "It's creating a better safety net," said Kelly. The police meet with perpetrators and let them know their behavior is unacceptable and that the DART team has been alerted.

In 2009, CASDA initiated a collaborative program, known as SART (Sexual Assault Response Team), with the Superior Police Department and Douglas County Sheriff's Office, the Douglas County Community Health Clinic, UWS, St. Mary's Hospital, and the county's Victim

Witness Assistance program. The intent of SART is to improve communication among area agencies for a collaborative response to sexual assault. Thirty other counties in Wisconsin also have SART programs.[10]

CASDA's relationship with the schools has also improved. When CASDA changed the focus of its program to talking with youth about healthy versus unhealthy relationships, the doors began to open. CASDA works with youth of all ages, from Head Start through senior high school and college. All students in their first year at Superior High School take a "Keystone Class," and CASDA's presentation on healthy relationships is a regular part of that curriculum. When the organization began to focus on risk reduction and protective measures youth should take if adults were hurting them, they began to see effective change. Kelly remarked, "If we want to see a difference in violence against women and kids, we need to be working with the younger generation. They're the ones that are going to be making that difference."

The CASDA Bayfield County Outreach office has a growing collaboration with the other domestic violence programs in the area: New Day shelter in Ashland, the Red Cliff Reservation domestic violence program, and the Bad River Reservation program in Odanah. The office also provides an alternative, if needed, to people in Red Cliff and Bad River. "It [the reservation] is a small tight-knit community," outreach coordinator Kim Marble-Follis said. "Every once in a while there'll be an individual that's been abused that doesn't want to go and confide to someone that is related to them. We exist as an alternative."

While CASDA has made significant strides in several areas, CASDA staff continue to encounter significant hurdles in certain aspects of the justice system. In her outreach work in Washburn, Ashland, and Bayfield Counties, Kim has encountered problems dealing with "the system." She has found working in the rural counties of Wisconsin to be like the early days of domestic abuse advocacy in Duluth. "The biggest challenges are the mentality of the people in the systems that we work with," she said. She added that in Bayfield and Ashland Counties, "sexual assault is handled by people who don't understand the dynamics. It seems no one is willing to make the big changes. Everyone says their hands are tied." Many in the criminal legal system still don't seem to understand that victims need help. "We don't see a lot of empathy," Kim said. "The 'Why doesn't she just leave?' attitude carries into the court system. . . . It is the judicial system in particular that I have seen many victims crumble over. They survive horrific abuse, but then they get into the court system. We [meaning the system] don't support victims."

She said that the use of Richard Gardner's parental alienation syndrome as a tactic by certain attorneys who represent abusers has "literally devastated the lives of clients and their children." The fathers' rights movement is particularly strong in rural Wisconsin, and according to Kim, "they find experts to come in and testify that mothers have been coaching their children to hate their father. It has been shocking and disheartening." They also have had problems with "book and release" of batterers and having cases prosecuted. "The offenders . . . get away with it over and over," Kim said. "Nothing serious happens until someone has been devastatingly abused." CASDA also lacks a visitation center where abusers can visit their children in a supervised environment and where parents can exchange children without having to have contact with each other.[11]

In addition, the laws and processes in Wisconsin make obtaining a restraining order much more difficult than in Minnesota. The victim must appear at the injunction hearing and sit in close proximity to the abuser. A new law requires that, in child sexual abuse cases, even a three-year-old is expected to articulate what happened to him or her. This has resulted in persons not being convicted.

CASDA's legal advocate, Elsa Swenson, whose role is to support victims as they navigate the justice system, has similarly found a lack of understanding and support for victims/survivors of stalking: "Even when they are able to get solid documentation and evidence, the crime often isn't taken seriously. The system doesn't sympathize with the violation of fundamental rights to privacy and safety that are threatened by these seemingly small gestures. An email, text, or 'coincidental' run-in with a stalker evokes an incredible amount of fear that, while justified, is completely misunderstood and underappreciated by people who have not experienced such violations."[12]

Nevertheless, CASDA continues to work to educate and raise awareness of those working in the criminal justice system, and to effect public policy change. The director and program coordinators regularly attend meetings with End Domestic Abuse Wisconsin. CASDA staff are encouraged to support legislative efforts regarding domestic and sexual abuse through calls to their representatives. They keep their coordinated community response team updated on legislative issues and raise awareness in the community about those issues.[13]

New Shelter

Since it began, CASDA had been running its shelter program, as well as its administrative offices, out of Hawkes Hall, which had become a nonprofit incubation center. This had worked well for several years, but

UWS needed to revert Hawkes Hall to dorm space due to growing enrollment. In 2007, the university notified CASDA that it would need to find a different space.

In 2008, CASDA bought land for a reasonable price where a previous business had burned down. The organization had planned to build on that spot and was making payments on the land while it strategized how to raise the funds to build a shelter and offices. Three months later, the stock market bottomed out, at which point the board decided it had no chance of raising the necessary $3 million to build a new building. "We had to go back to the drawing board," said Kelly. The university graciously gave CASDA another year in Hawkes Hall, but after that CASDA had to move the shelter temporarily to a three-bedroom house, which housed only half the number of women and children.[14]

CASDA suffered a significant financial loss selling the property it had just bought, but it soon heard through the grapevine that Essentia Health wanted to sell its old Duluth Clinic building in Superior, and CASDA was able to purchase it. The organization received a short-term loan through Forward Community Investments, which gave them $100,000 in seed money to kick off a capital campaign in late 2011. CASDA received tremendous support from community members and funding partners and was able to raise the $1.1 million needed to renovate the building. The capital campaign helped establish new connections with business leaders and others in the community.[15]

CASDA encountered little resistance to its plans to build a new shelter. At the city council discussion about having the area rezoned for the shelter, one neighbor protested that this would drop property values and wanted CASDA to build a fence, but nobody else objected to the rezoning proposal. "We're by Zion Lutheran [Church], and the pastor stood up and talked about what a service CASDA does for our community," said Kelly. "We had other neighbors [support us], too. . . . We built the fence, and we have not had complaints."

The new shelter opened its doors in April 2013. In addition to housing up to ten families, it has space for CASDA's offices, so the staff is able to provide comprehensive services to victims of abuse under one roof. Director of program services and former shelter director Dana Doyle said, "We love it here because we're all together now. We were fragmented when we were not in the same place as the regular staff. Now we can offer feedback to each other, support if needed." CASDA quickly began a visioning process to determine what its next project would be. The CASDA staff regularly examines the current programming as well as the goals and visions for the future. "We go back and visit where we are with our mission, our programs, and our services, and [think about] what we want to be in another ten years. We're always growing," said Kelly.

Conclusion

For nearly three decades, CASDA has provided shelter, support, and advocacy to thousands of women and children, and outreach and education to the wider community. On an annual basis, it provides direct service to nearly four hundred fifty individuals and answers well over 2,000 crisis line calls. At the heart of its ongoing work is "truly seeing a victim progress. Clients (for lack of a better word) have come to us and said, 'I'm doing better, and I'm safe.' That's a highlight," said Kim.[16]

CASDA survived a major crisis and became a respected organization in the community. "Throughout my years at CASDA I have seen more and more people standing behind us," said Kelly. "Watching that community grow . . . has been a huge highlight." Former director Linda Kelly added that "the agency would not be able to function without the dedication and commitment of the volunteers . . . and the financial support of the community."

They attribute their effectiveness to continuing to go back to their core mission of seeking better to serve the women and children who come to them for services, and to have the victims' needs drive the services they provide. "We work for them," said Kelly. "It's not like 'This is what we can do.' It's truly, 'What do you need, and how can we support you in getting those needs met?'" She went on to say, "We worked hard at CASDA to put our mission in the forefront of any decision we make on programming." The staff strive "to listen to the women and kids and men we serve about what we could do differently, what would make it easier, whether we are setting up barriers." Because of this, said Kelly, "I've seen our emergency shelter come [to embody] that kind of family-centered, victim-centered kind of philosophy that we've always dreamed of."

Those working for CASDA say they would like to work themselves out of a job, but they don't see that happening anytime soon. Nevertheless, they have been effective agents for change, "albeit, a lot of times slower than I'd ever want, but I've seen change," said Kelly. "I'd like people to know that we can make a difference." And they have.

{ 9 }

Women's Transitional Housing Coalition/ Women's Community Development Organization and Women in Construction

For many survivors of domestic violence, the typical stay in an emergency shelter is about thirty days. However it can take several months for women and families to secure safe and affordable permanent housing. Designed to be a stepping-stone between a crisis shelter and long-term self-sufficiency, transitional housing programs for survivors fill an important function. In Duluth, almost a decade after the Women's Coalition opened its first emergency shelter, women who saw a need for such a program stepped up to create it. For more than twenty years, Women's Transitional Housing provided safe, affordable, and supportive housing for hundreds of women and children who were experiencing violence or homelessness, and assisted them in bringing their personal visions of their lives into being.[1]

Origin Story

Time and again, advocates at the battered women's shelter in Duluth saw women return to their batterers when their thirty days at the shelter were up, not because they wanted to, but because they had no place else to go. "I was always struck by how difficult it was for women to successfully leave a violent situation," said Nancy Burns, a former advocate. "Even if they did leave, the forces arrayed against them made it difficult for them to stay out of the relationship. It could be something as small as a toilet that was broken or a car that had a flat tire. So often they had so few resources other than their partner that they would just drift back into the relationship because there were just too many challenges to make it on their own." One of the greatest challenges was the lack of safe and affordable housing in Duluth.[2]

When Kate Regan, who worked for the YWCA, learned that so many women go back to their abusers because they have no other options, she called Nancy and Michelle LeBeau, who also worked at the shelter, and the three met to discuss creating a place for women to go rather than return to their partners. The YWCA had a residence with single room occupancy units for women, and Kate, Nancy, and Michelle briefly considered using rooms at the Y for this purpose, but the Y was not adequately equipped to run a housing program. Also, most of the women had children, and the rooms at the Y were small. Nor was there any play space. For many reasons, the rooms at the Y were not a viable option.

Seeking more input, in the spring of 1986, Kate, Nancy, and Michelle called together advocates from the shelter, Community Action, and other organizations—including Catherine Peterson from the Community Action Program (CAP), Pam Kramer with city planning, community member Hildred Sunbear, and Barb Lund, who was a counselor at Fond du Lac—to discuss establishing a transitional housing program for women in Duluth. "It was such an exciting time," said Kate, "because we were all committed to this idea. It was grassroots. It was what we wanted it to be, what it could be."

The small group called together by Kate, Nancy, and Michelle was still in the visioning stage when they discovered that the State of Minnesota had put out an RFP (request for proposal) for more transitional housing programs, like the one in Minneapolis, and the proposals were due in five days. "We didn't have a board. We didn't have a 501(c)(3). Nothing. We were just meeting," said Michelle. They decided to jump in anyway. Everyone in the group took portions of the proposal to work on, and Catherine did most of the work of bringing the pieces together. "It was so invigorating," said Kate, "the exhilaration of getting it together and doing it in five days, everybody working on it together." They sent in the proposal and were awarded the grant to set up a transitional housing program in Duluth.

At that point, they formed a 501(c)(3) and became the Women's Transitional Housing Coalition. They got together a board and hired Nancy part-time to do grant writing and other necessary start-up tasks. To assess the needs of the target population, they surveyed women at the shelter and in the displaced homemaker program, asking them about the obstacles that kept them from leaving a violent situation or becoming more independent in their living situations. "The data came

back consistently that the obstacles were affordable housing, safe housing, childcare, transportation, and a generalized need for support for
the changes they wanted to make in their lives," said Nancy. From the
data and their own considerable knowledge of the needs of survivors of
domestic abuse, the group developed a concept for a women's transitional housing program. They raised enough money from the McKnight
and Bush Foundations, as well as several smaller funders, to buy a building and fund the program for the first year.

The board hired Nancy and Michelle to be co-directors. "We knew
a lot about women's lives and obstacles and we had some pretty good
thoughts about what would make a difference in their lives," Nancy said.
"The things we didn't know a lot about, that were challenging, were what
it would be like to be owning and managing property and all the things
that can go wrong with that." But, as Kate said of Nancy and Michelle,
"You couldn't ask for better staff people. . . . They had the history of working with battered women. . . . Michelle and Nancy were the spirit and the
heart and the brains, and did the bulk of the work."

The next step was finding a building. Nancy and Michelle together
looked at buildings around Duluth for possible occupancy. A few members of the planning group also went to the Twin Cities and visited the
Harriet Tubman transitional housing program. Though it was a much
larger operation than what they had envisioned for Duluth, the Harriet
Tubman program gave them useful ideas.

The organization bought and renovated two side-by-side brick buildings at 1401 East Second Street and 216 North Fourteenth Avenue East,
which would provide twenty-four units of housing. It developed programming to provide women with the skills to move beyond transitional
housing. After a year-long process of working with city, county, and
state agencies, Women's Transitional Housing officially opened its doors
in 1988.

"It was just the right moment in time," said Nancy, "the right group
of women to get on the board, the right foundations, and just the right
people to put together a program that made a significant difference in
women's lives." Kate recalled the excitement of those first years. "There
was so much hope," she said.

Early Years

To be eligible for housing at Women's Trans, as it was known, a woman
had to be "homeless, low income, and willing to participate in the pro-

gram." The application process was straightforward. The board interviewed potential residents to determine whether the applicants' goals fit what Women's Trans could provide. Prior to opening, Michelle and Nancy had sent application forms to the shelter, the Salvation Army, and other appropriate places around Duluth, so when the facility opened it was immediately filled with twenty-four women and twice as many children. The women could stay at Women's Trans for eighteen months, but could extend their stay to twenty-four months, which most of the residents did.[3]

The staff consisted of Nancy, Michelle, and Michelle's sister, Lindy Askelin, who lived on-site as the maintenance person. Not long after opening, they hired Sadie Green as Lindy's assistant. Nancy and Michelle worked together as a team, dividing the administrative tasks to match their respective strengths. Nancy did the grant writing and administered the program. Michelle kept the books. They both did advocacy and programming. "They were a fabulous team," said Sadie.

A year later, Victoria Ybanez came on board as the first women's advocate. Victoria worked with the residents and developed programming. She remembered the work being difficult: "With an emergency shelter, people are in and out so fast, you just touch the tip of the iceberg. When they move into Transitional Housing and they stay for a longer period of time, you get involved in deep stuff. People had so many hard, complicated, challenging issues that they were dealing with. It required that we pull together a ton of resources."

The founders quickly recognized a gap in the initial plan for the program. "Women come with children," said Victoria. "At any given time during the summer, you could conceivably have sixty children on site, and the place would vibrate." Besides the playground between the buildings, they hadn't made any other accommodations for the children. They soon hired Jean Baribeau (Thoennes) to be the first Children's Program coordinator. She was responsible for overseeing childcare during the women's groups. She also acted as a liaison with the court system and the schools; advocated in the courts and with social services for women whose children had been temporarily placed in foster care to have their children returned to them; got children enrolled in school; and connected children who had a history of sexual or physical abuse with therapists. "I did more supporting families and supporting women in their roles as mothers, at least initially, than direct work with the children," said Jean. Though as Victoria noted, she also developed "some incredible programming for the kids." The Children's Program offered support and assistance to families "to create a space for children to be happy, healthy and learn ways of being nonviolent."[4]

Women's Trans also offered programs to assist residents in their transition to independent living. These included life and career assessment and goal-setting programs, which combined on-site services with aid from other community agencies to help the women foster their personal and family growth, as well as obtain education and employment. Residents could work with an employment advocate to identify their strengths and barriers to employment, and to obtain information and resources for finding work. Several years later, Women's Trans added a follow-up program for participants who had moved out of the program and into the community. Women who were parents were required to attend parenting classes, where they were given information and tools to create healthy and respectful home environments. Other education and support groups focused on such issues as family intervention, supportive services for children, and parenting. The program also provided access to a computer lab and tutoring.

The founders of Women's Trans were very clear, however, that they did not want to be a social service agency. One of the most important pieces of the programming was empowerment, which the organization did through building women's community, consciousness raising, educating the women on their political and legal rights, and involving them in the political process. One way they fostered community was holding classes on such topics as fair housing, tenant rights, domestic violence, DAIP's Power and Control Wheel, racism, and homophobia. They ran educational groups based on DAIP's *In Our Best Interest* curriculum. "That was one of the best things I ever did," said Michelle. "The women loved the groups. . . . Every group ended with a social change action. People did some great actions." Victoria remembered, "We talked about patriarchy and systems of oppression, and how that plays itself out, and worked on a lot of education about that."[5]

The women themselves started doing some of their own organizing. One woman, Suzie Forevermore, was an artist who ran a book group for the other residents and did collages with them; some of these she gave to other agencies in town with which she was connected. "Here's these women who are living in poverty and have all these problems they're dealing with, but they can rise above that and become community and help each other out, and want to do something to change their lives and other women's lives," said Michelle.

Women's Trans collaborated with other nonprofits to bring in national experts to speak and run workshops, and it also brought in people from a variety of local organizations to do trainings and workshops. For instance, Jill Abernathy and Babette Sandman from DAIP ran a group on women's culture "to figure out who we were as women if we weren't defined by men," said Jill. "[It] was a celebration of being female."

On the political front, the organization invited candidates for local office to come speak, and the staff members taught residents about the political process, precinct caucuses, voter registration, and the importance of knowing who their representatives are. They involved the women in political action. In the early 1990s, a group from Women's Trans and other folks from Duluth involved in housing issues took a bus to Washington, DC, where they connected with housing advocate Mitch Snyder from the Community for Creative Nonviolence. Together they staged what was essentially a sit-in in Vice President Dan Quayle's office, refusing to leave until he came and listened to them about the need for affordable housing. Women's Trans brought the women to the state capitol and to city council meetings when elected officials were discussing matters that affected their lives. Residents made presentations at city council hearings for Community Development Block Grants. Women from the program remained politically active and involved long after they had moved out of Women's Trans. The women speaking up for themselves in public forums—"talking about their life and having other people hear and respect that"—was profoundly important for their self-concept and empowerment. "That is something that is seldom factored in to how you help people grow," said Nancy. "We confirmed for us it was true." She thought that educating residents and encouraging their participation in the political process was "the most potent and powerful thing we did with women. For many women, it helped to make the most significant internal changes about possibility in their lives."[6]

Finding the best way to "provide an environment that allows women to grow in the way they want to grow" was an ongoing challenge. The staff and board of Women's Trans had an idealistic vision of women becoming fully empowered to enact the vision of their lives in the short time they were at Women's Trans. For some, this vision and the empowerment tools that Women's Trans offered were exactly what they needed to move on to the next stage of their lives. Others, however, simply needed an affordable and safe place to raise their kids, and were dealing with too many other basic survival issues to work on their own self-actualization. "I was both continually impressed and amazed at the changes people would make and the movements people would start toward a life that they envisioned, and also disappointed and surprised at how difficult it was sometimes," said Nancy. "Sometimes there was too much in their lives that we couldn't address. . . . On the other hand, sometimes people accomplished amazing things in a short period of time. All they needed was that safe space and they were on their way. Seeing that happen was exciting and gratifying and supportive of why we were doing what we were doing." Victoria fondly remembered taking four women to their first day at the community college. One of the women said she couldn't wait to be a college student, and when Victoria reminded her that she was a college student right then, "these four women started jumping up and down on the sidewalk and hugging each other. . . . There were lots of those moments."[7]

Women's Trans also fostered empowerment by including the women in decisions that affected their lives in the program. "Every project we did, we went to the women," said Victoria. When the staff started hearing about gaps or unmet needs in the program, input from the women guided the decisions. For example, the decision to remodel one of the properties into single-room units for single women came about as a result of single women telling staff they needed their own unit apart from families with children. When it came time to design those spaces, staff talked with the women. Given the option of a shared kitchen or bath to stretch the budget, the women were clear that they wanted their own bathrooms and kitchens. They didn't care how small the living spaces were, but separate bathrooms and kitchens were important. "We responded to that and women loved their spaces," said Victoria. "We could listen to what women had to say and move it into something real." Jean regarded this as the very nature of Women's Trans: "see a need, figure out how to address it."

Women's Trans also provided support for families that had finished their two years at Women's Trans and were successfully moving forward, but needed assistance to keep from falling backward. As the SAFAH (Supplemental Assistance for Families At Risk of Homelessness) coordinator, Sadie, who fairly early on had transitioned from doing maintenance to being an advocate with women in the program, helped families find permanent housing off-site and met with them on a monthly basis. As the women progressed in their goal plans, they could access financial assistance from Women's Trans for goal-related expenses and were welcome to stay connected to groups and community events held at Women's Trans.[8]

Women's Trans demonstrated its commitment to its mission of race, class, and gender justice in several ways. About half the residents at

Women's Trans were women of color, and about half of those were Native and the other half African American and Hispanic. Women's Trans wanted the makeup of its staff and board to reflect the population that came through the program, and it made hiring decisions with that in mind. "We do not just say we're 'Equal Opportunity Employers,'" said Melissa Taylor, an advocate at Women's Trans. "We do recruitment to make sure we get a pool of individuals who are diverse in race. . . . We also want our staff [to be] not far removed from the experiences of the women in our programs. Many of them have backgrounds in the same struggles, and that's important." Priority was also given to individuals who had lived in Women's Trans housing or had gone through one of the programs, though Women's Trans required that a certain amount of time elapsed between their residency and their working for the organization. In addition, the majority of board members and staff had personal experience with issues of poverty, welfare, single parenting, and/or domestic violence. While Women's Trans was committed to having residents represented on the board, this created difficulties if those residents were required to keep information confidential from other residents. "We ended up having [on the board] women who were low income, women who had been homeless, women who were in the same situation as the women who were in the residence, but not women who were actually in Trans," remembered Kate. One of the difficulties of a grassroots board was that the members sometimes lacked the experience, confidence, status, or skills to step in on difficult administrative and personnel decisions when necessary. To further its commitment to social justice, Women's Trans was also scrupulous in funding, making sure sources had no role in exploiting women or low-income people. "We walk the talk," said Melissa. Despite the desire to walk the talk, Women's Trans faced ongoing issues of racism, both within the organization and directed at the organization from the outside. Diversifying the staff was not easy. "I was the first not-white person on staff and it stayed that way for a while," said Victoria. "I don't believe we ever achieved [full diversity], but we got a higher percentage of staff that were people of color, and there were two times when they had women of color as co-directors."[9]

Women's Trans also struggled with racism among the residents and directed at the residents. "You had this very diverse population, so of course issues of racism are going to come up," said Michelle, as are sexism and homophobia, she added. She recounted a life-changing lesson she received from an African American resident, who during a particularly awful racist event in the community explained to Michelle, "You will never understand what I'm talking about until you can see racism from my perspective, until you have my consciousness in your consciousness all the time." This made Michelle aware of the limitations of her perspective, that it was a white perspective, and this incident changed how she dealt with racist incidents from then on.

Jean also spoke of how her work with women of color at Women's Trans gave her deeper understanding of the daily struggles of being a person of color in Duluth. An African American woman in the program told of how she feared for her twelve-year-old son every day he went off to school, because he was big and looked like a grown man, but acted like an adolescent. She didn't know what situations he might find himself in in this town. Jean remembered listening to her and "being struck like being hit in the chest" about what it must be like as a mother "to send your child out the door and feel that they're at risk. I can't imagine what kind of courage it takes to get up and do that every day."

Victoria recalled a difficult time when some residents were receiving death threats from white supremacists in the mail. Years of dealing with struggles of racism had been exhausting for many on the board and staff, and for some this was the final straw. As a result, one staff member and a few board members quit. Despite these negative consequences, Victoria did see one positive outcome. Following the threats, Victoria hired Pow-wow Security so that the women could get outdoors with their kids on a beautiful spring weekend and feel safe. However, the neighbors started calling the police to arrest the Native men they saw walking around the property. After the women at Women's Trans explained to the police and neighbors that the men were providing security and were not a threat, the neighbors brought over food for the men. "It turned out to be a positive neighborhood relationship thing," said Victoria. Nevertheless, battles in the neighborhood and community were ongoing. "There were messages that we were going to Chicago and recruiting people to come back and be in our program because we had such a diverse population. Some people felt threatened by it because they weren't used to having communities of color in concentration in Duluth," said Victoria.

The centerpiece of Women's Trans was the residents, who had a rare opportunity to live in intentional community with other women. The diversity brought, as Victoria said, its own "unique challenges," but it also brought opportunities for the women to learn from one another and figure out how to live together. Trying to enforce rules for adult women presented other challenges. The restriction against residents having live-in partners, either male or female, arose as a point of contention at times. A program participant occasionally would have someone move in with her surreptitiously, and that would need to be dealt with. Sometimes the staff felt like they couldn't win. If unbeknownst to staff a lesbian had a woman living with her covertly, straight residents would complain to the staff about men not being allowed, yet when the staff enforced the rule for female partners, the residents would be upset as well. The women were allowed a few nights of overnight guests, but, as Kate said, "nobody was standing at the door counting."

Women's Trans had rules and structure, and mandatory meetings twice a week, but it also allowed considerable autonomy and independence for the residents. "It was open in that people were coming and going, but it was also a very safe community with boundaries," Sadie remembered fondly. "Kids played together on the playground. Women shared childcare all the time. We'd go to the Capitol. We'd go grocery shopping together. It was a real community." The women had space and time in which to create relationships. "People living in community are not always harmonious, but especially at the beginning, there was a real sense of joy and support," remembered Kate. Sadie described life at Women's Trans as "living very close to the bone," without "a lot of distractions. . . . It was a basic love human connection."

Growth and Transition

As demand for housing continued to increase, Women's Trans added other buildings over a period of about a decade. They purchased and renovated a triplex in the East Hillside and created three units of permanent supportive housing for families exiting Women's Trans. The program had been set up primarily for families, but many single women needed supportive and safe housing as well, so the organization added thirteen more units specifically for single women. They also purchased a parking lot next to their transitional housing buildings on Fourteenth Street, and constructed a new building with five units of permanent supportive housing. Beneath the housing was a large community space that could be used for groups, meetings, and gatherings both by the Women's Trans community and the community at large.

Not only did Women's Trans develop safe and affordable housing for women, it did "absolutely *beautiful* housing," said Victoria. Women's Trans valued providing quality housing. The staff wanted to "create a space [where] people can live in dignity. Just because you're low-income doesn't mean you deserve a shabby kitchen," said Victoria. "Everything that we did was beautiful. When people would look at it, they would love it. . . . Many times women would cry, they were so happy, and couldn't believe that this was . . . going to be their home for a while. . . . The goal and commitment was to offer a quality living space for people to make hard decisions about their lives. They deserved good space to do it in."

Jean—who was not directly involved in purchasing and rehabbing the buildings but witnessed the skill and dedication that it required—said, "I was absolutely amazed at the knowledge and the skills and the collaboration and the connections of the women I worked with. I was in awe of the things they did." She remembered walking through the triplex on Fifteenth Avenue East and First Street right after they bought it, and wondering, "Why would anybody buy this?" She explained: "There were no stairs. There was rubble. It was dilapidated, a nearly condemned building. What was done with that building was amazing." The rehabilitation of the triplex earned Women's Trans a national award from the Fannie Mae Foundation for being one of the top low-income housing developments in the country by a nonprofit organization.[10]

As with so many of the grassroots feminist organizations, growth brought organizational challenges. Women's Trans became more institutionalized and more hierarchical, both among the staff and between the staff and the residents. As staff took on more specialized roles, the organization ran more efficiently, but it undermined the collective vision. In the beginning, all the staff had been advocates. The organization used a management team approach which for the first few years was quite informal. When the organization was small, the management team included most of the staff, including part-time people in childcare, fill-in people in maintenance, and caretakers. Eventually the management team was a small group of more regular staff. Sadie thought the first several years worked well because Women's Trans had a stable staff. "We had our own jobs and no one micromanaged," she said. "Everyone had something important to bring to the table. . . . The structure of having two women's advocates, two childcare advocates, two maintenance, two admin gave each autonomy and yet we worked together." The structure was formalized by the board around 1996 or 1997. When the management team became more formalized, team members would ask permanent staff who had been with Women's Trans to fill out an application to be on the team. "We tried to make sure that not only was each program represented—such as Admin Program, Women's Program, Children's Program, Maintenance—but also that personal diversity was represented. For instance, Wanda Maldanado did not particularly want to be on the management team, but was persuaded to be there as a cultural representative," remembered Sadie. The organization tried to combine a co-director leadership structure with collective decision-making, but the two management styles continually clashed. Despite holding multiple meetings and hiring consultants, Victoria said, "we never achieved that full management structure that we wanted."[11]

Also, personal experience with poverty, homelessness, or domestic violence became a less important factor in hiring, and gradually there came to be greater separation between the staff and the women they served. Women's Trans began with incredible energy and enthusiasm, and a clear and strong vision of creating a women-centered, women-run program. As with so many of these organizations, the paradigm that initially inspired Women's Trans became more and more difficult to maintain within the context of a society that ran on a different paradigm.

Gradually, almost imperceptibly, the women-centered paradigm faded away. Looking back, Nancy said that while the mission of Women's Trans to empower the women residents was "the most powerful and the most meaningful" aspect of the organization, it was "also the hardest thing to hang on to." She felt the founders had internalized the mission from the work they did and from their own lives, but with new people in the organization and systemic pressures to the contrary, it was difficult to sustain the dream of a women-run organization committed to working in solidarity with women. Sadie remembered thinking they had invented a new paradigm, a different way of doing things, but unless that new paradigm is deeply embedded in the individuals and the organization, the more entrenched mainstream paradigm returns and takes over. "We lost it somewhere along the way," said Sadie.

As increasing numbers of residents were coming into the program with complex clusters of problems that needed to be addressed, such as mental illness or drug addiction, the staff and board often felt overwhelmed. Michelle said, "We were used to working with women who came into the shelter, but a lot of women who came into transitional housing were not from shelters. They might have whole different issues than what we were used to." Because Women's Trans did not have the capacity to deal with these difficulties, the temptation to exclude women struggling with mental illness or substance abuse problems, for the sake of the rest of the residents and the stability of the program, was strong. Yet, as Kate said, "these were the people who most needed housing. . . . There was nowhere else for them to go."

Increasingly, the residents were having men move in with them, and some were conducting illegal activity. In January and again in April 1996, police arrested suspected crack cocaine dealers who had moved in with women at Women's Trans. The January arrest was the largest crack bust in the history of the city, and the dealer's conviction added evidence to an ongoing investigation that finally broke a ring of dealers from Detroit selling drugs in Duluth. The woman with whom the man was living was not charged, but she was asked to leave Women's Trans.[12]

The arrests sparked attacks on Women's Trans by some in the community who said that the program was attracting people with ties to "big city problems." A local talk show host criticized Women's Trans for the number of police calls to the apartment block where the women lived. Women's Trans responded by pointing out that most of the police calls were for intruders, not for women in the building. The drug arrests were the first such problem they had had with women residents. Duluth city councilor Marcia Hales, who was not a supporter of Women's Trans, told reporters, "We are reaching out of our community. I just wonder if we are providing beds to people from outside that could be better used for our own." In fact, most of the residents in Women's Trans were local, but by law the organization was not permitted to deny housing to someone solely because they were from out of state. Victoria said at the time, "The beating that Women's Trans has been taking has had the effect of draining resources and stressing the participants."[13]

It also drained the staff. After several years of staff stability, in the mid- to late 1990s, Women's Trans experienced several staff transitions. Nancy Burns left for a time, and Victoria Ybanez stepped in as co-director with Michelle from 1993 to 1996. Then Victoria left to head the American Indian Community Housing Organization (AICHO) in 1996, though she stayed on with Women's Trans as a board member. Nancy came back in a development capacity and then served again as co-director from 1996 to 1998. Tragically, Lindy Askelin was lost to breast cancer early in 1996. Michelle gave her letter of resignation to the board in October 1997, though she stayed on in a limited capacity as the bookkeeper and to oversee the administration. Sadie Green moved into the position of administrative coordinator after Michelle's resignation, and Sadie's move necessitated hiring a replacement for her position as SAFAH coordinator. Nancy Burns and Jean Baribeau both resigned in 1998. Other members of the management team took leaves for personal reasons, and three new staff were hired onto the management team, which placed additional burdens on the two remaining experienced staff. In addition, over a very short time period, more than a dozen staff were let go for various reasons. After much soul-searching, Sadie left Women's Trans at the end of 1999. The board hired Zoe LeBeau, Michelle's daughter, and Deyona Kirk (Norvel) as co-directors of Women's Trans.[14]

Women's Community Development Corporation and Women in Construction

As co-directors, Zoe and Deyona brought an expanded vision to Women's Trans of doing far more property development. A major rehab of fifteen of their units started them down the path of becoming a development corporation, but the main impetus was the growing need for permanent housing among the resident population. "When it [Women's Trans] first opened, the target population was women who were victims of domestic violence that didn't have a lot of other barriers, just needed some shorter term support," said Zoe, but the Women's Trans population had changed, and the problems the women faced were more long-term. Living in continual transition was particularly difficult on children, and the women dealing with mental health and chemical dependency issues needed the stability of more permanent living situations. "That's how transitional housing morphed into looking at more permanent housing," said Michelle, "realizing people can't [always] leave in twenty-four months."[15]

To provide permanent affordable supportive housing, Women's Trans invested in buying, rehabbing, and building considerably more housing. Over the next few years, it went from fifty to a hundred units of housing, all subsidized by government funding. In 2000, the organization was renamed Women's Community Development Organization (WCDO) to reflect the shift to more permanent housing.

During this period, WCDO was struggling with two recurring issues: the inability to find women construction workers to hire for its many building projects and the inability to find stable employment in decent-paying jobs for the women in the program. As part of its commitment to women's empowerment, Women's Trans prioritized hiring women and companies that hired women for its construction projects. However, the percentage of women in the building trades is quite low, around three percent nationally and five percent locally. At the same time, most of the employment opportunities available to the residents in the WCDO program—primarily jobs in tourism, telemarketing, housecleaning, and cooking—paid below $10 an hour and provided no benefits. "Women that came into our program who didn't have any schooling and didn't have any skills usually had to find jobs in service industries," said Michelle. "They didn't make enough to support themselves or, if they had children, to support their children." The construction trade, on the other hand, provided higher-wage jobs with greater stability and benefits, but it was very difficult to get women jobs in the construction industry.[16]

Michelle recalled, "We were sitting there talking one day and all of a sudden this idea came about that if we're a housing developer and we can't find women to build housing, why don't we create a training program, and [train] women in shelters and transitional housing and other low-income women . . . and then help them find jobs in the construction industry." It seemed a win-win situation, a creative solution that would enable WCDO to provide job training and skills for women in the program, and also employ more women in the construction and rehabilitation of its buildings.

People they talked with in the trades were supportive of the idea of training women in construction trades, but urged them to get the women into already-existing apprenticeship programs, rather than create their own training program. But because Michelle, Zoe, and Deyona knew that part of the barrier to getting women into the trades was sexism and harassment, they thought the best strategy was to train the women themselves. They knew they could provide a more supportive environment for women who were just beginning to acquire construction skills. Michelle reflected: "A woman who's going on a job site, who's never held a tool in her hands before, doesn't want to . . . not do well. If . . . there's five other women there and most of them have been in her shoes, it's going to be much easier for her to feel comfortable and confident about her skills." However, finding women with the skills to provide the training was no easy task, nor could they find any women contractors. They needed another approach.[17]

Michelle thought back on how she had learned construction skills. As a girl, she had learned basic skills in the way men traditionally do: from her dad. Later on she learned from other women—her sister, Lindy, and women in the community who were building their own homes. "There'd always be these work parties," Michelle said. "You'd go over there and help people build. I got enough hands-on experience to know what it was about." They modeled this approach of learning-while-doing for their training program, and drew on their own contacts and resources to develop it. They set up the training program so that the women would work alongside one or two skilled workers, usually men, who would train the women as they worked on the buildings.

In 1999, in an initial partnership with Women Build, a division of Habitat for Humanity, the fledgling Women in Construction (WiC) program put out flyers informing women of the new program to train women in construction. "We had hundreds of women who called in who wanted to work on the 'Women's Build,'" said Michelle. Twenty-five of these signed up for the training program.

One of the first projects was repairing a large flat roof on one of the WCDO buildings that had been severely damaged in a storm. "All of the women in the training program said, 'Let us do the roof!'" remembered Michelle. She talked the roofing contractor into letting some of the women join his crew. The women learned quickly. "These were women who would get up at 6:00 AM," Michelle remembered. "It was July, so up on this roof it would get to be 115 degrees. When they got off the job site at night, they'd go home and take care of their children. Every day they showed up for work enthusiastic and wanting to do this." When they completed the job, the contractor said that he'd hire any of the women, if they wanted a job. That's how WiC proceeded from then on: connecting with contractors and sending out women crews to learn on the job.

The original idea had been to train women to work in the existing construction industry. However, the women in the training program hit barriers of sexism. When they completed their training and started applying for jobs, they were invariably told the company wasn't hiring secretaries. "Sometimes they wouldn't even be handed a job application," remembered Michelle, "and if they were . . . they weren't called back for jobs." Even the few who did find jobs encountered such a negative atmosphere and so much harassment that it was difficult for them to stay. Frustrated with the discrimination and harassment the women faced and the women's inability to be hired for jobs they were trained to do, in 2002 Michelle got her contractor's license and formed Women in Construction Company, LLC.[18]

The training program was the centerpiece of the company's mission to enable low-income women to acquire the skills they needed to obtain employment in the well-paid construction industry. Some came into the training program from WCDO. Others came from the Duluth Workforce Center, Northeast Minnesota Office of Job Training, and the Minnesota Chippewa Tribe. Michelle hired skilled laborers who taught the women as they worked on jobs. "We train on the job," said Michelle. "That person might go out to pour slabs. She might be going out to gut a building. She might be going out to install windows. . . . The next job, they might be learning how to do finishing work, trimming out windows and doors, and installing cabinets."

"It exploded," recalled Zoe. "Women in the program absolutely loved the training." As one of the participants, Deborah Santiago, said, "It's been fun, really fun. Coming to work, not knowing what I'll be doing the next day, learning new things every day." The approach to the training proved successful, and the women quickly learned a variety of construction skills. "Ninety-nine percent of the company, when they started with us, had no skills at all," Michelle commented, "and within a short period of time they were very skilled and wonderful craftspeople."[19]

Michelle began conservatively in terms of the scope of the work the women were being trained to do, limiting it to gutting rooms and installing windows, doors, and cabinets. But the women asked to learn more skills, like laying ceramic tile and refinishing hardwood floors. "Everything we did was based on what the women wanted to learn," said Michelle. She would find people with the appropriate skills to train the women, and then those who had been trained would in turn train those who came into the program after them. Michelle credited the women's desire to learn for WiC's becoming an all-purpose company. "We never would have done metal siding or metal roofs ourselves if I'd listened to the men in the program," said Michelle. Instead, WiC became known as the company to hire.

Because Michelle regarded it as a project of radical economic justice, the training program also gave women the empowerment tools they needed to work in the construction field. Participants received leadership training and attended workshops on racism, sexism, and homophobia. "Women must steel themselves against the bias they will face on a job site and explore some of the differences faced by women crews," said Michelle. The women were also encouraged to examine their own latent prejudices about race, sex, and age in diversity training sessions.[20]

Despite its name, only 60 percent of WiC's employees were women. Men were often hired to teach the women skills. While the men occasionally encountered entrenched attitudes and wearisome harassment about being "women" from their suppliers and subcontractors, most loved working for the company. Nevertheless, the men sometimes carried these habituated ways of thinking into WiC. Often men would pick other men first to be on their crews, and Michelle often found her role to be bringing these latent prejudices to light.

WiC and WCDO worked hand in hand. WCDO acquired more buildings and apartments, which were then renovated by WiC. When WCDO told prospective funders that WiC crews would do the work on any new project, they had no trouble finding funds. "We had homeless women training to have livable wage jobs working on homeless housing projects. The funders went crazy," said Zoe. WCDO continued to add housing to meet the ever-growing need for affordable, safe, and decent housing for low-income and homeless women and children. It developed partnerships with UMD, from which WCDO leased a house to use for large families, and with St. Mary's Hospital, which donated a four-unit building. In addition, WCDO purchased the Endion School building and developed it into twenty-six one- to three-bedroom apartments. They converted a dilapidated triplex into three units of housing, built a new duplex, and developed and built Women in Construction's worker-owned condos, all on Fifth Street in the Central Hillside area of Duluth. Nearly all of WCDO's residences became permanent housing, with less than a third of its housing being transitional.

One of the high points in 2005 was WCDO's purchase and rehabilitation of an old convent next to the Damiano Center that was being used by a slumlord for, among other things, prostituting women. The building had been condemned by the city in May 2001, though people continued to live there illegally. The project for WCDO grew out of a conversation between Zoe and musician Charlie Parr, who worked for the Human Development Center (HDC), about the need for housing for women who were currently using drugs. The result would be an eleven-unit apartment complex, run in partnership by WCDO and HDC, for women who hadn't succeeded in other programs; HDC would have an office on-site to help residents who were struggling with mental illness or addiction.[21]

WCDO hired WiC to do the renovation. "This is a nightmare," Michelle thought at the time. "It's vacant, abandoned, burned out. . . . We can't do this." But the women in the program were confident, and their dedication and vision drove the historic rehab as they restored the building to its original beauty. That WiC was doing the rehab pleased Zoe, who said at the time, "That means it's going to be a building for homeless women built by women who used to be homeless themselves, and in a building that was one of the first places for social services in the Hillside and in Duluth." Because the convent had once belonged to the Benedictines as part of the Sacred Heart parish, WCDO asked the Sisters of St. Scholastica if they would be interested in partnering with them on the project. The sisters were delighted. Sister Mary Christa Koenig, who had once lived in the convent, said, "I used to drive by and say a prayer that something good would happen with the building. Now it is." She was joined by Sister Romana Ewen, another former resident, who said, "We're very excited the building is going to be used again, especially with the way it's going to be used—to help women." During the time the nuns had lived there, they also served the homeless population, giving sandwiches, coffee, and any leftovers they had to homeless men, whom they referred to as "St. Josephs." Zoe remarked, "The building is coming full circle now. It's going to be a place where people go for help again." Of the sisters, Zoe said, "They were amazing. They were radical. They came in and did a blessing, and we had somebody come in and do a sage at the same time." Not only did the sisters provide financial support, but when WCDO was facing resistance from the city council, the nuns came to the council meeting dressed in their full habits. "That was pretty hard to say no to a room full of nuns," added Zoe.[22]

The building was named Alicia's Place in honor of Sister Alicia Panger, who had reached out to the poor in the Central Hillside decades before. For eighteen years, she checked on residents in the neighborhood, saved many from fire, starvation, and suicide, and rescued children from abuse and neglect. "She was an angel in the hillside," said Zoe. "She definitely is an inspiration for our project."[23]

Zoe left WCDO shortly after the construction of Alicia's Place, and Deyona left a couple years after that. With their departure, Wanda Sayers became executive director. As WiC's reputation grew, WiC began working for other nonprofit developers and for private individuals, building single-family homes in addition to taking on substantial rehab jobs. WiC remained committed to its mission to serve low-income women and people of color. Brian Murphy, vice president for banking for North Shore Bank, the primary lender on many of their projects, said of WiC and its work, "We were very impressed. Key is finishing a project, according to specs. They did both. The fact that they are mission-based also adds a level. There's not just a profit motive here."[24]

The company became financially self-sufficient, with revenues averaging about $2 million per year. Michelle was surprised by how quickly the company had become a success, and she credited that in part to community support. In a 2005 interview she said, "It speaks to the community who does want to see social enterprise and does want to support economic justice. A lot of the jobs that we get are people who want their project to be a good quality project, but they also want to support the mission of our business."

In keeping with this mission, WiC did several major construction jobs for organizations that provide housing and services for women fleeing domestic violence and facing homelessness. In addition to Alicia's Place, WiC also did building and renovation for North Shore Horizons, a domestic abuse shelter in Two Harbors, and the Family Justice Center for Safe Haven Shelter in Duluth. WiC developed a particular niche building energy-efficient housing, most notably Eco-Home, built in the Hawk Ridge development in 2007 in partnership with Minnesota Power, the Minnesota Pollution Control Agency, the City of Duluth, HRA of Duluth, and other private and public entities. It featured solar panels to provide electricity and solar-heated hot water. Patrick Garmoe, who reported on the Eco-Home for the *News Tribune*, was impressed: "The home, and the company that built it, are both extraordinary."[25]

Over the years, WiC built and renovated hundreds of units of housing, from single-family homes to condominiums. It also had several large commercial jobs, including the renovation of a downtown Duluth building for the Hanabi restaurant. In 2008, WiC built nine energy-efficient studio apartments with modest rent for lower-wage downtown workers. At its peak, WiC was bringing in about $4 million in sales annually, employed twenty-five people full-time, and was working on as many as five projects at a time. "It was fun and creative," Michelle recalled fondly. "We had some of the best, talented people." The concept and the project of training women for jobs that would enable them to move out of poverty and homelessness and support their families, while building housing for others coming out of homelessness, was original and inspiring. In 2004, the nonprofit National Law Center on Homelessness and Poverty in Washington, DC, honored the City of Duluth with a Solutions through Alternative Remedies (STAR) Award, in recognition of the Women in Construction program.[26]

Women's lives were changed for the better because of WiC. Not only were the women able to earn decent wages, they also gained skills that enabled them to be self-sufficient. "They can maintain their own home, build their own home. They can work on jobs on the side for other people and always be independent," said Michelle. Many of the women WiC trained and employed came from the domestic violence shelters and WCDO's transitional housing program. "I love it because it's a full circle," said Melissa Taylor of WCDO. One of the women, Katie Piasecki, had dropped out of Lake Superior College and was working at a gas station when she decided to apply for a job with WiC. She intended to stay in construction the rest of her life. "I just fell in love with it," she said. Elsie Robinson, a single mom trying to make ends meet, was working as a cashier at a Salvation Army store during the day and as a stocker at the local Wal-Mart in the evening when she applied to WiC. She learned everything from putting up siding and installing windows to building staircases. "I love it," she said. "It's hard work and you see the results." Delaneyah "Delly" Fritze was delivering pizzas when she joined

WiC. Michelle encouraged her to go back to school and allowed her to work part-time for WiC so she could attend college. They made similar scheduling accommodations for women with children. Kara Schneider, who had dropped out of high school, said her job with WiC gave her self-confidence. "At the end of the day, you actually see what you have made. . . . I've grown so much because of the job." "They just want the chance," said Michelle, and WiC was willing to give them that.[27]

Michelle encouraged women in WiC to develop their own construction businesses. One of these was Lindy's Dream Builders, named after Michelle's sister, Lindy, who was the inspiration for WiC. Like WiC, the purpose of Lindy's Dream Builders was to build and renovate low-income housing. Lisa Lyons, one of the founders of Lindy's Dream Builders, said of WiC, "Being in the program is an inspiration, not just to my children but to other women out there—showing them that everything is possible."[28]

Final Chapter

In the late 2000s, WCDO found itself in financial difficulty. At the same time that WCDO was developing more properties, it had gone from two co-directors to a single executive director, leaving one person in charge of managing one hundred rental units. When the recession hit, the demand for affordable housing and support services increased, but the economic downturn also dried up funding. Cheryl Witzenburg, WCDO's board chair at the time, said, "The organization grew beyond its capacity." With several vacancies and overdue rents, WCDO had a severe cash-flow problem, and while not in foreclosure or bankruptcy, the organization owed about $50,000 to its various creditors. Amy McCulloch, vice president of programs for the Greater Minnesota Housing Fund, observed that "problems with unexpected vacancies, inadequate rent payments, or unanticipated repair costs quickly can push an organization into trouble."[29]

Concerned about the state of WCDO, stakeholders from Duluth Local Initiatives Support Corporation (LISC), the City of Duluth, the Greater Minnesota Housing Fund, and other funders put together a group of about thirty individuals who met monthly to discuss WCDO's situation. The WCDO board's top priority was finding a way to maintain the maximum number of affordable housing units in the community. Michelle, on the other hand, was concerned about the future of WCDO's mission. She said that while the stakeholder group wanted to salvage the housing for low-income people, it "wasn't all that concerned about [WCDO's] vision or about the fact that it should remain a women's organization." In early 2010, the stakeholder group put out an RFP (request for proposal) for someone to step in and take over WCDO's properties. WiC, which also had been hit hard by the recession and was having difficulty staying afloat, submitted a proposal. "The [WiC] employees wanted to do it, because most of them had done the renovations," said Michelle. "They were really invested, and we wanted the mission to stay the same. We wanted this to be about women's housing, and women-run." But within a week of the RFP, the funders accepted a proposal from Center City Housing and with funding from the Minnesota Housing Finance Agency, Greater Minnesota Housing Fund, and the City of Duluth, gave them $2 million to do the renovations. "The thing that makes me furious," said Michelle, "is that . . . if they had given Women in Construction that much money, we could've not only kept that [WCDO] going, but it would've stabilized Women in Construction." Instead, both Women in Construction and WCDO ended in 2010.[30]

It was a bitter pill for the founders of Women's Trans to swallow. During the first five years of Women's Trans, they were told repeatedly that they should go under the umbrella of Center City Housing and let it do the "sticks and bricks" and "let the *girls* do the programming." Michelle was livid about that attitude, which she said "never went away" and led to the buildings going to Center City. "Center City Housing, that was a painful transition," echoed Kate. "It was the right thing to do to maintain the housing . . . but we always felt this competition that the big boys thought we were the little sisters. To have to give that up to them was bitter." Nancy voiced everyone's disappointment: "A lot of time and energy were put into forming that organization, and it makes me sad that it's not in its original mission or that that empowerment piece is not there in that same way."

Conclusion

"It was all born out of those few women saying we really have to have housing," said Melissa, reflecting on Women's Trans's legacy and the hundreds of women it had enabled to make better lives for themselves and their children. "It was a group of women wanting to do something," said Victoria, "and [who] did it because we believed we could." As Michelle said, "If you give women the same opportunity that you give men, you fund them, you give them the tools and the skills they need, women can create amazing housing and amazing programs." Said Melissa, "I would hope that any grandchildren I had would be inspired by how we at every level walked the talk. . . . I would want them to know you don't have to follow the same path as everyone else. You can make your own path."

"A lot of women's lives were changed by going to Women's Transitional Housing," said Nancy. "For some it was a space from which they could move into safe, affordable, permanent housing . . . that gave them a long-term base out of which to raise a family and have a good chance of making it economically. Then there was another group that also got a sense of who they could be and got back to school, or got to school for the first time, or got their GED, or got their kids connected in school and were able themselves as parents to connect with that school, or got into some counseling."

What was most moving to the former staff of Women's Trans was witnessing and being a part of the growth of the women who moved through the program onto major accomplishments in their lives. The staff valued educating the women, making them aware of opportunities, and then watching them take those opportunities and run with them. "All you had to do was provide a garden plot, and what they did with their lives was amazing," remarked Jean. "I learned so much about resiliency and tenacity and growth and strength. . . . I think about all the life, all the joys, all the celebrations, all the sadness, all the losses—how much life happened on that block."

All the former board members and staff interviewed said that the years and the work at Women's Trans were some of the best of their lives. Victoria reflected, "It was some of the hardest work I ever did and it was also some of the most rewarding work I ever did. I got to participate when people recognized they were college students or went to court and faced their abuser for the first time in their life and were empowered, and made strong strides for something positive." As Sadie put it: "It was an incredible experience for me. A lot of people put a lot of love and passion [into it]. . . . I loved being a part of it. I loved going to work. I loved the people I worked with. I loved the whole idea of it. I just loved Transitional Housing. . . . I loved the community. It was life-changing for many of us. For a while I had a job as a community organizer. How good can that be?"

Of her coworkers, Nancy said, "The heart that they brought to the workplace and to the women was amazing. There was so much energy made available to people and so much compassion and just good cheerleading, too." Michelle was amazed by the accomplishments of Women's

Trans—from developing a hundred units of housing to building a staff that represented the people Women's Trans served. "We were a group of women who had this commitment to making sure that women and children were part of everything that we did," she said. "Some of the most important lessons of my life I learned at Women's Transitional Housing. My whole experience at Trans was amazing."

Women's Trans had an enormous impact on the lives of the hundreds of women who lived there and went through the program. "We gave a number of women and children breathing space and a stabilization point for a couple of years to get their acts together, to go to school, to get free of whoever it was they were wanting to be away from," said Michelle. They gave them a supportive community in which to grow their dreams. As Sadie said, "I still to this day believe that's the most important thing you can give anybody, or be a part of—[to] talk and explore and learn from each other."

Referencing the term *kairos*, a Greek word meaning "the exact right time and moment" that Nancy Burns had used to describe the beginnings of Women's Trans, Victoria summed up the significance of Women's Trans in this way: "It was the right time and moment. . . . We worked with women in ways that engaged them in making their own choices about their own lives, envisioning their future, and moving toward what they envisioned."

{ 10 }

Mending the Sacred Hoop

P re-contact, women were held sacred within Native cultures. Rape
was unheard of, and a man beating a woman would have been unthinkable. Today, both nationally and locally, Native women are,
in the words of Holly Oden, "at the highest risk of violence than [*sic*]
women of all other races nationally. They are over three times more likely
to experience sexual assault and intimate partner violence."[1]

One of the main reasons for this change is the boarding schools Native children were forced into from the 1870s through much of the twentieth century, where they experienced violence and abuse as means to
force assimilation. There they were taught that physical violence was a
tool to compel obedience. While many Native women are assaulted and
beaten by non-Native men, according to Eileen Hudon the effect of the
boarding schools has contributed to the "serious problem" of domestic
violence Native American women face today.[2]

Since 1991 Mending the Sacred Hoop has been working to restore
the safety, sovereignty, and sacredness of Native women in their tribal
communities and, by so doing, to move toward ending violence against
Native women and children. Providing training and technical assistance
on domestic violence to tribes across the country, Mending the Sacred
Hoop is committed to restoring the leadership of Native women, thereby
strengthening the voice and vision of Native peoples.

Origin Story

In the late 1980s, an informal group of Native women and men from
Minnesota, South Dakota, and Wisconsin involved in domestic violence
work began meeting together to talk about creating a response to domestic violence specifically for Native women. Among those involved were
Karen Artichoker, Dick Diver, Eileen Hudon, Marlin Mousseau, Sonny

Peacock, Rose Robinson, Dorothy Sam, Babette Sandman, Norma Wall-gren, Mary Ann Walt, and Chet Welch, along with Ellen Pence from the Domestic Abuse Intervention Project (DAIP). DAIP had been working on domestic violence issues for nearly a decade but recognized it was not adequately addressing the specific needs of Native women.[3]

Ellen asked Tina Olson, a Native woman who was working at the Women's Coalition for Battered Women, to work at DAIP for fifteen hours a week to assess the needs of Native women and the criminal jus-tice system's response to meeting those needs. Tina began monitoring the police department, reviewing police reports and police handling of domestic abuse cases involving Native women to ascertain whether they were following proper policies and procedures. Tina found the police response to Native women to be "disrespectful and insufficient." The of-ficers usually assumed the women were drunk and threatened to take their kids away if they called again, which of course deterred women from calling the police if they needed help. She also gained a sense of how Native women were treated in the criminal justice system by the way she was treated when she would go in to pick up the reports. "Those desk sergeants were pretty rude," she recalled. "They had this patriarchal, paternalistic attitude and [would] make me wait for twenty minutes, and talk disrespectfully, like I was nobody to them." She decided the best way to stop the disrespectful treatment and to change the officers' stereo-types of Native women was to establish relationships with the people in power in the police department. "I went through three chiefs of police, a couple lieutenants . . . and ended up creating healthier relations based on respect and my work being credible, promoting an image of a Native woman that was contrary to what their image was in their heads. We're not all a bunch of homeless drunks living off welfare."

Tina's work benefited from DAIP's location in the Damiano Center, where she often met women who were battered or homeless. "I started to do more advocacy," she recalled, "especially for Native women be-cause of my coloring. Women were comfortable with me. We'd end up talking for a long time." Mary Ann Walt, a Native women's advocate, was working across the street at the Center for American Indian Re-sources (CAIR), a branch of the Fond du Lac Reservation. She had been trying, without success, to get Native women who had been abused to come to support groups. DAIP had $5,000 from the Minnesota Depart-ment of Corrections earmarked for women's groups, and Ellen, Tina, and Mary Ann began talking about how they might use that money to raise more interest and facilitate women coming to the support groups.

Instead, they decided to develop a coordinated community response for Native women.

To launch this initiative, Tina and Mary Ann held an invitation-only feast with key people involved in the community response to violence against Native women. The community encompassed Carlton County, the city of Cloquet, and St. Louis County, because the reservation crosses three law enforcement jurisdictions. In consultation with other Native women, Tina and Mary Ann determined the people who should attend, and they invited Sonny Peacock, then chairman of the Fond du Lac tribe, to give the keynote speech. To spark a conversation about, as Tina said, "why women were getting run over on the Rez, why women were getting stabbed," she and Mary Ann presented real-life case scenarios of Native women who had been affected by domestic violence. "Nobody in the criminal justice system or in programming was focusing on the response to Native families until we had this gathering that brought all the decision makers together and opened the door for a dialogue," said Tina. The gathering was a great success. This was the beginning of Mending the Sacred Hoop.

Early Years

Ellen, Tina, and others developed the formal structure of Mending the Sacred Hoop (MSH), which officially began as a program under Minnesota Program Development, Inc. (MPDI) alongside DAIP, in 1991. Tina became the director. She created a strategic plan and received a grant from the Blandin Foundation to continue developing a coordinated community response for Native women. MPDI hired two half-time people, Liz LaPrairie and Jenny James, to work with Tina. Tina said they called themselves "The Three Musketeers."

The three women conducted listening surveys at White Earth and Fond du Lac Reservations. They also approached Carlton County sheriff Dave Zebo, Carlton County judge Dale Wolf, Carlton County Probation, and the St. Louis County Sheriff's department with the idea of using the Duluth Model to build relationships and develop procedures and protocols for domestic assault incidents involving Native people. The women met with these representatives from the criminal justice system at early breakfast meetings at the Stage Stop restaurant in Carlton, which the women dubbed the "Nonviolence Council" meetings. Tina recalled, "We decided that we would slowly educate them until they got to know us. Then if we showed them how the response wasn't sufficient, they on their own would think to start to change." That's exactly what happened. Dave Zebo, whom Tina remembered as being one of their staunchest opponents at first, became one of their most avid supporters.[4]

Though MSH was breaking ground with its initiatives on one front, Tina recognized that the work was continuing a long tradition that existed within Native communities. "There's always been Native women in tribal communities doing this work, but they'd never had the recognition for it. They've always taken women into their homes and given them rides." When they were just beginning the work, Tina, Liz, and Jenny drove to South Dakota to get the advice of one such woman, Karen Artichoker, on the Pine Ridge Reservation, who had dedicated her life to meeting the needs of Native women who had been battered. This was at a time when the church, which had a shelter for battered women on the reservation, and the state were doing everything they could to disrupt the efforts of Native women on Pine Ridge, who had just opened their own shelter. Tina recalled, "It dawned on me the struggles that Native women have [to face], whether you're in an urban community or in a rural community like Pine Ridge." She was moved by Karen Artichoker's commitment to advocating for the women, often driving miles to connect with women, and taking them to the hospital or the shelter. Tina was inspired by the many women who have influenced the work of MSH. "You don't do any of this by yourself," she said. "You do it with other women."

Tina described that early work as "grassroots—from the community." While they did some work with DAIP's National Training Project, MSH's focus was more on direct service. Liz LaPrairie had strong connections at Fond du Lac, which enabled them to work closely with the Fond du Lac band on several projects, including advocacy and systems monitoring.

As part of the work with DAIP, MSH held Native batterers' groups. Rebecca St. George, an advocate with MSH, had worked with men in both the Native batterers' groups and the regular ongoing batterers' groups run by DAIP. Rebecca said that the batterer's curriculum developed by DAIP didn't work for Native men, so MSH adapted the original model to meet its needs. One of the ways the curriculum for Native men's groups was different was that it was grounded in Native history. Rebecca reflected, "One of the things that was easier about working with Native men is that when you talk about battering in our communities, you can generally find a point of origin. You can say, 'It happened when Grandpa went to the boarding school.' Usually . . . that's when the violence in our families started." To Native men who said that wife beating was "natural," the facilitators could identify that point of origin as a powerful counterargument. "Let's talk about a very recent history," said Rebecca, "and how that has led to violence in our communities, and the racism that has twisted our cultural ways."

Rebecca found other differences between working with Native and white men as well. One was the different understanding each had of the term "respect." Native men, she said, tended to understand "respect" in the way that they respect and honor the life of a deer in a hunting culture. (She recognized that this was just before they kill the deer, but the point is that the recognition is for the life-sustaining role that the deer has in their culture.) So, it was easy to use the word "respect" when addressing their attitudes toward women and have that be understood as honoring. "But for the white men," Rebecca explained, "respect is about fear. . . . 'I'm gonna make you respect me.' It's something they used as part of their control."

She also noted significant differences between the two in terms of entitlement: "The white guys had such a massive sense of entitlement," she said, "what the world owes them, and what they get to have and why they get to control these women. The Native men's battering was coming from a different place. It was still about control and ownership, but they had their own oppression to deal with on top of it." In addition, it was easier for MSH advocates to include a spiritual basis in their work with Native men. "Almost every man who came through there understood how the dynamic of the room changed when we smudged before every group," said Rebecca.

MSH had a Native women's advocacy project, a large part of which was monitoring the criminal justice system's response to Native women. Rebecca explained how the system treats Native women differently than it does white women: "It's so much more likely to label [Native women] as 'problems' and 'uncooperative.' 'They're all drunk. They're all angry. They're all violent.' There's two stereotypes of Native people. They're either the noble savage—spiritual, gentle—or they're this horrible drunk and disgusting human being. You can see how that ends up playing out, particularly when . . . people who are battering them are not Native."

Much of MSH's role was to educate people working in the system about how Native women's needs and issues are different from the mainstream, and what approaches were or were not helpful and effective. Additionally, advocacy involved keeping a watchful eye on Child Protective Services, as well as on custody issues. Native women have a long history of losing their children, "starting with boarding schools, and then the foster care system, and then Child Protection, and then batterers being able to take women's children away," Rebecca explained. "You've got a white father saying, 'I'm gonna take my kid away from you if you don't do what I tell you,' and they do, over and over again. If [the fathers] don't, Child Protection will take them. We've been losing our children for generations, and in this system it continues. . . . Those intersections of racism and sexism are so intense."

The work of MSH often involved sorting out complicated jurisdictional matters among the tribal, federal, and state governments. While not a problem locally because Fond du Lac is a Public Law 280 tribe, for many Native women on or near reservations, "jurisdictional problems can . . . make it difficult, if not impossible, for them to have any justice," said Rebecca.[5]

MSH advocated for Native women's issues at the state and federal levels. Of this Tina said, "I talk to tribal chairmen, to U.S. attorneys, and the director of the Violence Against Women office, and to women who are battered and homeless. I think that's what advocacy is. I don't speak for women, but I help to raise their issues. . . . When you start speaking for women, you're no better than their partners. Women can speak for themselves. They've been doing it for years—it's just that people haven't been listening."

An ongoing challenge for MSH is that the work of Native women across the country to end sexual and domestic violence continues to go unrecognized. As they suffer the double invisibility of being both Native and women, their knowledge and wisdom fall on deaf ears. Native women's initiatives and practices go unseen, until said or done by those who hold status and legitimacy, who then receive accolades for their "unprecedented" or "visionary" work, as if no one had thought of this or done this before. As an example, Tina pointed to the 2005 congressional hearings on an Amnesty International report about sexual violence against Native women. This was a bittersweet victory for Tina, who while glad for Amnesty's work expressed frustration that even though Native women had been doing this work for years, Congress didn't pay attention until Amnesty did the report: "Women like myself . . . that have been organizing for twenty years have been saying the same thing, but we can't get any credibility." To be "credible" is "to be worthy of being believed." The credibility given to Amnesty but denied to Native women who had been doing the work added insult to injury. It only perpetuated the message that Native women are not worthy, a message that has contributed to the widespread violence against them.

In doing direct advocacy for Native women locally, MSH tried to maintain respectful boundaries between the role of MSH and the role of Safe Haven Shelter. In her advocacy work at MSH and DAIP, Rebecca had been part of discussions on DAIP's and Safe Haven's separate roles and had often heard things to the effect of, "DAIP's not allowed to do advocacy. That's Safe Haven's job." She added, "I've always tried to be careful to respect what they know, respect what they do, and try to work together." Safe Haven has sent Native and non-Native women who have been arrested for perpetrating violence to MSH. "There's this understanding that over here we're better able to work with women, who, for whatever reason, [strike back]," said Rebecca.

New Role: Training and Technical Assistance Provider

The work of Mending the Sacred Hoop changed substantially after the passage of the Violence Against Women Act (VAWA) in 1994. At this time, the Office of Violence Against Women (OVW) in the U.S. Department of Justice approached MSH to provide technical assistance to fourteen tribes. MSH became the first Training and Technical Assistance (TA) provider to Native women in the country.

The project initially was run out of Minneapolis, with Tina on staff in Duluth, but when the Minneapolis office was not fulfilling its responsibilities, MPDI brought the program back to Duluth, and Tina gathered her own team. Being the first and the main TA provider for tribes in the nation has been a source of pride and accomplishment for MSH. In that role, the organization has helped tribes across the country develop domestic violence programs. "There's a lot more Indian programs, more Indian women doing this than ever before," said Tina. "In 1989 you could count on one hand how many people were doing it, but now in every state there's some sort of program." As a TA provider, MSH consults with OVW tribal grantees, offering assistance, guidance, site visits, in-person and online educational opportunities, and expertise to new programs or programs that are struggling. Because of centuries of colonization, many tribal communities have picked up the dominant culture mentality that blames women for their victimization and have adopted mainstream programs that don't work in Native communities and that focus on short-term measures, such as orders for protection and filing safety plans. MSH focuses on the broader issue of how to change the community in a way that will bring an end to violence against Native women. Oftentimes Tina has found that tribal communities are struggling to address the issue adequately because they frame it in terms of family violence rather than violence against women, and MSH helps them reframe it. "One of our jobs," said Tina, "is to go into a community and focus on what violence is, what it does to a woman's body and spirit, how it breaks down her ability to control her body and then how that manifests in how she parents, how she works, how she perceives herself, how she heals."

MSH uses DAIP's Duluth Model when providing technical assistance. "Part of what's amazing about it," Rebecca said of the Duluth Model, "is its ability to meet different communities' needs." The model involves listening to the community to find out what the needs are, which is especially helpful given the diversity of the tribes with which MSH works. "A tribe in Arizona is so different from a tribe in Washington State, which is so different from a tribal village in Alaska, which is so different from the Fond du Lac band," said Rebecca. Marilu Johnsen, who worked with MSH in its early years, also remarked on these differences: "Tobacco, turtle shells, owls, and so on, may mean something for one tribe and the opposite for other tribes." Rebecca was especially struck by how different the situation of tribes in remote villages in Alaska is from that of tribes in the lower forty-eight states: "There are villages in the interior that saw the first white people thirty years ago. The colonization up there is so recent, and the isolation of some of those villages is like nothing you've ever seen." The law enforcement response MSH has developed for use in the lower forty-eight is unworkable in these Alaskan villages, which often have no local law enforcement, and must rely on state troopers who may be three days away.[6]

Rebecca learned she had to pay attention to the language she used to talk about domestic violence with tribes whose situations were different from what she knew. In response to her questions about whether they had safe houses, the women in the villages often said that they did not, but if she asked what happened if a woman was beat up by her husband, they might say something like, "She goes to Violet's house." As Rebecca explained, "They totally had a safe house, but they did not use that language to describe it." Tina also spoke of interviewing elders in Alaska who had no word for domestic violence. Rather, they talked about domestic violence in terms of relationships and the way they used to be, and about what they had lost. The work of MSH was to listen and learn from the women in the villages, and adapt the response to meet the needs and the resources available.

Wherever they went, the MSH TA providers felt privileged to work with the women in the communities. Tina related a particularly memorable time working with people in a remote Alaskan village: "They invited us to a feast and all the community came. They gave us moose stew and spaghetti. . . . A grandma made fish ice cream. It was such a delicacy. They made it with berries and the blubber of whale. I thought, 'I can't eat fish ice cream,' but we had to be respectful. They served all the ice cream to all the guests first. You could see all these kids just waiting to get a dish of ice cream and they served us first. It was a great sacrifice that they did this [*tearing up*]."

Reflecting on this and her work with so many different tribes, Tina said, "The greatest thing about this work is that you're going into these communities with the focus of educating and training them, and they give you so much more back."

Later Years: 2005–2015

In 2005, Congress reauthorized VAWA with the inclusion of a new provision, Title IX, which Tina described as being "dedicated to the sovereignty and safety of Native women." "That's historical," she said, crediting this unprecedented inclusion of Native women to a decade of Native women's organizing after VAWA was first passed.

The implications for MSH were several. Federal funding rules were changed so that MSH could access TA money only if it was a strictly Native organization, and as long as it was under the umbrella of MPDI, it wasn't. So, in 2006, MSH broke from MPDI and DAIP, and it became a separate nonprofit organization. DAIP retained its Native advocate position, partly because the position was no longer covered by OVW funds, and MSH no longer provided direct local services for Native women. Another significant implication of Title IX was that it allowed MSH to increase significantly its outreach to tribes throughout the United States. Much of MSH's work involves traveling around the country training tribes on domestic violence issues. "If you look at this map, those are all the tribes we've worked with," said Rebecca, pointing to a map that was covered with pins dispersed across the United States. (Rebecca admitted with a smile that the map was not entirely accurate—"sometimes little kids move the pins around.") When MSH began its work as a TA provider, it was the only one in the country. Since the inclusion of Title IX in VAWA, it has been joined by the Tribal Law and Policy Institute in California; the Southwest Center for Law and Policy in Arizona; Red Wind Consulting, Inc., and First Nations Development Institute in Colorado; Institute for Native Justice in Oklahoma; and the Minnesota Indian Women's Sexual Assault Coalition. The number of tribes MSH consults with at any given time fluctuates depending on funding, but MSH has served 172 tribes nationwide, including all eleven tribes in Minnesota. Though that seems like a high number, Tina felt it wasn't enough, considering there are 566 federally recognized tribes in the United States.

Lastly, through Title IX, OVW created a new formula grant, called Tribal Coalitions. Coalitions of agencies that work to end domestic and sexual assault exist in just about every state across the country, including the Virgin Islands and Puerto Rico. However, Native women knew that these state coalitions were not providing adequate representation and services for Native programs and Native women, under the guise that Native programs had their own separate tribal governments. In an effort to promote policy change and resources for tribal communities, Native women organized to obtain funding for tribal coalitions, resulting in the Tribal Coalitions grant program. The grant led to the creation of nineteen tribal coalitions across the country that focus on organizing Native women in different states. These coalitions have enabled tribes to inform one another and work together to overcome barriers to providing safety and training for women, and have created opportunities for more women to attend conferences and to develop skills. "When the coalitions first started, almost all of the women who started new tribal coalitions were women who had come through Mending the Sacred Hoop trainings," said Rebecca. "It was wonderful to see that sort of wave happening from our work."

While its association with the Department of Justice and OVW has brought positive changes to MSH in terms of the significance and scope of its work and in providing regular funding, it has also created some negative implications, such as increased professionalism. Tina remarked that, although professionalism shouldn't necessarily carry negative connotations, a frequent consequence was that women who had been working in the trenches in Native programs for years were being replaced by professionals who had never worked directly with Native women. Professionalization brought a change to the terminology that was used, and changes in language affect the nature of relationships. "They [OVW] call battered women 'clients.' We never called battered women 'clients,'" explained Tina. "You have to provide advocacy to women in a way that upholds their dignity and integrity, not as a 'welfare mom' or a 'client.'" She said such changes have been difficult to navigate. MSH was also required to bring a more professional appearance to its products and presentations in order to meet federal approval, which could potentially compromise MSH's authenticity. "It's a challenge to grow and figure out how to be true to our mission and true to ourselves and keep the money," said Rebecca. Some Native domestic violence agencies refuse to use OVW money for this reason. The MSH staff have had "long, deep, hard discussions" about whether to use OVW funds but, recognizing the importance of the work, have continued to commit themselves to working with OVW, despite the challenges.[7]

MSH's association with OVW required the organization to change its internal structure. As a subsidiary program of MPDI, MSH was part of the collective and continued to maintain a consensus structure even after MPDI changed to a team management structure. OVW required "a point person. 'Take us to your leader,'" said Rebecca. "Tina is the leader," but "she gets mad at me when I refer to her as my 'boss.'"

Wanting to ensure that programming and policies come from the community, not from the top down, Tina was concerned that too much federal direction could lead to advocacy that was based on a dominant culture model of social service, rather than ones that genuinely meet the needs of the community. "Even the fact that we're in relationship with the Department of Justice is like we're sleeping with the enemy," she said.

Having its work so tied to OVW has meant that MSH must adjust to every change in federal administration. During President George W. Bush's two terms, MSH lost funding. "They cut us off for a while because we were being too radical," said Rebecca, "because we were talking about things like 'genocide.'" The Bush administration did not allow MSH to use the word "genocide" in any of its trainings or training materials. Tina also recalled a painful incident during the Bush administration. A coworker from MSH spoke openly at a conference about how MSH's funding had been cut, and she questioned aloud where the money that Congress had mandated for Native programs was, because MSH wasn't getting it. She made the comment that the Bush administration "doesn't like Indians very well."

As a result, MSH funding was frozen, and Tina was called to Washington, DC, where she had to apologize in person to OVW director Diane Stewart and several non-Native program specialists. Tina remembered "walking into a room with all these white people . . . and being real contrite for the things that I'd said." They told her that MSH was only allowed to say "celebratory" things about the Bush administration. They called her on what her staff person had said, and made her promise to exercise greater scrutiny and control over the staff. "I sat there very quiet and I said, 'I understand the issues and I understand my error. . . . I will do my best to insure that my staff and coworkers do not say anything negative.'"

Characterizing herself as "this tiny little woman and this huge institution," she said she felt like David facing Goliath. "I wonder how proud they must be . . . to sit around and have this tiny little Native woman say, 'I'm sorry.'" MSH funding was restored. "I walked out with my dignity and integrity," Tina said. "I did what I had to do. There's a greater purpose down the road." The incident also shed new insight: "Not that I agree with it, but I can understand why tribes had to modify and adapt to dominant culture ways in order to survive, not knowing how it was going to impact their future." She thought having to apologize was small in comparison to the sacrifices that tribes made for survival.

Rebecca was hopeful that Title IX's requirement that all staff of Native domestic violence programs be trained by Native technical assistance providers would help to counteract some of the negative changes under OVW. The staff had watched more and more Indian programs be run by non-Indians with academic credentials and degrees. Degrees had been given priority over "any sort of connection or real understanding of what's going on in your community," said Rebecca, "so for them [OVW] to say we want Indian programs to be trained by real Indians, that's not a bad thing."

In the late 2000s, OVW began putting more emphasis on addressing sexual assault, which it previously had regarded as separate from domestic violence. With this change, MSH put more effort into becoming educated on sexual assault. "The longer we're doing this work, the more we're seeing the need not to put these issues in a silo," said Rebecca. MSH had experienced reluctance on the part of the criminal justice system, and even the Program to Aid Victims of Sexual Assault (PAVSA), to respond to incidents of sexual assault of Native women. So, despite the relatively high numbers of Native women who had been sexually assaulted, Native women often didn't turn to the police or PAVSA due to a lack of trust. After convincing Ellen Pence to train MSH in the institutional audit process she had developed, in 2006 Tina wrote and received a grant for a collaborative project with PAVSA to do a Safety and Accountability Audit of the Duluth Police Department and PAVSA to investigate the response to Native women who had been sexually assaulted. MSH's *Safety and Accountability Audit of the Response to Native Women Who Report Sexual Assault in Duluth* was the first time the audit process had been used specifically to assess the response to incidents of sexual assault.[8]

The audit team, headed by Rebecca St. George of MSH and Sterling Harris of PAVSA, included five Native women, five non-Native women, and representatives from vested agencies. Tina's years of work building relationships with people in the criminal justice system in Duluth,

Cloquet, and St. Louis County facilitated their willingness to make the two-year commitment to be a part of this audit. The team interviewed and observed everyone in the system who worked with victims of sexual assault, from the police chief on down. They held focus groups with more than forty Native women who had suffered sexual assault. Rebecca recognized two-thirds of the women from MSH's work with victims of domestic violence: "The crossover and the sort of misogyny that goes into what happens, particularly to Native women . . . are startling sometimes," she said.

The audit team went on ride-alongs with police and watched how they interacted with victims. According to Rebecca, "The process we went through with the audit was tough on them [the police]. We uncovered a lot of unpleasant things about how they were doing their work." The team reported that Native women who were victims of sexual assault in Duluth felt "brushed aside" by law enforcement and legal systems and did not feel that "there was any justice for them." The audit also found that Native victims were asked questions, such as whether they had been drinking, that came across more as stereotypical Native victim-blaming than as a necessary part of the investigation.[9]

The audit revealed flaws in the criminal justice response and identified seven gaps between the needs of sexually assaulted Native women and how the system responded. Among them was a lack of follow-up with victims once the initial report had been filed. According to Sterling Harris, "One of the things that quickly changed once we found the problem was that every single one of the reports were being followed up on and the women were being called back. . . . It was a small fix, but it had a huge impact."[10]

Deputy police chief Mike Tusken said, "Within the organization you can get into practices and procedures that you think are absolutely tip-top, but when you open it up to people outside law enforcement to come in and question 'Why do you ask a question this way?' you get a different perspective." He said that feedback was invaluable and helped them create more victim-friendly protocols. As a result, officers took more time with victims to explain why they had to ask sensitive questions to prepare cases for trial. The department also worked in conjunction with the county attorney's office, MSH, and PAVSA to develop a checklist of procedures officers should follow in investigating sexual assault and decided to have a sexual assault advocate from PAVSA in the police department.[11]

Rebecca appreciated the fact that the police were willing to work with the audit team as community partners and make necessary changes.

Sterling was impressed with the way the leadership of the police department was "willing to hear negative things about their organization, take a step back and make changes that were going to make life better for Native women that were being hurt in Duluth." In 2012, the Duluth Police Department earned the Community Policing Award from the International Association of Chiefs of Police for its work to improve the response to Native victims of sexual assault. However, the role of MSH in its groundbreaking work on the audit was overlooked. As Tina said: "It was the Duluth Police Department that was given recognition. It mentions our name in passing. That's the standard operating procedure for a lot of things. . . . I wrote the grant; I got it funded; I got the audit team together; I trained them; I was part of the audit team; Rebecca and Sterling were the coordinators; and the Duluth Police Department was recognized for the award."[12]

While Tina acknowledged that she's in this work to improve the lives of Native women, not to receive awards, being rendered invisible was hurtful. The fact that MSH received little to no recognition was just another example of the continual invisibility of the work of women, of Native Americans, and of Native women in particular in this society.

The Safety and Accountability Audit on Native women who had been sexually assaulted was the first to combine the efforts of Native and non-Native programs on a project of that sort. It established a national model for such collaborations. Now state funding and pass-through money from the federal government often require Native and non-Native partnerships, and every state must demonstrate how they are serving Native communities. "The work informs the future," Tina said in reference to the audit. "It changes the language; it changes the scope of the work, and the priority areas."

A significant finding of the audit was the extent to which Native women were being disproportionately affected by trafficking. With Duluth being a port city, Native women have long been trafficked onto the boats in the harbor. The study found that more than 90 percent of Native women who reported sexual assault were involved in prostitution, and because of this their reports of sexual assault were discarded. Since that time, MSH has been working informally on the trafficking of Native women on state and national levels, speaking with state legislators, participating in conferences, and working with tribes around the country.[13]

In response to the audit findings, a Duluth Trafficking Task Force, including members from MSH, PAVSA, and other organizations, was formed, with a special focus on Native American women and girls, who are at the highest risk of being trafficked. A major goal of the task force was to reframe the issue by recognizing prostitution as sex trafficking and as sexual violence against women and a violation of human rights. To this end, the task force has worked to educate the community on trafficking issues and has worked with a variety of agencies to develop a more appropriate response to the needs of trafficking victims. MSH has been working on the issue of Native women who are trafficked on an unfunded and voluntary basis since 2007. In 2014 the Sacred Hoop Coalition, the statewide Tribal Domestic Violence Coalition of which Mending the Sacred Hoop is a part, entered into a collaboration and partnership with the Minnesota Indian Women's Sexual Assault Coalition to provide technical assistance on the trafficking of Native women. MSH also became involved in the Native Sisters Society, which works on the prevention of the trafficking of Native women locally.[14]

The environment for MSH, in general, improved during the administration of Barack Obama. Funding for tribal governments increased, and President Obama visited Native communities to witness their situation firsthand. People in OVW also made more of an effort to witness and learn what is happening in Native communities. OVW director Bea Hanson toured the Bakken oil fields in North Dakota, where violence against women, especially Native women, had increased more than tenfold.

The reauthorization of VAWA in 2013 included a landmark provision in its Title IX that allows tribal governments to prosecute non-Native offenders. Tina again credited its passage to the work of Native women "to bring together stories, going in front of Congress, testifying that this is what our life is like." She said that while it was important not to let Native men off the hook, non-Native men are by far the majority of the perpetrators of violence against Native women, and the assaults by non-Native perpetrators are often trivialized by the criminal justice system. "Non-Native men are extremely brutal. Their violence injures Native women at a higher rate than any other ethnic group." In order to implement this provision, a tribe must provide a public defender, and it must be able to establish that the non-Native offender has some ties to the community through marriage or work, and the judge and prosecutors must have law degrees. Tina viewed President Obama's signing of the VAWA Reauthorization Act as a major indicator of the supportive attitude of the Obama administration toward MSH's work and the needs of Native communities. Among the administration's initiatives was making funding available for changes in Indian Health Services to create protocols for forensic exams. Prior to this, a woman who was sexually assaulted had not been able to get a forensic exam, except on her own, and perhaps hours away.

Being so dependent on the political winds in Washington brings much uncertainty to MSH's work. Tina expressed the insecurity that comes with every change in the political leadership and landscape. "For every ten steps we get forward," she said, "sometimes with a change in administration, we get five steps back." The fate of MSH rests not only on the presidential administration, but also on Congress and the judiciary. "To have your lives in the hands of Congress, the Supreme Court, or the president is pretty scary," said Tina. The people voting on bills that decide MSH's fate are largely ignorant of the conditions of the lives of Native people, and Tina fears that unless they saw the "epidemic proportions of violence against Native women" for themselves, they would not understand the vast need for funding. For example, in Congress's decision to limit the recent VAWA reauthorization to the lower forty-eight states, one lone congressperson from Alaska succeeded in excluding tribes in Alaska from the Title IX provisions that had been celebrated elsewhere in the country.

Over the years, the nature of MSH's work has changed. Because MSH receives many more calls for assistance in dealing with "repeat clients" and women who are dealing with mental health and chemical dependency, MSH has begun to address the root problems in its trainings. Native women often have multiple victimizations. Tina said that a battered woman might be "brought up in an abusive home where the parents are coping with being addicted to either alcohol or drugs because of this trauma [of abuse], and then just pass that on." She noted a hopelessness in some communities, but, not one to focus on that, she has chosen to concentrate on the healing of Native women.

Another change in MSH work is examining other strategies of addressing domestic violence that are not solely focused on criminal justice. "This is based on our years of experience of seeing the criminal justice response, how our women lack credibility when law enforcement arrives to a domestic violence call, and how our women and men are overrepresented in the criminal justice system as perpetrators and yet we are a small percentage of the population," said Tina. Mending the Sacred Hoop is prioritizing creative strategies of providing services and resources to Native women survivors. One such strategy is to provide and train on trauma-informed services and care that offer a holistic approach that engages women in their own healing at a pace and in a way that is more traditional and takes into account the physical, emotional, spiritual, and mental elements of their healing journey as survivors. "Our work has to stay true to learning as much as you can about the issue and the ways in which to solve it, and reaching out and educating communities about women's sacredness," she said.[15]

In November 2013, MSH moved its offices to Gimaajii-Mino-Bimaadizimin, the American Indian urban center that houses the offices of the American Indian Community Housing Organization (AICHO) and other agencies. "We moved our program here from DAIP because we wanted to be around people who were doing the work and to support that work," said Tina. MSH has had a long-standing relationship with AICHO. Members of MSH have served on AICHO's board, and some of the women from AICHO served on the Safety and Accountability Audit team. The organizations frequently share resources and are able to work more closely now that they are in the same building.

MSH continues to train across the country, and for Tina, the work is its greatest reward. "I love the work that I'm doing," she said. "I love meeting people, from the villages of Alaska to some pueblo out in the boonies of New Mexico or some reservation out in Washington. . . . I have a passion for my work and I can't imagine doing anything else."

Conclusion

Artist Sam English created a visual representation of the work of Mending the Sacred Hoop with a depiction of three Native women dancing. "It's these grandmothers that are standing watching us," said Tina. "These three women [are] dancing because we're celebrating the sacredness of women. That's what we keep in our heads when we're doing this work. . . . The reason these women can celebrate is because these grandmothers went before us. We're doing it for them."

The lives of Native women have been and continue to be improved by the work of Mending the Sacred Hoop. Tina has seen evidence of this in things ranging from the disappearance of the word "squaw" from national databases to the changed lives of the women in her own family. She sees the results of the work in the lives of her daughters, who are strong and assertive women. She knows that "if anything happens to their relationships, they can stand and support themselves; they can support their children, and not have to stay in a relationship like my grandmother and my mother and my great-grandmother did because they had no place else to go. . . . That is a legacy . . . for all the women I've served. I don't put a value on that. It's lived."

Rebecca said, "The name Mending the Sacred Hoop comes from a story that Black Elk told about our hoop, that the sacredness of the circle and all that goes into it is broken and we need to mend it." The organization's work has been about mending that sacred circle. Tina has sensed "a renaissance of pride in identity and sovereignty and sacredness," and she feels grateful to be a part of it. Rebecca agreed. Watching her daughter run around the office, she was appreciative of how welcoming and honoring Mending the Sacred Hoop is of womanhood, "to recognize the sacredness of that and to not pretend that it has to be separate from the work we do." As she said, the wonder and sacredness of motherhood, of auntiehood, of womanhood motivates the work they do.

"Our role on Earth is not to gather the most materialistic thing that we can," said Tina. "It is to put back into life. Your legacy is the footprints you leave in the world." The footprints of Mending the Sacred Hoop are of women dancing.

{ 11 }

Aurora: A Northland Lesbian Center

The headline from the May 1991 Aurora newsletter read, "Karen Thompson lost battle to gain custody over her partner, Sharon Kowalski." This landmark Minnesota case was indicative of the times in which Aurora: A Northland Lesbian Center played such a vital role for lesbians in the northland. It was a time when most lesbians could not be out to their friends or families, or even themselves, let alone have the legal right to visit their life partner in the hospital. Aurora was formed with the mission "to increase self-acceptance, self-esteem and positive social identification among lesbians in the northland and promote awareness, education and advocacy regarding lesbian issues in the community at large."[1]

For more than twenty years, Aurora provided a welcoming and safe space and community for lesbians in Duluth and the surrounding area. Through its outreach, education, and community organizing, Aurora contributed to the widespread acceptance of lesbian, gay, bi, and transgender peoples in the region, which led to increased civil rights and eventually the right to marry in the state of Minnesota. So successful were they in their mission that in only a couple of decades, their existence as an organization was no longer necessary.

Origin Story

Women in the lesbian community in Duluth had been talking for quite a while about the need for a lesbian center. An early document detailing this need noted that in the late 1980s, lesbians in the northland had "no visible place for new women to connect with the community; . . . no available place to meet openly other than two bars, and a coffeehouse which operates once monthly; no established means of providing networking, support, or organized outreach for ourselves, and no channel of communication to help those who are questioning their affectional preference; and . . . no concrete means for educating ourselves and the community at large regarding our issues, our oppression, our legitimacy, and our existence."[2]

While the Northcountry Women's Coffeehouse provided cultural events and a once-a-month gathering place for lesbians, it was primarily social and, as Aurora member Deb Anderson noted, "there was a strong stripe in the community that wanted a political entity, that wanted contact, that wanted resources available to people." "Something that women could find in the phonebook," added Dianna Hunter, "and drop-in space, support groups." So on March 9, 1988, a group of lesbians met as the Task Force for the Lesbian Center to develop plans for such an organization and space.

As the story goes, task force member Randi Freesol, then the secretary for the Women's Studies Department at the University of Minnesota Duluth, needed to write a grant for a class assignment, so she wrote a grant to fund the formation of a lesbian center in Duluth. To everyone's surprise, the task force received the grant, which enabled them to go forward and form a 501(c)(3) nonprofit. (The document was obviously drafted from the Coffeehouse incorporation papers, as "Coffeehouse" is crossed off in several places. The Coffeehouse papers were based on the incorporation papers for the Northcountry Women's Center—and so the legacy continued.) On November 17, 1988, the Elsie Center, as it was legally named at that time, was incorporated by task force members Ann Richtman (attorney) and JoDei Marcella, Linda Estel, Suzanne Steinbeigle, Trish O'Keefe, Diane R., and Lee P.[3]

Early Years

The group rented space in the Temple Opera Building in downtown Duluth. They had two rooms, one for office space and one where people could hang out. Lee Hemming recalled the excitement when it first opened. It was "old and a bit musty," Linda Estel remembered, "but with plenty of character." The group concentrated on programming. Within a few months, it established support and discussion groups, developed a mailing list, sent out a monthly calendar of events, held gatherings, and conducted trainings on homophobia, lesbian battering, and legal rights.[4]

The name "Elsie"—code for "LC," meaning "lesbian center"—was commonly used by lesbian centers around the country. "Lesbian Center," or "L.C.," could be communicated covertly by using the common name

"Elsie." The incorporators and board soon decided that the Duluth center needed a more distinctive name, so they formally amended it to Aurora: A Northland Lesbian Center in the spring of 1989. Members hotly debated whether to include the word "lesbian" in the name, because it would effectively out anyone visibly affiliated with it. As Deb said, "There were people like me who said, 'There is no way that I can be affiliated with something with lesbian in its name because I'll lose my job.' And I would have." Trish O'Keefe remembered that they didn't want to deter women "who aren't comfortable being associated with an organization that has the word 'lesbian' in the name," and at the same time they wanted people to "know who we are; otherwise, how are lesbians going to find us? . . . People felt strongly both ways." Although they eventually settled on Aurora: A Northland Lesbian Center, most knew it simply as Aurora.

Many lesbian and feminist organizations at the time were reclaiming names of goddesses and mythic figures as the names of organizations and enterprises, such as Artemis Productions, Pleiades Records, and Demeter Publishing. Aurora was the name of the Roman goddess of the dawn, and the women of the center saw their organization as the dawning of a new era. As was explained in Aurora's first newsletter: "Aurora is Aurora Borealis, the northern lights which can easily be seen from here. . . . Being a northland organization, the association is pleasing to the Task Force. Whether because of the association with the colorful lights that sometimes light the northern sky, or the image of the rising sun so vividly present to us every morning over Lake Superior, or the ideas of rebirth and renewal we find behind the goddess, we feel her name is appropriate to what we hope to be the dawning of a new age for lesbians in Northern Minnesota and Wisconsin."

That first year Aurora hired a paid staff person, Betty Hupperich, and with her work and the help of many volunteers—who did everything from advocacy and facilitating support groups to providing childcare, doing office work, and working on the newsletter—Aurora accomplished much. Grants from the Minnesota Women's Foundation, the Chicago Resource Center, and the Philanthrofund Foundation enabled Aurora to sponsor workshops and forums and to participate in community and university events, including cosponsoring lesbian comedian Chris Cinque's performance of "Growing Up Queer in America." Aurora established an Adult Daughters of Alcoholics Group, as well as over-thirty-five, mothers, and spirituality discussion groups; printed and distributed brochures; and marched behind an AURORA banner at the Gay/Lesbian Pride march in Minneapolis.[5]

With an initial mailing list of close to two hundred names, the Aurora newsletter was intended "to provide lesbians with information on AURORA events, programs and services; to open a dialogue between the task force and the lesbian community, as well as within the lesbian community itself; and to provide pertinent information on lesbian issues locally, nationally and globally." Aurora also provided resources and publications about lesbians. Rose Frye, a librarian with the Duluth Public Library, was well positioned to provide resources to the lesbian community. Because she had the ability to order books for the Duluth Public Library, she was largely responsible for supplying Duluth with information on lesbians. Moreover, "when she culled collections [at the library], she would channel books to people she knew needed books," said Deb. "She was truly fulfilling her professional role. She was incredibly brave in those years."⁶

In 1990, the task force formalized Aurora's structure. It established bylaws and formed five standing committees: financial management, fundraising, community education, public relations, and board development. Anyone who ascribed to the mission and purpose of Aurora and who contributed to the organization either financially or with volunteer time was considered a member. A small handwritten note on the initial bylaws indicated: "Men can be non-voting members," with "non-voting" underscored twice. The group chose its first board of directors at a meeting of the lesbian community in November 1990.⁷

At a time when it was not safe for lesbians to be out, Aurora made the bold decision to invite the *Duluth News-Tribune* to do a story on the center. Betty Hupperich and Linda Estel talked about how members of Aurora were always concerned about their safety, but they had decided it was time to be more visible. "Fear is something that we live with all the time," said Linda. "That is the oppression we feel. We are doing things anyway."⁸

Northern Lights Womyn's Music Festival

Women's music festivals were well established around the country by the time Aurora began, and Aurora members Pat K. and Kat S. envisioned "a field full of womyn with music, dancing, socializing, and just feeling safe" in the northland. That vision became the Northern Lights Womyn's Music Festival. Pat and Kat volunteered the use of their land about thirty miles north of Duluth, and women from Aurora and the Northcountry Women's Coffeehouse volunteered to cut trees and clear the land for the festival. With musicians Ann Reed and Ruth MacKenzie headlining and a few hundred women in attendance, the first Northern Lights Womyn's Music Festival, held in September 1990, was deemed a "huge success." As a member of the festival committee wrote in Aurora's newsletter: "The first annual Northern Lights Womyn's Music Festival will always stand out in my mind as a tribute to our community. . . . Words of support and goodwill given to the committee gave us the courage to go on despite what came to be overwhelming odds. All the women that came early the day of the festival fell into work alongside the committee . . . simply finding out what needed to be done and doing it!" It was an event that brought the community together and seemed to bring out the best in everyone.[9]

The annual festival, which attracted a broad cross-section of women, was an important event for the regional lesbian community, and it became a major fundraiser for Aurora. It eventually became a two-day event, and camping was allowed on the property. Among the performers over the years were Heather Bishop, Faith Nolan, Alix Dobkin, and Buffalo Gals, as well as several local performers. Advertised as a "woman-only" festival, the perennial question of who qualified as a woman inevitably arose. It was the consensus of those attending the first festival's wrap-up meeting that "a woman does not have to be a woman at birth to attend the festival; transgender women are welcome."[10]

Pat and Kat called the festivals a "thrill . . . as our field fills with wonderful womyn, sharing a day of music, fun and laughter on our land." However, after five years, they were ready to be "festival free." "Once Kat and Pat decided not to do the women's festival on their land anymore, a big piece of glue for the organization went away," remembered Laura Stolle Hesselton. Searching for a new venue brought out divisions in the board. Some wanted to hold the festival in Grand Rapids, eighty miles from Duluth; others thought that was too far and, as a more conservative community, potentially unsafe. These discussions caused deeper divisions surrounding issues of trust and classism to surface, and some board members felt silenced and unheard. The festival was not held in 1995 but returned for a short time in later years on land owned by members of the Women's Action Group, with campsites available on Betty and Lee's land.[11]

A Watershed Year for Aurora: 1994–1995

The years 1994 and 1995 saw major turning points for Aurora, with changes in staff, location, mission, and the music festival. Coordinator Betty Hupperich, who as the public spokesperson for Aurora had done so much to educate people in the larger community about homophobia, stepped down. Laura Stolle (now Hesselton) was hired as the new coordinator in June 1994. She recalled, "When I arrived in town and had my first meeting with the board, they told me they had run out of money and they couldn't pay me!" Having moved to Duluth for this job, she had "a little moment of crisis," but she thought the women in Aurora were "so amazing" that she didn't want to pass up the opportunity to work for them. She made a contract with the board whereby she would work without pay until they got the funding to pay her back. Aurora had always received funding from the Minnesota Women's Fund. However, nobody had submitted the grant application, so Laura's first job was to write the grant to fund her position, which, fortunately, Aurora received.[12]

After three years in the Temple Opera Building, Aurora had moved its offices to the Damiano Center, where it shared a community room with the Women's Action Group (WAG), and Aurora developed a strong relationship with WAG. (See Chapter 5: Domestic Abuse Intervention Project and Praxis International.) Some WAG members served on the Aurora board, and four WAG members hosted the re-birthed music festival on their land. Laura loved sharing space with WAG. "They were super, on-fire women," she recalled. So it was with some disappointment that she learned, shortly after starting work there, that Aurora had made a commitment to move its office to the Building for Women in the coming year—a decision that would prove to be very controversial.

The Aurora board had made an informal agreement to move into the Building, but the move stalled because so many Aurora members were opposed to it. As reported in the Aurora newsletter, "every board member feels connections at Damiano with other organizations who work in interest of women and children. . . . With a greater representation of low income women on the board, there is a natural alliance with Damiano." Staff turnover and financial problems further complicated making a move at that time. In June 1994, the Aurora board temporarily reneged on its agreement to move Aurora to the Building for Women, but did not rule out that possibility in the future.[13]

The board remained deeply divided over the issue of the move, and the discussion did not end there, as several heated board meetings about the move ensued. Class considerations drove some of the opposition to the move. Some board members felt that the Building would not feel welcoming to poor and working-class lesbians, that it would feel, in Laura's words, "too 'social worky,' or too fancy." Supporters of the move argued that, in addition to being supportive of the organizations and the intent of the Building itself, the location would also be more secure. The office in Damiano had been broken into twice, which was of particular concern since the membership of Aurora was confidential. They also argued that the Building would provide increased accessibility, safety, longer open hours, availability of office equipment and meeting spaces, and solidarity and networking opportunities with other women's organizations. For Aurora members who had separatist leanings, or at least wanted to be in women-only space, the fact that it was a building *for women* was also appealing. After months of discussion, the board made the consensus decision, with one or two members standing aside, to move to the Building for Women. At least one board member resigned over the decision.[14]

Laura had mixed feelings about the new space. "It was more isolating because we were down in the basement, and there weren't other offices down there at the time," she recalled, but she acknowledged that there was "a lot more support. The women who put together the Building for Women were right there." She could go upstairs to solicit their opinions on various issues, but still remain tied to the low-income women from WAG she had met in her first few months at Damiano. "Being part of the community of the Building for Women was significant," said Laura.

The move to the Building made financial sense for Aurora because of the incubator space the Building offered for new and fiscally unstable organizations. The agreement was they could rent space at reduced cost for two years, and then would need to find a different location. As it turned out, Aurora was never asked to move and remained in the Building for Women for its duration.[15]

Many saw the move as part of a positive rebirth of Aurora, but this rebirth did not come without labor pains. With the concerns about classism that arose with the move and the discussions about relocating the music festival later that year, the board brought in trained facilitators to help identify key issues that were causing rifts and feelings of being silenced between board members, and to help build back trust within the board. The facilitators noted how well the board members listened to each other, and the sincere attention and desire shown, and they made several suggestions for further work. It's not clear if board members ever followed through on this, as other issues soon diverted their attention, including an impending fiscal crisis.[16]

Financially, 1995 was a difficult year for Aurora. The Northern Lights Womyn's Music Festival—a significant source of funds—had been cancelled. Aurora also suffered when a woman who had been hired to do the books disappeared with all their papers. Over the years, Aurora received substantial grants from the Minnesota Women's Fund, the Minneapolis Foundation Gay and Lesbian Funding Partnership, RESIST, and

Philanthrofund, but it relied primarily on donations and optional dues from members to stay afloat. In the December 1995 newsletter, the board made a plea for additional donations from Aurora supporters, noting that the organization barely had enough money to pay its bills. Paid staff hours had to be reduced from fifteen to five hours per week. Within a year or two, Aurora could no longer afford even a five-hour-a-week staff person, and it became an all-volunteer organization.

The board and membership were also grappling with the changing mission of Aurora. Although it began as a center to provide space, support, and resources for lesbian women, the question of the inclusion of bisexual and transgender women in the mission statement increasingly became a topic of debate. Many felt that to include people who were making a male-to-female transition "would threaten their sense of safe space," as Laura put it, and insisted that Aurora was to be only for women-born-women. Others felt equally strongly that it was important to respect all those who in any way self-identified as lesbian, and that bi and transgender women should be included. In December 1994, the board approved including bi and transgender women and spent 1995 drafting a new mission statement. The final version stated: "As lesbian/bi/trans women, our society denies us the safe expression of sexual identity that is our basic right. Aurora: A Northland Lesbian Center exists to ensure that this expression is valued within all areas of our society—at work, at school, at home, at play—without the negative consequences historically enforced upon us." Aurora's mission would change at least twice more over the years, to include working to eliminate not only heterosexism and homophobia but also other forms of discrimination, such as classism, sexism, racism, ageism, and ableism. The inclusion of trans women was never again an issue.[17]

Aurora did, however, resist efforts to connect with the Northland Gay Men's Center. "There was kind of a separatist vibe where people didn't want to work or talk to anybody at the Gay Men's Center," Laura recalled. "I was making the case that we can have separatist time and space, and we also can benefit from working with our brothers, but . . . some people were never going to do that."

1995–2002: An Active and Flourishing Community Resource

Throughout all these changes, Aurora consistently provided resources, support, programming, and education to the community. The center offered books, magazines, and newspapers of interest to the LGBT community. Laura remembered how excited people would be when they found just the book they wanted to read. Trish O'Keefe remembered the center as "that sweet little space with the library," and Sue Maki remembered it as "a place to sit and come and hang out."

Aurora operated a drop-in and call center and provided information and referrals about local LGBT-friendly medical, legal, counseling, parenting, and social resources. People would call looking for bars and other places to meet other lesbians. Sue, who voluntarily staffed the office for about ten years, remembered getting calls from people looking for LGBT-friendly establishments, from restaurants to B&Bs. "My famous phrase was, 'We were there for the people who didn't know we existed,'" she said. "They were looking for some kind of connection, for community, and there we were." Having a lesbian center at that time opened up the world for a lot of women and gave them a way to connect with each other and be in spaces where they could thrive. This was evident in member responses to a 1996 survey question about what they liked about Aurora: "It's critical for the specific and general community." "I know how much it meant to me when I was new to the area. To have a place like Aurora to go to learn about our community & meet people." "Warms those Minnesota nights for me."[18]

People sought out Aurora to deal with their questions and confusion. In an e-mail featuring the subject line "Confused," a twenty-three-year-old woman wrote: "I am terribly confused with my sexuality, although I am certain that I am gay . . . and actually just came out to my mom this weekend. I work at a church here and everything is so complicated, and I just need some kind of advice, although I am not sure what I am asking for." Aurora sent a detailed response with advice, resources, and support.[19]

Despite the early controversies, Aurora provided support for transgender people as well. Laura remembered, "My friend who did a whole medical social gender transition had gone to the Lesbian Center in Duluth and had talked to someone there (probably me). . . . [She was] so excited that a transgender person could come into Aurora."

Occasionally people expressed frustrations that Aurora was not as welcoming as it might be. Some respondents to the 1996 survey wrote about how they felt that Aurora was cliquish and elitist: "I have heard comments regarding a less than warm/open welcome to new and not so new lesbians." "It is invisible! Except to a small select group of women." Unfortunately, as is often the case in small, tight-knit communities, long-time members tend to cluster together, making it difficult for newcomers and outsiders to feel the same sense of belonging. Though Aurora did make efforts to reach out to the community, it was not always successful. But for many, Aurora provided a place of welcome and support to women at critical times in their lives.

Aurora offered a range of services for gay, bisexual, and transgender women. It ran support groups on spirituality, parenting, and bi issues, and hosted a book club. Sue co-facilitated a coming-out group with Marj Carol for a number of years. For a while Aurora sponsored a twelve-step program for women wanting to lose weight. They had social events, game nights, and holiday parties. Aurora also answered the phone for Together for Youth, a resource and support organization for LGBT teens. Laura remembered having conversations with teenagers from the Iron Range who felt isolated and some of whom were suicidal. Laura assured them that there were other teens who felt the same, and she encouraged them to come to a Together for Youth meeting. She said Aurora provided a lifeline to teens dealing with homophobia.

Deb and Dianna recalled fondly the potlucks for lesbians over thirty-five. Some of the older women did not feel entirely welcome at the Coffeehouse, which was the main place lesbians came to socialize and which was run by mostly younger women, and Aurora's potlucks gave them an alternative where they could feel comfortable. "They didn't want any alcohol; they didn't want rowdiness; they didn't want youth and vigor," said Deb, laughing. "They just wanted people who would come and have nice food and nice conversation." Laura, who was too young to go to the over-thirty-five potlucks, remarked that she was jealous, saying the potlucks were "the place to go to find your sweetie."

Once or twice a year, Aurora held meetings for the larger lesbian community of the Twin Ports, usually at Chester Creek House. "It was hard to get business done because everybody wanted to visit so much," remembered Laura. "To me, that was fine, because that was a good business to have." Throughout its existence, Aurora put out its monthly newsletter, the *Aurora Borealis*, which included a calendar of events and was the key source of information and connection for LGBT women in the Twin Ports and beyond. Though a great thing for the community, the newsletter was a chore for staff and volunteers, because so few people contributed. Caroline Pelzel, who was in charge of the newsletter in later years, was often the only person willing to write front-page stories. Volunteers got together to help fold and mail the more than four hundred copies. Financing the newsletter was often difficult as well, but some members made significant contributions that helped keep it going.

Preserving the confidentiality of the mailing list and the mailings themselves was an important issue. Aurora received an angry letter from one recipient who lived in a small town and was upset about being outed by the newsletter because "Aurora: A Lesbian Center" was printed on the return address. The letter said in part, "Just because you have relative anonymity and acceptance in Duluth/Superior, doesn't mean we do in more rural areas. . . . I greatly resent your just sloppily doing it [outing] for me and others. . . . Get it together. Have some consciousness." Despite such challenges, the newsletter was a lifeline for many people in the LGBT community, especially those living in more isolated, rural areas. In a letter expressing her appreciation for the newsletter, one woman wrote: "I would like to thank you for all of your work, your energy, your inspiration. . . . My partner and I live in Ely, Minnesota. . . . I appreciate your presence. . . . Aurora is my people. . . . I feel a connection to the community. I belong. I can truly be myself with you. I appreciate not only that, but also that you folks who are more involved are out there for me. You're pulling for me. You're giving your time and energy to me and to us."[20]

Aurora did a lot of work toward furthering acceptance of lesbians and gays in the larger community. Through its Speaker's Bureau, individuals would speak on LGBT issues to businesses, high school and college classes, churches, and other organizations. "I went to so many community groups and college classes, by myself or with other volunteers, to do panels, so people could see gay people and talk to us," said Laura.

Laura recalled attending an educational town hall meeting about tolerance set up by one of the television stations. "I remember going there wearing my big pink dress, because I was trying to code-up as straight enough to be a credible lesbian," she recalled with a laugh. "I stood up and said something about how important it is for people to know that their loved ones, neighbors, friends, and co-workers are gay. They might think they didn't know anyone who was gay, but we're all here." In the 1970s, the Northcountry Women's Center had begun an effort to establish a Human Rights ordinance in the city of Duluth, and that effort was still going on when Aurora was established. Members of Aurora were a visible presence at hearings about the ordinance, which made them vulnerable to threats, harassment, and physical harm. Laura remembered "being scared" attending the hearings, particularly after someone called out, "I call for the public execution of all gays, including the ones in this room tonight." The passage of the Human Rights Ordinance in 2002 was due in large part to Aurora's work in the community.

Aurora did a lot with very little. As an all-volunteer organization, it constantly needed more people to do the work. Sue, who almost singlehandedly kept the office open, described the difficulty of "getting people to serve on the board; getting bodies to help with things; finding people willing to volunteer, to participate, to be part of the community." Every newsletter had a blurb entitled "Volunteers Needed."

Even though few people stepped up to volunteer, many used Aurora's resources. A 1996 survey of Aurora's membership indicated that all thirty-two respondents utilized the newsletter and monthly calendar of events and two-thirds attended social and cultural events hosted by Aurora. Data from 1997–98 showed that Aurora received more than six hundred phone calls from people seeking information and assistance, and more than two hundred individuals used the drop-in center. The center provided key services, support, and camaraderie for the LGBT community, as well as education and resources for the community at large.[21]

Final Years

By the 2000s, the very nature of Aurora was challenged by the emergence of a more broadly defined queer community. Many of the younger people joining Aurora identified more with being queer than with being lesbian and wanted to change the name of the organization and the newsletter. Caroline recalled that the young people wondered, "What does 'Aurora Borealis' mean? How does that relate to being GLBT?" In 2002 the Aurora board voted to change the name of the organization to the Queer Action Resource Center. However, many of the older members didn't like it, and the name change lasted only a few months. "It hurt us to try to change the name," Caroline reflected. "It hurt people's hearts, so their commitment to donating money [and] . . . to being present for Aurora functions decreased."[22]

As Aurora's early separatist leanings gave way to queer culture, more efforts were made to collaborate with the Gay Men's Center. The two organizations had worked on Pride together, and in 2001, some members of Aurora developed a formal proposal that the LGBT organizations in the Twin Ports and the Arrowhead Region—Twin Ports GLBT Pride, Word of Mouth, Out, Up North, the Northland Gay Men's Center, and Aurora—come together to form an umbrella organization. These efforts were not welcomed by others, however, especially those outside of Duluth. Over the next several years, the possibility of merging with the Gay Men's Center was often discussed, primarily for purposes of sharing expenses. The two groups hosted joint social events—brats and pool, game nights—and eventually the Gay Men's Center moved into the office across from Aurora in the Building for Women, but the two groups never formally merged. "Aurora was pretty determined not to do that," said Sue. "It's nice to combine resources when resources get thin, but we wanted to maintain our autonomy and our own sense of who we were and what we did."[23]

An emerging queer culture and greater acceptance of the queer community by the larger society contributed to waning interest in Aurora. Membership and donations declined; fewer people volunteered; and not as many people used the resource center. Seeing the dire straits in which Aurora found itself, Caroline and a few others stepped up to revitalize Aurora. Younger people, including some from Together for Youth, became more involved. Occasionally they got interns from local colleges to help with operations. "We did what we could to make sure Aurora kept going," said Caroline. Annual community meetings revolved around challenges facing the organization: the lack of board members, a failure to reach a quorum at monthly meetings, the shortage of funds, and general waning interest. Aurora also lost energy after a few key members and strong advocates died.[24]

For a short time, Aurora and the Northcountry Women's Coffeehouse, which had many overlapping memberships and had collaborated on the Northern Lights Womyn's Music Festival, considered forming an umbrella organization as a way to keep both organizations going. They already shared space and had decided to combine their mailings to save money. However, most people wanted to keep the two organizations separate, because the two organizations had separate identities and purposes. They didn't want to contribute to the growing confusion over which was which. In 2007, Aurora board members identified a rift between older lesbians who had been involved with the center since its formation and younger queer and lesbian-identified women who were not involved. In response, Aurora collaborated with the Coffeehouse in intergenerational potlucks and conversations, for "Dyklings, Dykosaurs, and Queergrrrls," as the Coffeehouse flyer said. The conversations, while contributing to deeper understanding among the generations, did not serve to bring the generations together or spark interest in Aurora among younger members of the LGBT community.

As fewer people attended community meetings, Aurora slowly ground to a halt. The organization stopped paying rent sometime in 2010, and other outstanding bills went into default. Aurora closed its doors permanently in the summer of 2012. Laura, who had put so much of her life into Aurora, said, "Sometimes I mourn the passing of things that helped connect lesbian, bi, and trans women . . . but now people have other social structures that have replaced that. The anti-homophobic pressure is better now than it used to be. It feels less physically dangerous in most cases." Sue responded to the end of Aurora by saying, "It served its purpose. We don't need to be hiding in the closet anymore. . . . Things have evolved."

Conclusion

Given the widespread acceptance and inclusion of lesbians in the culture at large, the need for an organization like Aurora no longer exists. However, the impact that Aurora had on the lives of those who came to it for information, resources, and support in a previous era is immeasurable. "People's lives were so changed because Aurora was there for them when they needed it," said Laura. Aurora helped many people gain confidence in coming to terms with their sexual identities and in their coming-out process. "People who felt they had to keep a big secret about being lesbian from their family could come to the support group or to the office and have this expansion of their life," continued Laura. Meeting people who were like them helped lesbians overcome feelings of being alone and different and gave them the confidence to be themselves out in the world. As Sue said, "Aurora was a charging port for people to gain strength and go out into the community and be who we are."

For many, the relationships formed through the organization lasted far beyond their days at Aurora. Women who were otherwise isolated and closeted found friends and partners. "It was a good opportunity to connect with people like myself, and people who were not like myself," said Sue. "It changed my life completely in my coming out. I met my partner—a couple of them—there. I met lifelong friends there." Laura added, "It was connecting people with each other—to do feminist work, or their work, or just have a good life."

Due to its outreach and education, its work to include gay rights in the Duluth Human Rights Ordinance, its visible presence in the community, and most significantly, its support that enabled lesbians confidently to be out and actively involved in the community, Aurora played a significant role in fostering a climate that is more accepting of LGBT people in the larger community. As Laura said, "Aurora changed the world." The dawning of the new age they had envisioned had arisen to the full light of day.

{ 12 }

American Indian Community
Housing Organization

T he area around the Great Lakes, from Minnesota to Wisconsin, Michigan, and Canada—where the food grows on the water—is the home of the Anishinaabe. Almost entirely, the Anishinaabe have been displaced from their original homes through colonization. Colonization also brought the social acceptability of violence toward women that before contact would have been unheard of and abhorrent in Anishinaabe culture. Fleeing violence and domestic abuse, and finding themselves and their children without homes, has been part of the legacy of colonization affecting many Native women in Duluth and the surrounding area. Yet when Native women sought shelter with mainstream organizations that provided services for women leaving abusive situations, they still did not find "home," a place that provided shelter and support that was sensitive to their cultural practices and beliefs.[1]

For more than twenty years, the American Indian Community Housing Organization (AICHO) has provided for these needs. The organization operates with the philosophy that "every American Indian woman and child deserves to live in a safe, non-threatening environment and should be treated with dignity and respect." AICHO has grown from a transitional housing program for Native women to a multifaceted organization offering not only housing but also a Native American cultural center for the entire community.[2]

Origin Story

Like so many of the organizations in this book, the idea for AICHO began with women talking with one another. Victoria Ybanez, the program coordinator at Women's Transitional Housing, Toni Sheehy, the director of the Minnesota Clients' Council, and Mary Ann Walt, of the Minnesota

Council of Churches, had numerous conversations about the challenges battered women who were Native had in finding a shelter where they felt comfortable. "We kept saying, 'We should create our own,'" Victoria recalled. In 1993, when the three once again found themselves at a conference together having the same conversation, they decided it was time to stop talking and do something about it.[3]

They held a gathering of people in the area who worked with large populations of Native women. Victoria recalled, "Mary Ann, Toni, and I dug into our pocketbooks and pulled together the resources to put together a feast." About thirty, primarily Native, women attended. After an opening prayer, they began a conversation about what the needs were for Native victims of domestic violence and those who were homeless in the Duluth area. "Everybody thought there's a lot of Native victims that are falling through the gaps," said Victoria, but they lacked the evidence to document it. "When we looked at community data, Native people were practically nonexistent or invisible, so there wasn't any solid data to say, 'This is the number of homeless we have. This is the number of Native victims of domestic violence.'"

With a grant from the Minneapolis Foundation, the three developed their own needs-assessment survey, gathering input on what people saw as the needs, what would be helpful in meeting those needs, and what a Native-specific response to those needs might look like. They administered the survey at Women's Transitional Housing, the Women's Coalition, Wren House (a chemical dependency halfway house), the WIC (Women, Infants, and Children) clinic, and events attended by large numbers of Native people. They also surveyed community practitioners in social service agencies that served large populations of Native women and reached out to people at the Fond du Lac treatment center and the Center for American Indian Resources (CAIR). The assessment became the foundation of all the work they would do.

In 1994, AICHO officially became a 501(c)(3) nonprofit organization. The intent in creating AICHO was both to provide services and "to build people's capacity to provide their own services," said Victoria. "We were working with those that were most disenfranchised, but doing it in a way that was fostering leadership from within."

Early Years

For the first couple of years, AICHO had no staff, but rather was run by an active working board. The first board included Toni, Mary Ann, and Victoria, as well as Karen Diver from Fond du Lac, a woman from Grand Portage, and Lucille and Don Goodwin from White Earth. The decision to include Don came only after a long discussion about what it meant to have men involved in AICHO. Victoria, who had come from strong feminist organizations, recalled struggling with the idea of including a man on the board, but ultimately decided with the others that "in our community, having a community that was responsive in a balanced approach, we needed to be including our men." However, the board was clear that because AICHO was focused on issues of domestic violence against women, men could be involved in policy decisions only, not in shaping the space and programming for the women. Victoria came to value having Don on the board and appreciated the "solid cultural beliefs" he brought to their conversations and decisions.

In 1994, when AICHO received its first round of funding, Victoria resigned from the board so she could be hired to do development for the organization. Board member Karen Diver described Victoria as "entrepreneurial and such an incredible woman, and so incredibly capable. She carried a ton of water. She called people out on their institutional racism, and their bias, and their differing expectations of us than other groups." Victoria appreciated her working relationship with the board. Karen said, "We had her back, and she called upon us if necessary. . . . We were all in it together."

When AICHO began its search for an executive director in 1996, Victoria was still working full-time at Women's Trans and doing development for AICHO on the side. Victoria recalled, "Mary Ann Walt showed up at my office at Women's Trans one day, shut my door, and said, 'Tell me three reasons why you're not applying for this job.' I said, 'I love my job. I love my job. I love my job.'" But by the time Mary Ann left, she had convinced Victoria to apply, and Victoria was hired as the executive director of AICHO in May 1996. Lucille Goodwin was already on staff as the director of Oshki, AICHO's first transitional housing program that had opened in April of that year. Liz LaPrairie was hired two years later. As executive director, Victoria continued to work closely with the board and encouraged Lucille and Liz to come to board meetings. Although Victoria had the ultimate authority, she would consult with Lucille and Liz on decisions and did what she could to encourage their involvement. "I worked at educating them about their voice, their responsibility to shape and guide their work, and . . . fostering their own leadership and ability to make decisions, to get people to take ownership for shaping and defining the Indian community in Duluth," she said.

Karen valued "seeing grassroots Indian women find their voice," but in mentoring them, she taught them to develop a range of tools and good advocacy skills. "The flip side of grassroots organizing and empowerment is you give people their voice, [and] they tend to shout first," she explained. "Then you teach them to moderate it and develop other tools in the toolbox. We're not going to get stuck in the '70s. Everything's not going be a protest."

The philosophy that informed AICHO was to treat everyone as a peer and with respect, and to recognize the leadership and authority within each person. This had implications not only for the way the AICHO staff interacted with the people they served, but also for the way the AICHO staff members themselves were treated. "You work in a way that also empowers and liberates your staff, not just those that you're working with," said Victoria. When she started as director, Victoria negotiated a salary for herself that was comparable to that of directors of male-led nonprofits in the area. She also made sure that the staff's wages and benefits reflected an appreciation for their dignity and worth, and enabled them to care for themselves, given the intense nature of the work and the vicarious trauma and compassion fatigue they were likely to experience. "It was key for me to know that they had living wages, so that they were not on the edge of poverty while working with people in poverty," said Victoria.[4]

Creating Shelter and Programming

The assessment survey conducted by AICHO showed an urgent need for transitional housing for Native women coming out of abusive relationships, so AICHO quickly acted to create a transitional housing program, Oshki Odaadiziwini Waakan 'Igan, meaning, "a place where we dream of new beginnings" in Ojibwe. Because AICHO wanted to have a large presence in the parts of Duluth where the Native population was most concentrated, they looked for property for Oshki in the city's Central Hillside neighborhood. With support from the Ordean Foundation, the Minnesota Housing Finance Agency, Fond du Lac Reservation, and others, AICHO purchased and rehabbed two houses at 419 and 421 North First Avenue West for $15,000 each. The decision to acquire the property from the slumlord who owned it was a bit anguished. A few years earlier, two Native men had died in a fire there as a result of building code violations. "We had a difficult conversation about whether or not we'd give money to this man," recalled Victoria. As much as they didn't want him to profit off of Indian people, AICHO thought it better to take the property out of his hands and make it safe for Indian people. The board and staff of AICHO, along with their attorney Bill Burns, worked out a satisfactory purchase agreement and were eager to begin renovations on the property. But the controversies were only just beginning.

Shortly after the purchase, the city building inspector's office notified AICHO that the buildings had 118 code violations, and if the buildings were not up to code within thirty days, they would be shut down. After consulting with AICHO's board, Victoria presented to the building inspector's office a plan to address any potentially life-threatening violations within ninety days, with the rest to be completed soon thereafter. After laying out the plan, Victoria told the inspector, "If you can't accept this plan, then I'm going to have to take it to the media for us to discuss how it could be that I purchased a property that was a rental property under your watch and [you] have allowed it to get to this point of 118 code violations." The building inspector's office backed off, accepted AICHO's plan, and thereafter worked in cooperation with AICHO on the project. "That was a major coup for us," said Victoria, "to be able to exert some authority in addressing housing and safety for Indian people."

However, new struggles arose within the neighborhood. The newly acquired property was filled with garbage and debris. As part of its commitment to spend money within the Indian community, AICHO hired some Native men from Thunderbird Halfway House to help with the cleanup. Neighbors assumed the men were stealing things from the property and called the police. Victoria had to run intervention with the police, but this ultimately led to AICHO building a relationship with the community police station and leading the community block watch.

Some non-Native neighbors organized and wrote letters opposing AICHO's efforts to build transitional housing for Native women in the neighborhood. "It was that whole attitude around 'not in my backyard,'" said Victoria. One complaint was that the neighborhood residents had not been consulted beforehand. In fact, early on, AICHO had put flyers out all over the neighborhood inviting people to meet with them to discuss Indian housing issues and the properties they were considering, but no one took interest until AICHO had actually acquired the property. Leaders of the Central Hillside Community Club and the Central Hillside Neighborhood Coalition also expressed concerns about increasing crime in the neighborhood and explained that keeping AICHO and other low-income housing projects out was part of their effort to attract more middle-income families "to stabilize the neighborhood." Victoria's response was that because Indians aren't included in the neighborhood meetings and are left out of the discussions, they are often the ones blamed for crime. The community club and the neighborhood coalition were overwhelmingly white and elderly and not welcoming of Native Americans, who were shouted down when they attended a neighborhood coalition meeting to challenge the coalition's leadership.[5]

AICHO decided to take a proactive approach. During a spring cleanup event in Duluth, they put flyers around the neighborhood with the message, "If you need help . . . give us a call and we'll come clean up your yard." "We got active in neighborhood cleanup to dispel some of the stereotypes we were dealing with," said Victoria. "We still had challenges and issues, but we felt good about what we were doing."

AICHO moved ahead with its plans for Oshki and partnered with an architect, an engineer, their attorney, and the Housing Authority, which oversaw the construction. AICHO put more than $250,000 into the buildings to make them livable and to correct the code violations. "Hardwood floors were restored, windows replaced, new appliances installed, new porches built and vinyl siding put up," said the story in the *Duluth News-Tribune* on the day Oshki opened its doors in April 1996. While renovations were still underway, five eager families moved in.[6]

True to its name, Oshki has served as a place for new beginnings for hundreds of women. In addition to providing eighteen months of safe and affordable housing and six months of follow-up services, Oshki supports women in obtaining education and training, internships, job placement, and parenting courses, all designed to help the women become self-sufficient. Lucille Goodwin, Oshki's first program coordinator, said, "When you talk about welfare reform, this is it. Our programs are the kind of things we need to do . . . to prepare them to live on their own." One of the first residents, Kelly Sullivan, a twenty-two-year-old mother of a four-year-old daughter, said that the programming at Oshki was just what she needed. The staff at Oshki had helped her make arrangements to take a money management course and enroll at Lake Superior College to study social work. They also helped her put together the necessary paperwork to get child support for her daughter. "I just needed someone to push me along," she said.[7]

Native culture and spirituality provides the framework and infuses every aspect of the program at Oshki. Wanda Sayers, an employment coordinator at Oshki, said, "We try to tell women that they have to walk in both worlds. . . . They need to walk in the [modern] world to survive . . . but they also need to walk in the traditional world to become whole people to find themselves." Madeleine Tjaden, who was AICHO's director in 2002, underscored the organization's ongoing commitment to cultural programming: "We try to reconnect [Native women] with their Ojibwe culture, with the sweat lodge, medicine people, spiritual healing." Oshki staff reconnect the women with their roots and the land through wild ricing and maple sugaring and time in the woods and by the lake. They also explore the connections between centuries of oppression as Native people and the interwoven issues of domestic violence, alcoholism, and poverty with which the women may be struggling. "They inspired me to work on myself, to respect myself and other women and our spirituality," said Oshki resident Lisa Lyons. Through Oshki, she had reunited with her children, completed her GED, connected with the Women in Construction training program, and become part of the women-owned construction company Lindy's Dream Builders.[8]

Former resident Theresa Johnson expressed appreciation for the cultural programming at AICHO. "I'm learning a lot," she said in an interview when she was living there. "I didn't know much of anything about my culture because my mom was adopted [by a white family] when she was ten. Learning all of this is like . . . a major-league bonus." She was studying Minnesota American Indian history from the books in AICHO's library and was looking forward to learning from an Indian dream interpreter and a medicine man.[9]

Oshki was only the beginning for AICHO in meeting the needs of Native women escaping abuse. The AICHO board knew that Native women who chose not to use the services of the Women's Coalition had critical needs for safety that were not being met. A remote property on the Fond du Lac Reservation was available for use as an emergency shelter, "but nobody ever wanted to go out there," said Victoria, "because it was so far away and isolated. It felt like it could be dangerous if an offender wanted to get hold of that victim."

As Victoria set about assessing the need and exploring funding for a Native-specific shelter, it brought about an abrupt and harsh rift with the Women's Coalition. "I think their biggest concern wasn't competition," Victoria recalled. "It was more about stability of funding." She knew the importance of working with and learning from similar programs and was disappointed not to have that opportunity with the Women's Coalition. Instead, AICHO worked with Women of Nations Eagle Nest Shelter in St. Paul, as well as a short-term Native-specific treatment program, to learn how they approached working with people in short-term communal living situations. However, just as AICHO began investigating funding options, Minnesota Crime Victim Services, the main source of state funds for domestic violence shelters, put a moratorium on funding for any new shelters.

AICHO feared its vision of a Native-specific shelter had just come to a screeching halt. On Ellen Pence's advice, AICHO contacted Julie Tilley of the Minnesota Coalition for Battered Women (MCBW), who connected AICHO with a group of shelters from southern Minnesota that also were seeking legislative appropriation to fund shelter programs. The group had sufficient resources to hire a lobbyist and legislative specialists. What it did not have was diversity. The partnership proved beneficial for both groups. They were successful in getting legislation passed that provided more funding for shelters in Minnesota. "It created another piece to the pie, so we didn't take anybody's funding," said Victoria.

While seeking funding for a shelter, Victoria had explained to Cindi Cook, the director of the Minnesota Crime Victim Services, the need for a Native-specific shelter in the community and why it was not a duplication of services already offered. Victoria said her argument "must've struck a chord," because after she submitted a written proposal, Victim Services dedicated a portion of its discretionary funds to a Native-specific shelter in Duluth. This plus the funds from the state enabled AICHO to buy the property for a shelter and hire its first staff, Liz LaPrairie.

Liz and Victoria worked together closely on developing the shelter, which they named Dabinoo'Igan, meaning "a place where you are safe, comforted, and sheltered." They also formed a special advisory committee made up of victim advocates, formerly battered women, Mending the Sacred Hoop's director Tina Olson, and the advocate from Fond du Lac. Together they developed the building and the programming.

Opened in 1999, Dabinoo'Igan was the third Native-specific battered women's shelter in Minnesota and the second urban Indian shelter in the nation. "We were paving ground in those early days," said Victoria. Soon after opening, a church youth group from Maryland landscaped and built a playground between the Oshki buildings and Dabinoo'Igan. Funds from the Office of Violence Against Women enabled AICHO to put in place a project to support and educate victims on the civil legal remedies to domestic violence. It was able to work across multiple tribes and hire a full-time on-site attorney, as well as an advocate for victims going through legal proceedings.[10]

As with Oshki, the heart of Dabinoo'Igan is its culturally specific approach. Though open to women of all races, the shelter is focused on meeting the needs of Native women. Providing a strong cultural component helped Dabinoo'Igan to be intentional about how its program differed from the non-Native program—and ensure it incorporated Native values, beliefs, and teachings into everything they did. To that end, AICHO hired Esther Nahganeb, a local medicine woman, as a cultural liaison who would bring Native values and beliefs into the work at both Dabinoo'Igan and Oshki. "It was an enormously valuable resource to have Esther working there," said Victoria.[11]

One of the early residents, Lara, a member of the Leech Lake Band of Ojibwe, talked about how valuable the cultural program at Dabinoo'Igan was to herself and her five-year-old daughter. Though Lara's adoptive white parents had tried to expose her to her tribal roots, she said she never felt like she fit in with the Native community. Through her participation in the cultural activities and spiritual practices at Dabinoo'Igan, she said, "I've learned that . . . there's nothing wrong with being Native American."[12]

The staff of AICHO quickly recognized that they also needed to reconnect with their cultural heritage. The staff had various layers of connection to the Native community; some were strongly assimilated into mainstream culture, others were strongly connected to their culture. According to Victoria, the staff recognized that "if we were going to work with our participants in a way that helped them to embrace their own culture—to go to a sweat or full moon ceremony or take sweet grass or sage—that we ourselves will only be able to take them as far as we've gone." So Esther also did monthly in-services with staff to engage them in exploring their own culture. Victoria remembered that in preparation for these trainings, Esther would pray about what was needed until she was clear about which teachings she needed to bring to the group. The staff often talked about what these sessions meant to them personally and how they might use them to inform the programs.

The interactions with the women who came to Oshki and to Dabinoo'Igan were guided by what Victoria called "creating sister space": "When someone's in crisis, you treat them as you would your sister. You don't think about them as a client and a case to be managed. You see them as a peer. [You] recognize you have some authority and power for their lives, but you work at engaging in an equalizing manner, not putting yourself above them; working in ways that recognize where they're at and supporting them through whatever transition process they're going through at the time. [You] recognize them as an intact human being who has something to offer the world."

Establishing and maintaining the housing and programming AICHO offers requires a steady supply of funding, and for AICHO, the challenges of acquiring funding are compounded by the challenges of racism—from blatant, everyday encounters with stereotypes and prejudice to the less-visible barriers of institutional racism and historical trauma, to the pervasive and painful invisibility the organization encounters on a regular basis. Institutional racism makes accessing services more challenging. "As a Native population, we're more likely to hit barriers to accessing different systems," Victoria explained, "so the advocacy requires not only being able to work with the domestic violence or poverty or alcoholism that people are dealing with, but to recognize that access into systems and the way that people engage with you is going to be different just by virtue of being Native." This, combined with the complexity of issues arising from historical trauma, makes providing services for Native women in crisis all the more difficult and imposes tremendous demands on AICHO's staff. Victoria pointed out that the system itself contains so many layers of institutional racism "that have to be peeled back and cleaned up and fixed and repaired," and at the same time AICHO was also working with "people who [also] have constant layers that need to be peeled back, cleaned up, repaired, and healed."

AICHO constantly has had to fight for city and county funding. "It required constant, proactive strategies to be heard, to be funded, to be respected," said Victoria. Being able to leverage both tribal and municipal funds was critical for AICHO, but the fact that AICHO had some tribal funding was often used against it as a reason it should not be supported by city funds. As an example, once when AICHO was up for a Community Development Block Grant (CDBG), a city council member argued that AICHO should not receive CDBG funds "because it's for the public," as if a Native organization wasn't part of the public. "We were Indians, so [he thought] we should go after Indian money," said Victoria, who stressed that AICHO is an urban program, not a tribal program. So endemic was the anti-AICHO sentiment that an ally on the city council urged Victoria not to attend council meetings when CDBG funding was discussed, fearing that her very presence would "inflame" members who opposed AICHO receiving the funds. As the executive director, Victoria very much wanted to attend and be able to argue on AICHO's behalf and answer any questions. She listened on the radio from home, and when the councilor who was opposed to funding AICHO disparaged Victoria using racist stereotypes, she said she had to restrain herself from running down there. AICHO did receive the CDBG funding, but this incident was indicative of the hurdles AICHO had to clear. An examination of the

records of CDBG fund allocation over several years shows AICHO consistently at or near the bottom of the list. AICHO had similar battles with
St. Louis County, the Rural/Urban Housing Council in particular, where
it often found itself at the bottom of the rankings for funding. Only after
Victoria met with HUD officials in the Twin Cities and raised questions
about the rankings was AICHO able to get funds.[13]

After several AICHO residents had difficulties securing their mandated funding from the county, AICHO conducted a survey of county
financial workers. Most of the survey questions were based on simple
rankings, but the survey did leave space for comments. "People went out
of their way to write comments on what was wrong with Indian people,"
said Victoria. "The racism . . . was all over these forms." When AICHO
took this information to the county, the county hired AICHO to train its
workers.

Transition Years: 1999–2004

Victoria Ybanez left AICHO and Duluth in 1999 for personal reasons,
though she has continued to be involved with the organization as a consultant. Following her departure, AICHO went through a difficult transition. Several different people served as interim director over a short span
of time, including Liz LaPrairie, Madeleine Tjaden, and Dawn LaPrairie.
Even though the staff and board were consistent during that time, and
Mary Ann Walt remained very involved as board chair, the frequent
turnover in leadership caused problems for the organization. AICHO
missed deadlines for filing reports, which jeopardized future funding.
Problems arose at Dabinoo'Igan and Oshki when several residents did
not abide by the rules prohibiting the use of drugs and alcohol. Police
were called to the residences more than fifty times for fights, domestic
violence, and other trouble. AICHO suffered a huge blow in October
2001 when, after reviewing AICHO's program, the city's Community
Development Commission voted to take away $10,000 from the orga-
nization. Employment coordinator Wanda Sayers said at the time, "That
$10,000 may seem like a small amount to a lot of people, but it represents
a lot to us. It maintains our connection with the city of Duluth." AICHO
hired a financial manager and successfully completed an audit in the fall
of that year. The commission monitored and worked with AICHO on
a monthly basis and, believing that AICHO was making a "good-faith
effort," ultimately reversed its earlier decision.[14]

During this time, AICHO lost significant amounts of funding, wages crept backward, and staff members lost all of their benefits. In response to the high number of trouble calls to the police, the structures of accountability and operating practices at Dabinoo'Igan and Oshki became excessively rigid. Dabinoo'Igan even installed a time clock for residents to check in. The employee handbook and the written personnel and program policies that had been put in place in the early years literally disappeared. (They were discovered many years later in the attic.) "It all was slipping away," said Victoria.

Stability, Growth, and the Establishment of Gimaajii-Mino-Bimaadizimin

During the transition years, the American Federation of State, County, and Municipal Employees (AFSCME) organizers convinced AICHO staff to form a union. They were just finalizing their first contract when AICHO's next executive director, Sherry Sanchez Tibbetts, was hired in November 2004. Sherry remembered Mary Ann Walt telling her during her interview for the position, "We have some issues with the union right now, but we have an attorney to take care of that. Tell us about your plans for development." As soon as she came on board, Sherry found herself in the midst of union negotiations, and these, plus unexpected funding challenges, absorbed her immediate attention.

Shortly before coming to AICHO, Sherry had learned from Joe Geary, AICHO's head program officer in Minneapolis, that its continuing funding from the Department of Justice was being questioned. Developing stable, long-term funding had been a continual challenge for AICHO, so this was quite a blow. A particular challenge for AICHO has been educating funders on the fact that AICHO was providing unique and much-needed services. Because a transitional housing program and a domestic violence shelter already existed in Duluth, many believed that AICHO was simply duplicating available services—"never mind," said Sherry, "that both shelters were usually full at any given time, and that there was a waiting list for transitional housing that was six months long."

Ellen Pence, who was on the AICHO board at the time, told Sherry that it was time for AICHO to "wind down gracefully." This is not what Sherry expected, but it did not deter her from going ahead with her vision. The more she worked with staff and funders, the more she fell in love with AICHO and the vision that had been established by its founders. Sherry recalled thinking, "No, we are not going to wind down gracefully. We're going to continue." She gave each staff member a tie of tobacco as a show of honor and respect, and she told them, "We can't close. We are the only organization in Duluth that is focused on Native women. If we go away, what's going to happen to the women who come to our program?"[15]

Thus began a renewed commitment and revitalization of AICHO. Sherry instituted changes that helped to create a greater sense of the collective, rather than an assortment of individual programs. In order to gain financial stability, she fostered a more professional culture at AICHO, doing long-term strategic planning and building basic infra-structure, such as high-speed Internet and dedicated e-mail. She never-theless wanted to preserve AICHO's Anishinaabe ikwe perspective, integrating it into professionalism to show that these could coexist. Vic-toria said that Sherry's efforts enabled the organization to reclaim its original vision and philosophy of empowering Native women, and she saw this in the staff. Program director Patti Larsen said, "We're primarily a female-dominated organization. Ojibwe tradition is a matriarchal-led tradition. When we come to work, we all make decisions." Victoria said that "to see the leadership of Native staff in the different aspects of what they're doing is phenomenal." As funders saw the changes, AICHO was able to garner more funds, and the budget doubled to $1.2 million. "Sherry brought it back," said Victoria, "putting in place the programs and moving it toward its vision."[16]

A highlight for Sherry was bringing full moon ceremonies back into practice in the community. Of the monthly ceremonies on the shores of Lake Superior, Sherry said, "How many years has it been since Native women gathered and sang these songs in Ojibwe with their daughters there?" She recalled one time in particular, during the moon of the open-ing of rivers, "where you cast away those things that are holding you back." On her drive home, she saw the northern lights for the first time and was awestruck. "In Ojibwe, the word for northern lights is 'dancing spirits.' I thought, 'That's because we were having full moon. The spirits heard us and they were there with us.'"[17]

Among the new programs put in place under Sherry's leadership was a collaborative venture with the Northeast Regional Project funded by Hearth Connection, a nonprofit organization dedicated to ending long-term homelessness in Minnesota. This was the beginning of Giiwe, meaning "he or she goes home," a program of scattered site housing for thirty-five families. The program is for families and individuals who are the hardest to house, such as those with mental health and chemi-cal dependency issues. Hearth Connection pays rents and deposits, and

AICHO provides case managers who work with individuals and families to maintain their housing, which is the primary goal. Patti Larsen calls project coordinator Penny Wait "the guru of Giiwe housing," because of her skill in keeping people housed long-term in even the most difficult circumstances. Giiwe is based on a "harm reduction model," meaning they don't try to work on the chemical dependency or mental health issues of the people who use their services. "We meet them where they're at. We just try and keep them housed," said Patti. Penny has developed relationships with landlords who are willing to rent to this population. "People would call them slumlords," said Patti. "[Penny] will tell you that they serve a purpose in this town. Had it not been for them, some of her people would not be housed. They will take people that nobody else will give a chance to."[18]

Two case managers also work with program participants to find and maintain permanent housing, obtain benefits, and develop basic life skills like grocery shopping and housekeeping. The managers provide transportation; referrals to therapy, Legal Aid, and other agencies; and advocacy for housing, legal, and medical issues. In 2014 AICHO purchased a ten-unit building in the East Hillside, enabling AICHO to provide quality housing for the Giiwe program.

Of the nearly eight years that Sherry Sanchez Tibbetts was with AICHO, six were devoted to developing an urban Indian Center in downtown Duluth, with apartments intended to provide housing for the many Native people in Duluth facing homelessness. Three things motivated this drive. The first was a needs assessment Sherry had done to identify gaps in AICHO's programming, which showed a need for permanent housing. Second, AICHO staff also knew, anecdotally, that women who left Oshki sometimes fell back into homelessness or difficult living situations. Many still needed a supportive network and environment, in Sherry's words, "to continue on, to maintain their sobriety, or their family integrity, or just their personal autonomy."

Third, a 2006 Wilder Research Center study conducted with the American Indian Commission (now the Indigenous Commission) in Duluth confirmed what everyone had known: "that Native people in the Duluth area were disproportionately impacted by homelessness, poverty, and violence against women." The Wilder study also showed that Native people wanted housing that was culturally specific and run by an organization that had Native staff.[19]

The result was Gimaajii-Mino-Bimaadizimin, which was to provide permanent supportive housing for women and their children, elders, and families, as well as space for an American Indian Center. It was to be "a place for people to gather and share their culture with others," said Sherry. Gimaajii-Mino-Bimaadizimin means "We are, all of us together, beginning a good life" in Anishinaabe. "I always think it's important to say that exact meaning of the word," said Sherry. "That's the translation the woman who gave the name to Gimaajii gave to me." When first envisioning the center, Sherry gave tobacco to Barb Wilson, a Canadian elder, grandmother, and first-language speaker, and told her about her dream for a place that would provide safe housing, primarily for women and children. Barb took the tobacco and, after some thought, told Sherry that its name was to be "Gimaajii Mino Bimaadiziyaan."[20]

AICHO worked with the American Indian Commission to identify buildings and services they could develop. Providentially, the YWCA wanted to relocate its offices to the Building for Women and was seeking buyers for its building. The Y had ninety units of SRO (single room occupancy) housing, which could be converted into apartments to address some of the housing needs in the American Indian community. Despite certain unanticipated obstacles presented by the Y and extra costs, AICHO, along with the American Indian Commission, purchased the building and developed it into twenty-nine units of long-term supportive housing. The lobby areas, meeting spaces, and gymnasium were also part of the center. A few years later, AICHO purchased Trepanier Hall, a large meeting space also owned by the Y, where AICHO holds its community and cultural events.

The team that developed Gimaajii was made up of the chair of the Duluth American Indian Commission Bob Powless, Sherry Sanchez Tibbetts, Rick Smith, Maria Danns, and Zoe LeBeau, with the Corporation for Supportive Housing. Zoe called it "the project that gave me grey hair," in part due to the stress of finding funding, but also, she said, because of "the level of racism that exists toward the American Indian community."

Dr. Powless was instrumental in securing funds for the project from the Minnesota Housing Finance Agency (MHFA), which had turned down the team's applications a few times before. At the meeting with MHFA, Dr. Powless spoke of the large numbers of homeless Native people in the city of Duluth and of the vision the commission had for an American Indian Center. Afterward, the second in command of the MHFA, on a handshake, said, "We will give you $3 million if you come up with the other three." The team spent the next two years raising the rest of the money from nearly a dozen sources, including support from the Grand Portage and Shakopee tribes, and the Minnesota Chippewa Tribe

Foundation. "All of the tribes in Minnesota were very supportive of this project and helped in one way or another," said Zoe. Bob and Linda Powless generously donated $50,000 of their own. "People who know us know we're not a wealthy family," said Bob, "but there are other people out there who could make a donation. I hope this will encourage them." The final piece was $600,000 from the City of Duluth that had been set aside from revenues from the Fond-du-Luth Casino.[21]

The City of Duluth annually received $600,000 from the Fond du Lac tribe as part of its revenue-sharing agreement for proceeds from the Fond-du-Luth Casino that is located in the city. In 2005, at the request of nonprofit affordable housing and community development agencies, the Duluth City Council earmarked five years of this money, $3 million, for affordable housing. The money went into the city's Housing Investment Fund to support housing efforts where finance gaps existed. In an op-ed piece for the *Duluth News Tribune*, Tadd Johnson, a member of the Bois Forte band and special counsel on government affairs for the Mille Lacs Band of Ojibwe, explained that "by ordinance, up to $600,000 from the fund is designated for a housing project with an attached American Indian Center, as endorsed by the Duluth American Indian Commission." The development team, which had managed to put together nearly all the funds for the $7 million project, was counting on that $600,000 to complete the funding.[22]

In previous years, other low-income housing projects—Center City Housing, the Community Land Trust, Women in Construction, and Women's Transitional Housing—had been able to access these funds. This would be AICHO's first time dipping into them. "To me, Gimaajii was a no-lose situation," said Sherry: "Why wouldn't people support this? We were going to preserve a historic building—the YWCA building in downtown Duluth. We were going to provide affordable housing for families and elders and individuals. We were going [to] stabilize a marginal neighborhood . . . bring in millions of dollars of funding and construction jobs, and create another community center. . . . Who wouldn't love this project? [But] there were some people who didn't."

Even though the city had set aside those funds, final approval for their disbursement needed to come from the city council. On September 24, 2007, the city council voted on AICHO's and the American Indian Commission's request for these funds to finalize development of Gimaajii, and in an unexpected turn of events, on a 5–4 vote, the council turned them down. "It was a shock," said Sherry. "We thought the city council review was a formality because we not only met but we exceeded the statutory guidelines." They also were denied low-income housing tax credits for the project, even though nearly all the mainstream housing organizations in Duluth had received tax credits from the city for their projects.

Much to their surprise and dismay, city councilor Roger Reinert, whose support they had counted on, voted against the project. Reinert told reporters that he voted against the project because he was uncomfortable with the proposed location. Other councilors who voted against the project said they thought the money should go to street improvements instead. One councilor even said he did not want public moneys to support a building that had turtles in its motif and design, because he claimed that turtles are considered a symbol of death in some cultures. Sherry regarded the events surrounding the council's vote to be thinly veiled racism: "I think it was very intimidating for people to realize that this small organization that they had written off four years before actually had the capacity to do something like this, but more importantly, that they were going to create a visible urban land base for Duluth's Indian population at the time. And, it's women-led," she said.[23]

The council's decision was met with considerable opposition. The editors of the *Duluth News Tribune* came out in support of Gimaajii, saying that "the project is still ripe with merit, so much so that the council's 'no' vote last week shouldn't be its final vote." St. Louis County commissioner Steve O'Neil, who cochaired the mayor's commission to end homelessness, said that not being awarded the funds was "like getting a hammer over the head out of the blue." In his op-ed piece, Tadd Johnson wrote: "People in our community have worked hard to develop a plan for this project. . . . The Duluth Indian community was stunned, and the sense of betrayal was deep. . . . Housing advocates from across Minnesota were equally shocked." He pointed out that the no vote jeopardized AICHO's application for $3 million in financing from the MHFA, as well as hundreds of thousands of dollars in federal and private funding. He also made the pertinent point that, "if nothing else, councilors should keep in mind that Housing Investment Fund money is generated from revenues from Fond-du-Luth Casino through an agreement between the Fond du Lac Band and the city of Duluth. . . . This plan has worked well to serve all citizens of Duluth. It would be a travesty if the only population left out in the cold was Indian."[24]

The proposal came before the city council for reconsideration two weeks later. Over two hundred people gathered both in and outside council chambers that night. Many testified that the project was needed to help end homelessness in the city. Others testified that the vote against the project was an attack on their race. Craig Grau, a political science professor emeritus at UMD, reminded the council that had it not been for the casino and the American Indian people, the city would not have these community investment funds. He cautioned the city council, "Your legacy is in this decision."[25]

Supporters participated in a rally outside city hall that night. Recalling that night eight years later, Sherry was still visibly moved as she remembered aloud:

> It was everyone—from the women's hand drum group
> to folks from Spirit Valley. All the affordable housing
> providers. . . . The Sisters Benedictine were out there. We
> had tribal leaders. We had women's advocates. . . . We had
> affordable housing preservationists, as well as Mille Lacs
> Band of Ojibwe. . . . I was very moved by it—I still am—by
> the support that people showed for the project because
> it was the whole idea of what Gimaajii was supposed to
> be. It was a very rare opportunity where so many different
> groups who had such specific interests were able to come
> together around a project. Maybe that was the cosmic
> reason behind the first shot being not given—to bring the
> community support around it.

In the end, Roger Reinert changed his vote. The council's reversal secured the final piece of funding for the project. "The city council battle was dramatic," said Zoe, "but there were battles like that every single month. Every month that project died and had to be revived."

Five years later, in 2012, Gimaajii-Mino-Bimaadizimin opened its doors. It is a beautiful space: light, airy, its walls filled with art by local Native artists, with comfortable chairs arranged for conversation and community. Its four efficiency, five one-bedroom, eleven two-bedroom, and nine three-bedroom units offer modern urban loft living. Within its first month, AICHO had four hundred applications for twenty-nine units of housing, and the demand has never lessened.

Though Sherry devoted most of her time at AICHO to developing Gimaajii, she continued to examine how the organization might address other unmet needs in the community. The most pressing need quickly revealed itself. One day, a mother called AICHO's office and told advocate Wanda Sayers, "If you see my daughter, call the police, because she has run away. I think her boyfriend is pimping her out at the candy shop."

The Hip-Hop Candy Shop, which unbeknownst to AICHO was being used as a trafficking front, was in AICHO's backyard. Police investigations later discovered that the store owner had trafficked at least four Native girls between the ages of thirteen and seventeen. The girls said the owner promised them new clothes, shoes, manicures, and haircuts if they would work at strip clubs and have sex with him and other men of his choosing.[26]

Around this time, the Minnesota Indian Women's Resource Center (MIWRC) in the Twin Cities started developing its work around trafficking of Native women, and Sherry worked with Suzanne Koepplinger of MIWRC on that. "Through surveys and talking circles we came to realize that almost one out of two Native women in our shelter and our transitional program had been somehow sexually exploited in their life," said Sherry. Addressing this issue became part of AICHO's mission. "If we as a Native women's organization didn't stand up for Native women and didn't help policy and make the situation better, who would?" asked Sherry. "It was a sovereignty issue for us," she added. "We were Indian women who needed to stand up for Indian women and children." AICHO became so invested in this that the U.S. Senate Committee on Indian Affairs invited Sherry to testify when it was gathering information on trafficking. This awareness also went into the shaping of Gimaajii. Five of the units were to be reserved for women coming out of domestic violence situations, and AICHO worked with the management company to make sure that sex offenders would not be housed in Gimaajii. "We wanted to help those women and children . . . who have been victimized, and help them rebuild their lives," said Sherry.[27]

2012–2014

Sherry Sanchez Tibbetts stepped down as AICHO's executive director shortly before Gimaajii-Mino-Bimaadizimin opened. Interim executive director Michelle LeBeau remembered Gimaajii's first year being difficult. Opening Gimaajii roused anti-AICHO backlash from the community. In addition, during that first year, AICHO experienced internal difficulties with much staff turnover, and it took a while to get the right mix of people and policies. Despite the challenges, Michelle expressed appreciation for AICHO's board of directors, who, she said, "have a vision for what they want to see and happen here. They always want to move forward in a positive way." She said that any time a problem would come up, they would respond, "We're going to keep moving forward positively. We're not going to get into the negativity." Michelle also witnessed many wonderful things happen for the residents of Gimaajii.[28]

When AICHO moved its offices to Gimaajii, Dabinoo'Igan, which had shared the building with AICHO, was able to move to a house of its own. The new shelter houses up to ten women. Patti Larsen and Dabinoo'Igan director Janis Greene have been impressed by how few conflicts have arisen among the women who live in close quarters. "We're talking about women in trauma," said Patti. Janis added, "They leave behind everything they've known. Plus they are dealing with abuse. . . . The majority of women bond with each other. Some make . . . lasting friendships that will go beyond the shelter." "Women are amazingly resilient beings," Patti added.

A cultural specialist spends twenty hours a week with the women at Dabinoo'Igan doing anything from beading to Native cooking, and an elder has done storytelling and the seven teachings. The staff holds weekly talking circles with the women and has continued to do full moon ceremonies. They bring residents to events like powwows, language camp, and the sobriety feast. They also provide "small things like smudging in the morning and smudging in the evening," said Janis. "We started giving small shells and sage to each woman as she comes in, so they have their own and they can smudge whenever they want to." Patti said they try to offer activities for the women without being overwhelming. "Sometimes it's just about having women come and start conversations," she said. They have often found it easier for women to open up when not pressured by an expectation to talk, and the activities help them do that. Dabinoo'Igan staff credit the work they do with the women, as well as the work the women do themselves, with their success in finding permanent housing for the residents.[29]

When Patti started working at Dabinoo'Igan, which takes women of all ethnicities, very few Native women sought out the services. To reach a greater number of Native women, Patti and Janis changed some of their screening practices. "A lot of women will call in and they'll present [themselves] as homeless, but if you start asking the right questions, the core of it is they are homeless due to domestic violence," said Janis. The advocates found that as they were more indirect in their questioning, such as asking if the woman was staying with family, which is often the case with battered women, the fact that the woman was homeless because she was battered would reveal itself. The staff recognizes that

Native people are leery of systems in general, and changing the conversation has been very helpful, as have conversations with women out in the neighborhood and women on the streets who have been trafficked.

An incident at Gimaajii prompted AICHO to make sure the Duluth police were fully aware of the services they offer for Native women who have been battered. A man had come into Gimaajii threatening to shoot up the place. The police came and began asking questions of the Native woman who had been victimized by the man. In the process, they let the woman know that she could go to the shelter. Patti was relieved at first, because she often worried that the police weren't telling women about Dabinoo'Igan, but instead the officers told the woman they could take her to the Safe Haven Shelter. Patti told the police, "This is AICHO! We have our own shelter. This is a Native woman. We have Dabinoo'Igan." "Right in our own building," said Janis, "telling a Native woman . . . that she can go to Safe Haven."

This is just one of many examples of the painful reality of invisibility faced by those outside of the mainstream, especially Native Americans, and even more so Native American women. Patti and Janis related experiences of being at meetings where they, the only people of color in the room, would make a point that would go unacknowledged, but if a non-Native person later made the same point, other people would hear it—"Now, all of a sudden it's validated," said Patti—or of attending meetings where someone says, "AICHO's not here," and the person from AICHO is sitting right beside him. "This is the biggest battle we fight all the time," said Patti. "When I think about the story of AICHO, that's it," said Victoria. "Indian people have been invisible for so long; people want to keep it that way. When we start to show up, either they don't know what to do with us or they don't want to do anything with us. Our challenge is how we push through that in a way that tries to build bridges and not create enemies."

After the incident with the police, AICHO staff made a point of talking with police about AICHO programming and Dabinoo'Igan. They sought to increase awareness of the programs available for Native people in hopes that the police in turn would make Native people aware of the culturally specific housing and programs available to them. They also talked with police about the importance of having conversations with and getting to know Native women on the streets. The women would be more likely to report to an officer with whom they had developed a relationship. Late in 2014, Janis and Patti started a domestic violence support group for women at the county jail, and they recognized at least half of the women in the group as Native. When they asked the women to introduce themselves and to say whether or not they had experienced domestic violence, every single one had.

The number of Native women coming to Dabinoo'Igan continues to increase. Janis estimated that about 80 percent of the women coming through the shelter are Native. AICHO hoped that as more Native women used the shelter, word would spread to others. AICHO could use a bigger shelter, but the organization is wary of the shelter becoming too big. Many of the women who come to Dabinoo'Igan from Safe Haven have said they feel more comfortable in the homier environment of Dabinoo'Igan. "We want to keep that," said Janis, but added that "adding even up to fifteen beds would be awesome."

Five years after it opened, Gimaajii-Mino-Bimaadizimin continued to have a long waiting list for its housing, with one hundred fifty being a fairly consistent number. The need is great. "We just housed a woman who had been on the waiting list for a year and a half. That's a long time for an Indian woman . . . to be homeless," said Patti. Another had been homeless for ten years.

A 2014 HUD initiative, "Continuum of Care," threatened to make housing Native people at Gimaajii more difficult. Modeled on a successful program in Dayton, Ohio, it was designed to coordinate efforts in the community to find homes for homeless individuals and families more quickly. But the program is particularly inappropriate for AICHO. Legally, AICHO may not discriminate on the basis of race, but the new HUD program could undermine the intent and vision for Gimaajii to provide culturally specific housing for the large Native homeless population. The HUD initiative requires that people who are homeless fill out an application for every housing program available in the city. Michelle said that the program is frustrating for AICHO because the application process, designed to distribute housing on the basis of "need," gives points for such things as being a homeless youth or a veteran, but not for being a victim of domestic violence living in an emergency shelter or to American Indians or African Americans, both groups that are disproportionately homeless in Duluth. Also, points are awarded for having barriers like criminal histories, including violence, so while these individuals do need housing, "they are often not appropriate for housing that includes children." When a unit comes open in any of the housing programs that are part of HRA housing, HRA takes the top three names and gives them to the program, which then must choose one of the three to receive the apartment. The problem for AICHO, said Patti, "is what if

I get three non-Native people? What if that happens a bunch of times? Now my program, that was developed because of a vision of the Indian Commission, [is no longer housing Native people]." HRA has agreed that it will send more than three names if AICHO can document why the first three are not "appropriate" for their housing. However, AICHO may not request priority for people who want culturally specific housing or for women who are in Dabinoo'Igan or Oshki. One way AICHO will remedy some of this is to create new housing units without HUD funds so those units will not have to go through this system.[30]

AICHO has considered adding on to Gimaajii-Mino-Bimaadizimin. They need more housing units and more office space. Mending the Sacred Hoop, the Leech Lake Reservation urban office, and Research for Indigenous Community Health all have offices in Gimaajii. In addition, White Earth Reservation has a therapist and an Adult Rehabilitative Mental Health Services (ARMHS) worker at Gimaajii to provide mental health services for people living there. University Day Care is housed there as well. Adding more facilities requires funds, and funding continues to be a challenge. The CDBG program has created a process whereby programs receiving its funds have to meet certain benchmarks, and all the participating programs have to determine who among them will not get funding. Janis and Patti expressed frustration that in 2014, a new affordable housing program that had not yet opened, the Steve O'Neil Apartments, was ranked number one on the CDBG list while AICHO was ranked twenty-second. They did not question the value of the new apartments for the community; they simply wondered why it was ranked number one because, having not yet opened, it could have no benchmarks. Nobody could explain this to AICHO. "That's the kind of governmental, systemic racism that AICHO organized around. . . . [We've] been battling the city forever," said Patti. "We got all of $3,000 from the city for CDBG funding last year; others got $140,000."

Nevertheless, the services and programming at Gimaajii have expanded greatly. A Native leader comes in three times a week to do a prayer circle and talking circles for adolescents and adults. Another man offers a language camp. Alcoholics Anonymous holds meetings at Gimaajii. Life House, a resource center and street outreach program for homeless teens, uses AICHO's gym for basketball games. AICHO also set up a trade with Men as Peacemakers, whose offices are across the street, where the women at AICHO participate in Men as Peacemakers' restorative justice circles, and the men do tutoring and have fun in the gym with the kids.

One of the most successful additions to Gimaajii's services has been providing meals to the residents. Gimaajii participates in Second Harvest, which distributes surplus food to charitable organizations offering meals to the hungry. "When you get people a place to live, and you get them food . . . it's stress that people don't have to live with," said Patti. "Everything's about food," she added, which is why AICHO enhances all of its community events with abundant offerings of food.

AICHO emphasizes inviting the public into Gimaajii by hosting events and holding community forums. It regularly hosts art openings for local Native artists, many of whose works are displayed on Gimaajii's walls. It has hosted poetry readings, plays, powwows, and other gatherings. "I love the Indian Center," said Victoria. "It's great to create that space for the Indian community, but also it . . . helps educate the non-Native community of the presence . . . and the richness of the Indian community within Duluth and the surrounding area." "Gimaajii is becoming this bridge between the Native community and the non-Native community," said Michelle. "Slowly but surely this whole image of who AICHO is and what we do has changed. There's a lot of support in the community now."

Conclusion

AICHO began with "this very small group of women, and this is what became of it," said Janis Greene, reflecting on the organization's growth from Oshki to Gimaajii. "As I look at AICHO and where it's going," reflected Victoria, "they are leaders, not only in Duluth, but in other parts of the country." Featured as a cover story in the national publication *Indian Country Today*, Gimaajii-Mino-Bimaadizimin has become a national model. "AICHO has a great reputation," said Michelle LeBeau. "People from all over the United States come here, tour the facility, and talk about our programs, and want to learn from us what we're doing so they can replicate it in other communities." "There's not another program like it," echoed Patti. "I'm proud of it," said Karen Diver. "I didn't envision it being as large as having Gimaajii. We just wanted to have a good place for Indian women to heal, and to get a start, and hopefully leave there in a better place. And it worked."

"The women that came to AICHO were what made AICHO happen," said Sherry. "They were the ones who had the resiliency. They kept the staff going too—by seeing the difference you made in someone's life." The victories, triumphs, and celebrations in the lives of the women and children were the highlights—from the small triumphs of a woman who by learning to cook saved enough money to buy the big-screen TV she had been wanting, and the children who glowed at seeing their artwork hung up in Gimaajii, to the larger victories of gaining education and skills, finding employment and safe housing, and becoming self-sufficient. AICHO's legacy lives on in the transformed lives of the women and families it has served.

One of the few things that Sherry kept from her time at AICHO was a shell given to her by a little girl who used to live at Oshki. "It has a little crack on it," she said. "Seashells are very delicate, and when they get a crack or are marred, the underlying lip becomes stronger where that damage was." She said that same resiliency was evident in the women who came to AICHO: "That's what AICHO is about: creating that space for people who may not have had other options, to help them realize their own potential and develop some sort of resiliency. That was our tagline, 'honoring our resiliency.' To me that meant not just the resiliency of our clients, but of Native people. . . . We were on the verge of not being around and we're still here; the organization was on the verge of not being around and is still there."

AICHO's new logo of figures in front of a teepee with rays coming out of it provides a visual representation of AICHO's vision of its future. Said Sherry, "It can be a family. It can be a community. It can be adults and children. The teepee could be home; it could be a mountain; it could be a new day. It's everything that we wanted to see moving forward."[31]

{ 13 }

Lessons Learned

What can I learn from you?
In your lifetime, in what you've been through?
How'd you keep your head up and hold your pride
In an insane world how'd you keep on tryin'? . . .
Heroes appear like a friend
To clear a path or light the flame
As time goes by you find you depend
On your heroes to show you the way.

ANN REED, "HEROES"

C ollecting the histories of these grassroots feminist organizations from the Twin Ports of Duluth and Superior presented a unique opportunity to gather wisdom from those who have been doing the work of feminist organizing, in many cases, for decades. Many of these women were the pioneers, the ones who broke the ground and made a feminist future possible. This book was an opportunity to learn from them: What had allowed the organizations to thrive? What sustained and nourished them? What were the pitfalls and how might they be avoided in the future? What would they have done differently, in retrospect? What enabled them to do effective feminist work in the world? What lessons had they learned and what would they pass along to future generations? Some of the lessons are pragmatic—the basics of keeping any organization going—but most show the way to create and sustain feminist transformation of the world.[1]

Nearly all those involved in the beginnings of these organizations said something to the effect of, "We didn't know what we were doing, but we jumped in anyway." The lesson here is simple: If you have a vision, go for it. Those early years also taught them the importance of gathering allies and being willing to ask for help, learn from others' expertise, and pass the wisdom on.

As they went along, these women had to learn such pragmatic lessons as maintaining a balance between the work of the program and the administrative work that keeps it all in place. For many, their passion for their mission was their overriding priority, but organizations came to value the fact that day-to-day maintenance of administering an organization secured the structural and fiscal health that enabled them to carry out their missions.

Transitional times, when strong leaders left organizations, often were difficult times. Many women emphasized the importance of developing a transition plan, so that the vision of the organization may be carried forward. They also underlined that building more than one leader within an organization by continually developing staff leadership and mentoring up-and-coming members is critical to an organization's success and long-term stability. A smooth transition was also facilitated when those serving in leadership positions for a long time were adaptable to new ideas and new perspectives, knew when it was time to leave, and were willing to let go and let others step in.

The importance of taking the time to nurture relationships, both within and outside the organization, was also a common lesson. As Erika Leif stated, "We can't do this work alone, can't be the single captain in the community, save the world. . . . We have to have other system players on board. We all need to work together." In this regard, many women spoke of how, in working with organizations and community partners, it was important to provide agency for all involved and to create a win-win situation. "You can't go to the community people and tell them how to do their job," said Coral McDonnell. "We go as partners in a work and together try to do some problem-solving." Tina Olson, Jen James, and Liz LaPrairie forged relationships with law enforcement partners over weekly breakfasts, and DAIP met with community partners every two weeks over lunch. Coral recalled, "Everybody liked those meetings; everybody learned something; and it was a good opportunity to share, to get to know each other personally. . . . Friendships were formed."[2]

Within the organizations, taking the time to talk and reflect together on a regular basis is a vital practice. Taking the steps necessary to ensure that, as mission-driven organizations, they are keeping their mission at the center of their work has been critical to the ability of these organizations to effect change in the world. Victoria Ybanez said: "Many organizations don't build in time and space to think, so they're running, running, running like worker bees, and they don't tend to see the unintended consequences. . . . Maybe they're having what appear to be good outcomes, but they're actually moving away from their mission." "We continuously have discussions about where we are with our mission," said Kelly Burger, to ensure that the mission is at the center of the work. Janice Wick talked about how the very meaning of praxis—integrating theory and practice—requires advocates at Praxis International to "keep looking at the center and making sure that the things they are doing are what they should be doing for or with victims." Even more important is taking the time to sustain relationships with one another outside of the day-to-day work of the organizations. Some camped together, some swam together, some did full moon ceremonies, some cooked, some shared meals. All spoke of how important taking that time was and how much their organizations suffered when it disappeared. "If you don't have that connection, it's impossible to sustain . . . the work that you're doing together," said Laura Hesselton.

As part of the work of relationship building—whether with organizational partners, the people they served, or each other—an important lesson was to meet people where they are and respect others' points of view. Ellen Pence learned not to judge men too quickly. There were times she would feel such anger toward the batterers she worked with, but she came to recognize that most of them weren't the men "holding up the patriarchy." They hadn't chosen to be batterers, but had unwittingly been brought down that path. She said the key for her was "to hang on to the commonality between us." Sue Maki passed along this bit of wisdom: "I'm always willing to listen to your journey, no matter what it is, and be respectful of it. I think if we expect people to treat us well, we need to treat everyone well. . . . I learned you can never judge another person until you've walked in their shoes. Everyone has a story. You just have to sit and listen and respect their story." Jean DeRider urged activists also to treat each other with the same respect they gave the women they served.

Because people in positions of authority were quick to pass judgment on the women in the organizations, especially women of color, a difficult and oft-repeated lesson was to choose words and battles wisely. It was disturbing and telling how many women had learned to be "careful" and "circumspect" in their choice of words. Otherwise, as Tina Olson said, funders "can take your funding away in a New York minute." Victoria Ybanez learned the importance of determining when to engage an issue and when not to, based on careful discernment of whether her engagement carried the probability of making a significant difference or was merely a vehicle to express her thoughts, with the potential of making things worse. Sheryl Boman recognized the difficult line between being an advocate in a way that is respectful to people in power and not buying into the status quo, and she emphasized the importance of always choosing to maintain advocacy.

Many stressed that those involved in doing anti-oppression work need to do this same anti-oppression work among themselves. "If staff don't get it, staff are not going to be able to recognize some of it coming at those they're working with," said Victoria Ybanez. "They're not going to be able to work at helping to unravel or dismantle some of that, and may even be perpetuating it." Laura Hesselton suggested building in regular times for members to talk about how we reproduce oppression with each other. Sheryl Boman, recognizing that "race has been used to separate us," stressed that activists do their work "from an anti-racist perspective, because if we aren't doing our work with an anti-racist lens, then everything we do will only benefit white people, because it's already built into the system to do that." Similarly, activists and advocates dealing with violence and abuse on a daily basis benefit from doing their own "internal healing and practice around violence and abuse," said Lora Wedge. She added, "If you have a shadow part of yourself that you're not seeing that you're putting out there in the world, that's just adding to the violence and abuse." Honestly examining these issues in oneself enables advocates to "do the work from a place of peace and wholeness." Others spoke of the importance of grounding the work in some form of spirituality. Njoki Kamau of the Women, Gender, and Sexuality Studies Department at UMD spoke of how important it is "to have a spiritual center in your own heart, so that you're not broken, because life will be difficult." Ellen Pence wished she had taken a more spiritual approach to her work early on. While she was initially resistant to this, her attitude changed when twenty years of working in the movement left her feeling so despondent that she knew she needed something to replenish her "depleted soul." She ended up going to a peace center with Buddhist and Christian origins, where she learned what compassion and love meant. "It gave me a different kind of energy," she said. "When I practiced meditation, I found that within all of us is this potential for love." This enabled her to approach her work from a sustaining place of love.[3]

Balance, spiritual centering, and taking time for friendship all contribute to perspective. Also vitally important in sustaining oneself in the difficult work is a good sense of humor. "My son used to tell me, 'Mother, don't ever take yourself too seriously," said Tina Welsh. "Humor is very, very important."

Many noted the importance of continuing to work on social change. A paradox for many organizations was that their very nonprofit status limited their ability to do lobbying and political work. Others spoke of the limitations of relying on government funding. As Ellen Pence said, even though Praxis was doing feminist work, because of restrictions placed on them by the government, their feminism could no longer be "cutting edge." Feminist nonprofits need to take care not to be drawn into and perpetuate the white patriarchal governmental and social services systems they sought to change, so staff development in systems-change work is vital. "We have to be creative," said Sheryl Boman. "There are systems in this country that want to maintain the status quo that have thought ahead many years." By contrast, she added, these feminist organizations are "going from one crisis to another." She advised the organizations to work in ways that were more forward thinking. In part, this requires that organizations not always let funding dictate their decisions. Too often they have to abandon successful programs and start new ones based on what grantors are funding next. In order to ensure that the needs of those they serve and the organization's own vision, rather than those in power, drive their program initiatives, some have learned not to "run for the money just because it's there," because, warned Kelly Burger, if you do that, "you're not running well."

A central piece for the women and organizations in staying true to their feminist work is listening to those they serve. As Jean DeRider said, "listen to whomever has issues. Don't assume that you know. . . . It needs to come from whomever you're serving." The common refrain was to let the needs of those you serve guide your work, and this means including them in your decision-making. "Do not do things without the people you're serving," said Babette Sandman. "We need to know the effects on people." Trish O'Keefe agreed, saying that it was critical "to have the people who are experiencing the problem be the ones who are leading the vision."

In that regard, Ellen Pence wanted to pass on this lesson: "If you want to make a difference in women's lives, keep talking with women in real ways all the time." Toward the end of her life, she reflected, "What's missing [in agency work these days] is the art of dialogue. [Say] 'Talk to me about your life,' and then listen. Let her drive and define the kinds of things she needs." If what the organization offers doesn't match what a woman needs, then find others who can meet those needs. Like many, Ellen expressed concern about the turn that advocacy had taken toward a more professionalized and distanced relationship in which advocates refer to women as their clients. "That's a very different relationship than 'I work with a woman who is like me, and we're working together.'" She continued: "When a woman walks into our building and she's got three or four or five kids and she's getting beaten up and she's poor, when I recognize that she and we that are on the other side of the door are the same, that's when I know that I'm still there as a feminist. But when I look at her and start to psychologize her or see her as a victim . . . and see a client come through the door, then you've lost something big. To me, that's the heart of it."[4]

This is similar to what Victoria Ybanez had described as "creating sister space." "That lesson that you treat people just like your sisters treated you has never left me," said Michelle LeBeau, reflecting on her work in several of the organizations. "We need to go back to some of those grassroots ways of being." Jill Abernathy said, "Remember that women are your sisters. Give the benefit of the doubt that she has somehow been coerced, abused by the system, this woman-hating patriarchy we live in. . . . If we aren't there for each other, we'll never make any progress."

Acting in sisterhood also has implications for how one uses one's power. Rosemary Rocco said the lesson she most wanted to pass along to future generations was that for a "true feminist," acting as a sister implies using whatever power she has at any given time "to make sure there are more women in the room, as opposed to just being able to rise to the level of getting to play with the boys." Kim Marble-Follis of CASDA added that she would remind everyone of the importance of continually asking, "What are you doing to protect people?" and to use the power they have in a way that supports the people they serve.

The importance of valuing women and women's wisdom was central to all who began this work. As Babette Sandman said, "If we don't get into the core of valuing women as a gem . . . we should be out of the business." In an era when, in the name of inclusivity, gender neutrality is once again decentering and occasionally silencing the voices of women, Shirley Oberg's wisdom deserves reiteration: "Listen. Listen to each other and the women. The process is the product. How we are with each other determines the success of our endeavors."

Conclusion

Each of the stories of the featured organizations is unique, and yet together they tell a common story—of women who shared the stories of their lives, created community and connection, and responded to the truths that were revealed. It is the story of women who persisted in the face of great resistance and hostility to create new systems and ways of relating, and who occasionally succumbed to forces of divisiveness and old habits of mind. It is the story of women who succeeded, against all odds, to repair and restore, heal and transform both individual lives and the life of the collective.

The basic premise of all of these grassroots organizations was to listen to the women, and then develop programs and resources guided by their needs. Every one of these organizations evolved and changed in response to the needs of the women they served. They also recognized that simply addressing immediate needs was, as Sheryl Boman remarked, like pulling drowning women out of the river, when they needed to stop women from being thrown into the river in the first place. To do this they needed to transform the system, attitudes, and an entire culture of patriarchy. Grounding their vision in the concrete experiences of women's lives, they worked to change laws and policies and worked directly with systems, training police, courts, attorneys, social workers, and physicians, educating them about the need for a victim-centered response.

These organizations did outreach to community groups, churches, schools, and universities to raise awareness and to change attitudes. But most important for enacting a new paradigm was the education for awareness and empowerment that took place in groups run by DAIP, the Women's Coalition, Women's Trans, and Aurora, as well as in Women's Studies classrooms at UMD and in the cultural grounding at Dabinoo'Igan and Oshki. Without this critical consciousness, the dominant paradigm remains unchallenged, and women will continue to be thrown into the river. The theme of women's empowerment runs throughout all these organizations—whether acting on the premise that women are their own best decision-makers; educating women on their political rights; affirming women's cultural, sexual, racial, religious, and gender identities; or listening to women in ways that allowed them to feel heard. Many founders sought to institutionalize models of decision-making within their own organizations so as to equalize power and give everyone equal voice. As Patti Larsen said of AICHO, in the Ojibwe tradition of female leadership, "When we come to work we all make decisions." The core value grounding the work, and that the organizations often had to struggle both internally and externally to maintain, is to treat women with dignity and respect: *dignity*, from the Latin *dignus*, meaning "value" or "worth," and *respect*, from the Latin *re*, meaning "with strength or emphasis," and *specere*, meaning "to see." I am reminded of the passion with which Babette Sandman and Marvella Davis spoke of how valued they felt in the Women's Action Group—they felt seen.

Throughout these stories, women speak of the pain of invisibility, of not being seen or heard. That invisibility underscores the "nonbeing" of women, of Native peoples, and of Native women in particular, in mainstream culture. Accompanying this invisibility is the frustration of not being able to move ahead with concepts and actions for change because one's wisdom is not respected and is regarded as worthy only if someone who is accorded legitimacy signs on. It is not unlike needing someone to cosign a loan if one is not considered to be credit-worthy, or a woman being regarded as "real" only if she is attached to a man.

I suspect that invisibility and inaudibility stems from not being seen as human, or at least not as humans of a type worthy of attention. Humans' physical ability to see something is attached to our ability to place it in a context of meaning. If only men of privilege define the category of human, then women, especially women of color, are not seen or respected. In patriarchal culture, the inherent dignity and worth of women, and of indigenous peoples, fall outside the regard of those in power. This is precisely why the work of creating a new paradigm, or in the case of Anishinaabe ikwe, restoring the former paradigm, is so necessary. Had the Euro-Americans who came to this land approached the indigenous peoples with respect and regard, and learned from them to respect the sacredness of women rather than impose their dominating ways toward women onto the indigenous population, none of the work of these organizations would even be necessary. To listen to women, to give attention and loving regard, is to enable women to be seen by themselves. Cultural change begins here. Listening to the women is core to this work.[1]

And this is what too often disappeared in the work of these grassroots feminist organizations. The story of a loss of focus on women and a peer connection with the women is one I heard repeated many times in many variations, and most often with a sad awareness that something precious had been lost. Nearly all these organizations came to a point in their development, usually ten to twenty years from their beginning, where they began to lose touch with the voices of women—the voices of the women they served, their own inner voices, the voices of each other. Many factors contributed to the slow creep of patriarchy back into the organizations: lack of time, expansion and specialization, imperatives of funders, loss of places to celebrate and renew, and the persistence of patriarchal habits of mind and social institutions. All lamented the loss of time to listen to each other and to the women they served. Swamped with paperwork, grant writing, the energy-draining need to respond to backlash and attack, they no longer had time. As the organizations institutionalized they became professionalized, with one consequence being that staff were expected to have gained more of their knowledge from "experts" instead of from the expertise of their own lived experience. Gradually the staff became the experts who told the women they served what they could offer, rather than meeting the women where they were and with what they needed. The women they served became "clients," not women who were like them.

Part of the reason for the changing focus and nature of the organizations has come from the enormous expansion of services and programming. Each of the organizations is deservedly proud of this expansion, but it also rendered them so big that they no longer could gather together easily, or make decisions collectively, or even know what each was doing. One of the main driving forces for organizational change is outside their control. In order to secure funding, an organization needs to show that it is not duplicating services that another organization in the region is providing. Thus, an organization that might function better as a small collective, or as several small collectives with particular specialties, is often forced to grow to incorporate so many different programs that hierarchy and specialization become necessary. However, there is something to be said for maintaining several smaller agencies, perhaps each with a particular niche, that can stay in more direct contact with women and with each other, and thus be more flexible and responsive to ongoing and changing needs.

In addition, nearly every organization in this study expressed the same desire that foundations and government agencies would provide funding for the ongoing maintenance and sustenance of existing programming and administration, instead of the constant demand for new programs. When organizations must create new programs based not on the needs of the women they serve but on the whim of the funders, they can no longer respond as effectively to the women they serve. They can no longer respond as grass roots—by paying attention to the soil and fertility conditions—but rather must grow what someone hundreds or thousands of miles away deems a marketable crop. From what I have heard and seen, the need to meet requirements of funders frequently eats away at the heart and soul of the very organizations that the funders intend to support. As an example, HUD's imposition of a model of prioritizing applications for housing that could fill Gimaajii with non-Native residents undermines the very foundation of AICHO's mission to provide shelter for the homeless Native population. The government might as well be planting domesticated rice in indigenous wild rice beds.

But some critical pieces are within the power of these organizations to maintain and restore. Person after person who was involved in these organizations in the early days spoke of a deep sense of loss of the solidarity that was at one time such a vital and energizing part of these organizations and the feminist movement in Duluth. One reason for this is the cessation of the work of education for critical consciousness that once occurred in small consciousness-raising groups throughout the community, as well as in the programming at Women's Transitional Housing, and which was at one time so central to the work of many of the organizations. Most have moved from emphasizing educating for critical consciousness and feminist political awareness and action to become service organizations, and from consciousness-raising groups to support groups. Such a move assumes that once the work of consciousness raising has been accomplished for one generation of women, it is no longer needed. Yet as long as patriarchy persists, every successive generation needs to engage in this work. Most of the work of education for feminist critical consciousness is now confined to the privileged halls of academe and the elite few who are able to access it in courses that include feminist scholarship on women, gender, and intersectionality. While students do carry that education out into the world, and many of them work in these organizations, it is neither sufficient nor wide-reaching enough, nor is it inclusive enough of the perspectives of those outside the academy to create the kind of paradigm shift needed to move from patriarchy to partnership.[2]

Solidarity has also suffered due to loss of collective gathering spaces. While lesbian women no longer need the Coffeehouse as a place to meet because they can be out in the world, the feminist community as a whole lost a great deal with its demise. A central gathering place for the feminist community would serve to sustain, connect, and nourish the relationships, friendships, and vision that have contributed to the vitality and longevity of the feminist movement in the Twin Ports. My hope is that the gatherings held by AICHO at Gimaajii are coming to serve this purpose.

Times have changed, and one factor in the destabilization of so many feminist organizations nationally in the 1990s, and in the Twin Ports in the 2010s, was the emergence of the Third Wave feminist movement and its efforts to problematize and refocus the feminist movement around issues of gender fluidity. Increasingly, these organizations emphasize incorporating a more expansive understanding of gender. It is too early to know its full effects. While this perspective may indeed open a new approach to changing the dominant paradigm, some organizations expressed concerns that in doing so, once again women and the honoring of women's wisdom and experience might become invisible in the process. These organizations strive to keep women at the center of their focus. As feminist scholar Cynthia Enloe suggests, gender neutrality hides the political workings of masculinity and femininity still very much at play in the dominant culture, which in turns stunts our curiosity about patriarchy, enabling its persistence.[3]

It is concerning for the future of feminist organizations that feminism is being disowned by those who have so benefited from its struggles and sacrifices. Even many of the women in these organizations wanted to disassociate from the term "feminist," regarding it as not being inclusive of gender, race, and class perspectives. In this regard, while the recognition of gender fluidity is important, it is also vital to appreciate the fact that that discussion about gender fluidity began decades ago among feminist scholars and activists, and the awareness of gender fluidity in the larger population has been made possible largely through the work of feminists. Similarly, the recognition that the majority of feminist organizations in the Twin Ports have suffered and struggled as a result of being framed from white perspectives is critical. Organizations' work to decenter white perspectives and become organizations that are truly inclusive of all voices and perspectives is only beginning. But to perceive the feminist movement as only and always a white women's movement is to ignore the vital role that women of color have played in the full spectrum of the movement. The very concept of intersectionality of race, class, gender, sexual orientation, nationality, and physical ability originated in and is at the core of contemporary feminism.[4]

In addition, some of those interviewed expressed concern that individuals coming into the work of these organizations today often share the view commonly held in society at large that the need for feminism is over. If that were true, the work of these organizations would be finished. The meaning of feminism has been distorted by antifeminist pundits who have labeled feminists "feminazis" and "man-haters," and, sadly, these are the associations held by the vast majority in this society. These epithets are a far cry from the life- and love-affirming philosophy and movement that I know feminism to be. I have elsewhere defined feminism as resistance to injustice and oppression in affirmation of the dignity of all, in solidarity and friendship with each other and the earth. With this in mind, I concur with the sentiment expressed by Tina Welsh: "I would like people to have a deeper appreciation and respect for the word feminism."[5]

That these organizations must continually struggle to maintain their vision for a more egalitarian and inclusive society in which women, and all beings, are treated with dignity and respect, and occasionally slip back into patriarchal habits of mind may be wearisome, and cause for discouragement. But as Adrienne Rich wrote, "Many of us would be grateful for some rest in the struggle . . . [but] the politics worth having, the relationships worth having, demand that we delve still deeper." Those who have persisted in these organizations through all of the challenges know the truth of Rich's wisdom and continue to rise up to meet that demand.[6]

Reasons for hope remain. Many people working for these organizations persist in their vision and deliberately take time to remind themselves of the need to keep their mission central to their work. In the long arc of history, these organizations have accomplished much in the relatively short time of their existence. Though the numbers of women who are assaulted and abused remain largely unchanged, women are more likely to find themselves treated with sensitivity by the medical and criminal justice systems and have far more resources to aid them in their healing. The culture has shifted from one of victim-blaming and belief in men's right to beat and dominate women to one of widespread recognition that no such "right" exists and it indeed is a crime; and from the need for lesbians to be closeted to the legal affirmation of their right to marry. These organizations have saved many lives, and those lives have been made better.

The conditions of place that led to Duluth/Superior being such a thriving feminist community still exist. Due to the expansive and innovative work of Mending the Sacred Hoop and AICHO, the influence of the women-honoring culture of the Anishinaabe is even more vital than it was in the 1980s. The continuing cross-fertilization of people and ideas is evident at local conferences, meetings, trainings, and cultural events, as well as in new and creative collaborations. The spirit of the community continues to energize and inspire. Writer Linda Hogan once expressed to me that she loves to do readings in Duluth because people here genuinely care. Shunu Shrestha, who came to Duluth in 2010 to begin the Duluth Trafficking Task Force, has found this quality of care to invigorate her feminist work: "Duluth is very proactive. I call it a village. People know everybody, and there's a very communal feeling . . . which actually works in a very beautiful way. Because of that communal feeling, people are really passionate when something like this [the trafficking issue] comes out. . . . People are always up in arms about what they can do, how they can help. . . . I feel blessed to be working here in Duluth."

What has most impressed me in the course of listening to the stories of the women, and a few men, who have been a part of these organizations is what Nancy Burns called the "heart" they bring to this work—the passion, steadfastness, courage, and pluck of dedicated individuals, who self-admittedly jumped into the work not knowing what they were doing, only knowing that somebody needed to do it. This spirit led to the rise of organizations that have changed the world and transformed countless lives for the better. Many spoke of their love for the work, of how deeply rewarding it is to know that they are making a positive difference in the lives of the women and children they serve, and in the world at large. What has meant the most to each of them is witnessing the transformations and triumphs in the lives of the women they have touched.

The legacy of grassroots feminist organizations in Duluth/Superior lies in the visionary and transformational work that continues today. The concepts, frameworks, practices, and models created by individuals in these organizations have spread throughout the state, nation, and world.

Transforming just one life for the better is a success, and these organizations have touched and transformed the lives of thousands. They
have persisted and they have inspired. In their daily work and lives and
in the hope they engender for the future they live out that which is expressed in the name of AICHO's new gathering space: Gimaajii-Mino-
Bimaadizimin—"We are, all of us together, beginning a good life."

Timeline of Events

1970–71
- Northcountry Women's Center opens.
- Women's Liberation of Duluth begins meeting.
- First women's studies–related courses are taught at UMD.
- Northcountry Housing and Cooperative Association (Chester Creek House) is established as a social justice intentional community.

1972
- Woman to Woman Conference is held at Pilgrim Church.
- Duluth Community Health Center opens, providing health care, STD testing, and pregnancy testing and counseling.

1973
- Randi Goldstone from the Neighborhood Improvement Center, the first rape crisis shelter in the Twin Cities, holds a workshop in Duluth for the Duluth and Superior Police Departments and other interested parties, starting early conversations about the need for a rape crisis center in Duluth.
- Following passage of *Roe v. Wade*, abortions are provided at St. Luke's hospital for a few years.

1974
- Provost Ray Darland establishes Special Committee on Women's Studies at UMD to investigate possible Women's Studies program.

1975
- Community meeting is held at YWCA to discuss the need for a rape crisis center in Duluth.

1976
- Aid to Victims of Sexual Assault Program officially begins.
- Wo/men's Center opens at UMD library.
- Duluth chapter of the National Organization for Women is established.
- Feminist therapists at Human Development Center hold women's support group sessions.

1977
- Woodswomen begins wilderness trips for women in the BWCA.
- Speak-out and workshop on domestic violence is held in Duluth that leads to task force investigating the need for a domestic abuse shelter in Duluth and creation of hotline.

1978
- PAVSA officially incorporates.
- Women's Coalition for Battered Women opens its first shelter.
- New Women's Network begins.
- Community Action Program in Duluth begins weatherization program with a commitment to hiring women.

1979
- March for the Equal Rights Amendment happens in downtown Duluth.
- Superior chapter of the National Organization for Women is established.

1980
- Domestic Abuse Intervention Project begins.
- Members of Duluth and Superior NOW travel to Chicago for the national march for the ERA.
- Project SOAR begins.
- Women's Coordinating Committee at UMD works on developing a Women's Studies minor and women's resource center on campus.
- Human Resources Rape and Incest Victim Advocacy (RIVA) unit is established in Douglas County Human Resources Department in Superior.
- Dr. Jane Hodgson of the Midwest Health Center for Women explores the possibility of establishing a clinic in Duluth.

1981
- Women's Health Center opens.
- Northcountry Women's Coffeehouse begins.
- UMD Women's Studies minor is established.
- Wise Women Radio has first broadcast.
- Greater Minnesota Women's Alliance holds kick-off event with Gloria Steinem.
- Chester Creek House becomes a lesbian housing collective.
- A Woman's Bookstore opens in downtown Duluth.
- Take Back the Night rally and march is held in Duluth.

1982
- Wise Women Radio sponsors Holly Near in concert.
- Artemis Productions begins.
- Grandmothers for Peace is founded in Superior.

1983
- Coalition Against Domestic Violence (CADV) begins in Superior.

1984
- *Ruby Red Slippers* has first broadcast on KUMD.

1985
- Local chapter of Women Against Military Madness is founded in Superior.

1986
- Women's Studies at UMD establishes a major in Women's Studies and becomes a department.

1987
- The Institute for Women's Studies is established at UMD.
- The Family Visitation Center opens at the YWCA.

1988
- Aurora: A Northland Lesbian Center incorporates as "Elsie."
- CADV and RIVA combine to form the Center Against Sexual and Domestic Assault (CASDA).
- Women's Transitional Housing opens its doors.
- Women's Resource and Action Center at UMD is established.

1989

- The National Training Project is established as part of the former DAIP, which by now has incorporated as Minnesota Program Development, Inc. (MPDI).
- Early beginnings of Mending the Sacred Hoop.

1990

- First annual Northern Lights Womyn's Music Festival is held north of Duluth.
- Journeys Bookstore opens storefront on Superior Street.

1991

- Mending the Sacred Hoop officially incorporated as part of MPDI.
- At Sara's Table opens at its London Road location.

1992

- Women's Health Center faces eviction from Arrowhead Place building and plans and fundraising for the Building for Women begin.

1993

- Women's Health Center moves into the Building for Women.
- *New Moon Magazine for Girls* publishes its first issue.
- Norcroft: A Writing Retreat for Women is established.
- The Battered Women's Justice Project begins as part of Minnesota Program Development, Inc.

1994

- American Indian Community Housing Organization (AICHO) incorporates.
- Building for Women is fully operational, and PAVSA, the Northcountry Women's Coffeehouse, and Aurora move in.
- Men as Peacemakers is established.

1996

- Praxis International is incorporated.
- AICHO opens Oshki Odaadiziwini Waakan 'Igan transitional housing.

1998
- Praxis International begins work as an organization.
- Women's Coalition opens new shelter.
- Crossroads project begins through MPDI.

1999
- AICHO opens Dabinoo'Igan shelter.
- Women's Transitional Housing becomes Women's Community Development Organization.
- Women in Construction begins as part of Women's Transitional Housing.

2001
- Women's Coalition collective ends and becomes Safe Haven Shelter for Battered Women.

2002
- Women in Construction Company, LLC, becomes its own company.
- Northland Birth Collective begins.

2006
- Mending the Sacred Hoop becomes a separate nonprofit and begins the *Safety and Accountability Audit of the Response to Native Women Who Report Sexual Assault in Duluth* in collaboration with PAVSA and the Duluth Police Department.

2007
- MPDI becomes Domestic Abuse Intervention Programs.
- Praxis International develops Blueprint for Safety with the St. Paul police department.

2008
- Safe Haven's Family Justice (now Resource) Center opens.

2009
- Northcountry Women's Coffeehouse closes its doors.

2010

- Women's Transitional Housing and Women in Construction end.
- North Central Windows Program begins.
- Duluth Trafficking Task Force begins.

2012

- Gimaajii-Mino-Bimaadizimin opens its doors.
- Aurora: A Northland Lesbian Center ceases operation.

2013

- CASDA opens new shelter.
- Mending the Sacred Hoop moves into Gimaajii.
- Native Sisters Society begins.

2014

- Hildegard House, a hospitality house for trafficked women, opens.
- DAIP receives Future Policy Award for Ending Violence Against Women and Girls from the UN World Future Council.

Notes

Note to Methodology

1. Rossi, *Feminist Papers*, 245.

Notes to Introduction

1. Epigraph, Steinem, *Outrageous Acts*, 384.
2. Gilmore, *Groundswell*, 135.
3. The feminist movement in the United States traditionally has been defined in terms of waves, with First Wave feminism being from around the time of the women's rights movement, beginning with the first Women's Rights Convention in Seneca Falls, New York, in 1848, to the achievement of women's suffrage in 1920, and Second Wave feminism beginning about 1960 and merging into the Third Wave sometime in the 1990s. Some speak of Third Wave feminism being very short-lived, saying that we are now in the era of Fourth Wave feminism.

   Some of the widely referenced studies include Alice Echols, *Daring To Be Bad: Radical Feminism in America, 1967–1975*; Anne Enke, *Finding the Movement: Sexuality, Contested Space, and Feminist Activism*; Sara Evans, *Tidal Wave: How Women Changed America at Century's End*; Ruth Rosen, *The World Split Open: How the Modern Women's Movement Changed America*; Winifred Wandersee, *On the Move: American Women in the 1970s*; and Nancy Whittier, *Feminist Generations: The Persistence of the Radical Women's Movement*.

   Jo Freeman first made the two cohort argument in *The Politics of Women's Liberation*. Many others, including Alice Echols, Sara Evans, and Ruth Rosen, have followed suit.
4. Evans, *Tidal Wave*, 61–97.
5. The phrase "the personal is political" is often attributed to Carol Hanisch, who wrote a piece with that title in *Notes from the Second Year: Women's Liberation* (1970). In fact, Shulamith Firestone and Anne Koedt were the ones who gave the piece that title (Hanisch, "The Personal Is Political: The Women's Liberation Movement Classic with a New Introduction," http://www.carolhanisch.org/CHwritings/PIP.html). On the Miss America pageant, Evans, *Tidal Wave*, 40, 51.

6. Freedman, *No Turning Back*, 279, 287, 295, 296, 305; Rosen, *World Split Open*, 184–86, 292; Wandersee, *On the Move*, 56, 80, 91, 92, 184; Evans, *Tidal Wave*, 49.

7. Whittier, *Feminist*, 195; Evans, *Tidal Wave*, 139, 143–44, 149, 207; Wandersee, *On the Move*, 69, 97, 100; Rosen, *World Split Open*, 175; Freedman, *No Turning Back*, 265; Ferree and Hess, *Controversy and Coalition*, 211.

    Historian Alice Echols traces the genesis of lesbian feminism's visibility, in part, to the Lavender Menace action on the opening night of the Second Congress to Unite Women and the presentation of the Radicalesbian position paper, "The Woman-Identified Woman," which she claims used the term "woman-identified" to assuage heterosexual feminists' fears about lesbianism (*Daring*, 214–15).

8. Calling the years from 1983 to 1992 the decade of "defensive consolidation," Myra Ferree and Beth Hess said that during the Reagan and Bush administrations the feminist movement took two steps forward, one step back (*Controversy and Coalition*, 159). Ferree and Hess, *Controversy and Coalition*, 183; Evans, *Tidal Wave*, 178; Whittier, *Feminist*, 184, 197.

9. Whittier, *Feminist*, 88, 197, 207.

10. Freedman, *No Turning Back*, 323–24; Cobble, Gordon, and Henry, *Feminism*, 151–55; Reger, *Everywhere*, 119, 161; Whittier, *Feminist*, 234, 236.

11. "End Bi-Coastal Arrogance" was the slogan printed on T-shirts of the 1983 National Women's Studies Conference in Columbus, Ohio. It was the first NWSA conference held in the heartland.

    On national versus local, for example, Stephanie Gilmore states that "sweeping nationally based narratives of a movement cannot possibly capture completely the nuance and texture of feminist activism in this era" (*Groundswell*, 4). Judith Ezekiel similarly regards overarching explanations of the national movement as inadequate in describing and explaining the "immense, multifaceted grassroots movement in a decentralized country" (*Feminism*, ix). As Anne Enke states, such a generalized national narrative "distorts even as it explains" (*Finding*, 9). Others concur—see Ferree and Hess, *Controversy and Coalition*, ix; Reger, *Everywhere*, 6.

    Gilmore, *Groundswell*, 7–8.

12. Gilmore, *Groundswell*, 10; Reger, *Everywhere*, 6; Enke, *Finding*, 11. Adrienne Rich first used the term "politics of location" in her piece "Notes Toward a Politics of Location," originally published in 1984 and reprinted in *Blood, Bread, and Poetry*.

13. Ferree and Martin, *Feminist Organizations*, 4.

Notes to Chapter 1

1. Sara Evans, Judy Remington, Diane Kravetz, and Alice Echols all detail similar patterns of development of these small feminist organizations in New York, Boston, Chicago, and Washington, DC. In her classic piece, "The Tyranny of Structurelessness," as well as in *The Politics of Women's Liberation*, Jo Freeman expounds on the problems created by the structureless qualities of these organizations. Echols also discusses what she found to be an "obsession with process" in these organizations (*Daring*, 17).

On moving into the mainstream, Ferree and Hess, *Controversy and Co-alition*, 145–47; Wandersee, *On the Move*, 94.

For further discussions of a lack of inclusivity in feminist organizations, see Echols, *Daring*, 254–55; Evans, *Tidal Wave*, 114, 156; Reger, *Everywhere*, 140, 155; Whittier, *Feminist*, 98, 207; and Enke, *Finding*, 9.

2. Michelle LeBeau, interview with author, 2014; Nancy Loving Tubesing, interview with author, October 24, 2013; Nancy Gruver, interview with author, March 28, 2015; Pence quoted in Domestic Abuse Intervention Project, Annual Report, 2011, accessed April 12, 2015, http://www.theduluthmodel.org/cms/files/2011%20annual%20report%20indesign%20web.pdf.

3. Winona LaDuke, presentation at Northern Prints Gallery, Duluth, MN, August 23, 2015.

4. Rossi, *Feminist Papers*, 249.

5. On fracturing of the movement, Evans, *Tidal Wave*, 125, 202; Echols, *Daring*, 202; on Twin Cities feminist organizations, Remington, *Need to Thrive*, 65.

6. Linda Gordon has argued that while these appeared to be two movements, their separation did not last long, and for women outside larger cities, it never existed (Cobble, Gordon, and Henry, *Feminism*, 69, 71).

7. Whittier, *Feminist*, 112.

8. Raymond, *Passion*, 13.

9. Morgan quoted in Echols, *Daring*, 245; Whittier, *Feminist*, 211.

10. In 1980, Duluth had a population of about 93,000 and the population of Superior was about 30,000.

11. Remington, *Need to Thrive*, 69; Miller quoted in Remington, *Need to Thrive*, 39; O'Neil quoted in Remington, *Need to Thrive*, 60; Ezekiel, *Feminism*, 246–47.

12. Duluth has sister cities with Vaxjo, Sweden; Petrozavodsk, Russia; Ohara–Isumi City, Japan; and Rania, Iraqi Kurdistan.

13. Evans, *Tidal Wave*, 202; Michelle LeBeau interview.

14. Whittier, *Feminist*, 234.

15. Wandersee, *On the Move*, xii; Cobble, Gordon, and Henry, *Feminism*, 81; Rosen, *World Split Open*, 199; Taylor, "Watching," 224, 231.

16. Taylor, "Watching," 229, 232; Freeman, *Politics*, 126.

17. Raymond, *Passion*, 8, 9, 28.

18. The women of the indigenous tribes of the Haudenosaunee (Iroquois) nation (the Cayuga, the Onandaga, the Oneida, the Seneca, and the Mohawk) were a significant inspiration and model for women's rights activists in upstate New York in the mid-1800s. As historian Sally Roesch Wagner argued, "They believed women's liberation was possible because they knew women who possessed a position of respect and authority in their own egalitarian society—Haudenosawnee women" ("Indigenous Roots," 248). Associations and friendships between Native and Euro-Americans were particularly strong in upstate New York, and through these the white women learned of the freedom, equality, and respect the Haudenosaunee women experienced. Rape was virtually nonexistent among the Haudenosaunee. Women were honored, and physically violent or punishing behaviors would have been unthinkable and unacceptable. A Haudenosaunee woman could "divorce"

her husband by placing his things outside their home and telling him to leave and return to his own clan. Haudenosaunee women had an equal voice in the governance of their tribes. Even their loose-fitting tunics and pants inspired the Euro women of the area to adopt the new fashion. Elizabeth Cady Stanton, who unlike many white women of her day reportedly gave birth to her seven children with relative ease, practiced a Native-directed form of natural childbirth. In Stanton's living room, where many of the conversations about women's rights occurred, activists all sat in a circle and, using the practice of local tribes, passed a talking stick to ensure that everyone had an equal voice. All of this would come to shape their vision for an egalitarian society as well as the specific reforms they called for in the Declaration of Sentiments, the Married Women's Property Act, the dress reform movement, and their work to reform sexual mores and to bring an end to wife beating, as well as their work for the full inclusion of women in political decision-making and women's suffrage.

19. Babette Sandman, interview with author, December 11, 2014.
20. Tina Olson, interview with author, January 2, 2008.
21. Gilman, *Stand Up!*, 1.
22. So many Finns settled in the Twin Ports that it was known as "the Helsinki of America." The Finns also established a large network of consumer cooperatives, for everything ranging from food and dairy to insurance, credit unions, and burial-aid societies (Kolehmainen and Hill, *Haven*, 139). Central Cooperative Wholesale Records, 1916–69; Karvonen, "Three Proponents," 197–98.
23. Of particular note, women published their own feminist newspaper, the *Toveritar* (*Woman Comrade*), in 1911. Though its publication changed locales, in 1930 it returned to Superior, where it continued to be published under the title *Naisten Viiri* (*Women's Banner*) until 1978. The widely read newspaper was influential in improving the lives and status of women. The women also published separate pamphlets on women's issues that were used for discussion in the many women's "sewing circles," where women read, studied, and debated these issues (Brown, "Legacy," 31–32.). Karvonen, "Three Proponents," 197; Brown, "Legacy," 26.
24. Echols, *Daring*, 85; Evans, *Tidal Wave*, 125.
25. Over a million acres in size, the BWCAW extends nearly one hundred fifty miles along the border with Canada, adjacent to Quetico Provincial Park, a similar wilderness area. It contains over 1,200 miles of canoe routes.
26. Dacher Keltner, "Awe: For Altruism and Health?" John Templeton Foundation, accessed August 8, 2015, http://www.slate.com/bigideas/why-do-we-feel-awe/essays-and-opinions/dacher-keltner-opinion.
27. LaDuke presentation.
28. Chittister, *Heart of Flesh*, 44.

Notes to Chapter 2

1. Further information on and detailed histories of many of the secondary organizations that are mentioned in this chapter are available electronically at Archives and Special Collections, Kathryn A. Martin Library, University

of Minnesota Duluth, http://www.d.umn.edu/lib/. These include: Artemis Productions, At Sara's Table, CAP Weatherization Program, Chester Creek House, the feminist therapists, Grandmothers for Peace, Greater Minnesota Women's Alliance, Journeys Bookstore, Men as Peacemakers, the local branch of the National Organization for Women, *New Moon Magazine*, Project SOAR, the School of Social Development, Wise Women Radio, Woodswomen, Women's Liberation of Duluth, and the Women's Studies program and the Women's Resource and Action Center at UMD, including the Northcountry Women's Center.

HMO is the acronym for health maintenance organization. The first HMO in the country was founded in St. Paul, Minnesota, essentially as a health care cooperative, offering a means for health care consumers to work collaboratively with health care practitioners to manage costs. The idea spread throughout Minnesota but was quickly taken over and reconceptualized by insurance companies, who saw control of the health care system slipping from their grasp.

2. Saul Alinsky, author of *Rules for Radicals* (1971), is widely considered to be the founder of modern community organizing.

3. For the first several years, Loaves and Fishes operated as a station on the overground railway sanctuary movement, helping to house Central American refugees fleeing civil strife and to transport them to Canada, where they were granted political asylum (Angie Miller, interview with author, May 1, 2015.). They were also involved in draft resistance and civil disobedience actions—including the successful effort to shut down a naval base in Clam Lake, Wisconsin, whose extra-low-frequency transmitters acted as a trigger for first-strike nuclear war. The Loaves and Fishes community has done much to create a climate of care and concern for the homeless population in this community, as well as to inspire many to take action on issues of peace and justice.

4. According to Judith Niemi, the Northcountry Women's Center came about primarily "because there was nothing much going for lesbians in Duluth. We were pretty invisible." She had met other lesbians from Duluth at lesbian bars and gatherings in the Twin Cities, and eventually they started connecting up with others in the Twin Ports. The NWC was one of the places where openly lesbian and straight women met and began working together. As Judith said, "There was never a division between the lesbians and the married women."

5. Daly quoted in Margaret Ulvang, "'Option' Is the Key Word When Women Get Together," *Duluth Herald* (MN), October 29, 1972, Mary Ann LucasHoux collection.

6. Photo, *Duluth Herald* (MN), February 19, 1976, A4. UMD Women's Studies Collection, Archives and Special Collections, Kathryn A. Martin Library, University of Minnesota Duluth, http://www.d.umn.edu/lib/.

7. Joyce Benson, interview with author, June 2006.

8. A city initiative originally begun as part of President Johnson's Great Society program, Duluth CAP separated from the city in 1982 and became its own nonprofit. Among its many initiatives were affordable housing development, the Senior Coalition, and neighborhood empowerment efforts. The

weatherization program, established in the mid- to late 1970s, weatherized, at no cost, the homes of people who met certain low-income guidelines.

On Susan's hiring, Wendy Ruhnke, interview with author, January 25, 2015. Susan's sister, Lindy Askelin, who was part of the weatherization project, would go on to be the maintenance person for Women's Transitional Housing and the Building for Women. Their sister, Michelle LeBeau, would later found Women in Construction.

9. Shirley Duke, interview with author, January 25, 2015.

10. The feminist therapists were influenced by Anne Wilson Schaef, Noel Larson, Virginia Shapiro, Sandra Butler, and others. Gloria Singer, interview with author, October 24, 2013.

11. The Equal Rights Amendment had passed both houses of Congress in 1972, but by 1977 still was three states short of ratification. In the last few years preceding the 1982 deadline, most of NOW's national and local activities were focused on ratifying the ERA.

On the ERA rally in Duluth, Cynthia Hill, "ERA Rally Draws Support and Stares," *Duluth Herald Tribune* (MN), August 26, 1979, A1, 12, Joyce Benson collection. On the Take Back the Night rally, Jan Conley, phone interview with author, March 28, 2015.

12. The first federal legislation to address displaced homemakers was the 1976 amendment to the Vocational Education Act, which directed states to use federal money to meet their needs. In 1978 and for many years to follow, programs were specifically targeted for funding through the federal Comprehensive Employment and Training Act (CETA) program ("Displaced Homemakers: Programs and Policies—An Interim Report," Washington, DC: U.S. Office of Technology Assessment, OTA-ITE-292, October 1984, 15).

The Minnesota legislature established funding for displaced homemaker programs in 1977 and began two pilot programs in 1977 and 1978. Due to their success, the legislature authorized funding for two additional programs. By 1994 all counties in Minnesota had displaced homemaker programs (Office of Employment Transition, Workforce Partnerships Division, Minnesota Department of Employment and Economic Development, "Report to Legislature," state fiscal year 2004, St. Paul, MN, accessed January 5, 2016, http://archive.leg.state.mn.us/docs/2005/mandated/050223.pdf).

Tina Welsh, "Feminism in Twin Ports," keynote, October 25, 2002, Tina Welsh collection.

13. Office of Employment Transition, "Report to the Legislature"; Michele St. Martin, "The Little Program that Could," *Minnesota Women's Press*, April 1, 2008; Cullen-Dupont, *Encyclopedia*, 282–83.

14. Sandy Battin, "Women Form Network Like Railroad Line," *Duluth Herald* (MN), August 31, 1980, Mary Ann LucasHoux collection; Lucas quoted in Ann Glumac, "Women Form Answer to 'Old Boys' Network,'" *Duluth Herald* (MN) [1978], parentheses in original, Mary Ann LucasHoux collection; Tierney quoted in Glumac, "Women Form Answer." In 1993, an all-volunteer organization with similar purposes, the Professional Women's Network, was formed. It continues to hold monthly luncheon gatherings in Duluth.

15. Joyce Benson, Patricia Pearson, Mary Ryland, and Marilyn Krueger, "Greater

Minnesota Women's Alliance: GMWA Accomplishments: Yesterday, Today and Tomorrow," address, Third World Conference on Women of the UN Decade for Women (1976–1985), United Nations, Nairobi, Kenya, July 1985, Joyce Benson collection.

16. GMWA Newsletter, September 25, 1981, Joyce Benson collection; Benson interview.

17. Ann Glumac, "Alliance Gives Duluth Women Political Clout," *Duluth News-Tribune & Herald* (MN), October 17, 1982, C1; Benson, Pearson, Ryland, and Krueger, "Greater Minnesota."

18. Stephanie Hemphill, interview with Tineke Ritmeester, July 18, 2007; Jean Johnson, memo to "Interested Person," WDTH, February 11, 1981, Stephanie Hemphill collection; Brenda Dziuk Latourelle, e-mail correspondence with author, March 19, 2015.

19. Brenda Djiuk, "Meeting Notice: Women's Radio Project," Stephanie Hemphill collection.

20. Information on program content and events comes from dozens of Wise Women Radio programming notes in the Stephanie Hemphill collection.

21. Hemphill interview.

22. The material on Artemis derives primarily from an author interview with Linda Estel, July 2006.

23. Michigan refers to Michigan Womyn's Music Festival.

24. Tineke Ritmeester, interview with author, July 2006.

25. *North Shore Visions*, May 1988, UMD Women's Studies Collection, University of Minnesota Duluth.

26. The information on Men as Peacemakers derives primarily from an author interview with Frank Jewell, October 15, 2014.

27. Neubert quoted in Rachel Kraft, "Lesbians Share Experiences of Living in Duluth," *Lake Voice News* (Duluth, MN), March 7, 2013.

28. The material and quotes on *New Moon Magazine* are derived primarily from an author interview with Nancy Gruver, March 28, 2015.

29. Suzanne Kelsey, "The End of a Dream: Norcroft Writing Retreat Closes This Month After Nurturing More Than 600 Women Writers," *Minnesota Women's Press*, October 2005.

30. Information on the Northland Birth Collective derives primarily from an author e-mail correspondence with Jana Studelska, May 16, 2015.

31. Susan Meyers, e-mail correspondence with author, May 13, 2015; Michele Naar-Obed, e-mail correspondence with author, April 29, 2015.

Notes to Chapter 3

1. Nancy Massey, quoted in "PAVSA 35th anniversary: 35 Years of Working to End Sexual Violence," compiled by Em Westerlund, 2009–10, author's collection.

2. "PAVSA 35th Anniversary."

3. Quoted in "PAVSA 35th Anniversary."

4. Much material from this chapter derives from interviews with Phyllis Cook, Candice Harshner, Rosemary Rocco, Shunu Shrestha, Tina Welsh, and Inez

Wildwood, as well as Tina Welsh's keynote address to the "Making Women's History Now" conference that inspired this book.

5. "PAVSA 35th Anniversary"; Doug Smith, "New County Rape Program Begun," news article, n.d., PAVSA collection.

6. Gillespie quoted in "PAVSA 35th Anniversary"; Welsh, "Feminism in Twin Ports."

7. Welsh, "Feminism in Twin Ports."

8. Rosemary Rocco, interview with Em Westerlund, April 17, 2013.

9. First and third degree involve penetration of the mouth, vagina, or rectum by physical contact or an object; second and fourth involve sexual assault without penetration. Minnesota State Statutes on sexual assault (609.341–609.3451) have been revised and amended multiple times. A fifth degree of sexual assault was added in 1988.

    "Aid to Sexual Assault Victims Available," news article, Gilbert, MN, n.d., PAVSA collection.

10. St. Louis County is the largest county, by area, in Minnesota and the second largest east of the Mississippi. Extending from Duluth to the Canadian border, it covers a total of 6,860 square miles, about the size of the state of New Jersey. Adding Lake, Carlton, Itasca, and Aitkin doubled that, and with Cook, they encompass all of northeastern Minnesota.

11. Todd Beamon, "Showers Fail to Dampen Spirit of 'Take Back the Night' Rally," *Duluth News-Tribune & Herald* (MN), September 12, 1982; Inez Wildwood, interview with author, December 1, 2014.

12. "PAVSA 35th Anniversary."

13. MN Statute §5300.0340, 2008.

14. Coral McDonnell, Letter to Take Back the Night Planning Committee, May 16, 1990, PAVSA collection.

15. Candice Harshner, interview with author, October 14, 2014.

16. Schomberg and Fries quoted in Mark Stodghill, "Duluth Area Groups Collaborate to Train Nurses to Care for Sexual Assault Victims," *Duluth News Tribune* (MN), April 3, 2008; Harshner interview.

17. "PAVSA 35th Anniversary."

18. "PAVSA 35th Anniversary."

19. Bhy Ron Brochu, "Schools Develop Response to Harassment—Duluth's Policy Would Include Training for Teachers," *Duluth News Tribune* (MN), May 12, 2002, A1.

20. Harshner interview; Mark Stodghill, "Methods Focus on Helping Sexual Assault Victims—Public Safety: The SMART Team Aims to Improve the Way Victims Are Treated in the System," *Duluth News Tribune* (MN), February 25, 2005, D3.

21. Harshner quoted in Mark Stodghill, "Duluth Police Receive Prestigious Award," *Duluth News Tribune* (MN), September 18, 2012.

22. Shunu Shrestha, interview with author, March 11, 2015. A challenge Shunu has faced in her work in trafficking is needing to adapt continually to changing ways that perpetrators find to victimize. Not long ago, pimping primarily happened on the streets; now it's online.

23. Safe Harbor: MN Statute §145.4716; see exclusions at MN Statute §260B.007, Subd. 6.

24. Editorial, "Victims not Criminals," *Duluth News Tribune* (MN), August 17, 2014, D8; Littman quoted in Mark Stodghill, "Rubin Supports Bill to Protect Exploited Children," *Duluth News Tribune* (MN), May 5, 2011.
25. The seven counties are St. Louis, Carlton, Pine, Kennebec, Koochiching, Lake, and Itasca. For more information on the ten-week program, see Justice Research Institute, "My Life, My Choice," accessed June 14, 2015, http://www.fightingexploitation.org/.
26. Harshner interview; Shrestha interview.
27. Fifield quoted in "Meet a Volunteer," *Duluth News Tribune* (MN), August 14, 2011, C6; Perpich quoted in "Meet a Volunteer," *Duluth News Tribune* (MN), August 12, 2012.
28. Harshner interview.

Notes to Chapter 4

1. Safe Haven, "History," n.d., Jean DeRider collection.
2. Mary Chagnon disappeared under suspicious circumstances in August of 1973. She had not withdrawn money from her bank account. Scheduled to give a keynote address the day she disappeared, she had never shown. Most of her friends felt sure she had been murdered (Judith Niemi, phone interview with author, January 5, 2015). "There's no doubt in our minds that something violent has become of Mary. It would not be like her to just run away," said Nancy Marschke, who had been in the Women's Liberation support group with Mary [quoted in Larry Oakes, "Getting Away with Murder," *Duluth News-Tribune & Herald* (MN), June 24, 1984, C1]. Many suspect that Mary's husband, who several years later was convicted of assault with the intent to commit murder of his girlfriend at the time, had murdered her. Her body was never found.

   John Myers, "Lincoln Hotel Demolished," *Duluth News Tribune* (MN), April 17, 2005, http://attic.areavoices.com/2011/09/20/hotel-lincoln-comes-down-2004/.
3. Susan Utech, Jean DeRider, and Shirley Oberg, "Safe Haven Shelter," lecture presented for University for Seniors, University of Minnesota Duluth, April 2012. Much of the material for this chapter derives from interviews with Sheryl Boman, Cathryn Curley, Jean DeRider, Michelle LeBeau, Shirley Oberg, Trisha O'Keefe, Tina Olson, and Susan Utech.
4. Shirley Oberg, interview with author, December 16, 2014; Utech, DeRider, and Oberg, "Safe Haven."
5. Oberg interview; Utech, DeRider, and Oberg, "Safe Haven."
6. The original members of the collective were Nancy Ahmed, Linda Breiman, Jean DeRider, Linda Freeman, Pat Gosz, Pat Hoover, Sharon Karas, Michelle LeBeau, Kathie Moore, Shirley Oberg, Cathy Tickle (Curley), and Carolyn Torvick. "10th Anniversary Celebration" program, Jean DeRider collection.

   Jean DeRider, interview with author, November 19, 2014.
7. Cathryn Curley, "Acknowledging 25 Years," Safe Haven Shelter, accessed November 20, 2014, http://www.safehavenshelter.org/wp-content/uploads/2012/09/Acknowledging-25-Years.pdf.

8. Utech, DeRider and Oberg, "Safe Haven"; Quie detail from Oberg interview.
    A civil order for protection is a court order that sets conditions on the respondent (the person the order is against) when domestic abuse is alleged. "The conditions may include, but are not limited to: no harm, no contact, exclusion from residence/employment, custody/parenting time, child support, etc." ("OFP FAQs," Second District, Minnesota Judicial Branch, accessed May 29, 2015, http://www.mncourts.gov/ofpfaq.aspx).
9. Utech, DeRider, and Oberg, "Safe Haven."
10. Utech, DeRider, and Oberg, "Safe Haven."
11. This was adopted by the State of Minnesota in 2002: "The policy shall discourage dual arrests, include consideration of whether one of the parties acted in self-defense, and provide guidance to officers concerning instances in which officers should remain at the scene of a domestic abuse incident until the likelihood of further imminent violence has been eliminated" [MN Statute §629.342, subd. 2(a) (2002)].
12. In her groundbreaking work on curricular development, scholar Peggy McIntosh first raised the point that simply to "add women and stir" was not a sufficient approach to incorporating gender into curricula.
13. Trisha O'Keefe, interview with author, November 13, 2014.
14. *Aurora Borealis*, January 1990, Aurora Collection, Archives and Special Collections, Kathryn A. Martin Library, University of Minnesota Duluth, http://www.d.umn.edu/lib/.
15. O'Keefe interview.
16. Cathryn Curley, "The Women's Coalition Visits Russia," Building for Women Newsletter, June 1999; Jason Begay, "Women's Coalition Grant To Aid Russians Sister City To Learn from Duluth Shelter," *Duluth News-Tribune* (MN), May 30, 1998, B5.
17. Curley, "The Women's Coalition."
18. Noam Levey, "New Women's Shelter Unwelcome, Lower Chester Residents Want Open Space Left," *Duluth News-Tribune* (MN), January 27, 1997, A7.
19. Levey, "New Women's Shelter."
20. Cathryn Curley, interview with Susana Pelayo Woodward, 2008.
21. Lisa Michals, "Kenyans Learn To Fight Domestic Violence—Activists Come to Duluth To Participate in Exchange Program for Women's Shelter," *Duluth News Tribune* (MN), August 1, 2002, B2.
22. The center was designed by architects Susie Vandersteen and Sarah Sidleman and rehabbed by Women in Construction.
    Mark Stodghill, "Fundraiser Tonight in Duluth To Help Pay for New Shelter for Abuse Victims," *Duluth News Tribune* (MN), September 14, 2007.
23. Safe Haven, Lake Superior Regional Family Justice Center brochure, author's collection; "Safe Haven Statistics," n.d., collection of Safe Haven Shelter, Duluth, MN.
24. "Safe Haven Statistics."
25. "Safe Haven Statistics."
26. The full statement of the core values are as follows: "1) safety—striving to overcome fear and create a safe environment for all through nonviolence, shelter, and confidentiality; 2) equality—working toward justice and shared power through fairness, diversity, and respect; 3) teamwork—

collaboration with trust, integrity, passion, and competence to meet our goals through positivity, enthusiasm, supportiveness; 4) empowerment— creating independence through education, respect, and awareness by putting the needs of the woman first through healing, strength, and growth; and 5) compassion—providing support and resources with non-judgmental advocacy through empathy, dignity, and understanding" (Collection of Safe Haven Shelter, Duluth, MN).

27. Curley quoted in Chris Olwell, "Women's Shelter Celebrates Milestone, Accomplishments," *Duluth News Tribune* (MN), February 29, 2008.

28. Curley quoted in Mark Stodghill, "Battered Women's Advocate Honored at Duluth Crime Victims' Event," *Duluth News Tribune* (MN), April 16, 2008.

Notes to Chapter 5

1. Shepard and Pence, *Coordinating Community Responses*, 16. The eight key components of the intervention model, as identified by Melanie Shepard and Ellen Pence, are: 1) creating a coherent philosophical approach centralizing victim safety; 2) developing best practice policies and protocols for agencies that are part of an integrated response; 3) enhancing networking among service providers; 4) building a monitoring and tracking system; 5) ensuring a supportive community infrastructure for battered women; 6) providing sanction and rehabilitation opportunities for batterers; 7) undoing harm violence to women does to children; 8) evaluating the coordinated community response from the standpoint of victim safety.

2. Oberg interview. Much of the material in this chapter derives from interviews with Jill Abernathy, Marvella Davis, Lee Hemming, Coral McDonnell, Shirley Oberg, Ellen Pence, Linda Riddle, Babette Sandman, Carol Thompson, Lora Wedge, Janice Wick, and Maren Woods.

3. Pence and McMahon, "A Coordinated Community Response"; Pence, "Duluth Domestic Abuse Intervention Project," 6–3.

4. Pence, "Duluth Domestic Abuse Intervention Project," 6–3; Oberg interview; Pence and McMahon, "A Coordinated Community Response."

5. Paymar, "Duluth Model?"

6. Pence, "Duluth Domestic Abuse Intervention Project," 6–3; Utech, DeRider, and Oberg, "Safe Haven"; Oberg interview.

7. Utech, DeRider, and Oberg, "Safe Haven."

8. Pence and McMahon, "A Coordinated Community Response"; Shepard and Pence, *Coordinating Community Responses*, 17, 28. For a fuller discussion of the philosophy underlying the DAIP, see Pence, "Some Thoughts on Philosophy," in Shepard and Pence, *Coordinating Community Responses*, 25–40.

9. Pence, "Advocacy," 332.

10. Pence, "Advocacy," 332.

11. Pence, "Duluth Domestic Abuse Intervention Project," 6–4, 6–5, 6–6; Pence, "Advocacy," 338; Oberg interview.

12. Paymar, "Duluth Model?"; Pence, "Advocacy," 338; Pence, "Duluth Domestic Abuse Intervention Project," 6–7.

13. Coral McDonnell, interview with Tineke Ritmeester, July 14, 2008.

14. DAIP's views on the prison system were informed in part by the work of

Barbara Smith and Lisa Leghorn on domestic violence and prison reform (Pence, "Duluth Domestic Abuse Intervention Project," 6–8).

On the men's groups, Paymar, "Duluth Model?"

15. The basic premise of the Freirean approach to education, as developed in his *Pedagogy of the Oppressed*, was "problem-posing" rather than the traditional "banking method" of providing a predetermined knowledge set. Following this approach, DAIP adopted a particular educational process for use in women's groups. It includes five main steps: 1) conducting a survey to discover the issues the participants want to discuss; 2) choosing a theme from the surveys, allowing the facilitator to pose a problem; 3) analyzing the problem from three perspectives: personal, institutional, and cultural; 4) developing a "code," that is, a teaching tool such as a picture, role play, or story to focus and generate discussion; and 5) discussion of possible actions for change. For a more detailed description of the process, see DAIP's women's curriculum, Pence, *In Our Best Interest*.

16. Marvella Davis, Jean DeRider, Coral McDonnell, Shirley Oberg, Babette Sandman, and others separately recounted this protest. It is also described in Pence, *In Our Best Interest*, 97.

17. Among WAG's members over the years were Jill Abernathy, Rose Anderson, Leah Carr, Marvella Davis, Julia Dinsmore, Robin Erickson, Kelly Fenstamaker, Shannon Knasolla, Julie Merrian, Stephanie Meyer, Susan Moore, Darlene Moyer, and Babette Sandman (Marvella Davis, interview with author, December 11, 2014, and Sandman interview).

18. The skits were the "codes" they had developed in their initial consciousness-raising sessions.

19. Linda Miller-Cleary, interview with author, December 1, 2014.

20. "Ellen Pence: Battered Women's Movement Leader," December 6, 2009, YouTube video, https://www.youtube.com/watch?v=r9dZOgr78eE; Pence, "Duluth Domestic Abuse Intervention Project," 6–13.

21. Lenore Walker developed her "cycle of violence" theory based on a pattern she found after interviewing 1,500 battered women. The stages of the cycle are: tension building; acting out; reconciliation/honeymoon; and calm. In abusive relationships, this cycle keeps repeating.

Quoted in "Ellen Pence," YouTube video, and in Pence, "Duluth Domestic Abuse Intervention Project," 6–16.

22. "Ellen Pence," YouTube video. The core tactics are: intimidation; emotional abuse; isolation; minimizing, denying, blaming; using children; using male privilege; economic abuse; coercion and threats.

23. "Values," http://www.theduluthmodel.org/about.html. The curricula are designed to help members critically examine and reflect on the various aspects of a given theme or problem; to provide a process that is liberating to the group as a whole; and to expand the facilitator's own knowledge (Pence, *In Our Best Interest*, 29). The curriculum lays out the steps of the process. It also develops themes, "codes," discussion questions, and so forth, from several topics that emerged from the groups. For more information, see Pence, *In Our Best Interest*.

24. Pence, "Duluth Domestic Abuse Intervention Project," 6–16, 6–17.

25. Paymar, "Duluth Model?"; Pence, "Duluth Domestic Abuse Intervention Project," 6–13.
26. Pence, "Duluth Domestic Abuse Intervention Project," 6–10. The men's curriculum used the process adapted from Freire: the Power and Control Wheel, the Equality Wheel, and the "control log" —a series of questions designed for the men to tell their stories of when they have used abusive behaviors and to analyze them (Pence, "Duluth Domestic Abuse Intervention Project," 6–14) .

    The men's curriculum has been criticized for its cognitive approach to changing men's beliefs and attitudes, with some experts arguing that a focus on anger management and substance abuse, or marriage counseling, is more appropriate (Paymar, "Duluth Model?"). Some argue that the cognitive approach is ineffective in ending domestic violence; others that it is oversimplified, based on "a radical form of feminism" [Donald Dutton and Kenneth Corvo, "Transforming a Flawed Policy," *Aggression and Violent Behavior* 11.5 (September–October 2006): 457–83, doi:10.1016/j.avb.2006.01.007]. This critique has been countered by the research of Edward Gondolf, who found that those completing a cognitive program were far less likely to batter again. Five years after offenders had gone through the program, 70 percent were not using physical violence. DAIP has also found that only a quarter of the men who complete the program end up back in the criminal justice system [Edward W. Gondolf, "Theoretical and Research Support for the Duluth Model: A Reply to Dutton and Corvo," *Aggression and Violent Behavior* 12 (2007): 644–57, doi:10.1016/j.avb.2007.03.001].
27. Curley quoted in McMahon and Pence, "Doing More Harm," 193; McMahon and Pence, "Doing More Harm," 194.
28. McMahon and Pence, "Doing More Harm," 188, 194.
29. Ellen Pence, interview with Tineke Ritmeester, June 27, 2006.
30. Pence interview.
31. Pence interview.
32. Linda Hanson, "In Defense of Women Duluth Advocate Tackles New Issue: Abuse Victims Who Fight Back," *Duluth News-Tribune* (MN), July 19, 1998, A1.
33. Marshall quoted in Hanson, "In Defense."
34. Lisdahl quoted in Daniel Bernard, "Anti-Violence Programs to Share One Roof," *Duluth News-Tribune* (MN), April 17, 1998, B4.
35. See for example, Miriam Ruttenberg's "A Feminist Critique of Mandatory Arrest: An Analysis of Race and Gender in Domestic Violence Policy," *Journal of Gender and the Law* 2 (1994): 171–99, http://digitalcommons.wcl .american.edu/jgspl/vol2/iss1/6.

    Paymar, "Duluth Model?" The controversy was spurred in part due to Murray Strauss's research that found women reported using violence in equal numbers to men. Many practitioners today argue that women are just as violent as men. Michael Paymar has countered that women using violence and battering by women, which happens very infrequently, are two different things. Nevertheless, an increasing nationwide trend has been to treat women who fight back as batterers [Murray Strauss, "Gender Symmetry and Mutuality in Perpetration of Clinical-Level Partner Violence: Empirical

Evidence and Implications for Prevention and Treatment," *Aggression and Violent Behavior* 16 (2011): 279–88, doi: 10.1016/j.avb.2011.04.010].

36. Many specifics were never made clear to me. Most people were reluctant to talk about the nature of the tensions, especially for the record. Ellen died before I had a chance to ask her more about this.

37. With the exception of Mending the Sacred Hoop, all the programs remained as part of the umbrella organization. Because of changes in VAWA, MSH slowly transitioned out of DAIP on friendly terms, becoming its own nonprofit.

38. Domestic Abuse Intervention Project, Annual Report, 2011, accessed April 12, 2015, http://www.theduluthmodel.org/cms/files/2011%20annual%20 report%20indesign%20web.pdf; Linda Riddle, interview with author, January 21, 2015.

39. Hanson quoted in Peter Passi, "Duluth Steps Up Battle Against Domestic Violence—City Again Held Aloft as National Model," *Duluth News Tribune* (MN), January 30, 2015, A8, 9.

40. Lora Wedge and a team of others—Carol Thompson, Barbara Jones Shroyer, Graham Barnes, Michael Paymar, and Scott Miller—worked on updating the curriculum to focus more on current practices. They also provided discussion questions and videos drawn from experiences of women at the visitation center.

    On Transitions, Jill Abernathy, interview with author, December 18, 2014; on post-separation violence, Domestic Abuse Intervention Project, Annual Report, 2012, accessed April 12, 2015, http://www.theduluthmodel .org/cms/files/2012%20annual%20report%20indesign%20web.pdf; Abernathy interview.

41. "Ellen Pence," YouTube video.

42. Shamita Das Dasgupta, "My Friend, Advocate Ellen Pence," *Violence Against Women* 16.9 (September 2010): 987, doi:10.1177/1077801210379254.

43. Regarding the work of others, Ellen referenced reform movements in Seattle and San Francisco; programs for men in Minneapolis, Boston, Seattle, and St. Louis; the Oregon mandatory arrest law; the work of Barbara Smith and Lisa Leghorn and Russell and Rebecca Dobash (Pence, "Duluth Domestic Abuse Intervention Project," 6–46).

44. "Interview with Ellen Pence, with Casey Gwinn," December 2009, YouTube video, https://www.youtube.com/watch?v=bZeppoVr5fo; Paymar, "Duluth Model?"

45. Pence, "Reflection."

Notes to Chapter 6

1. Tina Welsh, interview with Em Westerlund, May 4, 2012. Much of the material from this chapter derives from interviews with Laurie Casey, Karen Diver, Rosemary Rocco, and Tina Welsh.

2. Melanie Evans, "Abortion Pill Expected To Make Quiet Local Debut Late This Year," *Duluth News Tribune* (MN), November 25, 2000, A1.

3. McKnight Grant, 1981, in Tina Welsh collection.

4. Welsh, "Feminism in Twin Ports."

5. LeAnne Schreiber, "A Fortress of Their Own," *Self*, May 1998, 163.

6. Tina Welsh, "Testimony: Clinic Access," April 13, 1993, Tina Welsh collection.
7. Begun in 1986, Operation Rescue is in its own estimation the largest Christian "pro-life" anti-abortion organization in the country. It prides itself on closing down abortion clinics all over the country (Operation Rescue, "Who We Are," 2015, accessed May 19, 2015, http://www.operationrescue.org/about-us/who-we-are/).
8. Laura Fraser, "Hodgson's Choice," *Vogue* (July 1990): 206, 207; Tina Welsh, Physicians for Reproductive Choice, "Voices of Choice"; Karen Diver, interview with author, January 29, 2015.
9. Welsh, "Testimony: Clinic Access"; Welsh, Physicians for Reproductive Choice, "Voices of Choice."
10. Welsh interview.
11. Kron quoted in Chuck Frederick, "Abortion Clinic Scares County off Arrowhead," *Duluth News-Tribune* (MN), May 23, 1990; Welsh on crimes in Julie Gravelle, "Women's Health Center Loses Lease Due to Harassment," *Duluth News-Tribune* (MN), June 20, 1992, A3; on butyric acid, Welsh, "Testimony: Clinic Access." Butyric acid is a clear, colorless liquid with a rancid odor that can linger for months. Its use in clinic attacks has caused thousands of dollars of damage, requiring clinics to replace carpeting and furniture and conduct extensive cleanup of facilities.
12. NARAL Pro-Choice America, "Anti-Choice Violence"; Welsh, "Feminism in Twin Ports."
13. "Building for Women Project History and Overview," n.d., Tina Welsh collection. A longer, more detailed history of the Building for Women is available electronically at Archives and Special Collections, Kathryn A. Martin Library, University of Minnesota Duluth, http://www.d.umn.edu/lib/.
14. Rocco, quoted in Schreiber, "Fortress," 178.
15. Schreiber, "Fortress," 178.
16. Schreiber, "Fortress," 178.
17. "Building for Women Limited Partnership, Limited Partnership Agreement," Tina Welsh collection.
18. Welsh interview; Schreiber, "Fortress," 177; Drury quoted in Schreiber, "Fortress," 177.
19. Rosemary Rocco, e-mail correspondence with author, January 19, 2015.
20. There have been more than 6,800 acts of violence toward abortion providers since 1977 and close to 200,000 acts of disruption, including bomb threats and hate mail. Since 1994, eight clinic workers have been murdered. There have been seventeen other attempted murders (NARAL Pro-Choice America, "Anti-Choice Violence").

    Rev. Paul Jennings Hill was the director of Defensive Action, which advocated for and justified the murder of abortion providers as a "defensive action." In 1994, he was convicted of the murders of John Britton, an abortion clinic physician, and his bodyguard, James Barrett. He was executed in 2003 (NARAL Pro-Choice America, "Anti-Choice Violence").
21. Schreiber, "Fortress," 177; Andrea Novel, "Its Opponents Assail 'Secrecy,'" *Duluth News-Tribune* (MN), December 16, 1993, A1.
22. Janice Pilon, "All Should Know Abortion Clinic Had Role in Building for Women," letter, *Duluth News-Tribune* (MN), December 16, 1993.
23. JoAnne Axtell, "United Way Neutral on Abortion: United Way Does Not

Fund Abortion, If It Withdrew, Would Be Accused of Being Pro-Life," *Duluth News-Tribune* (MN), January 14, 1994, A5.

24. Schwietz quoted in Susan Hogan-Albach, "Bishop Quits United Way: Building for Women Is at Center of Controversy," *Duluth News-Tribune* (MN), December 21, 1993, B1; see also Bishop Schwietz, "United Way Not Neutral," letter, *Duluth News-Tribune* (MN), January 8, 1994, A7. Letters quoted in Larry Oakes, "Abortion Clinic Divides Catholics and Charities," *Minneapolis Star Tribune*, December 24, 1993, B1; letter to Women's Health Center, December 21, 1992, Tina Welsh collection (names omitted to protect the privacy of the correspondents); Susan Hogan-Albach, "A Surprise Move: United Way, Diocese Reunite," *Duluth News-Tribune* (MN), August 11, 1994, A1.

25. The ad, which read "Congratulations to Building for Women," was signed by Revs. Judy Ondich, Karen Gustafson, Douglas Paul, Jan Morey, Robert Hickman, Lynn Silva-Breen, Amy Dindinger, Kathryn Nelson, Joel Huenemann, David Wheeler, John Kemp, Beverly Hosea, and Cindy Peterson-Wlonizinski and Rabbi Martin Scharf and Deacon Helen Hanten.

    "Concerning Abortion, Bishop Issue: Pastors, Deacons, Oppose Building for Women," letter, *Duluth News-Tribune* (MN), January 16, 1994; Life, advertisement, *Duluth News-Tribune* (MN), January 13, 1994, B3; Sheila S. Fishman, Minnesota Assistant Attorney General, letter to Women's Health Center, June 23, 1994, Tina Welsh collection.

26. Kathleen Hofer to Karen Diver, February 21, 1994, Tina Welsh collection. One example was a letter from Robert Powless with a $400 donation for the Mother's Day Walk/Run, saying that it was to help defray the amount withheld by St. Mary's (Letter to Karen Diver, March 7, 1994, Tina Welsh collection).

27. Whitney quoted in Schreiber, "Fortress," 178.

28. Schwietz quoted in Schreiber, "Fortress," 181.

29. Gloria Steinem quoted in fundraising letter for the Building for Women, Tina Welsh collection; Welsh interview.

30. Welsh interview.

31. Susan Hogan-Albach, "Mixed Blessing: Ceremony Dedicates Building for Women," *Duluth News-Tribune* (MN), October 11, 1994, C1, 2; Tricia Booker, "Risk-Takers, Miracle Workers: Rosemary Rocco, Tina Welsh, Karen Diver," *Minnesota Women's Press* 10.21 (January 11–24, 1995): 8.

32. The other women's buildings are in Minneapolis and San Francisco. Smeal quoted in Schreiber, "Fortress," 180.

33. "Building for Women: A 'Community Dream,'" Building for Women Newsletter, March 1997.

34. On violence close to home, NARAL Pro-Choice America, "Anti-Choice Violence"; Welsh interview.

35. MN Statute § 609.7495. In a victory for the protection of abortion providers and clinics, the U.S. Supreme Court in *Hill v. Colorado* (2000) upheld Colorado's eight-foot no-approach zone within one hundred feet of abortion clinics. However, a 2014 ruling by the court in *McCullen v. Cloakley* struck down a similar law in Massachusetts as a violation of free speech, placing buffer zone legislation and abortion providers at risk once again.

36. Candace Renalls, "Pro-Life Clinic to Open Near Abortion Provider in Down-

town Duluth—Pro-life Advocates Are Taking to a New Level Their Opposition to the Abortions Performed at the Women's Health Center in Downtown Duluth," *Duluth News Tribune* (MN), July 1, 2012.

37. Laurie Casey, e-mail correspondence with author, April 10, 2016.
38. *Belotti v. Baird* (1979) allowed states to mandate parental consent, or a judicial bypass, for minors seeking abortions; *Harris v. McCrae* (1980) allowed payments for medically necessary abortions to be excluded from Medicaid; *Webster v. Reproductive Health Services* (1989) allowed states to impose restrictions on the use of state funds, facilities, and employees in providing abortion services; and *Planned Parenthood v. Casey* (1992) upheld the right of states to impose laws that restrict access to abortion at any stage of pregnancy, as long as these do not impose an "undue burden" on a woman's access to abortion. Of several state-imposed restrictions, only spousal notification was held to impose such an "undue burden," but mandatory waiting periods, parental notification and consent, and presentation of biased information were not so regarded.

The 1981 law states that if each parent can be located through reasonable effort, they must be notified either personally or through certified mail at least forty-eight hours before the procedure.

Judicial bypass, *Hodgson v. Minnesota*, 497 U.S. 417 (1990); MN Statute §144.343.
39. *Jane Doe v. Gomez*, 542 N.W.2d 17 (1995).
40. MN Statute §§ 145.1421-145.1429; "Woman's Right to Know Act," Minnesota Department of Health, accessed March 20, 2015, http://www.health.state.mn.us/wrtk/.
41. For more information on legislation restricting abortion access, see Robin Abcarian, "Antiabortion Measures Flooding State Legislatures," *Los Angeles Times*, May 8, 2011, http://articles.latimes.com/2011/may/08/nation/la-na-abortion-legislation-20110508.
42. Welsh, Physicians for Reproductive Choice, "Voices of Choice."
43. Casey e-mail correspondence.
44. "Women's Health Center History and Overview," n.d., in Tina Welsh collection.

Notes to Chapter 7

1. Kathy Heltzer, interview with author, June 2006. Much of the material for this chapter derives from interviews with Deb Anderson, Jody Anderson, Shirley Duke, Linda Estel, Kathy Heltzer, Dianna Hunter, Fran Kaliher, and Caroline Pelzel, as well as from dozens of Coffeehouse monthly flyers, 1981–2006, Kathy Heltzer collection.
2. Enke, *Finding*, 118, 120, 125.
3. Deb Anderson, interview with author, November 21, 2014.
4. Quoted in Bob Ashenmacher, "Women's Nightspot Draws Standing-Room Only Crowd," *Duluth Herald* (MN), May 4, 1981.
5. *Radical Harmonies*, DVD, directed by Dee Mosbacher, 2002, San Francisco: WomanVision, 2002; Heltzer interview; Estel interview.
6. Northcountry Women's Coffeehouse, "By-Laws," Northcountry Women's

Coffeehouse Collection, Archives and Special Collections, Kathryn A. Martin Library, University of Minnesota Duluth, http://www.d.umn.edu/lib/.

7. "Women who weren't connected up": Heltzer interview.
8. Lesbian separatism, the theory that all feminists must necessarily be lesbian, otherwise they were giving energy and allegiance to patriarchy and male-defined culture, arose in feminist thought and practice in the early 1980s.
9. Heltzer interview; Enke, *Finding*, 221.
10. Heltzer interview.
11. Ashenmacher, "Women's Nightspot."
12. Most of the information about performances and events at the Coffeehouse come from monthly flyers (Coffeehouse Flyers, 1981–2006, Kathy Heltzer collection).

   Lois Jensen filed a class action suit against Eveleth Taconite Co. in 1988 for the abusive and demeaning sexual harassment she encountered while working for the company. It was the first class action suit for sexual harassment in the country. She won the case on appeal late in 1997, and the company made a $3.5 million settlement to the fifteen female employees in 1998 (Bingham and Gansler, *Class Action*).
13. Delattre quoted in Dominic Papatola, "Coffeehouse Audience Grows Through the Years," *Duluth News-Tribune* (MN), October 2, 1992, B8.
14. Dianna Hunter, interview with author, November 21, 2014.
15. Popeil's Pocket Fisherman was one of several innovations by Ron Popeil, an inventor who sold his gadgets only through television. To view the Popeil Pocket Fisherman commercial, go to Mike Duffy, "Popeil Pocket Fisherman 1972," January 30, 2013, YouTube, https://www.youtube.com/watch?v=ujW3qf9fyXk.
16. Papatola, "Coffeehouse Audience"; Shirley Duke, interview with author, July 2007.
17. "Limiting": Fran Kaliher, interview with author, July 2006.
18. Wikipedia contributors, "Mountain Moving Coffeehouse," Wikipedia: The Free Encyclopedia, accessed February 9, 2015, https:en.wikipedia.org/wiki/Mountain_Moving_Coffeehouse; Logan Wolfe, "Coffeehouse Meeting," e-mail to author, June 23, 2009.
19. Claudia Schmidt, "Beaver Island Jubilee / For the Birds / Replenish," *New Goodbyes, Old Helloes*, Flying Fish Records, 1983.

Notes to Chapter 8

1. Much of the information in this chapter derives from interviews with Kelly Burger, Dana Doyle, Linda Kelly, Bob Kinderman, Erika Leif, Kim Marble-Follis, Brita Rekve, Kim Storm, and Katrina Tobey. Katrina Tobey, interview with author, December 16, 2014.
2. Conley interview.
3. Linda Kelly, e-mail correspondence with author, February 23, 2016.
4. Kelly Burger, interview with Em Westerlund, July 2013.
5. "Superior To House Battered Women Transitional Housing; Will Offer Desirable Location, Accommodations," *Duluth News Tribune* (MN), Points North, 1B, *NewsBank*, March 4, 2015.

6. Burger interview.
7. Candace Renalls, "Former CASDA Director Faces Federal Charges; Feds to Investigate Suspected Embezzlement," *Duluth News Tribune* (MN), March 28, 2001, B2.
8. "Superior's CASDA Hires Interim Director," *Duluth News Tribune* (MN), August 18, 1999, C2; Shelley Nelson, "CASDA Survives Financial Crisis," *Duluth News Tribune* (MN), January 13, 2000.
9. Renalls, "Former CASDA Director"; "Superior Woman Charged with Embezzlement," *Duluth News Tribune* (MN), June 11, 2003, B8.
10. Laura Podgornick and Maria Lockwood, "Douglas County Agencies Meet To Evaluate Sexual Assault Response," *Duluth News Tribune* (MN), July 14, 2010, B2.
11. "Parental alienation" refers to a wide variety of symptoms from any sort of alienation from a parent. Richard Gardner popularized the term, and it has been used by parents seeking custody of their children to claim the other parent has deliberately alienated their children from them by use of (false) disparagement and denigration.
12. Elsa Swenson, personal Facebook page, January 7, 2015.
13. Kim Marble-Follis, phone interview with author, March 3, 2015.
14. Maria Lockwood, "Center Against Sexual, Domestic Abuse Opens New Shelter in Superior—The Center Against Sexual and Domestic Abuse Is Opening the Doors of Its New, Renovated Shelter to the Public on Tuesday," *Duluth News Tribune* (MN), April 6, 2013.
15. Lockwood, "Center."
16. Center Against Sexual and Domestic Abuse, Annual Report, June 23, 2013, accessed March 18, 2015, http://www.casda.org/wp-content/uploads/2014/06/2013-Annual-Report.pdf.

Notes to Chapter 9

1. On transitional housing in general, National Network to End Domestic Violence, "Domestic Violence Counts 2014: A 24 Hour Census of Domestic Violence Shelters and Services," posted June 8, 2015, http://nnedv.org/downloads/Census/DVCounts2014/DVCounts14_NatlReport_web.pdf.
2. Much of the material for this chapter derives from interviews with Jean Baribeau-Thoennes, Nancy Burns, Sadie Green, Michelle LeBeau, Zoe LeBeau, Kate Regan, Melissa Taylor, and Victoria Ybanez.
3. Women's Transitional Housing Coalition, brochure, n.d., author's collection.
4. Women's Transitional Housing Coalition brochure.
5. On classes, Melissa Taylor, interview with Joan Varney, 2006.
6. On empowerment, Taylor interview.
7. "Provide an environment": Nancy Burns, phone interview with author, February 12, 2015.
8. Sadie Green, e-mail correspondence with author, February 22, 2016.
9. Women's Transitional Housing, "Organizational Information," Sadie Green collection.
10. "Coalition Gets National Award," *Duluth News-Tribune* (MN), June 19, 1996, B2.

11. Victoria Ybanez, Skype interview with author, October 29, 2014; Victoria Ybanez, Facebook message to author, February 21, 2016.

12. Matt Nelson, "Crack Bust Biggest in City History; Detroit Gang Here, Police Say," *Duluth News-Tribune* (MN), January 4, 1996, A1; Matt Nelson, "Suspected Drug Dealer Arrested; He Struck Up Friendship with Transitional Housing Tenant," *Duluth News-Tribune* (MN), April 18, 1996.

13. Hales quoted in Noam Levey, "Advocates Say It's Unfair To Link Urban Trouble to Transitional Housing," *Duluth News-Tribune* (MN), January 14, 1996, B4; Ybanez quoted in Nelson, "Suspected Dealer."

14. Michelle LeBeau, memorandum to Finance Committee Members, n.d., Sadie Green collection; Sadie Green, phone interview with author, January 22, 2015.

15. A longer, more fully developed history of Women in Construction is available electronically at Archives and Special Collections, Kathryn A. Martin Library, University of Minnesota Duluth, http://www.d.umn.edu/lib/.

16. Linda Ocasio, "Building a Home and a Future: An Economic Justice Project in Minnesota Provides Women with More than a Job," *Shelterforce Online* 132 (November/December 2003), http://www.nhi.org/online/issues/132/womenconstruction.html.

17. Michelle LeBeau, interview with Joan Varney, 2006.

18. M. LeBeau, interview.

19. Santiago quoted in Ocasio, "Building a Home."

20. LeBeau quoted in Ocasio, "Building a Home."

21. Baird Helgeson, "Old Convent To Become Affordable Housing–Social Services: A Church Will Give $10,000 To Help Turn the Building Into Housing for the Homeless," *Duluth News Tribune* (MN), June 13, 2004, C1.

22. LeBeau quoted in Chuck Frederick, "Convent Conversion—Benedictine Sisters Work with a Nonprofit To Restore Their Once Proud Home," *Duluth News Tribune* (MN), January 9, 2005, A1.

23. Chuck Frederick, "Building Name to Honor 'Angel of Hillside,'" *Duluth News Tribune* (MN), January 9, 2005, A8.

24. Murphy quoted in Wayne Nelson, "Women in Construction, LLC Has a Busy Summer Lined Up," *BusinessNorth*, May 24, 2004, http://www.businessnorth.com/businessnorth_exclusives/women-in-construction-llc-has-busy-summer-lined-up/article_846d053e-1e5f-542d-86c7-a12f99b4c891.html.

25. "Eco-Home," Women in Construction Facebook page, accessed March 11, 2009.

26. "Duluth Nonprofit Earns Award," *Duluth News Tribune* (MN), March 9, 2004, B3.

27. Piasecki quoted in Patrick Garmoe, "Energy Efficient Approach Appeals to Construction Company—Women in Construction: Nonprofit Has Finished an Eco-Home at Hawk Ridge Estates in Lester Park," *Duluth News Tribune* (MN), May 29, 2007, B1; Robinson quoted in Ocasio, "Building a Home"; Schneider quoted in Wen-Yu Lang, "Construction Program Empowers Women—Women's Transitional Housing Coalition Provides Group with the Skills To Build Their Own Business," *Duluth News Tribune* (MN), August 6, 2002, B1.

28. Lindy Askelin, the inspiration for Women in Construction Company, was one of a small number of women carpenters working in Duluth in the 1970s through 1996, when she passed away from breast cancer. Lindy was a self-taught carpenter who gave her skills and knowledge to support many of the organizations in this volume—the CAP Weatherization Program, the Women's Coalition, Women's Transitional Housing, and the Women's Health Center. Lyons quoted in Lang, "Construction Program Empowers Women."
29. Witzenburg and McCulloch quoted in Peter Passi, "88 Affordable Housing Units in Duluth Saved," *Duluth News Tribune* (MN), March 20, 2010.
30. Michelle LeBeau interview with author, November 14, 2014; Passi, "88 Affordable Housing Units."

Notes to Chapter 10

1. Oden quoted in Julie Krienke, "Mending the Sacred Hoop Addresses Domestic Violence," *Lake Voice News* (Duluth, MN), April 8, 2013.
2. Hudon quoted in Mike Tobin, "Indian Battered Women Get Grant to Help Fight Domestic Violence," *Duluth News-Tribune* (MN), January 11, 1996, B9.
3. Much of the material for this chapter derives from interviews with Tina Olson and Rebecca St. George; Balzer, et al., *Full Circle*; Rebecca St. George, interview with author, January 2, 2008.
4. Tina Olson, interview with author, January 2, 2008. A follow-up interview was conducted on October 16, 2014, and we also corresponded by e-mail.
5. Public Law 280, enacted in 1953, transferred legal authority from the federal government to state governments, changing the division of authority for criminal and civil jurisdiction for tribal, state, and federal governments (Tribal Court Clearinghouse, "Public Law 280," Tribal Law and Policy Institute, accessed April 2, 2015, http://www.tribal-institute.org/lists/pl280.htm).
6. The model of intervention created by DAIP calls for development of policies and protocols for agencies that are part of an integrated response that centralize victim safety, are accountable for that, and provide a supportive community for battered women and rehabilitation and education services for batterers (Shepard and Pence, *Coordinating Community Responses*). For more information, see Chapter 5: Domestic Abuse Intervention Project.
   Marilu Johnsen, e-mail correspondence with author, February 12, 2015.
7. St. George interview.
8. Olson interview.
9. St. George quoted in Mark Stodghill, "Duluth Police Receive Prestigious Award," *Duluth News Tribune* (MN), September 18, 2012; Steve Kuchera, "American Indian Women Feel 'Brushed Aside' after Reporting Sexual Assaults, Report Says," *Duluth News-Tribune* (MN), December 3, 1999.
10. Harris quoted in Stodghill, "Duluth Police."
11. Tusken quoted in Stodghill, "Duluth Police"; Kuchera, "American Indian Women."
12. On leadership of police, Harris quoted in Stodghill, "Duluth Police."

13. Shunu Shrestha, "Local View: With Constructed Ignorance, Society Turns Its Back," *Duluth News Tribune* (MN), January 13, 2013.
14. On goal of task force, Shrestha, "Local View"; on MSH and trafficking of Native women, Tina Olson, e-mail correspondence, February 22, 2016.
15. Tina Olson, e-mail correspondence, February 22, 2016.

Notes Chapter 11

1. Lesbian partners Sharon Kowalski and Karen Thompson lived in St. Cloud, Minnesota, one hundred fifty miles southwest of Duluth. When Sharon Kowalski's partner, Karen Thompson, suffered severe brain injury as the result of a car accident, Karen's parents became her legal guardians, took Karen to their home, and denied Sharon access to her. When Karen's father could no longer take care of Karen, the court, at his request, appointed a family friend to be Karen's legal guardian. Hence the newspaper headline. On appeal, guardianship was awarded to Sharon. The case was followed closely by the LGBT and feminist communities in the northland.
   Aurora mission from *Aurora Borealis*, October 1989, Aurora Collection, University of Minnesota Duluth.
2. Quote, Aurora, "History," n.d., Aurora Collection. Much of the material for this chapter derives from interviews with Deb Anderson, Lee Hemming, Laura Stolle Hesselton, Dianna Hunter, Sue Maki, Trisha O'Keefe, and Caroline Pelzel, as well as *Aurora Borealis*, July/August 1990–December 1995, Aurora Collection, and other documents in the Aurora Collection.
3. Freesol story from Estel interview with author, December 5, 2014; Incorporation Papers, Aurora Collection.
4. Aurora, "History," Aurora Collection.
5. *Aurora Borealis*, January/February 1990, Aurora Collection.
6. *Aurora Borealis*, inaugural issue, Aurora Collection.
7. *Aurora Borealis*, January 1991, Aurora Collection; Aurora, Draft Mission Statements, n.d., Aurora Collection.
8. Estel quoted in Laurie Hertzel, "Lesbian Center Decides Openness Worth the Risk," *Duluth News-Tribune* (MN), February 21, 1990, B1.
9. Pat K. and Kat S. quoted in *Aurora Borealis*, 1993, Aurora Collection; Lee Hemming, interview with author, December 14, 2014; member quoted in *Aurora Borealis*, October 1990, Aurora Collection.
10. Hemming interview; "5th Festy Wrap-Up Meeting," Aurora Collection.
11. "5th Festival, Annual Northern Lights Womyn's Music Festival" program, September 10, 1994, Aurora Collection; Aurora Board, Meeting Notes, February 2 and 28, 1995, Aurora Collection.
12. Betty organized a series of trainings in Duluth on homophobia, internalized homophobia, and lesbian battering (*Aurora Borealis*, April 1994, Aurora Collection).
13. *Aurora Borealis*, June 1994, Aurora Collection.
14. *Aurora Borealis*, September 1994, Aurora Collection; Laura Stolle Hesselton, Skype interview with author, November 20, 2014.
15. Kim Surkan, "Aurora Lesbian Center Moves to Building for Women," *focuspoint*, December 22–28, 1994, 9.

16. On positive rebirth, Surkan, "Aurora Lesbian Center Moves," 9; on facilitators, Aurora, "Retreat of Aurora," November 4, 1994, Aurora Collection.
17. The original wording of the mission repeatedly referred to lesbians: "to increase self-acceptance . . . among *lesbians* . . . promote awareness . . . regarding *lesbian* issues . . . increase networking . . . among *lesbians* . . . etc." [emphasis mine] ("Mission Statement," Aurora Collection).
    The mission statements are as follows: 1999–2000: "We are a northland resource center working to eliminate heterosexism and all other forms of discrimination, while supporting lesbian, bisexual and trans gender women in our community through social outreach and education. We welcome all who share our vision." 2005: "We are a northland resource center working to eliminate homophobia in our society—as well as classism, sexism, racism, ageism, ableism, and all other forms of discrimination and oppression—while supporting lesbian, bisexual and trans gender women in our community through social outreach and education. In our own experience these 'isms' have limited our access to the rights and benefits we deserve. We welcome all who share our vision" (Aurora Draft Mission Statements, n.d.; Aurora Mission Statement, 1994; Aurora Mission Statement, 1995, Aurora Collection).
18. Survey, 1996, Aurora Collection.
19. Anonymous e-mail to Aurora, n.d., Aurora Collection.
20. Anonymous letter to Aurora, n.d., Aurora Collection; anonymous letter to Aurora, December 14, 2002, Aurora Collection.
21. Aurora Statistics, 1997–98, Aurora Collection.
22. *Aurora Borealis*, April 2002, Aurora Collection.
23. Talks of merging, Caroline Pelzel, interview with author, December 16, 2014.
24. Aurora Board, Meeting Notes, 2008–11, Aurora Collection.

Notes to Chapter 12

1. According to the Anishinaabe legend of their migration from the Atlantic seaboard, the Anishinaabe were to travel west until they reached the land where the food grows in the water. The food is *manoomin*, wild rice.
2. "Welcome," "About AICHO," AICHO website, www.aicho.org.
3. Much of the material for this chapter derives from interviews with Karen Diver, Janis Greene, Patti Larsen, Michelle LeBeau, Sherry Sanchez Tibbetts, and Victoria Ybanez.
4. In addition to health insurance, benefits included a small fund that could be used toward education and first-time home ownership.
5. Noam Levey, "Fearful Residents Ask Who Can Save Hillside? Is Community Club Best Hope," *Duluth News-Tribune* (MN), June 24, 1996, A1.
6. Chuck Frederick, "Mother Happy for Aid," *Duluth News Tribune* (MN), December 16, 2001, B1; Noam Levey, "American Indian Women Get Boost, Peeling Paint Hides Clean Units, Counseling Services," *Duluth News-Tribune* (MN), June 8, 1996, F1.
7. Goodwin and Sullivan quoted in Levey, "American Indian Women Get Boost."
8. Sayers, Tjaden, and Lyons quoted in John Myers, "Native Housing Program

Offers Much More—Social Service: Cultural Learning and Job Training Help American Indian Women Regain Control of Their Lives," *Duluth News Tribune* (MN), December 25, 2002, G5.

9. Johnson quoted in Frederick, "Mother Happy for Aid."

10. Jason Begay, "Teen Volunteers Aid Housing Effort; Landscaping at American Indian Project Seen As 'A Good Chance To Help Others,'" *Duluth News-Tribune* (MN), July 1, 1999, B1.

11. Ybanez interview.

12. Quoted in Begay, "Teen Volunteers."

13. For a sample see Noam Levey, "Councilors Walk Out: 4 Refuse To Vote on Duluth CDBG Allocations," *Duluth News-Tribune* (MN), October 21, 1997, B1; Martiga Lohn, "Residents Encouraged To Sound Off on Grants; Hearing Marks Last Time To Influence CDBG Committee's Funding Proposals," *Duluth News-Tribune* (MN), October 12, 1999, B1; Chuck Frederick, "City Council Will Consider Providing $4.6 Million for Variety of Programs," *Duluth News Tribune* (MN), December 16, 2001, B3; and "In the Public Interest," *Duluth News-Tribune* (MN), June 14, 1997, C2.

   Ybanez interview. The Rural/Urban Council was a self-selected group that formed in the 1990s to identify priorities for HUD applications for St. Louis County (Victoria Ybanez, Facebook message, April 9, 2016).

14. Leadership turnover, Sherry Sanchez Tibbetts, interview with author, February 19, 2015; Sayers quoted in Chuck Frederick, "Nonprofit Helps American Indian Women—Housing Group Has Fought Back from Its Own Financial Struggles," *Duluth News Tribune* (MN), December 16, 2001, B13.

15. Tibbetts interview.

16. Tibbetts interview. *Ikwe* is Ojibwe for "woman."

17. Tibbetts interview.

18. For more information on Hearth Connection see "About," Hearth Connection, accessed May 29, 2015, http://www.hearthconnection.org/about. AICHO, "Description," n.d., AICHO Collection.

19. Tibbetts interview.

20. Based on conversations with language specialists, the ending *yaan*, which is singular, was changed to the plural *min* in 2015.

21. Zoe LeBeau, interview with author, November 25, 2014; Powless quoted in "$50,000 Donation Helps Indian Organization," *Duluth News Tribune* (MN), April 5, 2007, D2.

   Fond-du-Luth Casino was the first urban tribal casino in the country. Agreements between the Fond du Lac Band and the City of Duluth in 1994 established that the city would receive 19 percent of the gross revenues, about $6 million a year. In an unrelated move, the band later stopped paying the city on the basis that the original agreement was illegal and the tribe should have sole proprietary interest in the casino. Lawsuits and appeals have ensued, each finding in favor of the band.

22. Tadd Johnson, "Casino Funds Should Go to Indian Housing," Opinion, *Duluth News Tribune* (MN), October 7, 2007.

23. Editorial, "Our View: Reconsider 'No' Vote in Homelessness Battle," *Duluth News Tribune* (MN), October 4, 2007; Jana Hollingsworth, "Backers Persist on Funding," *Duluth News Tribune* (MN), October 6, 2007; Tibbetts inter-

view. Not only had AICHO not begun any design work, the anthropologist AICHO hired to investigate this matter found no culture that held such views.

24. "Our View: Reconsider"; O'Neil quoted in "Our View: Reconsider"; Johnson, "Casino Funds."

25. Grau quoted in Brandon Stahl, "Council Approves Money for American Indian Housing Project," *Duluth News Tribune* (MN), October 10, 2007.

26. Liz Collin, "Sex Trafficking on the North Shore," WCCO TV, CBS News Minnesota, May 5, 2011, http://minnesota.cbslocal.com/2011/05/05/sex-trafficking-on-the-north-shore/.

27. Tibbetts interview.

28. Patti Larsen, interview with author, December 9, 2014.

29. The seven teachings that compose the Anishinaabe code of conduct are wisdom, love, respect, courage, honesty, humility, and truth.

30. For more information, see the Housing and Urban Development government website on the HUD Exchange program: https://www.hudexchange.info/. At the time this chapter was written, the HUD program was only in its beginning stages, and the actual consequences for AICHO had yet to be seen. Michelle LeBeau, e-mail correspondence with author, February 22, 2016.

31. The new logo can be seen on AICHO's website, www.aicho.org.

Notes to Chapter 13

1. Epigraph: Ann Reed, "Heroes," *Hole in the Day* (Turtlecub Records, 1993).

2. On creating a win-win situation, Janice Wick, interview with Tineke Ritmeester, July 14 and 18, 2008.

3. Victoria developed self-reflective exercises for AICHO staff that would be valuable for any organization. On an annual basis, each staff member created a "plan of how they were going to educate themselves on an area of oppression that they weren't comfortable looking at." They identified resources they would use to educate themselves. Twice a year they taught each other what they had learned (Ybanez interview).

4. "Ellen Pence," YouTube video.

Notes to Conclusion

1. Scientific experiments have repeatedly shown that people pay no attention to unfamiliar objects that are right in front of them. What we know frames what we see (Hawken, *Blessed Unrest*).

2. In *The Chalice and the Blade*, Riane Eisler develops the concept of the "dominator" and "partnership" paradigms as the two defining ways of thought in Western civilization.

3. Enloe, *Curious Feminist*, 4.

4. Women of color have been essential in feminist thought and movement from the influence of the Haudenosaunee in shaping the 1840s women's rights movement to the women who formed the National Organization for Women (see NOW, "Honoring Our Founders and Pioneers," National Organization for Women, accessed April 14, 2015, http://now.org/about/history/

honoring-our-founders-pioneers/) to the women of Kitchen Table Press and *This Bridge Called My Back: Writings by Radical Women of Color.* My concerns do not extend to the fact that for many Native women to be Native and to be feminist are redundant. Anishinaabe culture has always honored women, held women to be sacred, and valued the balance of female and male.

Feminist and critical race theorist Kimberlé Crenshaw first introduced the concept of "intersectionality" (Kimberlé Crenshaw, "Mapping the Margins").

5. Conservative political talk-show host Rush Limbaugh popularized the term "feminazi" in the 1990s. In his book *The Way Things Ought to Be,* he credited Tom Hazlett, a professor of economics at the University of California, Davis, with having coined the term.

On the author's definition of feminism, Bartlett, *Rebellious Feminism.*

6. Rich, *On Lies, Secrets, and Silence,* 193.

Sources

Interviews

All interviews were with the author, in Duluth, Minnesota, unless otherwise noted.

Abernathy, Jill. Personal Interview. December 18, 2014.
Anderson, Deb. Personal Interview. November 21, 2014.
Anderson, Jody. Personal Interview. July 2006.
Baribeau-Thoennes, Jean. Personal Interview. February 14, 2015.
Benson, Joyce. Personal Interview. June 2006.
Boman, Sheryl. Personal Interview. February 20, 2015.
Burger, Kelly. Interview with Em Westerlund. July 2013.
Burger, Kelly. Phone Interview. December 2014.
Burns, Nancy. Phone Interview. February 12, 2015.
Casey, Laurie. Personal Interview. December 19, 2014.
Christian, Sandy. Personal Interview. October 24, 2013.
Conley, Jan. Phone Interview. March 28, 2015.
Cook, Phyllis. Personal Interview. November 8, 2014.
Coultrap-McQuin, Susan. Phone Interview. July 2006.
Curley, Cathryn. Interview with Susana Pelayo Woodward. 2008.
Davis, Marvella. Personal Interview. December 11, 2014.
DeRider, Jean. Personal Interview. November 19, 2014.
Diver, Karen. Personal Interview. Cloquet, MN. January 29, 2015.
Doyle, Dana. Phone Interview. March 2, 2015.
Duke, Shirley. Personal Interview. July 2007, January 25, 2015.
Dwyer, Judy. Personal Interview. April 26, 2015.
Estel, Linda. Personal Interview. June 2006, July 2006, December 5, 2014.
Gosz, Pat. Phone Interview. March 27, 2014.
Graff, Mary. Personal Interview. October 24, 2013.
Green, Sadie. Phone Interview. January 22, 2015.
Greene, Janis. Personal Interview. December 9, 2014.
Gruver, Nancy. Skype Interview. March 28, 2015.
Gunderson, Constance. Personal Interview. January 25, 2015.
Harshner, Candice. Personal Interview. October 14, 2014.

Heltzer, Kathy. Personal Interview. June 2006.
Hemming, Lee. Personal Interview. December 14, 2014.
Hemphill, Stephanie. Interview with Tineke Ritmeester. July 18, 2007.
Hesselton, Laura Stolle. Skype Interview. November 20, 2014.
Hunter, Dianna. Personal Interview. November 21, 2014.
Jewell, Frank. Personal Interview. October 15, 2014.
Kaliher, Fran. Personal Interview. July 2006.
Kamau, Njoki. Personal Interview. March 16, 2015.
Kelly, Linda. Phone Interview. March 24, 2015.
Kinderman, Bob. Phone Interview. April 15, 2015.
Larsen, Patti. Personal Interview. December 9, 2014.
LeBeau, Michelle. Interview by Joan Varney. 2006.
LeBeau, Michelle. Personal Interview. October 16, 2014; November 14, 2014; November 19, 2014.
LeBeau, Zoe. Phone Interview. November 25, 2014.
Leif, Erika. Interview with Em Westerlund. Summer 2013.
Levings, Fran. Phone Interview. April 27, 2015.
Maki, Sue. Phone Interview. December 9, 2014.
Marble-Follis, Kim. Phone Interview. March 3, 2015.
Martin, Mary. Personal Interview. October 24, 2013.
McDonnell, Coral. Interview with Tineke Ritmeester. July 14, 2008.
Miller, Angie. Personal Interview. May 1, 2015.
Miller-Cleary, Linda. Personal Interview. December 1, 2014.
Niemi, Judith. Phone Interview. January 5, 2015.
Oberg, Shirley. Personal Interview. December 16, 2014.
O'Keefe, Trisha. Personal Interview. November 13, 2014. Phone Interview. December 26, 2014.
Olson, Tina. Personal Interview. January 2, 2008; October 16, 2014. Phone interview. January 7, 2015.
Pelayo Woodward, Susana. Personal Interview. June 2009.
Pelzel, Caroline. Personal Interview. July 2006, December 16, 2014.
Pence, Ellen. Interview with Tineke Ritmeester. June 27, 2006.
Provost, Jan. Personal Interview. Superior, WI. October 29, 2008.
Ravenfeather, Kelly. Personal Interview. January 25, 2015.
Regan, Kate. Personal Interview. December 4, 2014.
Rekve, Brita. Phone Interview. April 14, 2015.
Riddle, Linda. Personal Interview. January 21, 2015.
Ritmeester, Tineke. Personal Interview. July 2006.
Rocco, Rosemary. Interview with Em Westerlund. April 17, 2013.
Rocco, Rosemary. Personal Phone Interview. November 14, 2014.
Ruhnke, Wendy. Personal Interview. January 25, 2015.
St. George, Rebecca. Personal Interview. January 2, 2008.
Sandman, Babette. Personal Interview. December 11, 2014.
Seezaday, Darcy. Personal Interview. March 19, 2015.
Shrestha, Shunu. Personal Interview. March 11, 2015.
Singer, Gloria. Personal Interview. October 24, 2013.

Skomars, Diane. Personal Interview. October 22, 2014.
Stengl, Kathy. Personal Interview. January 25, 2015.
Storm, Kim. Phone Interview. January 9, 2015.
Taylor, Melissa. Interview with Joan Varney. 2006.
Tennis, Mary. Personal Interview. January 25, 2015.
Thompson, Carol. Personal Interview. January 23, 2015.
Tibbetts, Sherry Sanchez. Personal Interview. Cloquet, MN. February 19, 2015.
Tobey, Katrina. Personal Interview. December 16, 2014.
Torrison, Sharon. Personal Interview. October 22, 2014.
Tsai, Bilin. Personal Interview. June 2006.
Tubesing, Nancy Loving. Personal Interview. October, 24, 2013.
Utech, Susan. Personal Interview. November 28, 2014.
Van Hauer, Gretchen. Personal Interview. January 25, 2015.
Ward, Linda. Personal Interview. January 25, 2015.
Wedge, Lora. Skype Interview. January 26, 2015.
Welsh, Tina. Interview with Em Westerlund. May 4, 2012.
Wick, Janice. Interview with Tineke Ritmeester. July 14 and 18, 2008.
Wildwood (Wagner), Inez. Personal Interview. December 1, 2014.
Woods, Maren. Phone Interview. April 10, 2015.
Ybanez, Victoria. Skype Interview. October 29, 2014.
Zimmerman, Mary. Phone Interview. June 2006.
Zoff, Shary. Personal Interview. January 25, 2015.

Published Works

Balzer, Roma, Genevieve James, Liz LaPrairie, and Tina Olson, with contributions by Sandra L. Goodsky and Eileen Hudon. *Full Circle: Coming Back to Where We Began.* Duluth, MN: Mending the Sacred Hoop/Minnesota Program Development, Inc., 1994.
Bartlett, Elizabeth Ann. *Rebellious Feminism: Camus's Ethic of Rebellion and Feminist Thought.* New York: Palgrave, 2004.
Bingham, Clara, and Laura Leedy Gansler. *Class Action: The Landmark Case that Changed Sexual Harassment Law.* New York: Doubleday, 2002.
Brown, K. Marianne Wargelin. "The Legacy of Mummu's Daughters: Finnish American Women's History." In *Women Who Dared: The History of Finnish American Women*, edited by Carl Ross and K. Marianne Wargelin Brown, 4–40. St. Paul, MN: Immigration History Research Center, 1986.
Bunch, Charlotte. "Lesbians in Revolt." In *Feminist Frameworks: Alternative Theoretical Accounts of the Relations between Women and Men*, edited by Alison M. Jaggar and Paula S. Rothenberg, 3rd ed., 174–78. New York: McGraw Hill, 1993.
Chittister, Joan. *Heart of Flesh: A Feminist Spirituality for Women and Men.* Grand Rapids, MI: William B. Erdmans, 1998.
Cobble, Dorothy Sue, Linda Gordon, and Astrid Henry. *Feminism Unfinished: A Short, Surprising History of American Women's Movements.* New York: Liveright Publishing Corp., 2014.

Crenshaw, Kimberlé. "Mapping the Margins: Intersectionality, Identity Politics, and Violence Against Women of Color." *Stanford Law Review* 43:6 (July 1991): 1241–99.

Cullen-Dupont, Kathryn. *Encyclopedia of Women's History in America.* 2nd ed. New York: Facts on File, 2000.

Echols, Alice. *Daring to Be Bad: Radical Feminism in America, 1967–1975.* Minneapolis: University of Minnesota Press, 1989.

Eisler, Riane. *The Chalice and the Blade: Our History, Our Future.* New York: HarperOne, 1988.

Enke, Anne. *Finding the Movement: Sexuality, Contested Space, and Feminist Activism.* Durham, NC: Duke University Press, 2007.

Enloe, Cynthia. *The Curious Feminist: Searching for Women in a New Age of Empire.* Oakland: University of California Press, 2004.

Evans, Sara M. *Tidal Wave: How Women Changed America at Century's End.* New York: Free Press, 2003.

Ezekiel, Judith. *Feminism in the Heartland.* Columbus: Ohio State University Press, 2002.

Ferree, Myra Marx, and Beth B. Hess. *Controversy and Coalition: The New Feminist Movement across Three Decades of Change.* Rev. ed. New York: Twayne Publishers, 1994.

Ferree, Myra Marx, and Patricia Yancey Martin. *Feminist Organizations: Harvest of the New Women's Movement.* Philadelphia: Temple University Press, 1995.

Freedman, Estelle B. *No Turning Back: The History of Feminism and the Future of Women.* New York: Random House, 2002.

Freeman, Jo. *The Politics of Women's Liberation: A Case Study of an Emerging Social Movement and Its Relation to the Policy Process.* New York: David McKay Co., Inc., 1975.

Freire, Paulo. *Pedagogy of the Oppressed.* Rev. ed. Translated by Myra Berman Ramos. New York: Continuum, 1993.

Gilman, Rhoda R. *Stand Up!: The Story of Minnesota's Protest Tradition.* St. Paul: Minnesota Historical Society Press, 2012.

Gilmore, Stephanie. *Groundswell: Grassroots Feminist Activism in Postwar America.* New York: Routledge, 2013.

Hawken, Paul. *Blessed Unrest: How the Largest Social Movement in History Is Restoring Grace, Justice, and Beauty to the World.* New York: Penguin Books, 2008.

Karvonen, Hilja J. "Three Proponents of Women's Rights in the Finnish-American Labor Movement from 1910–1930: Selma Jokela McCone, Maiju Nurmi and Helmi Mattson." In *For the Common Good: Finnish Immigrants and the Radical Response to Industrial America,* edited by Michael G. Karni and Douglas J. Ollila. Superior, WI: Tyomies Society, 1977.

Kolehmainen, John I., and George W. Hill. *Haven in the Woods: The Story of the Finns in Wisconsin.* Madison: State Historical Society of Wisconsin, 1951.

Kravetz, Diane. *Tales from the Trenches: Politics and Practice in Feminist Service Organizations.* Lanham, MD: University Press of America, 2004.

Limbaugh, Rush. *The Way Things Ought To Be.* New York: Pocket Books, Simon and Schuster, 1992.

McMahon, Martha, and Ellen Pence. "Doing More Harm than Good?: Some Cautions on Visitation Centers." In *Ending the Cycle of Violence: Community Responses to Children of Battered Women*, edited by Einat Peled, Peter G. Jaffe, and Jeffrey L. Edleson, 186–206. Thousand Oaks, CA: Sage, 1995.

Moraga, Cherríe, and Gloria Anzaldúa. *This Bridge Called My Back: Writings by Radical Women of Color*. Trumansburg, NY: Kitchen Table Press, 1981.

Pence, Ellen. "Advocacy on Behalf of Battered Women." In *Sourcebook on Violence Against Women*, edited by Claire M. Renzetti, Jeffrey L. Edleson, and Raquel Kennedy Bergen, 329–43. Thousand Oaks, CA: Sage, 2001.

———. "The Duluth Domestic Abuse Intervention Project." In *Programs for Men Who Batter: Intervention and Prevention Strategies in a Diverse Society*, edited by Aldarondo Etiony and Fernando Mederos, 6-1–46. Kingston, NJ: Civic Research Institute, 2002.

———. *In Our Best Interest: A Process of Personal and Social Change*. Edited by Kate Regan. Duluth: Minnesota Program Development, Inc., 1987.

———. "Reflection." In *Violence Against Women: Classic Papers*, edited by Raquel Kennedy Bergen, Jeffrey L. Edelson, and Claire M. Renzetti, 388–90. Boston: Pearson / Allyn and Bacon, 2005. http://uknowledge.uky.edu/crvaw_book/19.

Raymond, Janice G. *A Passion for Friends: Toward a Philosophy of Female Affection*. Boston: Beacon Press, 1986.

Reger, Jo. *Everywhere and Nowhere: Contemporary Feminism in the United States*. New York: Oxford University Press, 2012.

Remington, Judy. *The Need to Thrive: Women's Organizations in the Twin Cities*. St. Paul: Minnesota Women's Press, Inc., 1991.

Rich, Adrienne. *Blood, Bread, and Poetry: Selected Prose, 1979–1985*. New York: W. W. Norton and Co., 1986.

———. *On Lies, Secrets, and Silence: Selected Prose, 1966–1978*. New York: W. W. Norton and Co., 1979.

Rosen, Ruth. *The World Split Open: How the Modern Women's Movement Changed America*. New York: Viking, 2000.

Rossi, Alice, ed. *The Feminist Papers: From Adams to de Beauvoir*. New York: Columbia University Press, 1973.

Shepard, M. F., and E. L. Pence. *Coordinating Community Responses to Domestic Violence: Lessons from Duluth and Beyond*. Thousand Oaks, CA: Sage, 1999.

Steinem, Gloria. *Outrageous Acts and Everyday Rebellions*. 2nd ed. New York: Henry Holt and Co., 1995.

Taylor, Verta. "Watching for Vibes: Bringing Emotions in the Study of Feminist Organizations." In Ferree and Martin, *Feminist Organizations*, 223–33.

Wagner, Sally Roesch. "The Indigenous Roots of United States Feminism." In *Feminist Politics, Activism, and Vision: Local and Global Challenges*, edited by Luciana Ricciutelli, Angela Miles, and Margaret H. McFadden, 267–83. Toronto: Inanna Publications, 2004.

Walker, Lenore. *The Battered Woman Syndrome*. New York: Springer Publishing Co., 1984.

Wandersee, Winifred D. *On the Move: American Women in the 1970s*. Boston: Twayne Publishers, G. K. Hall, 1988.

Whittier, Nancy. *Feminist Generations: The Persistence of the Radical Women's Movement*. Philadelphia: Temple University Press, 1995.

Electronic Resources

"Ellen Pence: Battered Women's Movement Leader." YouTube video. December 6, 2009. https://www.youtube.com/watch?v=r9dZOgr78eE.

"Interview with Ellen Pence, with Casey Gwinn." YouTube video. December 2009. https://www.youtube.com/watch?v=bZeppoVr5fo.

NARAL. Pro-Choice America. "Anti-Choice Violence and Intimidation." Fact Sheet. Accessed March 20, 2015. http://www.prochoiceamerica.org/media/fact-sheets/abortion-anti-choice-violence.pdf.

Paymar, Michael. "What Is the Duluth Model?" Webinar. Domestic Abuse Intervention Programs, Duluth, MN. November 18, 2014. http://www.theduluthmodel.org/u_whatistheduluthmodelwebinar.html.

Pence, Ellen, and Martha McMahon. "A Coordinated Community Response to Domestic Violence." Praxis International, 1997. http://files.praxisinternational.org/ccrdv.pdf.

Physicians for Reproductive Choice. "Voices of Choice." PRCH videos. January 21, 2013. http://prh.org/provider-voices/voices-of-choice/.

Unpublished Sources

American Indian Community Housing Organization (AICHO) Collection. Duluth, MN.

Aurora Collection. Archives and Special Collections, Kathryn A. Martin Library, University of Minnesota Duluth.

Bartlett, Elizabeth. Personal Archives. Duluth, MN.

Benson, Joyce. Personal Archives. Duluth, MN.

Central Cooperative Wholesale Records, 1916–69. "Historical Sketch," IRHC #118, September 8, 2010. Immigration History Research Center. University of Minnesota.

DeRider, Jean. Personal Archives. Duluth, MN.

Green, Sadie. Personal Archives. Minneapolis, MN.

Heltzer, Kathy. Personal Archives. Duluth, MN.

Hemphill, Stephanie. Personal Archives. Duluth, MN.

LucasHoux, Mary Ann. Personal Archives. Duluth, MN.

Northcountry Women's Coffeehouse Collection. Northeastern Minnesota Historical Society Archives. Archives and Special Collections, Kathryn A. Martin Library, University of Minnesota Duluth.

Program to Aid Victims of Sexual Assault (PAVSA). Collection. Duluth, MN.

Safe Haven Shelter. Collection. Duluth, MN.

Welsh, Tina. Personal Archives. Duluth, MN.

Index

racism, intersections with, 201; in trades, 186–88; among women, 179

sexual assault, 7, 43, 168; advocacy, 55, 58–60, 62, 65–66, 159; advocates, 54, 56, 58–60, 62, 64, 73, 158–59; anonymous reporting of, 67; on campus, 68; as crime, 7; and domestic abuse, 85, 160, 207; education about, 56, 59, 67, 161–62; ending, 75; feminist perspectives on, 9; issue of, 68–69; legislation, 25, 56–57, 161, 280n9; medical response to, 66; movement, 158; of Native women, 24, 70, 72, 198, 207–9; policies regarding, 74; public school protocol on, 68; in St. Louis County, 54–55; services for, 58–59, 61–62, 64–65, 67–68, 158–60, 163; trauma of, 37; victims of, 27, 53, 66, 118, 160

Sexual Assault Multidisciplinary Action Response Team (SMART), 64, 69–70

Sexual Assault Nurse Examiner (SANE), 64, 66–67

Sexual Assault Response Team (SART), 167–68

Sheehy, Toni, 48, 228–29

shelters. *See* battered women's shelters

Shrestha, Shunu, 71–73, 265

Simonson, Mike, 164

Singer, Gloria, 37

sister space, 24, 236, 258

sisterhood, 23, 105, 258

size of community, 18–20, 27

Skomars, Diane, 32–33

Smeal, Eleanor, 137

Smith, Barbara, 8, 233–34n14, 286n43

Smith, Dorothy, 113–14

Soeters, Adrianna, 152

solidarity, 151, 157; and Building for Women, 137, 220; feminist, 17, 23, 264; of feminist organizations, 16; loss of, 262–63; of Rosemary Rocco with Tina Welsh, 129; of women, 35, 183

Solon, Sam, 39, 63

Spector, Peggy, 54, 57

Spinsters Ink, 50, 140

spirituality: importance of, 256; Native, 233–34; women's, 8, 16, 146, 216, 223

stalking, 169

Stanton, Elizabeth Cady, xv, 276n18

state commissions on women, 6, 8

Steinbeigle, Suzanne, 215

Steinem, Gloria, 3, 38, 41, 50, 61, 136

Stewart, Carol, 159

Stewart, Diane, 206

Stoffel, Shelly, 115

Stolle, Laura, 219–20. *See also* Hesselton, Laura Stolle

Storm, Kim, 60, 158–60

Studelska, Jana, 51

Sullivan, Kelly, 233

Sunbear, Hildred, 173

Sunwood, Kayt, 152

support groups, 13, 262; and Aurora, 215–16, 223, 227; and CASDA, 164; at county jail, 248; and DAIP, 79; difference from education group, 105; of feminist therapists, 27, 37, 76; at Human Development Center, 37, 76; lesbian, 32, 47, 89, 215–16; for Native women, 197; and PAVSA, 65, 67; and Safe Haven Resource Center, 95; and Women's Coalition, 78–80, 89, 95; and Women's Health Center for menopausal women, 141; and Women's Transitional Housing, 176

Swenson, Elsa, 169

Take Back the Night marches, 7, 21, 38, 42; and PAVSA, 59, 62, 67

Taylor, Melissa, 179, 191, 193–94

Taylor, Verta, 23

Tellett, Anne, 148

Tennis, Mary, 35, 149

Third Wave feminism, 9, 263, 273n3

This Way Out, 44

Thompson, Carol, 104, 110, 286n40

Thompson, Karen, 214, 294n1

Thomsen, Sara, 149

with DAIP, 83–85, 90–91, 99–100; rules of, 90; shelter of, 79, 81; specialization of, 86; and support groups, 78–79, 89; two-pronged approach of, 82; unionization of, 86; volunteers, 78, 84. *See also* Safe Haven Resource Center; Safe Haven Shelter

Women's Community Development Organization (WCDO): beginning of, 185; building developments of, 188–90; end of, 193; financial difficulties of, 192–93. *See also* Women's Transitional Housing Coalition (Women's Trans)

Women's Coordinating Committee, 46

women's culture, in Duluth, 18, 42–43, 45, 149; importance of, 18

Women's Equity Action League (WEAL), 6

Women's Growth Center, 33. *See also* Northcountry Women's Center

Women's Health Center, 3, 4, 6, 38, 51, 122, 152, 298n28; allies, 125; and Building for Women, 51, 63–64, 128–38; dedication of staff of, 138, 142; financial challenges of, 140–41; funding, 124, 140–41; legal battles of, 139; origin of, 40, 122–24; move to Building for Women, 134; physicians, 126; protests against, 63, 125–28; and Safe Haven Resource Center, 142; volunteers, 127. *See also* Building for Women

Women's International League for Peace and Freedom, 19

Women's Liberation of Duluth, 32–33

women's music, 13, 24, 38; and Artemis Productions, 44; festivals, 8, 145; at Journeys Bookstore, 45; and Northcountry Women's Coffeehouse, 43, 143–45, 149, 151, 157; and Northern Lights Womyn's Music Festival, 45, 217–20; on Wise Women Radio, 43–44

Women's Music Show, 44. *See also* Wise Women Radio

Women's Resource and Action Center (WRAC), 20, 52, 68

Women's Studies, 5, 8–9, 24, 36; and gender studies, 9; influence of, 20, 259; at UMD, 20, 31, 33–34, 38, 46–47, 215, 259; at UWS, 47

Women's Transitional Housing Coalition (Women's Trans), 5, 25, 172, 229, 262, 298n28; board, 179; buildings, 174, 181–82; challenges of, 177, 180–84; children's program of, 175–76; community, 180–81; and diversity, 179; and empowerment, 176–78, 259; end of, 51, 96, 192–93; funding, 179; growth and transition of, 181–85; impact of, 193–95; legacy of, 193–94; management structure of, 182–83; mission, 178–79, 183; nature of, 178; origin of, 47, 122–25, 172–74; and political education and actions, 177; programming of, 174–78; and racism, 179–80

Woods, Maren, 115–16. *See also* Hansen, Maren

Woodswomen, 28, 36, 149

Woodward, Susana Pelayo, 3–5

Ybanez, Victoria: on AICHO, 240; AICHO, director of, 230–31; and AICHO, founding of, 48, 228–30; on anti-oppression work, 256; on choosing battles wisely, 255; and city building inspector, 231–32; on cultural heritage, 236; and Dabinoo'Igan, 234–36, 239; on Gimaajii, 251; on mission, 254; and Oshki, 231, 239; Petrozavodsk, 91; on racism, 232–34, 236–38, 248; on sister space, 24, 236, 258; and Women's Transitional Housing, 175–76, 178–81, 183–84, 193–95

YWCA, 16, 21, 34, 54; and AICHO, 242–43; and Building for Women, 51, 63, 129–30, 132–33, 135–36; and

Family Visitation Center, 112; and
Northcountry Women's Center,
32; and Northcountry Women's
Coffeehouse, 147; and PAVSA,
54; and Project SOAR, 39; and
Women's Coalition, 77–78; and
Women's Health Center escorts,
124; and Women's Transitional
Housing, 173

Zebo, Dave, 198–99
Zimmerman, Mary, 46
Zoff, Shary, 35

Making Waves has been typeset in Warnock Pro, a typeface designed by Robert Slimbach and released in 2000.

Book design by Wendy Holdman.